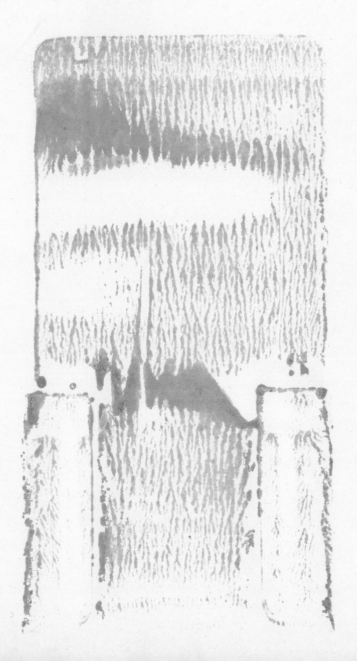

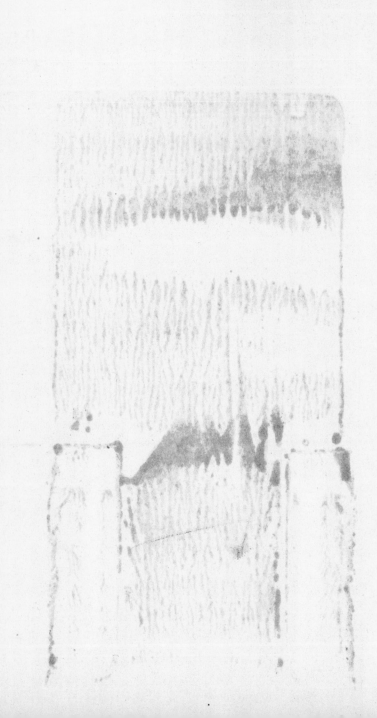

THE ROMAN STAGE

W. BEARE, M.A.

Late Professor of Latin in the University of Bristol

THE ROMAN STAGE

A SHORT HISTORY OF LATIN DRAMA IN THE TIME OF THE REPUBLIC

METHUEN & CO. LTD., LONDON
11 New Fetter Lane, E.C.4

First published November 30th, 1950
Second edition, 1955
Third edition, revised, 1964

Printed in Great Britain by
John Dickens and Co Ltd, Northampton
Catalogue No. 02/5187/31

3·1

PREFACE

MY ATTENTION was first drawn to Plautine studies by Robert Seymour Conway, at that time (1924) Hulme Professor of Latin in the University of Manchester. Much interest had been aroused among English scholars by the appearance in 1922 of Eduard Fraenkel's well-known work *Plautinisches im Plautus*, dedicated to Gunther Jachmann and acknowledging a special debt to Friedrich Leo. I found, however, in the course of time that my interest lay not so much in the relation of the Latin plays to their Greek originals, or in those linguistic, metrical and textual studies, which in this country are peculiarly associated with the names of W. M. Lindsay and E. A. Sonnenschein, as in the light thrown by the plays on the theatre for which they were intended. It seemed to me that nearly all modern discussions of Latin drama rested on certain assumptions, conscious or unconscious, which might seem reasonable in themselves but were incapable of proof and sooner or later led to serious difficulty. Ever since the Renaissance the scholars of western Europe, even while basing their standards on the supposed practice of the Greeks and Romans, have in fact allowed contemporary habits of thought to colour their conception of classical antiquity. It might have been well to pay more attention to the music, the art and drama of India and Java, of China and Japan, if only to remind ourselves that our western notions are not valid for all mankind, even at the present day. My own limitations and misgivings have confined me to a narrower field. I have tried to avoid using arguments which depended either on subjective judgments, or on evidence the validity of which was less than axiomatic. The reader may be disappointed by my failure to reconstruct for him the plot of some lost play, whether tragedy, togata or Atellane ; he may even think it perverse in me to have made so little use of the wealth of pictorial material which Dr. Bieber has put at our disposal, or the many references to drama which we find scattered throughout ancient literature.

On this last point perhaps I may quote what seems an apposite remark of Mr. L. P. Wilkinson (*Horace and his Lyric Poetry*, p. 19) : ' It is difficult for us, who use words primarily as a means of conveying what we believe to be the truth, to penetrate the mind of Roman writers, who, like the Italians of to-day, often used them primarily " for effect." ' I have placed little trust in the statements of such writers as the elder Pliny, and have even reserved judgment with regard to much of what is said by Vitruvius, however technical and detailed. On the other hand, when Lucretius (iv. 75–83) refers incidentally to the many-coloured awnings ' stretched over great theatres ' as they ' flap and flutter, spread every-where on masts and beams ', and in the subdued light of the enclosed theatre ' tinge the assembly in the tiers beneath, and all the bravery of the stage and the gay-clad company of the elders ', who can fail to detect the note of truth ? But in the last resort we come back to the plays as the primary source of evidence which is certainly valid and relevant. It is also evidence which is easily accessible to the reader, who may judge for himself whether the arguments which I base on it are sound.

I owe a debt for help and encouragement to many friends, including Professor P. J. Enk, of Groningen, Professor G. E. Duckworth, of Princeton, Professor J. F. Mountford, of Liverpool, and Professor J. A. K. Thomson, formerly of King's College, London. Since it has been my misfortune to have to differ from the views expressed on New Comedy by Professor Gilbert Murray and Professor T. B. L. Webster, I have special pleasure in acknowledging the courtesy with which they have received my criticisms. My colleagues, Professor H. D. F. Kitto and Dr. A. Momigliano, have read my book in proof : I owe it to them that the mistakes are not even more numerous. Mr. B. L. Joseph has allowed me to see an advance copy of his book on *Elizabethan Acting*, shortly to be published by the Oxford University Press. If the Elizabethan art of acting had closer affinity with Roman rhetoric than with the naturalistic technique of our modern picture-stage, how much more true must this be of the art of acting in ancient Rome ! Among the American scholars whose works I have consulted I would mention in particular Professor Tenney Frank, Professor Roy Flickinger and Professor P. W. Harsh. I have reserved to the last the names of Sir A. W. Pickard-

Cambridge, whose *Theatre of Dionysus in Athens* represents
perhaps the most important advance in our knowledge since
Dörpfeld's day, and Professor W. B. Anderson, whose work has
lain mainly in other fields, but whose standards of scholarship
are valid for us all.   To him I affectionately dedicate this book.

PREFACE TO SECOND EDITION

IN PREPARING the second edition I have taken into
account the very reasonable criticisms which have
reached me concerning its predecessor.   I have re-written the
chapters on New Comedy and Terence, relegating to an
appendix the technical problem of the meaning of ' contaminare '.   Other new appendices give the ancient evidence
(such as it is) for stage scenery and for the introduction of
masks on the Roman stage.   As much of my book deals with
the mime and kindred forms of sub-literary drama, I have
supplied the text, with translation and notes, of the Oxyrhynchus
Mime, which, if not Latin, at least belongs to the period of the
Roman Empire.   I have added a simple account of Plautine
metres, with some introductory remarks on the thorny
problems of accent and ictus.   The inclusion of ' Notes and
Sources ' and the extended bibliography will, I hope, make
the book more useful to students of the theatre, whether or
not they agree with my views.   For many of the passages
quoted from ancient authors I have supplied translations ;
when not otherwise attributed, these are my own.

I have tried to make use of recent publications, particularly
Professor Duckworth's *Nature of Roman Comedy* and the late
Sir Arthur Pickard-Cambridge's *Dramatic Festivals of Athens*,
which was seen through the press after the author's death by
Professor Webster.   My own point of view remains very much
what it was : that we know very little about the Roman
stage ; that much of the supposed evidence cannot be accepted
with confidence, and that many of our controversies arise
from uncertainty about the meaning of common words.
Lacking technical knowledge, I have tried to rely on common-
sense—well defined by Professor G. C. Field as ' a firm grasp
of the obvious '.   Logical analysis is not the best method of

approach to a literary work, such as a play ; but the hypotheses which scholars frame are self-condemned if they contradict themselves. Within the limited field where I have thought that study might prove fruitful, I have not intentionally evaded any difficulty.

It will be seen that I have modified my earlier views on the origin of comedy in fertility-magic and the accentual nature of Plautine versification. My views on staging are the meagre remains of many more or less fanciful theories which have not stood the test of further consideration. In the years before the war my wife and I visited the sites of many ancient theatres, and tried to relate what we had read to what we saw. The positive results, as set out in this book, may seem disappointing ; but the open-air setting, with all that it implies, has remained in our memory.

PREFACE TO THE THIRD EDITION

THE PREPARATION of the third edition was cut short by the untimely death of the author. He had completed the drafts of Chapters I and II, which are published here in place of the corresponding Chapters in the earlier editions. He had written a section on the ' phlyax ' vase-paintings, and this is published here as an additional Appendix. An article which he had published and a paper which he had delivered in April 1963 to the Seventh Congress of the Association Guillaume Budé form further Appendices. It is clear from his notes that he did not intend to make any considerable changes in the text of the other Chapters and Appendices. Thus the whole book is now in the form which Professor Beare had in mind. The final stages of this third edition owe much to the help of Mrs. Beare and Miss Rhona Beare.

UNIVERSITY OF BRISTOL   N. G. L. HAMMOND.
    October 1963

CONTENTS

CHAPTER   PAGE

I. THE AIM, THE METHOD AND THE PROBLEMS   I

II. THE ITALIAN ORIGINS OF LATIN DRAMA   10

III. LIVIUS ANDRANICUS AND THE COMING OF LITERARY DRAMA TO ROME   25

IV. NAEVIUS   33

V. PLAUTUS : LIFE AND LIST OF PLAYS   45

VI. GREEK NEW COMEDY   50

VII. THE FAMOUS PLAYS OF PLAUTUS   56

VIII. PLAUTUS : TREATMENT OF HIS ORIGINALS   63

IX. THE GENERAL CHARACTER OF ROMAN TRAGEDY   70

X. PACUVIUS   79

XI. COMEDY AFTER THE DEATH OF PLAUTUS   85

XII. TERENCE   91

XIII. THE OTHER COMPOSERS OF PALLIATAE   113

XIV. ACCIUS   119

XV. NATIVE COMEDY : THE FABULA TOGATA   128

XVI. POPULAR FARCE: THE FABULA ATELLANA   137

XVII. THE LITERARY ATELLANA   143

XVIII. THE MIME   149

XIX. THE LATIN PROLOGUES AND THEIR VALUE AS EVIDENCE FOR THEATRICAL CONDITIONS   159

XX. THE ORGANIZATION OF THE ROMAN THEATRE   164

XXI. SEATS IN THE ROMAN THEATRE   171

XXII. THE SPECTATORS   173

XXIII. THE STAGE AND THE ACTORS' HOUSE   176

XXIV. COSTUMES AND MASKS   184

XXV. THE ROMAN ORIGIN OF THE LAW OF FIVE ACTS   196

XXVI. MUSIC AND METRE   219

XXVII. EPILOGUE : DRAMA UNDER THE EMPIRE   233

APPENDICES

PAGE

A. SEATS IN THE GREEK AND ROMAN THEATRES. (*C.R.* liii. 51-5)   241

B. SIDE-ENTRANCES AND ΠΕΡΙΑΚΤΟΙ IN THE HELLENISTIC THEATRE. (*C.Q.* xxxii. 205-10)   248

C. THE ANGIPORTUM AND ROMAN DRAMA. (*Hermathena* xxviii, 88-99)   256

D. CREPIDATA, PALLIATA, TABERNARIA, TOGATA. (*C.R.* liii. 166-8)   264

E. THE ROMAN STAGE CURTAIN. (*Hermathena* lviii. 104-15)   267

F. CHANGE OF SCENE AND CHANGE OF SCENERY: THE QUESTION OF 'SETS'   275

G. THE DOORS SHOWN ON THE STAGE   285

H. PASSAGES IN ANCIENT AUTHORS SUPPOSED TO REFER TO STAGE SCENERY   295

I. THE INTRODUCTION OF MASKS ON THE ROMAN STAGE. (*C.Q.* xxxiii. 139-46)   303

K. CONTAMINARE AND 'CONTAMINATION'   310

L. THE OXYRHYNCHUS MIME   314

M. ACCENT, ICTUS AND RHYTHM: THE METRES OF LATIN DRAMA   320

N. THE SO-CALLED 'PHLYAX' VASE-PAINTINGS OF SOUTH ITALY AS EVIDENCE FOR STAGING   335

O. THE MEANING OF XOPOY   340

P. PLAUTUS, TERENCE AND SENECA: A COMPARISON OF AIMS AND METHODS   347

NOTES AND SOURCES   355

BIBLIOGRAPHY   377

INDEX   385

INDEX TO LINES OF LATIN PLAYS   391

KEY TO THE MEANING OF METRICAL TERMS   397

ILLUSTRATIONS IN THE TEXT

Iphigeneia in Tauris, illustrating so-called prothyron
Volute krater, Bunckingham Collection . . . *title page*
    (*Mon. d. Inst. IV, pl. 51*)
Reconstruction of Theatre at Oeniadae with thyromata *facing* 1
    (*Bieber,*[1] *fig. 322*)
Graeco-Roman Theatre Tickets . . . . *page* 175
    (*Bieber,*[1] *fig. 455 ;* cf. *D.F.* pp. 272–5)
Mechanism of drop-curtain, according to Mazois . ,, 274
    (*Fiechter,*[2] *fig. 119*)
Relation of house-doors to the side-entrances . . ,, 285
Construction of Greek or Roman doorway . . . ,, 290
Woman unlocking front door . . . . . ,, 293
    (*D. & S., s. v. ianua,*[3] *fig. 4128*)
Woman looking out of door . . . . . ,, 293
    (*D. & S., s. v. ianua,*[3] *fig. 4131*)

[1]From Bieber : *History of the Greek and Roman Theater* by permission of Princeton University Press.

[2]From Fiechter : *Baugeschichtliche Entwicklung des antiken Theaters* by permission of Becksche Verlagsbuchhandlung, Munich.

[3]From the article on *ianua* in *Daremberg et Saglio* by permission of Messrs. Hachette.

PLATES

  I. Spectators and Performers at the Etruscan Games *facing* 16
      1. Part of the Tomba della Scimmia at Chiusi
        (*Poulsen,*[1] *fig. 20*)
      2. Part of small frieze in the Tomba delle Bighe
        (*Poulsen,*[1] *fig. 19*)
      3. Scenes from the Etruscan Games . . ,,
        (*Poulsen,*[1] *figs. 4, 5 and 6*)
  II. ' Chiron goes upstairs ' : Phlyax Vase-painting . ,, 49
      (*Photo : British Museum*)
  III. Scene from Comedy : Relief from Pompeii in
     Naples Museum . . . . . ,, 80
      (*Photo : Alinari ; see Dramatic Festivals of Athens,* p. 201)
  IV. Jupiter and Mercury. Phlyax Vase-painting in
     the Vatican Museum . . . . ,, 113
      (*Phote : Alinari*)
  V. Poet (Menander ?), and Comic Muse: Choosing
     the Masks (?). Relief in the Lateran Museum ,, 176
      (*Photo : Alinari ;* see *D.F.* p. 201)
  VI. Street Musicians : Mosaic by Dioskorides, from
     Pompeii . . . . ,, 209
      (*Photo : Alinari ;* see *Theatre of Dionysus,* pp. 223–5)
  VII. The Roman Theatre, Orange . . . . ,, 240
      (*Photo : F. Beau, Avignon-Monclar*)
  VIII. The Large Theatre, Pompeii . . . . ,, 273
      (*Photo : Author*)
     The Roman Theatre, Vaison-la-Romaine, showing
     curtain-slot . . . . . . ,, 273
      (*Photo : Author*)

[1]From Poulson : *Etruscan Tomb Paintings* by permission of Oxford University Press.

Reconstruction of theatre at Oeniadae with thyromata

CHAPTER I

THE AIM, THE METHOD AND THE PROBLEMS

IN THIS book I shall attempt to give a connected account of
the drama of ancient Rome in its historical setting. We still
possess, under the names of Plautus and Terence, twenty-six
comedies translated from Greek into Latin and intended for
production on the stage. These works belong to the late third
and early second century before Christ. In addition we have
a number of fragments remaining from the drama of
Republican times, from tragedy, comedy and farce, from
translations of lost Greek plays and original compositions,
which help us to trace the story of Latin drama from the
earliest writer, Livius Andronicus, to the end of the Republic.
From early Imperial times we possess, under the name of
Seneca, ten tragedies, which seem to many modern readers, I
think rightly, to have been intended not for performance but
for declamation or private reading. Though framed on Greek
lines, these are not translations but independent compositions ;
indeed one of them, the *Octauia*, takes its subject from contemporary Roman history and has as its heroine the ill-fated
wife of the emperor Nero.

The historical importance of these plays is great. Their influence at the time of the Renaissance was far-reaching ; they
were the acknowledged models of dramatic art. The
Elizabethan world looked back with reverence on the days
' when Roscius was an actor in Rome '.* Polonius indicates
the versatility of the troupe of strolling players by saying that
for them ' Seneca cannot be too heavy, nor Plautus too light '.
The knowledge of Latin was common ; Greek was less widely
known, and the Greek plays were more difficult to understand. Not only Roman practice but Roman theory became
canonical. Our infant English drama came to be subjected to
rules, supposedly Roman, which were never known to the
Roman stage. This at least we must concede to the scholars of

* *Hamlet* II. ii. 419.

1

the Renaissance : they were influenced by Roman theories recorded in works which had survived and by Latin plays still extant.   The new vernacular drama soon drove its Latin models from the stage ; and towards the end of the eighteenth century even classical scholars began to turn their attention from Rome to Greece, from the Latin copies to the original Greek plays.   Indeed the Latin comedies came increasingly to be regarded chiefly as a source of evidence from which might be reconstructed their lost originals, the plays of Greek New Comedy.   The modern classical scholar, particularly, it may be, the German scholar, is only too ready to form an ideal picture of that unapproachable perfection which was Greece, and by such a standard to judge—and to emend—the material which has actually come down to us.   And at all times, from those of Cicero to our own, the plays of past ages have been treated by scholars as literature, written to be read, rather than as drama, designed for presentation on the stage.

No connected account of the Roman theatre and drama has reached us from Roman times.   What is commonly called the *Ars Poetica* of Horace is largely intended to guide future dramatists.   Livy gives us our most detailed account of the origins of the theatrical art.   Lucian writes about the panto-mime, and Choricius of Gaza about the mime.   Otherwise we depend on scattered references in ancient writers of various periods.   The theatre played a large part in ancient life, probably larger than it does today ; and writers on all sorts of subjects find apt parallels in drama.   Out of evidence of this kind our modern historians of Latin Literature have con-structed their accounts.   Evidence was supposed to be ' good ' if found in such an author as Cicero or Livy ; but often it was cited from post-classical authors, separated by centuries from the events or customs which they claimed to describe. Two simple questions should be kept in mind when weighing such evidence : first, is the writer likely to have known the facts, and second, is his most likely motive the desire to tell the truth.   There is ' good ' evidence that doors on the stage, as well as in real life, opened outwards, that is, into the street ; that Roman actors did not take to wearing masks until long after the time when our extant comedies were written ; and that in early times and indeed down to the first century B.C. the spectators were compelled to stand.   But in the plays themselves there is overwhelming evidence that all these statements are untrue. Ritschl used references to seats in the prologues as a proof that these prologues were post-Plautine. The truth is rather that these references (which occur not merely in the prologues but in some of the plays) are proof that some at least of the spectators in Plautus' day were seated.

It is often legitimate to draw an inference from some statement which cannot be accepted at its face value. Thus the remark by a character in a fictitious dialogue of Cicero that Plautus in his old age used to enjoy his *Pseudolus* and his *Truculentus** at least suggests that Cicero himself liked these plays. Livy's famous description of how the delivery of the *cantica* came to be entrusted to a vocalist while the actors were confined to accompanying his words with gestures, though incredible as an account of the normal performance of comedy, may well have some connection with the pantomime which was so popular in Livy's own day. Every document, however erroneous or fictitious, is at least evidence that someone thought it worth while to compose the document. But great as is our debt to antiquity, and our admiration for their intellectual achievement, we have to admit that they do not seem to have attached the importance that we do to the objective statement of fact. Writing was still an art, like painting or embroidery. For an example we may take the biographies of the dramatists. ' It has often been noticed ', writes Professor G. C. Field,† ' that the Greek idea of biography differs from our own. It is curious that the Greeks, who invented the scientific study of history, seem to have had so little idea of applying their historical methods to the biographies of individual persons. Even the best of them seem to write for edification rather than for truth. And in the average biography, when we are looking for an account of the events of the life, we find only strings of anecdotes and incidental comments, with little or no chronological connection and no coherent thread running through them '.

If we are to trace developments, we must try to get events into their chronological order. We want to know, for example, when a dramatist was born. Yet we do not know when Julius Caesar was born. We want to know in what year a particular

* *De Sen.* 14. 50.
† *Plato and his Contemporaries*, p. 2.

play was produced. This is just what we are never told. To quote Field again, ' one of the things that we should be most glad to have would be a single reliable date for the composition of any of the dialogues. Yet it appears likely that not even among the writings of his immediate successors was such information to be found '. The Latin dramatists were not in their day regarded as of such importance that anyone should trouble to record the facts concerning them while those facts were available. They were hard-working professional writers ; they gave their lives to earning a living, and went to their graves leaving, it may be, nothing to preserve their memory except the works which they had written. Somehow these works survived, and later generations of readers found themselves curious to know something about the authors whose names they found on the title-pages of the works they were reading. Attempts were made to satisfy this curiosity by examining the text of the plays for autobiographical details. This was a very natural and indeed legitimate proceeding, though any conclusions reached by mere inference from a text which we possess can have no independent authority. But a dramatist, of all writers, has small opportunity for talking about himself, except in his prologues, the value of which does not seem to have been realised by the biographers. Better evidence might be supplied by the manuscript, in which were entered (at least sometimes) notes concerning the opening or revival performances. Official records might make some reference to the Games at which the play had been produced ; noble families had their archives. Where there was no evidence, the biographers sometimes fell back on illegitimate inference from the text, or sheer invention, or popular gossip. We read in the Life of Aeschylus, for example, ' others assert that in the performance of the *Eumenides*, by introducing the chorus without order into the orchestra he so scared the people that infants expired and women miscarried '. When Varro made out his canon of the genuine plays of Plautus he seems to have applied two tests : was the play generally regarded as by Plautus, and did the style seem Plautine? Yet Varro was the greatest of Roman scholars, and such chronological information as we find in ancient sources seems to go back to him. Did he fully realise how important were early documents?

To treat the statements of ancient writers as reliable information, merely suppressing or toning down obvious contradictions and absurdities, is to repeat the very procedure for which we call Livy an unscientific historian. Manifestly if we think an ancient document worth quoting, we must be prepared to quote all of it. It will be seen that there are certain recurrent features in the Lives of the dramatists ; thus the supper-party which brings Caecilius and Terence together is paralleled by the meeting of Pacuvius and Accius. These anecdotes may have no more historical value than the story of King Alfred and the cakes ; but even if they are myths, they must be told. For the myth is itself part of history. But if we find that we have to reject certain details in a narrative, just because they are in themselves incredible, we cast doubt on the reliability of the narrative as a whole.

Modern historians of the ancient theatre rely increasingly on archaeological evidence. The remains of Roman theatres are impressive evidence of the importance of the theatre in ancient life ; and no one can doubt, after seeing such monuments, that an ancient performance was given in the daytime and under the light of heaven. But in all probability no extant theatre was used in antiquity for producing a play by Plautus, Terence or Seneca. The theatres belong to the Empire, when the prevailing types of performance were the mime and the pantomime ; the theatres of Plautus and Terence, slight affairs at best, had long disappeared, and the tragedies of imperial times were in all probability not meant for the theatre. Works of art are treated as evidence for details of stage production. It is thought that a painting depicting some incident in mythology was often inspired by the memory of a dramatic performance which the artist had seen and remembered so vividly that he showed the characters not simply as he imagined them in the story but as he had actually seen them on the stage. Of course paintings throw a great deal of light on ancient life, including the theatre ; we have pictures of spectators at a theatrical or similar performance, of actors looking at their masks, and (it would seem) of performances too. What is not clear is how closely such illustrations (very few of which contain details which suggest the stage) correspond with details of production. A few examples from more recent sources may make this plain. We are familiar with Sir John Millais' picture of the death of Ophelia; it shows her on the waters of the pool which will drown her. If this picture should be the only record of Shakespeare's *Hamlet* that will reach the 21st century, what inferences may not be drawn about the resources of the English stage, which could show a death by drowning! But we possess the play, and we know that this episode was narrated, not acted. No pictures can be more directly connected with drama than the engravings in the seventeenth century editions of Racine. Yet in these engravings by Chauveau and his successors subjects are often chosen which in the play were narrated not performed. Thus for the *Thébaïde* the illustrator shows Etéocle and Polynice killing each other ; in *Britannicus* we see the poisoning of the hero at the banquet ; in *Phèdre* we see Hippolyte lying on the shore between his wounded horses, while the monster breathes his last in the background ; in *Iphigénie* is shown the abortive sacrifice of the heroine ; Diana is seen sitting on a cloud. Similarly in illustrating *Corneille* Chauveau often chooses scenes which are described in speeches and not played on stage. Or, even when illustrating scenes actually performed, the artist may introduce some detail in absolute contradiction with the indications of the text. ' In short, the illustrators have systematically seized upon the sensational and the spectacular in Racine ; that is, upon all that is least typical of him '.*

The explanation of these discrepancies is very simple. The engraver is guided by the nature of his art. Pictorial art has its own resources and its own limitations, which are not the resources and the limitations of stage-production. The actor is subject to the law of gravity ; the engraver can suspend his characters on a cloud. He can show scenes of violence, bodies on the stage, dying horses, a dying dragon ; he does not have to consider how all these are in due course to be got off the stage. On the other hand the artist cannot easily tell a story in a picture which deals with a single moment in time ; he must speak to the eye alone, for he is not able to speak to the ear. In the begetting of Heracles, as all the world knew, Zeus assumed the likeness of the absent Amphitryon. In a phlyax painting (see Plate V) Zeus appears in his own character, accompanied by an equally undisguised Hermes, and he will have access to

---

* See Raymond Picard, *Racine and Chauveau*, Journal of the Warburg and Courtauld Institutes, vol. XIV, nos. 3 4, 1951, pp. 259–274.

Alcumena not through his divine power but by means of the ladder which he is carrying. This does not mean that the artist is illustrating a different play ; it does mean that, in illustrating this famous story, he is bound by the limitations belonging to his art.

We turn finally to the plays. The oldest surviving manuscripts of Plautus and Terence belong to the fourth or fifth century A.D. Early as these are, we can see that they do not preserve the original text unaltered. It is clear that Plautus was not the author of these lines in the prologue to the *Casina* which refer expressly to a revival of the play after his death. It is not likely that he was responsible for *both* the alternative last scenes of the *Pseudolus,* or that Terence provided *both* the alternative last scenes of the *Andria ;* indeed in each case it is evidently the second alternative which was added by a later hand. Some of the prologues to Plautus' plays refer to the author in the third person. It would seem that plays were peculiarly liable to alteration at the beginning and the end—where presumably there was room in the manuscript. The prologue of the *Casina* is expressly addressed to the spectators of a revival performance of the play ; the other interpolations presumably were also intended for a revival performance. Thus the remark at the beginning of the prologue to the *Menaechmi :* ' I bring you Plautus—on my tongue, not in my hand ', is evidently meant to let the spectators know that they are going to see a play by the famous dramatist of a former generation.

But what of the text of the play as a whole, apart from the beginning and the ending? Many attempts have been made to detect interpolations, chiefly on the ground of style : that is to say, critics consider particular passages unworthy of Plautus. Yet what do we know about the style of Plautus except what we infer from the text of his plays? Certainly there is no passage which is universally regarded on stylistic grounds as post-Plautine. It may be that for some time after the author's death his plays existed merely as acting editions, at the mercy of the producer who happened to own them. It would be possible, no doubt, for such a producer to make alterations—but we must assume that he would not do so without a reason. He might curtail a scene which seemed dull, or throw in a jest. But as these are precisely the methods by which Plautus is

supposed to have altered his Greek originals, it is not likely
that we should be able to detect the work of the producer who
carried this process a step further. Thus the theory of
retractatio, ' working over ', breaks down. There is an a
priori probability that producers would leave the text alone.
The prologue of Terence, written in reply to contemporary
critics, must have meant little or nothing to the theatre-going
public of later ages. Yet these prologues have come down to
us with the plays to which they refer. It is not easy to suppose
that the archaic plays of Livius Andronicus were popular on
the stage after his death ; yet they survived until the time of
Cicero, who read them (and pronounced them not worth a
second reading). It would seem that the bulk of the early plays
survived. Notes of revival performances were occasionally
jotted down on the title page ; acrostic ' arguments ' were
prefixed ; but we have no evidence of deletions, and the body
of the play probably remained in the form given to it by its
author. There was, it is true, some uncertainty about the
authorship of particular plays ; according to Varro plays of
other authors came to be ascribed to Plautus, no doubt to
enhance their value.

The most obvious feature of Republican drama is its
derivative character. All our Latin comedies are based on
Greek originals, themselves now lost. It is plain, moreover,
that the Latin plays are not exact translations ; the translators
omitted what they thought dull and added what they thought
would interest their public. It is self-evident that puns on
Latin words and references to Roman customs and titles cannot
have come from the Greek original. Beyond this it is not easy
to go. In any case the object of the present book is not to
reconstruct the lost originals but to consider the Latin plays
as they are, both as drama and as evidence for the Roman
theatre. It is agreed by all that we should try to read them as
plays and to picture them as performed on the Roman stage.
But modern readers are accustomed to a very different
theatrical convention ; we bring to our study of Latin drama
assumptions of which we ourselves may not be fully aware,
but which are only too likely to colour our picture and distort
our judgment. On few things do scholars differ more than on
the deductions about stage practice which they draw from the
study of dramatic texts.

How then are we to proceed, if every line of reasoning proves so unreliable? At least we can describe what is known. The plays exist ; each of them, whatever its source, is a unity ; it owes its present shape to some one mind ; and the comedies at least were evidently composed for production. About certain general principles there is a fair measure of agreement. We can begin with these and see whether the evidence supports them. One line of reasoning can be checked by another. Biographical information must be treated as unreliable ; statements made long after the events to which they refer must remain under suspicion, unless there is good reason to suppose that the writer is quoting a document ; actual quotations of old texts can generally be treated as authentic. On matters of staging the evidence of the plays outweighs everything else, provided that we can interpret it. Before we say that something is impossible, we must consider whether there is evidence for it on the stages of other times and peoples. If we must frame theories, the simplest are the best, at least to begin with. Very often we may find that our conclusions are negative. If we find the Latin dramatists using various expedients, sometimes far-fetched, to overcome a difficulty which would nowadays be met by the use of a technical device, we can infer that this particular device was unknown to these dramatists. We must try to keep an open mind, and be ready to discard our earlier conclusions and to re-examine our assumptions. We must be ready to learn from each other, remembering that to none of us is it given to be always right, or for that matter wrong.

Fashions in research change ; scholars are carried away by prevailing literary, artistic or even political theories. No change of fashion can alter the fact that the Latin plays are plays, and that, as plays, they may be studied in their own light.

CHAPTER II

THE ITALIAN ORIGINS OF LATIN DRAMA

TOWARDS THE close of the Republican period the theatre had become a dominating feature of Roman social life. Many writers—Lucretius, Virgil, Horace, Tibullus, Ovid, Livy, Valerius Maximus—tell us of the modest origin from which it had grown. I shall try to show in this chapter what can safely be extracted from their accounts concerning the prehistory of Roman dramatic performances, and I shall not take Greek influences into consideration for the moment.

I must try first to dispose of an unjust view of the Romans which would deny to them any dramatic gift. They had a marked taste for the theatrical, for action and miming. We can see this in their legal procedure, for instance in the sort of pantomime which was prescribed in a case concerned with the claims of ownership of an estate. Cicero, describing how the two contending parties utter the set formulas, pretend to set out for the estate in question, then are summoned back by the magistrate, is reminded of the stage. Roman religion shows us such rites as the festival of the Argei on May 15. These Argei were ' a number of puppets or bundles of rushes, resembling men bound hand and foot, which were taken down to the pons sublicius by the Pontifices and magistrates, and cast into the river by the Vestal Virgins '. Warde Fowler sees here a rite of dramatic character.* In dialogue and particularly in repartee, in their taste for satire, the Romans show some similarity to the Irish, who have made so marked a contribution to satire and comedy. Ranging as it did from bantering exchanges to savage abuse, Latin dialogue had in it a theatrical element. The Romans had an undeniable gaiety. They are said to have been the first people to dance for fun. †
Perhaps we have got the evidence out of proportion, and think that Cicero's remark ' nobody dances except when

* *Roman Festivals*, pp. 111 ff.
† See *Social Dance: a short history*, by A. H. Longrigg (1963).

drunk' sums up the Roman attitude. The solemn, impassive Roman presented to us as typical, as the 'image' of his country, may after all have been playing a part. The true Roman people may be pictured as they behaved in the festival of Anna perenna, on the Ides of March. They streamed out to the Campus Martius, near the Tiber, and either lay about in the grass in couples or set up tents or rude huts. They spent the day in drinking, dancing, singing and love-making. There, says Ovid, ' they sing whatever they have picked up at the theatres, and wave their hands to keep time with their song. They put the bowl down and dance round it, and the skilled girl-friend lets loose her hair and dances '.

The Greeks found the origin of their drama in the dance. For them ' dance ' included every kind of significant rhythmical movement. The feeling for rhythm lies deep in our nature. Graceful movement gives pleasure both to the performer and to the onlooker, especially if it is accompanied by music and song. In the dance primitive man finds expression for emotion of every kind ; in the dance, too, he gratifies his instinct for imitation. Among primitive peoples dancing is a communal activity. The tribe is faced at every turn with the need for preservation from enemies, disease or hunger ; from lack of game, of cattle, of crops, of children. Hence the war dance, the dances in celebration of birth and marriage, the magical dances intended to promote hunting and agriculture, to exorcise the demons of sickness and to lay the ghosts of the dead.

For a farming community the most important and the merriest event of the year is the harvest-home. Then, if ever, the farmer can forget his cares and join with his friends in unrestrained revelry, which may easily take a riotous or licentious turn. The chief dance of the Hos of Bengal is in January, when the granaries are full. During the dancing, as in the Roman Saturnalia, masters and servants treat each other as equals. There is much drinking of beer ; language and conduct are freed from the customary restraints of decency.*

Similar was the ' Fescennine jesting ' of the Roman harvest-home. 'Rival' scenes were dear to the Italian heart. Horace tells us[1] how he and Maecenas were entertained by an exchange of abuse between two clowns (one of whom was a

* Frazer, *Golden Bough*, ix. 136.

Campanian),* and even Marcus Aurelius Antoninus,[2] heir to
the Roman Empire, writes of how, after a day's work with the
labourers in the fields, finding himself too tired to study, he sat
in the kitchen and enjoyed the rustic quips exchanged between
his fellow-workers. In the Fescennine verses, the bantering
dialogue of clowns at the harvest-home, the Romans found the
germ of their own drama.

Virgil tells us (*Georg.* ii. 380 ff.) that goats are destructive
to vines, and that for this reason a goat was sacrificed to
Dionysus by the Athenians on the day when the dramatic
performances were taking place ; then, amid general rejoicings,
they would crown the poets. The Latins too, Virgil adds, held
wine-festivals in his day ; they amused themselves with improvised verse and wild laughter ; they covered their faces
with hideous masks made of the bark of trees ; in honour of
Bacchus they suspended on trees little figures (oscilla) which
swung in the wind. ' Then the vine is rich with fruit, and the
valleys, and the deep forests, and all the places looked upon
by the sacred image of the god '. Similarly Tibullus (II. i.
50–6) tells how the farmer, when resting from his labours,
would sing rustic words arranged in verse. After his meal he
would practise on the pipes the airs that he wished to repeat
before the flower-crowned statues of his gods. His face
covered with red lead, he would lead a clumsy dance. Horace
(*Ep.* II. i. 139 ff.) tells how the farmers of old, once their
harvest was home, took holiday, offered a pig to the Earth-
goddess, milk to Silvanus, flowers and wine to the Genius of the
household. For such occasions, he says, the Fescennine verse
was invented ; it consisted of rustic abuse in alternating verses.
This became an annual event and was at first inoffensive ; then
it began to attack members of noble houses. A law was passed
which forced the performers to observe proper limits.

What were the Fescennine ' alternating verses '? Festus
(P. 85 M) tells us that they were sung at weddings and that
they took their name from the town Fescennia or Fescennium[8]
in Etruria, or else from the word fascinum, black magic, which
they were thought to avert.

The connecting of Fescenninus with a place-name reminds

* Similarly Brutus and his officers were entertained by an exchange of abuse
between a Praenestine, Rupilius Rex, and a Greek, Persius—who was "drenched
with Italian vinegar" (Hor. *Sat.* i. vii).

us of the association of the fabula Atellana with the town of
Atella in Campania, and of the word caerimonium with the
Etruscan town Caere. Yet all these derivations[3] have been
doubted. The other derivation, Fescenninus from fascinum,
' black magic ', is more interesting. We find in Plautus the
expression praefiscini, ' save the mark '. Perhaps fascinum is
itself connected with fari, ' speak ', and denotes the ' speaking '
of magic spells. Now one of the ways of averting the evil eye
was to oppose to it a ridiculous or indecent object. Porphyrion
tells us (on Horace, *Epod.* viii. 18) that fascinum is used in the
sense of ' male member ', since in order to avert the evil
influence (praefascinandis rebus) an obscene representation of
this (haec membri deformitas) was employed. Varro (*L.L.*
VII xcvii) says that it was the custom to hang on the necks of
children an obscene object to avert evil (ne quid obsit) ; and
the elder Pliny (*H.N.* XXVIII. xxxix) informs us that such
an object was hung under the triumphal chariot as a protection
against jealousy, medicus inuidiae.

It is commonly supposed that the phallus is associated with
fertility magic, and that its use in comedy shows that comedy
originated in fertility magic. The Fescennine songs were
certainly connected with weddings*, where fertility rites would
be apposite. They were connected with harvest-homes and
vintage-festivals, as we have seen ; and St. Augustine† tells
us that in Latium, and especially at Lavinium, on the day of
the festival of Liber, a huge fascinum was conducted in
procession and then solemnly crowned by a matron ; in
return the god was expected to guarantee a bounteous vintage.
But fertility magic seems less relevant to the triumph, at which
ribald songs were sung and the phallus was attached beneath
the general's chariot. The elder Pliny (*loc. cit.*) tells us that it
was one of the sacred objects put in the care of the Vestals ;
the Vestals, who had taken vows of chastity, seem the wrong
priestesses for a fertility cult. Why, again, should a child
wear the emblem of fertility? Another explanation which will
apply to all the occasions when the ribald verses were sung or
indecent objects displayed is that these were occasions when

* Cat. lxi 126 f., procax Fescennina iocatio; Claudian, poems 11 and 12,
Fescennina de nuptiis Honorii Augusti.

† *Civ. Dei.* VII. 21: sic uidelicet Liber deus placandus fuerat pro euentibus
seminum, sic ab agris fascinatio repellenda. Cornford compares ' the gigantic
phallus-plough with its apotropaic eyes, carried by a row of naked men on the
black-figured vase figured by Dieterich ' (*The Origin of Attic Comedy*, p. 51, n. 1).

hostile spells were particularly to be feared* : the rejoicings over a successful harvest, the supreme moment of marriage, the superhuman glory of the triumph, and also the helplessness of infancy.

The antagonism between solemn ritual and indecent revelry seems clear enough to us, but may not have seemed clear to the Italians. Indeed the two extremes seem to have gone naturally together. The bride and bridegroom, about to enter into the high duties of their new state amidst all the solemnity which religion could afford, had to listen to the crudest jests, flung at them in accordance with ancient custom. The victorious general, riding through Rome in the superhuman pomp of the triumph, could overhear the songs of his soldiers,[4] which referred in the language of the camp to his bodily infirmities and moral peccadilloes. At the head of the funeral procession,[5] even at the funeral of a dead and deified emperor, might on occasion be seen an actor who wore the dead man's likeness and mimicked his characteristic gestures. It may be that indecency in drama owes its origin to ceremonies on which the very life of the tribe was thought to depend, but its continuance in more sophisticated times such as our own must be partly due to its power to raise laughter.

The Fescennine verses were in metre of some kind ; they were uttered in some form of song. What sense are we to attribute to these words, so easily uttered, but so vague in meaning?

The three great Indo-European languages of antiquity— Greek, Latin and Sanskrit—had in common certain features scarcely to be found in the world today—in particular quantity. Even in ordinary speech a clear distinction was made between short and long vowels ; versification seems to have been wholly quantitative, taking no account of the word-accent, which was one of pitch or tone, not one of stress or intensity. Latin differed from Greek and Sanskrit in the unity it gave to the individual word ; the initial syllable of each word seems from early times to have been given special importance. Thus alliteration is common in early Latin, whereas in Greek it scarcely exists. The gait of early Latin prose is quite different from that of Greek prose.

---

* ' The phallus itself is no less a negative charm against evil spirits than a positive sign of fertilisation ' (Cornford, *op. cit.*, p. 49).

Quantity, musical accent, importance of the initial syllable, alliteration, parallelism of phrases, all gave to early Latin a movement which, if not that of verse, nevertheless did not differ greatly from verse of a sort. The word carmen, which we translate ' song ', can mean (1) ' saying ', ' judgment ', ' motto '; (2) ' poem '; (3) ' song '. It can be used of the magical formula used in healing or cursing, or again of the formulas of oath-taking and of law, of treaty and declaration of war. Varro quotes the formula for curing a sprained ankle (*R.R.* I. ii. 27) :

> ego tui memini,
> medere meis pedibus ;
> terra pestem teneto,
> salus hic maneto
> in meis pedibus.

We have already seen that early verse is described by Roman writers as ' alternating '. The line tends to fall into two parts, with a break in the middle. Horace, after describing the part played by the Fescennine verses, tells of the changes brought about by Greek influences, one of which was to cast into the shadows the Saturnian verse, though that crude measure had long clung to existence and survived even to Horace's own day.

It seems to follow that the Saturnian metre was at any rate one metre used for the Fescennine verses. In the Saturnian a group of about seven syllables followed by a group of about six syllables tends to constitute the line. The break in the middle of the line is one of the constant features. The number of words also seems to be important ; three words often form the first part, two the second. Both parts often end with a three-syllabled word, the penultimate syllable of which is long. The second syllable of the second part is usually short. The stock example is

> dabunt malum Metelli   Naeuio poetae.

Other variants are

> (2) sancta puer Saturni   filia regina
>
> (3) carnis uinumque quod   libabant anclabatur
>
> (4) res diuas edicit   praedicat castus

The rustic dance mentioned by Tibullus was known as the tripudium. One can image the Saturnian recited with a triple beat in each half, indicating the places where the dancer's foot was set down, or a signal was given with arm or baton by the conductor. But we must not go on to assume that this beat was accompanied by a stress of voice, still less that this stress of voice could have the effect of turning a weak syllable into a strong syllable. Nor do we know on which syllables the beat fell.

Another occasion for Fescennine exchanges was the triumphal procession. We have some of the verses chanted by Caesar's soldiers :

> urbani, seruate uxores   moechum caluom adducimus

This metre is easy to define in Greek terminology as a trochaic tetrameter catalectic ; that is, the first half consists of four trochees, the second of three and a half—making a total of fifteen syllables to the line. It is a quantitative metre : the odd syllables must be long, and the fourteenth syllable must be short ; the other even syllables may be long or short. This metre too has a long history.

'In this and the following years' writes Livy (vii. 2), referring to 364–3 B.C. 'there was a pestilence. As the violence of the malady was appeased neither by human remedies nor by appeals to the gods, scenic shows were introduced, a novelty for this warlike people, which up till then had known no spectacle except in the Circus. These shows were on a small scale, like all beginnings. Dancers were summoned from Etruria and danced gracefully in Tuscan style to the strains of the piper, without any song or any gestures in imitation of songs. The young citizens took to imitating them, at the same time exchanging among themselves jests in improvised verse, with gestures to match their words. The innovation was a success and grew in favour by dint of frequent repetition. The native artists received the name *histriones*, *ister* being the Etruscan for *ludio* (player). They were no longer content with the old fashion of exchanging repartee in a verse like the Fescennine verse, improvised, unplanned and rough ; they now performed medleys full of varied metres, with music written out to suit the piper and with appropriate action. After a few years Livius took the bold step of abandoning the

I

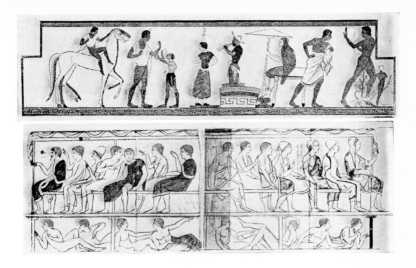

SPECTATORS AND PERFORMERS AT THE ETRUSCAN GAMES
1 Part of the Tomba della Scimmia at Chiusi
2 Part of small frieze in the Tomba delle Bighe

SCENES FROM THE ETRUSCAN GAMES

medleys and produced a play with a plot. He acted in his own pieces, as was the universal custom then. It is said that when frequent encores had injured his voice he got permission to put a boy singer in front of the piper and was able to mime the song all the more vigorously, because he was free from the necessity of using his voice. This was the origin of the custom whereby the actors mime the songs, reserving only the dialogue for their own voices. After the new rule governing plays had been substituted for merriment and uncontrolled jesting and the ' game ' had gradually turned into a profession, the young citizens abandoned to the actors the performance of plays and returned to the old custom of exchanging jokes set in verse ; their performances were later called ' after-pieces ' and were worked into plays, especially Atellane plays. These Atellane entertainments were derived from the Osci and were kept by the young citizens in their own control, unpolluted by the actors. Hence the rule that the performers of Atellanes do not lose their membership of their tribe and serve in the army, being held to have no connection with the entertainment profession. In my account of the small beginnings of many other things I think I should include the origin of the theatrical art, in order to show from what wholesome origins it has come to be the craze of our own day, a craze which would be almost beyond the means even of wealthy kingdoms '.

This famous passage is echoed by Valerius Maximus (II. iv. 4). In spite of the difficulties of interpretation, it is generally regarded as too detailed to be dismissed. Nevertheless Livy himself indicates that he is writing with a moral purpose, namely to show from what limited and wholesome beginnings the dramatic art has reached the intolerable vogue it possesses in his own day. He therefore emphasizes the native, amateur element and makes the professional and foreign element as small as possible. Yet his account implies the existence of professional actors in early Rome ; who else could have performed the ' medleys '? Emphasis is laid on the religious origin of the whole development. Most striking of all, he does not mention that Livius was a Greek, and that the plays which he produced were versions of Greek originals.

The Fescennine Verses, the Atellane plays, the activities of Etruscan dancers in Rome, the importance of the professional pipers—these are not in doubt. What is very much in question

2

is the rôle ascribed to the young citizens. Still more debatable is the reference to the satura, a word which we have translated ' medley '.

What does ' satura ' mean? The grammarian Diomedes (Keil, I. 485) says ' at the present day the name satire is given by the Romans to a malicious poem, which, like Old Comedy, is intended to attack vices ; such poems as have been written by Lucilius, Horace and Persius. In former times the name satire was given to a poem composed of pieces of different kinds (carmen quod ex uariis poematibus constabat), like those written by Pacuvius and Ennius. The word satura comes from the name of the satyrs, because this poem contains jests and indecencies like the licentious words and actions of satyrs. Or else it comes from satura lanx, a dish filled with first-fruits of all kinds which people in former times used to offer to the gods in sacrifice ; satura was so called because it was full to overflowing (a copia ac saturitate rei satura uocabatur). Virgil alludes to this kind of dish in the *Georgics*, when he writes (ii. 194)

> lancibus et pandis fumantia reddimus exta ;

and (ii. 394)

> lancesque et liba feremus.

Or else it comes from a mixed dish of various kinds of food, which, according to Varro, was called satura. Indeed we read in the second book of his Plautine Studies : ' the satura is a mixture of dried grapes, barley broth, edible fir-cones, soaked with wine and honey '. Finally there are those who derive the word from the combined law (a lege satura) in which different things are proposed en bloc to the people, just as different poems are included in a single satura. Lucilius mentions these combined laws in his first satire : per saturam aedilem factum qui legibus soluat ; and Sallust in *Jugurtha* (xxix) : deinde quasi per saturam sententiis exquisitis in deditionem accipitur.

Evanthius (*de fabula* ii. 5) says ' from this ' (the law controlling the Fescennines) ' arose another type of piece, the satura. It is so called from the satyrs, gods, as all know, always merry and unrestrained ; and it is a mistake to look for another derivation. This satura, while it attacked the vices of the citizens with biting jests which were rustic in tone, did not mention individual names. This form of comedy thus caused the poets much annoyance, for influential citizens suspected it of relating and making mock of their actions in a hostile manner. Lucilius was the first to change this type of piece ; he made it into a poem, that is, versified composition in several books '.

Paulus, abbreviating Festus, writes ' satura is a dish composed of different ingredients, and a law formed by uniting several laws, and a type of poem uniting several subjects '.

A modern philologist, L. R. Palmer (*The Latin Language* p. 48) derives satura from an Etruscan word meaning ' speak '.

I find it difficult to believe that this Latin word has anything to do with the Greek satyrs ; though the similarity would suggest to scholars some connection. The Latin derivation seems the right one : the word means a mixture. It could be a mixture of different themes, or of different metres (including prose), or of verse associated with music and dance. One can imagine a sort of music-hall performance flourishing in Rome about the period of the Samnite Wars. But we have to face the fact that no writer except Evanthius speaks of a type of drama called satura. He calls it a genus fabulae, genus comoediae, resembling Old Comedy. Livy's languáge is scarcely evidence for the existence of a specific form of drama called satura. In the words impletas modis saturas, descripto iam ad tibicinem cantu, motuque congruenti peragebant, we have to take saturas closely with ' filled with measures '. The satura evidently had a fixed text : the ' filling ' of this text with ' measures ' made it a medley. But it is not at all clear that Livy had in mind a piece of dramatic character, nor that he was speaking of a type which had really existed, still less a type which had borne the name satura. About this phrase, as about the passage as a whole, there hangs an artificial air.

In fact Livy is trying to prove a thesis. His expressed object in digressing about the despised subject of the theatre is to show from what modest and innocent origins had grown up what by his time had become a public nuisance. Like most educated Romans, Livy despised the theatre. By his day the stage had come to be occupied almost entirely by low farce and seductive pantomime, performed by artists who possessed neither legal rights nor moral reputation ; the only performers, he says, who in his day enjoyed citizen status were the actors of the traditional Atellane farce. Livy's general view of Roman history is that it represents a moral decline ; the theatre is a particular case of this. He therefore stresses the religious origin of the development ; he lays emphasis also on the amateur character of the native performers (iuuenes, ' young citizens '). On the relationship between these amateurs and the professional histriones Livy is so obscure as to suggest a doubt about the reality of the development described. It was the introduction by Livius Andronius of Greek plays in translation which finally, according to Livy, forced the amateurs to confine their theatrical activities to the performances of the Atellan farce.

We cannot understand the nature of the ' after-piece ' as described by Livy. The word exodium means ' end ', exitus, or something introduced at the end ; thus at the end of a tragedy a farcical scene. Festus-Paulus equates exodium with exitus. The term could mean something played during the ' going out ' of the company which had just finished the main piece ; thus it could denote the finale. The most striking use of the word occurs in Plutarch's narrative (Crassus xxxiii) of the campaign of Carrhae. After the Parthians had won the victory they had a performance of Euripides' Bacchae, at which instead of the head of Pentheus the actual head of Crassus was brought in and shown to the king. The actor playing the part of Agave declaimed the words : ' it was I who slew him!' But the soldier who had in fact killed Crassus made a protest ; this caused general merriment. It was said that the campaigning of Crassus had ended, like a tragedy, with an exodium—which seems to mean an amusing scene. Again, in Pelopidas xxxiv, Plutarch says that Dionysius' funeral was like a finale in the theatre after a great tragedy. The scholiast on Juvenal iii. 178 says : ' in former times the actor of an exode would come in at the end of the show to raise a laugh, in order that the gaiety of his performance might free the spectators from the distress caused by the passions of tragedy. This is what Lucilius alludes to when he says " the beginning is followed by a worthy end, an exode ".'

When Livy says these exodia were combined with plays, especially Atellanes (conserta fabellis potissimum Atellanis), he seems to be using intentionally obscure language in order to get from the ' after-pieces ' to the Atellanes. Perhaps these last were a well-known type of performance, themselves used as after-pieces. So Lydus, *de Mag.* i. 40., says the Atellana is one of the pieces known as exodiaria. Juvenal (iii. 174) says ' the well-known exodium appears on the stage, and the country child in his mother's arms trembles at the open mouth of the ghastly mask '. The words exodium and Atellana are sometimes found together ; sometimes they seem to be used interchangeably. A piece by Pomponius, a writer of Atellanae, was entitled Exodium.

Evidently there were several forms of farce or short amusing piece known to the later stage—the Atellana, the mime, the Rhinthonian burlesque. Livy seems to be saying that the exodium came to be combined with all of these, but especially with the Atellana. It is not easy to see how the presumably extemporary jesting of the exodium could have been ' combined ' with the equally extemporary jesting of a farce ; but we could understand that the farce, of whatever kind, could come to take the place of the exodium, i.e. after the main performance. Livy's account, if reliable at all, ought at least to be reliable for the practice of his own day. In other words, he may be taken as trying to explain how the custom arose of giving a short amusing piece—especially an Atellana— after a more elaborate performance. We can scarcely disbelieve his statement that the Atellanae were still, in his own day, performed by men of citizen class who had a right to serve in the army. Nevertheless in the Empire we hear of Atellanae performed by professional actors (Tac. *Ann.* IV. xiv).

In 264, the opening year of the First Punic War, came a more sinister importation from Etruria, the gladiatorial combat[6]. That prisoners should be set to fight each other for public entertainment was no great improvement on the primitive custom of putting all male captives to death—a custom which survived even to the time of Julius Caesar in the triumphal procession (also derived from Etruria), when captives were executed as the commander ascended the Capitoline hill. The gladiators fought in the Circus. The earliest known amphitheatre is that at Pompeii, built about 80 B.C. for the Sullan colony. Familiarity with gladiatorial combats may have affected the taste of the theatre-going public ; Roman tragedy, as we shall see, shows great interest in gruesome themes and details, and the later mime carried realism so far as to enact on the stage a real execution of condemned criminals, imported for the purpose into the performance.

These developments are admirably illustrated in the wonderful Etruscan tomb-paintings, which afford abundant evidence of the popularity in Etruria of dance and music and also of gladiatorial combat. In these paintings we see male dancers playing on the pipes and dancing-girls with castanets and bells ; a young man and woman dance merrily together near a wine-bowl to the music of the pipe and lyre. Everything is done to music ; boxers box and wrestlers wrestle to the sound of the pipes ; the piper keeps time for the cooks in the kitchen as well as for the guests on the banqueting-couch. We are reminded of the games of the Circus when we see processions of horsemen and chariots, or a picture showing the lassoing of a horse ; more interesting still is a picture of the aristocratic spectators, men and women, sitting side by side in curtained 'boxes'[7] on grandstands, while on the ground swarm the common people. Especially striking is a painting in the Tomba degli Auguri. On the left enters a spectator, beckoning to a boy who brings his stool (just as, in the Roman theatre of later days, chairs for the senators were set in the orchestra). In the middle are a pair of wrestlers, closely watched by the referee ; on the right is a grimmer contest. A masked figure, called Phersu in the inscription, holds a fierce dog by a long leash which he has wrapped round the legs of his antagonist, who holds a club but is unable to use it, because he has not yet succeeded in freeing his head from a sack ; meanwhile the dog has torn great bleeding wounds in his legs. In another picture we see the masked figure (again named Phersu) running away. Some philologists derive from the name of this masked gladiator the word persona[8], the Latin term for a theatrical mask. Masks, grandstands, curtains to protect the spectators, movable seats—these are all features which will recur in the theatres of Rome ; while the love for music, at least for instrumental accompaniment, will from the beginning exercise a powerful influence on Latin drama.

Thus the evidence of the tomb-paintings supports the Roman tradition that their theatrical art, in its early stages, was largely influenced from Etruria. Another early influence came, as has been seen, from Campania, where the rustic farce performed by masked actors (fabula Atellana)[9] had long been popular. Greek colonization had at an early date reached the shores of Campania, and long before the production of written drama at Rome, contact with such towns as Naples may have been familiarizing at least some Romans with Greek theatrical performances, especially those of a popular nature, such as the farces which seem to be shown on vases from south Italy. We can well believe that before the beginnings of Latin literature Rome had become familiar with stage-shows of some kind. Livy describes them as saturae or ' medleys ', presumably because of the formless mixture of different types of metre. It appears from his account that there were song-writers and composers of music in third-century Rome.

Nothing has survived of these early theatrical compositions. The word ' medley ' is merely Livy's description, not a title ; there was probably never a *form* of drama entitled Satura in contemporary speech. But that the Romans had at an early period formed a taste for dialogue mixed with declamation to musical accompaniment is strongly suggested by their later treatment of Greek New Comedy. Here they took over a form of drama which consisted almost entirely of dialogue, and added to it so large an element of metrical variety meant to be accompanied that the result seems to many scholars more like an opera than a play.

CHAPTER III

LIVIUS ANDRONICUS AND THE COMING OF LITERARY DRAMA TO ROME

BY THE middle of the third century B.C. we find theatrical activities established in various parts of Italy. In Etruria public taste seems to have been satisfied with music and dance, athletic, gladiatorial and equestrian performances. In Rome the merry banter of the harvest-home had developed under foreign influence into a professional but mainly improvised performance consisting of chant, dance and buffoonery. On Latium's southern frontier there had existed from early times the Atellane farce, a kind of Punch and Judy show, which displayed such stock types as the Clown, the Guzzler and the Gaffer in ridiculous situations.

How far these forms of entertainment were native to Italy, how far they were influenced by Greece, we cannot tell. But in the Dorian settlements of southern Italy and Sicily we have evidence for a very specialized kind of theatrical activity in the fourth and third centuries B.C[1]. This evidence consists of numerous vase-paintings showing rude stage-shows, in which, it is generally supposed, obscenely dressed clowns[2] performed the so-called 'phlyax' farces, scenes from daily life or burlesques showing the gods in various undignified situations— Zeus on a love-adventure, equipped with a ladder, his path lit by Hermes, while his fair charmer gazes from a window ; Apollo climbing the temple-roof at Delphi to escape from Heracles, and the like. If we may form a notion of the phlyax-farces from the vase-paintings, the actors stood on a stage.* Here we have a contrast with classical Greek tragedy and comedy, where the chorus danced and where, as it is now coming to be held, the actors stood in the orchestra.

At the beginning of the third century the mythological burlesque (hilarotragoedia) had been given a literary form by Rhinthon of Tarentum. We may be sure that the Tarentines

* But I cannot suppress a doubt as to how far the vase-paintings represent actual stage performances. Some of the scenes depicted on them seem to violate the conventions of ancient drama. They are essentially pictures of momentary situations. The supposed stage may be merely an artistic convention. The 'masks' and 'phalli' may be natural features exaggerated by the artist. The question is discussed fully in Appendix N.

were also interested in the higher forms of drama, both tragedy and comedy. The Greek comic writer Alexis, himself born at Thurii, had written a comedy entitled the *Ταράντινοι*. The love of the Tarentines for the theatre was proverbial, and Pyrrhus, when called in to aid them in their struggle against Rome, found himself (according to Plutarch)[3] compelled to close all places of public amusement in order to induce the citizens to take the war seriously. This suppression of theatrical activities (if we can believe the story) must have thrown a certain number of actors out of employment. Plutarch tells us that many Tarentines, unable to endure the new régime, left their native town, and we may suppose that in this way trained actors found their way to Rome, there to influence such dramatic activities as the city possessed. Towards the end of the war the Tarentines made honourable terms with the Romans, and they contributed ships to the Roman navy in the first Punic War.

The outbreak of war with Carthage brought Roman troops back to Magna Graecia. For twenty years they campaigned in Sicily. During that time they had an opportunity to become familiar with Greek drama and the Greek theatre. The new interest in the Greek way of life made itself felt at Rome in the first year of peace. In the year 240 B.C.[4] the Roman public were entertained by the performance at the Ludi Romani of a Greek play in Latin translation. The translation and the production were the work of Livius Andronicus, a Romanized Greek whom tradition connected with Tarentum.

Our records concerning the founder of Latin literature and drama are meagre and contradictory. We cannot hope to explain or reconcile them ; and when we have considered what we know or surmise about the man and his work, there may remain in our minds some sense of disproportion between what he was and what he did.

The dramatist Accius, born in 170 B.C., asserted that Andronicus had been taken prisoner by the Romans when they captured Tarentum in 209 B.C., and that he did not produce his first play until 197 B.C. In conformity with this chronology is the statement of another early writer, Porcius Licinus (*c.* 100 B.C.) that the Muse came to Rome in the *second* Punic War. Horace tells us that it was not till *after* the Punic Wars that the Romans began to apply their minds to Greek drama, and Jerome gives us 187 B.C. as the date when Andronicus was at the height of his fame. We can therefore understand the interest aroused in Roman literary circles when an early document was discovered which recorded the performance in 240 B.C. of a play by Andronicus. This document was seen by Cicero, who refers to the matter no less than three times. We can hardly doubt that Cicero was substantially in the right, and that Accius was wrong. The archaism of Andronicus' style would in itself prevent us from supposing that he was later than Naevius and Plautus. Cassiodorus, too, tells us that he produced a tragedy and a comedy at the Ludi Romani of 239. The only other event in his career which can be dated is his composition of the official hymn at the crisis of the Hannibalic War in 207 B.C., when Hasdrubal was invading Italy. His death seems to have occurred before 200 B.C., when the writing of a State hymn was entrusted to another poet.

Apart from the evidently erroneous statement of Accius, we have no evidence, other than general probability, to connect Andronicus with Tarentum. It has been suggested that Accius confused two captures of Tarentum—that of 209 and that which presumably took place at the end of the Pyrrhic War, in 272 B.C. But we cannot be sure that Tarentum *was* captured in the Pyrrhic War. Furthermore, if Andronicus was to write the State hymn in 207, sixty-five years later, he can have been little more than a child in 272. How then are we to suppose that he acquired that knowledge of Greek and of Greek literature which made him so significant a figure among the ' barbarous race of Romulus ' ? Jerome tells us (unfortunately in connexion with an impossible date) that he was the slave of Livius Salinator, whose children he taught, and that because of his talents he was given his freedom. Suetonius says that Andronicus, like that other ' half-Greek ' Ennius, gave lectures on Greek literature and read out his own Latin compositions to his class. There may be some truth in this ; Romans of the upper ranks were no doubt beginning to realize the disadvantage of not knowing Greek, and were willing to pay some one who would teach the language and literature to their sons. Indeed the need for a school text may explain why Andronicus made his translation of the Odyssey—a translation which certainly seems to have been used in boys' schools in the days of Horace, who retained a lively though not vindictive

memory of having been flogged through it by his teacher
Orbilius.[5]   That Andronicus, a Greek in Rome, became
associated in some way with the powerful Livian family is
suggested by his name Livius, and goes well with the fact that
in the year 207,[6] when he was chosen to write the hymn, a
Livius Salinator was consul.   So far our evidence presents him
as a teacher and writer who could be called in by the authorities
to translate a Greek play for a special occasion, or to compose
a hymn.   But there are three other references which show him
in a new light.   Festus tells us that after the decisive victory
of the Metaurus a grateful government, wishing to do honour
to Andronicus, assigned the temple of Minerva on the Aven-
tine as a meeting-place and shrine for ' penmen and actors ',
scribae histrionesque, ' because Livius both wrote plays and
acted in them.'   An unknown scholiast (Glossae Salomonis)
says that he was the first both to perform and to write tragedies
and comedies.   Best known of all the anecdotes, perhaps, is
the account given by his namesake, the historian Livy.   Livy
tells us that Andronicus was the first to bring on the stage a play
with a plot (instead of the old saturae) ; that he rendered his
own musical compositions (suorum carminum actor) as did all
the writers of his day (id quod omnes tum erant) ; that, as the
result of frequent encores, his voice gave way ; and that
accordingly he obtained the leave of his audience to employ a
boy (or a slave—Latin puer) to sing for him, while he himself
accompanied the song in dumbshow.   Whatever we think
of these statements in themselves, we have no a priori right
to reject, as some of the Germans do, the implied connexion
between the writing of drama and its performance in early
Rome.   As Livy himself declares, things had been different in
early times.

The introduction of drama at Rome raised a series of
practical problems.   Some one had to make arrangements with
the magistrates, to secure or build a stage and dressing-room,
to maintain and train a troupe of actors, to supply them with
costumes, to hire a musician.   It is not likely that a trained
actor-manager suddenly appeared to relieve Andronicus of
these burdens.   More probably he had to arrange everything
himself.   But whoever did it must have built on such foundations as already existed.   It appears from Livy's account of the
satura that there were already trained actors at Rome, who

were capable of giving a performance which included music, song and clowning. The songs with a score [8] ' written out for the flute-player ' must have been in some sort of metre. Here, perhaps, we see the explanation of the great difference between Latin plays and their Greek originals. All Greek plays, whether tragedy or comedy, appear to have had a chorus. The Latin comedies, at any rate, seem to have had no chorus. What they did have were the cantica. A large part of every Latin play was meant to be chanted or declaimed to musical accompaniment. Those who declaimed the cantica were the actors themselves. Thus the musical element, which had been diminishing in New Comedy, was largely developed by the Latin dramatists. It seems to me not quite enough to look for the origins of the cantica in Greek tragedy, or in some hypothetical development of opera among the Greeks. They must have been introduced into Latin drama because they were congenial to Roman taste. They occur in purely native pieces such as the Atellanae, togatae and mimes. Compared with the Greek originals, Roman plays in general might be described in Livy's words as impletas modis saturas, medleys in various metres. With the Greeks each metre had traditional associations ; variety for its own sake appealed to Roman taste.

We possess the titles of perhaps eight of Andronicus' tragedies and of three of his comedies—all, beyond doubt, adapted from Greek originals. We cannot tell how wide a choice of originals was made available by the book-trade of his day. What seems probable is that he chose tragedies from the fifth century as well as later, comedy only from the New Comedy which was so popular in the Greek theatres of his day. The tragedies are *Achilles, Aegisthus, Aiax Mastigophoros, Andromeda, Danae, Equos Troianus, Hermione, Tereus* and perhaps *Ino.* The fragments of the *Aegisthus* show that it dealt with the same subject as Aeschylus' *Agamemnon*—the return of Agamemnon from Troy and his murder by his wife Clytaem-nestra, aided by her paramour Aegisthus ; Andronicus' play is, however, a translation not of our *Agamemnon* but of some lost original. *Aiax Mastigophoros* dealt with the same subject as the *Aiax* of Sophocles—the madness which came upon Ajax when the arms of the dead Achilles were adjudged not to him but to Odysseus. We shall find madness frequently depicted in Roman tragedy and burlesqued in Roman comedy, and the culminating horrors of Senecan melodrama were to have their influence on the Elizabethan drama. The *Andromeda* dealt with the thrilling and romantic story of the maiden left as a prey to the sea-monster, and of her rescue by Perseus. Melodrama and romance had gained ground in later Greek tragedy and had a strong appeal for the Romans. The *Tereus* told the ghastly tale of how Tereus, king of Thrace, outraged Philomela, his wife's sister, and cut out her tongue to prevent her telling of his crime, and of the vengeance which the sisters wreaked on Tereus' son. It was indeed a novel and exciting world to which the Roman public were introduced by the new drama. Whatever Andronicus' weakness in execution, we must admire the judgment which led him to choose these tragedies as the drama and the Odyssey as the epic which were to thrill and instruct the people of Rome.

Of titles of comedies we have only three, the *Gladiolus*, the *Ludius* and the *Virgo* or *Verpus*. The *Gladiolus* or ' Blade ' may have portrayed one of those swashbuckling captains common in the troubled period which followed the death of Alexander ; the single extant fragment may be an ironic remark addressed to the captain by some one to whom he was boasting of the numbers he had slain : 'Were they fleas or bugs or lice ? Do tell me.' The word ludius [9] is used by Plautus of the professional dancer familiar on the Roman stage ; whether the *Ludius* was one of these, or a ' Lydian ', we cannot tell from the single fragment : ' He dropped just as if he had been pole-axed.' The title of the third comedy (' The Maid ' or ' The Circumcised Man ') is too uncertain to afford a foundation even for a guess as to the subject. If we may judge by the scanty number of titles, Andronicus took little interest in comedy. Terence,[10] when referring to his own predecessors in comedy, does not mention him, and his name does not occur in Volcacius Sedigitus' list [11] of the ten best comic dramatists. Perhaps he was disqualified from writing comedy by his lack of colloquial Latin ; Cicero, thinking [12] of his style, compares his Odyssey to some crude product of Daedalus, and says that his plays are not worth a second reading.

Trained on Greek lines, Andronicus had to create a literary style in a language which was not his own. No literary work, as far as we know, had been composed in Latin before. The language had its possibilities, but essentially it was heavier in movement, less adaptable than Greek. Its great merit was its gift of hitting the nail on the head. Alliteration emphasizes this quality. We find in Andronicus' fragments some remarkable examples :

confluges ubi conuentu campum totum inumigant,

' when across the flats in fury flow the watery floods amain ', as Professor Wight Duff [13] translates the line.

Metre was a great problem. Greek metres were based on quantity, the time a syllable takes to utter. The typical and primitive Latin metre, the Saturnian, seems to have been based on some other principle. Crude as it must have appeared when compared with the Homeric hexameter, this was the metre which Andronicus was content to adopt for his version of the Odyssey. In drama we find him using as the metre of dialogue the iambic senarius, modelled on the Greek iambic trimeter but characteristically Latin in rhythm. But we also find in the fragments the trochaic septenarius, a metre which, it is true, occurs in Greek tragedy and New Comedy, but which appears to have been much more widely used by the Latin dramatists. Indeed it had a long history in popular Latin usage. It was the metre used by the soldiers [14] who marched behind Caesar in Rome :

urbani, seruate uxores ! moechum caluum adducimus.

And we find it in the *Peruigilium Veneris* :

cras amet qui nunquam amauit, quique amauit cras amet.

In the ' Trojan Horse ' we have a passage in cretics :

da mihi hasce opes
quas peto, quas precor ;
porrige, opitula !

All these metres, except the iambic senarius, were declaimed to musical accompaniment [15] ; and all of them, including the senarius, seem throughout the existence of stage-drama to have departed in certain respects from quantitative rules as observed by the Greeks (see Appendix M).

The Romans looked back on Andronicus as a respectable but somewhat colourless figure. His importance is as a pioneer. He found Rome without literature or written drama. He laid down the lines on which tragedy and comedy were to develop for a hundred and fifty years.

CHAPTER IV

NAEVIUS

IN CN. NAEVIUS we have a man of strong, vivid and passionate temperament. He is the earliest Italian whom we feel we know as a human being. A greater contrast to his predecessor, the respectable but colourless Andronicus, can scarcely be imagined. In the whole of Latin literature we shall hardly find a more original figure.

He must have been born not much later than 260 B.C., if he was to take part in the First Punic War (264-241 B.C.). Perhaps he was by birth a Campanian. Aulus Gellius [1] records the well-known epitaph, which he supposes to have been composed by Naevius himself :

> If deities immortal their tears for men might shed,
> Our native Latin Muses would weep for Naevius dead ;
> For since we laid our poet in Hades' treasure-store,
> The true old Latin language is heard in Rome no more.

This epitaph Gellius criticizes as ' full of Campanian ' (or ' Capuan ') ' pride '. Are we to understand from this remark that Gellius thought Naevius to have been by birth a Campanian, or is ' Campanian pride ' merely a general, proverbial expression not intended to imply any connexion between Naevius and Campania ? This second interpretation seems rather unnatural. My feeling is that Gellius intends us to understand that Naevius came not merely from Campania but from the proud city of Capua itself. We have no further reference to this matter, and we cannot tell from what source Gellius derived his information, or whether it was correct. He is probably mistaken in thinking that the epitaph was composed by Naevius ; like that on Plautus which he quotes in the same passage, it is probably the work of some admiring reader—perhaps Varro himself, from whom Gellius derives so much of his information about Latin literature.

One thing is clear : Naevius either spoke Latin from his

infancy or acquired it sufficiently early to gain that mastery
of the language which is attested by the epitaph and by Cicero.
He must also have come to Rome early enough to regard
himself as a Roman and take a personal and active interest in
Rome's history and politics. We seem to be on sure ground in
affirming that he fought in the First Punic War. He said so
himself in the poem which he wrote on this war ; Varro
quoted his statement in his work on the Latin poets, and Gellius
in his turn [2] quotes Varro. In the course of his campaigns
he probably had opportunity to see something of Greek life
and the Greek theatre in the famous Greek cities of Sicily,
the main field of the tedious and bloody struggle. He may
also have brought back with him a bitter memory of harsh
military discipline and of the incompetence in high places
which sent so many splendid fleets and armies to the bottom
of the sea.

Peace brought with it the necessity to earn a living, and
the opportunity to do so. Andronicus had shown that even
in the ' barbarous ' city of Rome there was a livelihood for
any one who could successfully adapt Greek plays for the
Roman stage. Naevius did not long delay. We read in
Gellius that in the year 235 B.C. two interesting events occurred
in Rome : the first Roman divorce and the production of a
play by Naevius at the public games. The action of Sp.
Carvilius Ruga in divorcing his wife simply because she had
failed to give him children was remembered as an important
event, and perhaps some priestly chronicle of events of religious
significance recorded under one year both this case and the
public games at which Naevius produced his play. In truth
the development of the theatre and the weakening of the
marriage tie were two aspects of the impact of Hellenism on
Roman life ; and in the plays of Plautus we shall presently
find marriage treated almost consistently as a subject for
mockery.

For the next thirty years or so (including the years of Rome's
death-grapple with Hannibal) Naevius seems to have given
his energies mainly to the theatre ; we have the titles of about
forty of his plays, showing an average of more than one play
each year. In the main, like nearly all Latin dramatists, he
based his work on Greek originals. But in the translations
of Naevius there was something new. Terence speaks [3] of the

' carelessness ' (neglegentia) of Naevius, Plautus and Ennius as something more worthy of admiration than the dull pedantry of their successors. Evidently Terence found that the plays of these popular dramatists were somehow different from the Greek which they professed and perhaps believed that they were translating. Naevius, Plautus and Ennius may have tried, in a general way, to render their originals faithfully ; but their native genius and their instinctive knowledge of popular taste compelled them to infuse a Roman flavour into everything they wrote.

It is not always safe to judge a dramatist's outlook from isolated passages in his plays, spoken we know not by whom or in what circumstances. Nevertheless there is in the dramatic fragments of Naevius [4] a recurring note of independence, a love of freedom and of free speech, which seems typical of the author. ' We will speak with the tongues of freedom at the feast of Freedom's god.' ' I have always prized Freedom far above wealth.' ' I hate folk who mutter : say plainly what you mean.' The tragedy and comedy of the Roman republic were based almost entirely on Greek originals ; yet for a man like Naevius it would have been difficult to content himself with mere translation. Somehow or other he would find a vent for his native genius, his pride in Rome and his interest in contemporary life. Tragedy offered less opportunity than comedy ; and we know of only seven tragedies by him : *Andromache* (?), *Danae*, *Equos Troianus*, *Hector Proficiscens*, *Hesiona*, *Iphigenia* and *Lycurgus*. We notice the recurrence of two of Andronicus' titles, the *Danae* and the *Equos Troianus ;* it would seem that Naevius set himself the task of surpassing his predecessor on his own ground. The *Hector Proficiscens*, translated from an unknown Greek play, dealt with the subject so pathetically treated by Homer, Hector's last leave-taking of his loved ones before he goes to fight his fatal duel with Achilles. A line from his farewell to his father Priam was particularly admired by Cicero [5] :

laetus sum laudari me abs te, pater, a laudato uiro.

How different is such a Hector from the Hector of Homer ! Homer gives us a human being, Naevius' line suggests a formal, pedantic kind of hero, a Roman consul, very conscious of his robes of office, addressing in set phrase his father, himself an ex-consul. Listen again to Naevius' Lycurgus addressing his bodyguard :

> uos qui regalis corporis custodias
> agitatis, ite actutum in frundiferos locos,
> ingenio arbusta ubi nata sunt, non obsita.

In trying to achieve dignity, the Roman writers of tragedy sacrifice simplicity. They write as if, like Aeschylus and Euripides at the competition in Aristophanes' *Frogs*, they meant to be judged by the weight of their lines.

Comedy offered more scope to Naevius' original talent. Not that he composed original comedies ; indeed many of the surviving titles are Greek, the others are in all probability translated from the Greek, and the fragments bring before us the characters and situations of Greek New Comedy. Where Naevius' individuality appears is in his choice of plays to translate, the spirit which he infused into his translations and the unmistakable references to native Italian topics. The purpose of comedy, at least for the Romans of that day, was to arouse laughter. If jests, puns and topical allusions could serve this purpose, then they were to be admitted regardless of any incongruity with the context—in fact this very incongruity might make them more amusing. The titles of Naevius' comedies—we know more than thirty of them*—' The Charcoal Burners ', ' The Potter ', ' The Soothsayer ', ' The Races ', ' The Night-hawks ' and so on, suggest themes from common life, indeed from low life. It would not be difficult to insert into such plays references to everyday matters in Rome and its neighbour towns. There is an unmistakable Italian flavour in a fragment of conversation from ' The Soothsayer ' : ' Who dined with you yesterday ? ' ' Guests from Praeneste and Lanuvium.' ' I hope you gave each party its favourite food—empty sow's paunch boiled for the one, nuts in abundance for the other.'† In the *Tunicularia* (the tunic was the wear of humble folk in Rome, Horace's tunicatus popellus) some one says ' You would rob even Theo-

---

* *Acontizomenos, Agitatoria, Agrypnuntes, Apella, Ariolus, Astiologa, Carbonaria, Colax, Commotria, Corollaria, Dementes, Demetrius, Dolus, Figulus, Glaucoma, Gymnasticus, Lampadio, Leo, Ludus, Lupus, Nagido, Nautae (?), Neruolaria, Pellex, Personata, Proiectus, Quadrigemini, Stalagmonissa, Stigmatias, Tarentilla, Technicus, Testicularia, Tribacelus, Triphallus, Tunicularia.*

† Similarly Plautus inserts a description of Rome into the *Curculio*.[6]

dotus, who seated himself on an altar in a strong-room at the Compitalia and wrapped himself round with mats in order to paint with his cheap ox-hide brush a picture of the Lares at play ! ' Here the language, at any rate, is very Roman.

We have about a dozen references in Roman writers to a comedy of Naevius called *Tarentilla*, a title which probably means ' The Girl of Tarentum.' Though Tarentum is in Italy, the play was no doubt translated from the Greek ; Tarentum was a Greek colony, and mention has already been made of a play by the Greek writer Alexis entitled Ταράντινοι which described the life of that gay city, much addicted to dining, love-making and philosophy. But no Roman who saw Naevius' play would have forgotten that for many years now Roman soldiers had been campaigning among the Greek towns of southern Italy and Sicily and had come to know there a way of life more elegant and more dissipated than anything that Rome had to show. Many of them must have beguiled their off-duty hours in the company of girls like the heroine of Naevius' play * : ' Like a ball among a ring of players, she puts herself at the disposal of all ; to one she nods, to one she winks, one she fondles, one she hugs, to one she gives her hand to clasp, another's foot she presses with her own, she sings a duet with one while signalling a message to yet another.' To judge by the fragments, the play dealt with the adventures of two young men from the country who squander their savings in the luxurious town. They arrange a drinking-party ; one of them gets drunk and has to be supported by his mistress. Presently their angry fathers track them down. A stormy scene follows ; finally the young men receive solemn advice to leave the town and settle down to a sober married life on their farms.

In other comedies we find the usual characters of New Comedy. The *Colax* had not only the title-rôle, a ' flatterer ' or parasite, but also a braggart captain, miles gloriosus ; the play was translated from Menander, and Terence gives us the surprising and puzzling information that the translation was the work of ' Plautus and Naevius ' (or perhaps Plautus *or* Naevius). Did the two dramatists collaborate, or did Plautus re-write the play for a revival performance ? The

* If these lines belong to this play, or indeed to Naevius at all. Isidore[7] attributes them to Ennius.

Agitatoria (literally ' Charioteer Play ') told of a chariot race ; some one (perhaps his father) says to Demea, ' Lest you should say that I am thwarting you, I'll put them (the horses ?) at your disposal for this one day ; afterwards I'll sell them while they are actually running—unless you win.' We have another scrap of conversation about the result : ' What ? have we really won ? ' ' You have won.' ' I'm delighted ! ' ' I'll tell you how it happened.' We overhear a quarrel—perhaps between father and son : ' You seem to object on purpose to everything that I want, and to desire what I don't want.' The *Acontizomenos* (' Struck by a javelin ') had a prologue which recommended it as a ' first-rate play ' ; it seems to have told of someone who was falsely accused of killing his twin brother, and we also hear of a midnight murder. The *Agrypnuntes*, ' Those who keep awake at night ' (presumably for mischief) dealt with a band of brigands who infested the streets. One line seems to claim that the poet has shown up these ' night-thieves ' on the stage. Was the *Apella* a portrait of a Jew ? We remember Horace's Iudaeus Apella [8] ; the name is perhaps a pun on *a* and *pellis*, ' circumcised ', and one of Andronicus' comedies, according to Ribbeck, was entitled *Verpus*, ' circumcised '.* All that survives of the *Apella* is two remarks concerning onions. Elsewhere in the fragments we have references to the stock themes of Roman comedy—the power of love, the whipping of slaves, drunkenness, debauchery. Young men run after courtesans ; they promise them all their possessions ; one youth crudely wishes that the gods would put his parents out of the way, no doubt that he may bestow their property on his darling. References to banquets, parasites, exposed infants, twins, even quadruplets (no doubt all alike) and titles like ' The Madmen ', ' The Trick ', ' Dust in his Eyes ' (*Glaucoma*), suggest situations familiar to the reader of Plautus. That there was a spice of indecency is suggested by titles like *Testicularia* and *Triphallus*, and by some of the fragments. The title *Personata* has been taken to mean ' The Masked Play ' (implying that in other plays masks were *not* used), but it may only mean ' The Lady in the Mask ', implying, perhaps, that the heroine wears a special mask as a disguise for at least part of the play. It seems probable, on the whole, that all actors on the Roman stage, except the

* Another suggestion is that *Apella* means the ' Apulian Woman '.

mimes, normally wore masks ; there is nothing to warrant our attributing to Naevius the first literary fabula Atellana. Nor need we ascribe to him, because of his real or supposed references to Italian topics, the invention of the comedy on native Italian themes, fabula togata.

What he did, apparently, invent was the Roman historical play, fabula praetexta or praetextata. The toga praetexta was the purple-bordered toga worn by Roman magistrates ; the fabula praetexta dealt with the deeds of men who might have worn such a toga, the heroes of Roman history or legend. And so when Varro quotes [9] from the *Clastidium* of Naevius an iambic line referring to some one's triumphant return to his native land, we may be pretty sure that this work was a play dealing with the famous victory won at Clastidium in 222 B.C. by the consul M. Claudius Marcellus. We also hear of a play by Naevius entitled *Romulus*, perhaps the same as his *Lupus*, ' The Wolf ', from which latter we have a fragment of a conversation between Vibe, king of Veii, and Amulius, the usurping king of Alba Longa whom Romulus is destined to slay. It is sometimes said that this or another play dealt with the infancy of Romulus as well as with his triumphant achievements as a man. If that were the case, then indeed the fabula praetexta was completely free from the ' Unity of Time ' which limited most classical plays to a day or little more (two days in the case of the *Heauton* of Terence). The only support for such a belief is a remark of Donatus [10] (in reference to the proverbial expression ' lupus in fabula ', our ' Talk of the Devil ! ') that there was no truth in the story that a wolf appeared during the performance of a play by Naevius, in the scene of the suckling of Romulus and Remus. I find it equally difficult to suppose either that the Roman stage was ever capable of showing human twins being suckled by a she-wolf, or that Naevius would have thought it worth while to stage the suckling of the twins without the presence of the wolf. Apparently there was a play by Naevius dealing with Romulus (and that we knew already) ; and some one had the absurd notion of trying to explain ' lupus in fabula ' (which really means ' the wolf in the *story* ') by imagining that the suckling of the twins by the wolf was actually shown in this play.

Naevius' interest in Roman history and contemporary

affairs led to the composition of another work which was not
a play, his *Bellum Punicum*, or narrative in Saturnian verse or
the first Punic War.   Cicero makes Cato say [11] that this work
gave the poet great pleasure in his old age—from which remark it has been inferred that the poem was written during
Naevius' exile in Utica, when circumstances had cut him off
from his familiar literary medium, the stage.   I find this very
difficult to believe.   Possibly all that Cicero means is that
Naevius derived pleasure in his old age from re-reading his
poem ;   and if this is his meaning, it is hard to see what
evidence he had for such a statement.   We have other and
perhaps more reliable evidence that Naevius' later years were
clouded in misfortune.

According to a belief current in imperial times, Naevius'
jibes at the Roman aristocracy got him into trouble.   A
commentator of the fifth century A.D. [12] tells us that Naevius
lampooned the consular family of the Metelli in the line :

fato Metelli Romae fiunt consules,

' The Metelli are made consuls at Rome by Fate ' (and not
through any merit of their own).   The ancient law of the Twelve
Tables prescribed capital punishment for slander (si quis
occentauisset siue carmen condidisset quod infamiam faceret
flagitiumue alteri) ;   and an allusion to politics might be
rewarded with a flogging (cautum est ut fustibus feriretur qui
publice inuehebatur).   So the Metelli (one of whom was
consul in 206 B.C.) were within their rights when they replied
in the famous Saturnian :

dabunt malum Metelli Naeuio poetae,

' The Metelli will give a whipping to Naevius the poet.'   This
story may be apocryphal ;   but Gellius, too, quotes [13] lines of
Naevius which he thinks were in all probability a reference
to a scandalous episode in the life of the great Scipio :   ' even
he who has gloriously achieved such mighty victories with his
strong arm, whose deeds thrill the world, who is the foremost
man in the eyes of all the nations—even he has known what
it is to be hauled away from his lady-love by his father, with
nothing on but his cloak.'   (This passage may in fact have
referred not to Scipio but to some fictitious character, some
braggart warrior in a play.)   A character of Plautus (*M.G.*
210-1) remarks ' I have heard that a foreign poet has his

face fastened to a column, with two gaolers lying on him all day' (i.e. the two chains which bind him), and Festus [14] tells us that Plautus used the expression 'foreign poet' (poeta barbarus) of Naevius. Gellius [15] states that Naevius was thrown into prison for his incessant attacks on the nobles, and that in prison he wrote two plays, the *Hariolus* and the *Leo*, in which he begged pardon for his past offences, with the result that he was released by the tribunes. Jerome, however, tells us that he was driven from Rome by Metellus and other nobles, and died at Utica in 201.[16] These accounts are not easy to reconcile ; and if Naevius' imprisonment was as rigorous as Plautus appears to indicate, it is hard to see how he could have written plays in gaol. Cicero mentions [17] neither the imprisonment nor the banishment, but tells us that an ' early commentary' gave 204 B.C. as the date of the poet's death—a date which Varro thought too early. Evidently the date of Naevius' death was a matter of dispute even so early as Cicero's day.

On general grounds, the lines attributed in these anecdotes [18] to Naevius seem to me genuine ; as for the reply of the Metelli, I have some suspicion of a Saturnian which is so easy to scan. But even if we reject all the stories as mere gossip, it remains true that this was the sort of gossip which attached itself to Naevius. The best proof that his liberty of speech incurred some signal punishment is the care with which subsequent Latin dramatists resisted the temptation to allude to politics or mention contemporaries by name. Naevius had taken the first steps towards creating a new drama which would deal with the vital interests of the Roman people ; but the heavy hand of the State was to confine Latin playwrights to frivolous or foreign themes.

THE FABULA PRAETEXTA AFTER NAEVIUS

In Naevius' two praetextae, the *Romulus* and the *Clastidium*, we see already established the division of the praetextae into (*a*) plays dealing with remote Roman history or legend, and (*b*) plays celebrating victories won by Roman generals still living or only recently deceased. Examples of (*a*) are Ennius' *Sabinae*, ' The Rape of the Sabine Women ' (if that work was indeed a play), Accius' *Aeneadae* or *Decius*, which dealt with the victory of Sentinum in 295, achieved by the self-immolation of the consul P. Decius Mus, and Accius' *Brutus*, which told of how the tyrant Tarquin had been expelled by Rome's first consul. Examples of (*b*) are Ennius' *Ambracia*, which must have dealt with the capture of Ambracia in 189 by Ennius' patron, the consul M. Fulvius Nobilior (but it is not clear that this work *was* a play), and the *Paulus* of Pacuvius, if we see in this work a praetexta on the victory won at Pydna in 168 by the consul L. Aemilius Paulus. This short list includes all the genuine praetextae which we know to have been produced in Rome.

Contemporary history must have been a delicate matter to handle on the stage. It seems to have been a rule of the Roman theatre (at least after the time of Naevius) that contemporary personages should not be mentioned by name. Cicero (*Rep.* IV) says that in early Rome it was forbidden to blame or praise any *living* Roman on the stage. We know, however, that funeral games [19] were held in honour of L. Aemilius Paulus in 160, and that they included the performance of plays ; it is conceivable that the *Paulus* was a praetexta specially written for this occasion. The play dealt with a battle, and there was a reference to a mountain track—presumably the track used by the force under Scipio Nasica, which decided the issue at Pydna. I find it more difficult to suppose that such a praetexta could be performed at the triumphal games given by the victorious general. It would seem, at any rate, that praetextae dealing with contemporary history were written for some special occasion, and presumably at short notice. To make a play out of the events of a recent campaign must have been a fairly difficult task. The meagreness of the extant fragments suggests that such plays were short as well as few.

By way of contrast we must mention the praetexta written by L. Cornelius Balbus on his own achievements in 49 B.C., and staged by him at the games which he gave at Gades in 43. This must be regarded as merely one of the outrageous breaches of decorum of which he was guilty (see Cic. *ad Fam.* x. 32).

Roman myth or remote history presented a more attractive field for the dramatist. Some lines are preserved of Accius' *Aeneadae* or *Decius*, which evidently dealt with the battle and the ceremony of deuotio. From the *Brutus* [20] Cicero has quoted Tarquin's account of his dream, with the interpreter's reply, which ends with an impressive reference to the future greatness of Rome. Like Shakespeare's plays on English history, the praetexta found opportunities to appeal to patriotic sentiment, that refuge for dramatists as well as for scoundrels. Two other lines of this play deal with the etymology of the word consul and with the achievements of Tullius (i.e. King Servius Tullius). This latter line, according to Cicero, [21] was taken by the audience on one occasion as a flattering reference to the achievements of another Tullius (namely himself) in 63 B.C. The Romans, including Cicero, had a craving for reading such topical allusions into old plays ; this fact itself suggests that direct reference to current events and living persons was discouraged. The *Brutus* may have been intended to gratify Accius' patron, the consul Junius Brutus, who celebrated his Spanish victories with a splendid triumph in 136 B.C.

This seems to be all that can with probability be said about the praetextae produced on the Roman stage. It seems unlikely, indeed, that any other praetextae were ever composed for performance. The late grammarian Diomedes,[22] when citing examples of this form of drama, mentions only the *Marcellus* (i.e. the *Clastidium*), *Decius* and *Brutus*. The prologue to Plautus' *Amphitruo* (lines 41-4) tells us that mention had recently been made ' in tragedies ' of the service conferred on the State by Neptune, Virtue, Victory, Mars and Bellona ; but the normal sense of tragoedia makes it fairly certain that the reference here is to Roman adaptations of Greek tragedies.

We must conclude that the introduction of the historical play by Naevius proved comparatively sterile. This form of Latin drama has assumed undue importance in our eyes because of the Roman grammarians' love of classification and our own wish to find in Latin drama something corresponding to Shakespeare's historical plays. Generally speaking, it seems to have been beyond the power of the Roman dramatists to construct a plot quite independently of Greek models. Moreover the mention of national history, even of remote history, on the stage was rendered embarrassing by the sensitiveness of both people and government on this subject. The comedy of native manners (fabula togata) found its material in the ordinary life of humble folk and of the country town, and its plots may have owed something to New Comedy. In this way it achieved sufficient success to supply full occupation for the three writers whose names we know. The praetexta was never more than a parergon for a few writers of tragedy, and its remains do not extend beyond five or six certain titles and about fifty lines. As a purely literary composition it maintained its existence ; L. Cornelius Balbus circulated his manuscript among his friends, who read it with malicious enjoyment, and plays on remote or recent Roman history continued to be written under the Empire—but not for the stage. Our only extant example is the pseudo-Senecan *Octauia*,* written at some time after Nero's death and having as its heroine his unfortunate wife. This play seems to owe nothing to the genuine praetextae of Republican times ; it is a mere imitation of Greek tragedy, except that the subject is Roman. The author shows no more regard than Seneca for the necessities of stage-production ; he is clearly writing for private reading or the recitatio.

* See page 235.

CHAPTER V

PLAUTUS : LIFE AND LIST OF PLAYS

OUR HISTORIES of Latin literature present us with circumstantial details concerning the life of Plautus.[1] We are told that ' Titus Maccius Plautus ' was born at Sarsina, in Umbria, about the year 254 B.C., that at Rome he made some money as a craftsman in the service of the theatre (which perhaps means that he began as an actor), that he then engaged in trade, lost his savings and was forced to hire himself out as a worker in a mill, and that in such leisure moments as were afforded by this occupation he wrote some plays, which presumably were sufficiently successful to lead him to take up the profession of playwright in earnest. His death took place in 184. While there is nothing wildly improbable about this story, critical examination shows that the Romans themselves were by no means agreed as to the writer's name, his date and the authenticity of his supposed works. Beyond question there was a comic dramatist named Plautus, a highly successful writer of the generation preceding that of Terence. Possibly no record of him survived his death except the plays which he left in manuscript form, some of them perhaps bearing on the title-page the author's name in the genitive case, e.g. PLAVTI CASINA, ' The *Casina*, by Plautus '. A few details of first performances seem also to have survived, whether included in the magisterial records of ludi publici or jotted down on the manuscripts. In that unscholarly age these records soon fell into confusion. The fame of Plautus as a popular entertainer seems to have induced unscrupulous producers to pass off the works of other dramatists as his. His own practice (if Gellius is correct)[2] of working over the plays of earlier writers may have been partly responsible for the confusion. In the course of time the total number of works attributed to him rose to one hundred and thirty. Roman scholars strove to distinguish the true from the false, but their methods were subjective and their results were conflicting. Once they came to distrust the evidence of authorship given on the title-page of the manuscript, or by tradition, they had no criterion but their individual sense of style for distinguishing the genuine plays of Plautus (whether attributed by the manuscripts to him or to other writers) from the plays of other writers which were falsely attributed to him.   Finally, in the time of Cicero, the scholar Varro [3] made a determined effort to clear up the confusion.   He appears to have drawn up three lists : *first*, plays which were universally admitted to be Plautine ; *second*, other plays which he himself, on grounds of style, believed to be Plautine ; *third*, plays which, though attributed by some to Plautus, were in his opinion the work of other writers.   In the first list, the so-called Varronianae fabulae, were included twenty-one plays. Varro's methods were indeed uncritical, but his authority was great.   Though the controversy continued for centuries after his death, it cannot be a mere coincidence that our manuscripts of Plautus contain precisely twenty-one plays (of which the last is a mere fragment).   Evidently later editors saved themselves trouble by accepting the Varronianae fabulae, and only these.   Our manuscripts therefore give us only those plays which were, according to Varro, universally accepted in his day.   Varro himself did not claim that this list included all the works of Plautus ; as we have seen, he put in his second list those plays which, on grounds of style, he himself regarded as Plautine, though they were questioned by at least some other scholars.   As for his third list, the plays attributed to Plautus which, on grounds of style, he felt unable to accept, he seems absurdly to have invented a dramatist named ' Plautius ' who had written at least some of them.   Evidently, Varro had in his mind such titles or references as ' Plauti *Casina* ' ; as the genitive case of ' Plautius ' would be identical with that of ' Plautus ', the plays of Plautius would, he argued, in time come to be attributed to Plautus.

It seems clear that, apart from the Varronianae fabulae, there were genuine plays of Plautus which have not come down to us.   Terence [4] can hardly have been mistaken in attributing to Plautus the *Commorientes* ; yet this play does not appear in our manuscripts.   Terence also says, or appears to say, that there was a play by ' Naevius and (? or) Plautus ' called the *Colax*. If we can believe that these two authors collaborated, or that (as Gellius asserts) Plautus retouched the plays of earlier writers, we can well understand that confusion as to authorship had set in within a generation of Plautus' death. But if confusion had begun thus early, can we even feel certain that the twenty-one Varronianae fabulae are all from the hand of Plautus ? The prologue to the *Asinaria* gives the author's name (in the nominative) as ' Maccus ' ; the prologue to the *Mercator* gives it (apparently) as Maccus Titus. (These two plays are remarkably lacking in the metrical variety so characteristic of Plautus.) The other prologues which mention the author's name give it as ' Plautus '. The oldest manuscript [5] (fifth century A.D.) in one place gives the author's name (in the genitive) as T. Macci Plauti. It would seem that the Romans came to identify ' Maccus ', ' Maccus Titus ' and ' Plautus ' by supposing that the author's full name was Titus Macc(i)us Plautus ; but this identification was apparently denied (the passage is very obscure) by the dramatist and literary historian Accius,* who wrote more than half a century before the time of Varro. More than one scholar of the present day (e.g. Westaway [6] and Norwood) has found the *Mercator* different in style from the other plays. We must either suppose that Plautus bore different names in his lifetime, or that two or more individuals were confused by later generations. Whether ' Maccus ' and ' Plautus ' denoted the same person or not, it is curious that both look like stage-names ; ' Maccus ' was the clown in the Atellane plays, and ' Plautus ' is said by Festus [7] to mean planis pedibus, ' Flat-foot ', which reminds us of the Latin name for the bare-footed mime, ' Flat-foot ' (planipes).

On the whole, it seems reasonable to believe that Varro's list is substantially correct, though Havet and Freté attribute the *Asinaria* to ' Pseudo-Plaute '. As for Plautus' date, Jerome tells us that he died in 200, Cicero says that he died in 184, and Gellius speaks of him as a contemporary of Cato (234-149). Fortunately there is good evidence to show that Cicero's date is not far from the truth. There seems to be a reference in the *Miles Gloriosus* [8] to the imprisonment of Naevius. The prologue to the *Cistellaria* [9] speaks of the (second) Punic war as still going on. For two plays the didascaliae, or records of the first performance, have been preserved in our oldest

---

* See Warmington, *Fragments of Old Latin* II, 587. Accius distinguishes between Plautus and Titus Maccus, and says that the latter was *not* the author of the *Commorientes*.

manuscript ; these give the date of the *Stichus* as 200 and that of the *Pseudolus* as 191. Cicero's date for Plautus' death may have been inferred from the silence of the records as to new plays by Plautus after that year. There would naturally be no corresponding evidence as to the date of his birth. Cicero makes Cato speak[10] of Plautus in his old age as taking special pleasure in two works, the *Truculentus* and the *Pseudolus*. This passage is commonly understood to mean that these plays were *written* when Plautus was an old man, and it might conceivably be based on lost passages in Plautus' plays similar to the extant reference in the *Bacchides* to the *Epidicus* as ' a play which I love as I do my very self '. If the *Pseudolus*, produced (as we have seen) in 191, was written when Plautus was an old man (i.e. sixty or more), it follows that Plautus was born before 250. However doubtful the argument, the conclusion is reasonable ; it allows us to regard Plautus as a junior contemporary of Naevius, by whose original genius he seems to have been influenced and from whose melancholy fate he probably took warning.

The biographical details given by late writers may be nothing more than illegitimate inferences from passages in extant or lost plays. Legends are apt to gather about the early careers of famous men, particularly if there is no reliable information available. For example, the statement that Plautus was born at Sarsina[11] *may* be a mere inference from his mention of the town in his *Mostellaria*. When we come to the life of Terence we shall see how such biographies were concocted. Gellius' statement[12] that Plautus, when a mill-hand, wrote certain plays is rendered rather doubtful by the fact that the plays mentioned are not in our manuscripts, and were therefore not among those universally accepted as Plautine in Varro's day. Nevertheless it is not unlikely that Plautus acquired a practical knowledge of the theatre at an early age, that he knew poverty and hardship, and that he depended for his livelihood on the success of his plays with the common folk of Rome. If we hear of no patron, we may at least surmise that he was shrewd enough to avoid offending the great. In fact, he turns away from political affairs[13] with the remark that such matters should be left to the rulers of the state. If Puritans murmured (as they well might do) at the tone of his works or that of the new drama in general, he was ready to pose as a champion of public morals—that is if we regard as

II 'CHIRON GOES UPSTAIRS'
Phlyax Vase-painting in the British Museum

genuine the prologue and epilogue to the *Captiui*. With the possible exception of the *Mercator*, the extant plays seem sufficiently homogeneous in style (admittedly a fallible guide) to confirm the general reliability of Varro's list and reveal their author as essentially a man of the theatre, who troubled himself little with politics, philosophy or literary art but made it his business to win the crowd by plays which appealed to their sense of fun, their interest in intrigue and their pleasure in music, rhythm and rhetoric.

The twenty-one extant plays are :

	Date	*Greek original*	*Greek author*
Amphitruo	?	(Supposed by some to belong to Middle Comedy)	
Asinaria	Probably early	*Onagᵤs*	Demophilus
Aulularia	?	(Attributed by some to Menander)	
Bacchides	Perhaps late ?	(Contains a line which occurs in Menander's *Dis Exapaton*)[14]	
Captivi	?	?	
Casina	Late ?	*Clerumenoe*	Diphilus
Cistellaria	Before 201 B.C.	? *Synaristosae*	Menander
Curculio	Middle period ?	Unknown	
Epidicus	Before *Bacchides*	Unknown	
Menaechmi	(Various guesses)	Unknown	
Mercator	Probably early	*Emporos*	Philemon
Miles Gloriosus	About 205 B.C.	*Alazon*	Unknown
Mostellaria	?	? (A frequent suggestion is a *Phasma*; several Greek authors wrote plays with this title.)	
Persa	?	Unknown	
Poenulus	?	*Carchedonius*	Unknown
Pseudolus	191 B.C.	Unknown	
Rudens	?	?	Diphilus
Stichus	200 B.C.	*Adelphoe I*	Menander
Trinummus	?	*Thesauros*	Philemon
Truculentus	? Late	Unknown	
Vidularia	?	*Schedia*	Unknown

It seems appropriate at this point to consider the nature of New Comedy itself, and to compare it with its origins.

3

CHAPTER VI

GREEK NEW COMEDY

THE PECULIARLY Athenian form of political satire known as Old Comedy ended with the fall of Athens in 404 B.C. From now on comedy had to find other themes than the affairs of Athens ; it found them in the general problems of society and above all in domestic life. It was still prolific ; we hear of fifty-seven writers of the so-called ' Middle Comedy ' (404–338 B.C.), two of whom wrote more than two hundred plays each ; and of sixty-four writers of ' New Comedy ', of whom Menander, Philemon and Diphilus wrote about one hundred plays each. Of all this output we possess thousands of fragments, indeed, but only three complete plays—the *Ecclesiazusae* (391 B.C.) and· the *Plutus* (388 B.C.) of Aristophanes and the *Dyscolus* of Menander ; and although within the present century we have recovered considerable portions of five other plays of Menander, it must be admitted, in Pickard-Cambridge's words (*D.F.* 152), that ' the remains of Menander's plays are too fragmentary, and the assignment of lines to particular characters sometimes too uncertain ' to resolve our doubts. Our twenty-six Latin plays are indeed fairly complete examples of New Comedy,* but the difficulty is to distinguish between what the Latin translators took over from their originals, and what they themselves added. If we could be sure, for example, that the Greek plays were subject to the three-actor rule, we should then know that every scene in a Latin play which contains four speaking characters has been altered by the Latin writer. It is commonly supposed, too, that each Greek play had a prologue ; that it had a chorus, which was not connected with the action ; above all, that it was logically constructed. These assumptions are all open to question.

the speaking parts in any one scene to three (apart from the

---

* Attempts to claim the *Amphitruo* and *Persa* for Middle Comedy are without firm basis, and may be treated with reserve.

chorus). We hear that there were three actors, and are not told of a fourth. Nevertheless in several plays of Aristophanes there are scenes which require four, and sometimes five, speaking characters ; while as for New Comedy, ' what is certain is that there are extant scenes of Menander's plays which could not be performed without four actors ' (Pickard-Cambridge, *ib*. pp. 148–52). The Greek actors were, perhaps, evolved out of the chorus, and in the end all but superseded it ; but at no moment in this long process can we discover that they were separated by an absolute barrier. All performers, actors and chorus together, were classed alike as tragoedi or comoedi on the official records (*id. ib*. p. 128) ; and all alike seem to have stood and moved in the orchestra (*id., Theatre of Dionysus*, p. 163).

That comedy grew out of a primitive revel or riotous procession (κῶμος) is suggested by its name ; hence, perhaps, the nature of the parodos (' march on ') and exodos (' march off') of Old Comedy. Perhaps in the days of its decline it returned to the κῶμος. But in the *Ecclesiazusae* the chorus is still important, as representing, with the actors, the women who, putting on man's dress before our eyes, will go off to the Assembly and vote the State into the hands of women. (These scenes suggest strongly that there was no physical barrier or essential distinction in costume between actors and chorus.) In the *Plutus* the chorus of farmers are brought on merely to share in the benefits anticipated from restoring his sight to the God of Wealth. Still there *is* a chorus in each play, and it is given words to utter. Some manuscripts of these two plays show here and there the sign χοροῦ ' [performance] of the chorus '. This has been differently interpreted as (1) all that is left of a choral ode composed by Aristophanes which was suppressed by some post-Aristophanic producer or editor, (2) an indication from Aristophanes to the director, meaning that he was to introduce a dance or even a song, the words for which he was to provide as best he could.* Neither of these interpretations is free from difficulties ; and sometimes

---

* Contrast Rogers ad *Eccl*. 876 with Flickinger, *C.P.* vii, 24–34, and see Platnauer in *New Studies in Greek Literature*, ser. iii, p. 167, and note 3. Choral songs might conceivably be omitted in an edition meant for reading ; and we know that the *Plutus* was widely read (Platnauer, ib. p. 158). The *Ecclesiazusae* and the *Plutus* would both be suitable for reading, since they deal with themes of general interest.

χοροῦ seems to be a mere interpolation by some reader who
felt that a ' pause ' was desirable.

Defraying the expenses of the chorus was a heavy burden
on the choregus (Pickard-Cambridge, *Dramatic Festivals*,
pp. 87 ff.), and lack of choregi might conceivably lead to the
suppression of the chorus—a point made by the writer of the
first Life of Aristophanes, sect. 11.   But Aristophanes has *not*
suppressed the chorus.   In Menander, on the other hand, we
find no specific indication of a chorus except the sign χοροῦ.
There are, however, references in the fragments of Middle
and New Comedy to a band of revellers approaching down
the street, whom the speaker seems to wish to avoid.   At least
one and probably two of these references in Menander are
followed in the papyrus by the direction χοροῦ.   Apparently
in these cases the revellers are the chorus, and we have ' a
stock scene in which the actors make themselves scarce at the
approach of a riotous band ' (*Theatre of Dionysus*, p. 165).
This would be a return to the primitive kōmos ; and clearly
the incursions of a chorus at the sight of which all other
performers flee would divide the performance into sections.
Yet it seems certain that plays of Sophocles and Euripides
continued to be performed, and in those plays the chorus
takes part in the action.   Moreover, we have evidence that
in plays of the latter part of the fourth century the chorus
might still be addressed by the actors.   Even in Menander it
is supposed that the chorus might represent the guests in one
of the houses ; and Allinson makes Chaerestratus retire into
his house at the end of Act I of the *Epitrepontes* to avoid a group
of revellers who at the end of Act II themselves enter the house
of Chaerestratus as guests.

The one certain conclusion is that we know very little
about the chorus of New Comedy.   It may be that it was
declining towards ultimate extinction ; and our only extant
list of dramatis personae (in Menander's *Hero*) does not include
it.   Yet we have evidence that in 279 B.C. a company of
comedians included choreutae (*Theatre of Dionysus*, p. 241) ;
and on one occasion in the late second century B.C. a company
consisted of one comic actor, two assistants and four comic
choreutae (*D.F.*, p. 291, n. 6).

The view that New Comedy as a whole was of high artistic
quality in construction is connected with the view that it owes

much to Euripides. As Duckworth says (*N.R.C.* 33), ' the danger of such a theory is obvious ; if Euripidean art was so dominant an influence upon the development of Greek comedy, then that comedy acquired an artistic form of such regularity that flaws were impossible ; if flaws appeared in the Roman adaptations, these flaws must inevitably be due to the faulty workmanship of the Roman playwrights '. As evidence of Euripidean influence we are bidden to look at ' the dramatic treatment of modern problems, the profusion of moral maxims, the use of the monologue, the recognition scene, the isolated prologue and the prologue god ' (*O.C.D.*, p. 219). On one point there is indeed general agreement : the Euripidean formal prologue ' spoken sometimes by a god or by a human character, stating the circumstances in which the action originates, even (in many plays) forecasting the issue ' (Pickard-Cambridge, *O.C.D.* 349), was an innovation of his (for which he was criticized by Aristophanes) and probably pointed the way towards New Comedy. Our only complete surviving prologue from New Comedy itself,* the speech of Agnoia, the goddess Misapprehension, in the *Perikeiromene*, is on Euripidean lines—except that it is ' deferred ', i.e. spoken *after* the opening scene. There was probably a similar divine deferred prologue in the *Hero* (of which play we possess the opening scene, a dialogue, and the list of dramatis personae, which puts the ' Divine Hero ' third, after the speakers in the opening scene). If this device of deferring the prologue was an innovation of Menander, it may be that he found something unsatisfactory in Euripides' habit of putting his explanatory monologue at the beginning of the play, or he may have felt the need for something corresponding to the parabasis of Old Comedy ; but it is hazardous to assume that in every play of Menander (to say nothing of the sixty-three other named dramatists of New Comedy) there was a prologue of this type. In Plautus we find many varieties of prologue, and often no prologue at all ; in Terence no explanatory prologue anywhere.

The other supposed resemblances between Euripides and Menander, or New Comedy in general—the use of monologue, the moral maxims, the serious tone, the complex plots, etc.—

* Demiańczuk, pp. 96 ff., gives a large portion of a prologue spoken by a god—who discusses prologue-method and gives the argumentum.

are unconvincing. But on one important matter we have
ancient evidence. Satyrus' ' Life of Euripides ' speaks of
' the quarrels that we remark in comedy between husband and
wife, father and son, master and slave, and the climaxes
brought about by rape, suppositious children, recognitions by
rings and necklaces ; for these, of course, are the framework
of New Comedy, and were brought to perfection by Euripides '
(*Ox. Pap.* ix, p. 49). Is it true that ' as the creator of the love-
drama Euripides was the forefather of the New Comedy '
(Pickard-Cambridge, *O.C.D.* 349) ? The first Vita of
Aristophanes, sect. 10, tells us that one of Aristophanes' latest
plays, the *Kokalos*, contained ' seductions, recognitions and all
the other themes which Menander emulated '. These two
ancient authorities seem to be opposed to each other, and,
that being so, it is well to remember the famous question of
the Alexandrian critic, Aristophanes of Byzantium : ' O Life
and Menander, which of you imitated the other ? '

It was not from literary sources alone, nor from the fertility
magic supposed to lie behind Old Comedy, that Menander
took the theme of love (which, according to Ovid,[1] appears
in all his plays) ; it was from the world around him, the
political conditions which rendered all topics unsuitable
except domestic life, and the need to find in domestic life a
theme which would have in itself the driving-force, the
complications and the satisfactory ending necessary in a
comedy. Yet here Athenian convention imposed an apparently fatal difficulty. Young ladies did not appear in public ;
their parents married them off to men whom they had never
seen. Consequently, if a young gentleman is to fall in love,
it must be with some girl who is of inferior social class, and
whom therefore he will not be allowed to marry ; and a
young lady cannot fall in love at all. A costly sacrifice is
offered by society at the altar of female chastity. Young
gentlemen dangle after always expensive and sometimes
heartless courtesans ; they purchase slave-girls with money
which has to be extracted from the grasp of cantankerous
parents by intriguing slaves ; or else they fall in love with
some modest girl in humble circumstances and form illicit,
unstable unions which only the fairy wand of Comedy can
turn into real marriages by revealing the glad secret that the
girl is of better birth than she seemed to be. Young ladies

are still more unfortunate : if before marriage they are to
win a man's love without betraying their sex and social class,
they must be exposed as infants, or kidnapped in childhood ;
if they reach their teens in their parents' homes and venture
to attend a women's night-festival, they are raped by unseen,
unknown assailants ; if subsequently they marry, suspicion
and scandal soon darken their lives and alienate their husbands ;
the baby born as a result of outrage has to be exposed, and
still the young mother finds herself deserted by her husband.
It is satisfactory to be able to set on the other side the fact
that an exposed baby's chances of rescue are one hundred per
cent ; that kidnapped children are invariably recognized and
restored to good and loving parents ; that the drunken youth
who assaults a maiden at a midnight festival and the husband
who later disowns her for unchastity always turn out to be
the same individual ; that realization of guilt leads to remorse,
and remorse to reconciliation.

CHAPTER VII

THE FAMOUS PLAYS OF PLAUTUS

THE FOLLOWING summaries of some of Plautus' plays may serve to illustrate the variety and limitations of New Comedy.

(1) *Amphitruo*

The prologue is spoken by the god Mercury. He explains that his father Jupiter has fallen in love with Alcumena, whose husband, Amphitruo, is abroad in command of the army of Thebes. Jupiter has assumed the likeness of Amphitruo to deceive the virtuous Alcumena, whose company he is enjoying at this moment (the time is early morning, before daylight). Mercury has himself assumed the likeness of Amphitruo's servant Sosia. The gods, he tells us, wear tokens to help the audience to distinguish them from their human counterparts. The real Sosia now enters from the harbour with tidings for Alcumena : Amphitruo has won the war and will be home almost immediately. Mercury accosts Sosia, claims to be Sosia himself and drives the bewildered servant off the stage. Sosia goes off to report this incident to Amphitruo. Jupiter now comes out of the house, bids a tender farewell to Alcumena and departs. A little later the real Amphitruo appears, expecting a tender welcome. He is astonished to be received with cold surprise by his wife, who thinks he is playing some trick on her. His astonishment turns to fury when she tells him that he has only just left her ; he hurls charges of infidelity against her, which she receives with admirable dignity, conscious of her innocence. Amphitruo goes off to find witnesses ; Jupiter appears and cajoles the angry Alcumena into a good temper ; they go inside. When Amphitruo returns, Mercury, still in Sosia's guise, bolts the door against him, treats him as a stranger and pelts him from the roof. At this point some scenes of the play are missing or in a fragmentary condition ; evidently the real and the false Amphitruo are brought face to face, to the mystification of onlookers. Finally Jupiter reveals himself in his divinity, explains the trick which he has played, and soothes the unfortunate Amphitruo, who accepts the extraordinary situation that the twin brother of his newly-born son is Jupiter's child, the infant Hercules.

The *Amphitruo*, described in the prologue as a tragicomedy, is alone among the extant examples of New Comedy in bringing gods on the stage as characters in the play. Their behaviour is, indeed, unworthy of deity ; but we must not take these burlesques too seriously. Similar themes were popular in the farces of Magna Graecia ; a phlyax-painting shows us Zeus (Jupiter) on a love-adventure, escorted by Hermes (Mercury). What is remarkable is the noble bearing of Alcumena, who maintains in the most cruel circumstances her dignity, her calm consciousness of innocence and her affection for her husband. There is plenty of knock-about farce, but it is not suffered to touch this queenly figure.*

(2) *Aulularia.*

An old Athenian citizen named Euclio, who lives in a very poor way with his daughter Phaedria and his old servant Staphyla, has found hidden treasure in his house, and now goes in constant terror that some one else will discover his secret. He does not know that Phaedria has been wronged by a young gentleman of the neighbourhood ; this we learn from the prologue, spoken by the household god, who adds that the young gentleman's uncle (also unaware of Phaedria's situation) is going to ask Euclio for her hand in marriage. We are now given a vivid picture of Euclio's miserable state of suspicion. When his next-door neighbour, the wealthy Megadorus (uncle of the guilty Lyconides) comes to ask for Phaedria's hand, Euclio at once suspects that he has got wind of the treasure ; however, he gives his consent—provided that Megadorus does not expect the bride to bring a dowry. During Euclio's absence the cooks sent by Megadorus arrive to prepare the wedding breakfast in his house. When he returns he drives them out and hurries off with his treasure to find another place of concealment. He is shadowed by Lyconides' slave, who

---

* The spirit of the phlyax-painting (plate IV) is utterly different; and the situation which it represents is quite unlike anything that happens in the *Amphitruo*.

3*

finally manages to unearth the treasure ; when Euclio discovers his loss, his grief knows no bounds. Lyconides, who has come to admit the wrong he has done to Phaedria and his desire to make amends, imagines that Euclio's distress is due to knowledge of Phaedria's condition. Eventually the tangle is straightened out, Lyconides recovers the treasure from his slave, Euclio consents to the marriage of Phaedria and Lyconides and apparently makes a wedding-present of the treasure, much to his own ultimate relief and peace of mind.

Euclio is one of the outstanding characters of Latin drama. Though portrayed throughout as absurdly penurious and suspicious, he is perhaps at bottom just a poor old fellow, crazed by the sudden acquisition of wealth ; he is not a Shylock or a Harpagon, though these famous characters owe much to him. As is usual in New Comedy, the unfortunate heroine does not appear ; we only hear her moaning when in the pangs of childbirth. Among the subsidiary characters Megadorus and his sister Eunomia show a generosity of nature and a sense of social responsibility which contrast favourably with the selfishness of so many of Plautus' characters.

(3) *Captiui.*

An old Aetolian gentleman named Hegio had two sons ; twenty years before the play opens one of them had been carried off in infancy by a rascally slave to Elis and sold to a gentleman who had given him the name Tyndarus and made him personal slave to his own little son Philocrates. During the war which is now being waged between Aetolia and Elis Hegio's other son, Philopolemus, has been captured ; Hegio, hoping to arrange an exchange of prisoners, has purchased several Elean captives, his latest acquisitions being Philocrates and Tyndarus. They have secretly exchanged clothes and names, expecting that Hegio will send the supposed slave home to make arrangements for the ransom of his master. The plan works admirably, and Philocrates departs. Unfortunately Tyndarus is recognized by another of Hegio's captives, and the poor old gentleman is so infuriated to learn how he has been fooled that he orders Tyndarus off to the terrible quarries, there to be worked to death. Philocrates returns (with miraculous quickness, it must be confessed) from Elis, bringing with him Philopolemus and the rascally slave who had stolen Hegio's other son ; enquiries disclose that this son is Tyndarus, who is thereupon hastily fetched back from the quarries, and all ends happily.

As befits a comedy, the *Captiui* contains a lively plot and some capital fun ; but it derives its unique quality from the strong dramatic irony of the situation, the devotion of the Captives to each other and the noble and generous atmosphere which pervades the play.

(4) *Menaechmi.*

Two twin brothers had become separated in infancy ; Menaechmus I, kidnapped and carried off to Epidamnus, has had the good fortune to be made heir to a wealthy old gentleman, who has since died. Menaechmus II, having grown to manhood in his native Syracuse, has started on a search for his brother and is now newly arrived at Epidamnus with his slave Messenio. The exact resemblance of the two brothers leads to a ' comedy of errors ' which threatens to have serious consequences ; eventually the brothers meet, and all is explained.

The theme of mistaken identity was frequently exploited in New Comedy, to judge by the number of plays entitled ' The Twins ' or ' The Doubles '. The interest of the *Menaechmi* lies chiefly in its well-handled if improbable plot and its amusing scenes ; the two brothers alienate our feelings by their selfishness, but some of the minor characters are well portrayed, especially the doctor who is called in by the father-in-law of Menaechmus I to treat the young man's supposed insanity.

(5) *Miles Gloriosus.*

Pyrgopolynices, a vain, amorous and timid ' braggart captain ', has secured possession of Philocomasium, mistress of the young Athenian gentleman Pleusicles, and has also purchased Pleusicles' slave Palaestrio, who had been kidnapped by pirates. Palaestrio has managed to send word to Pleusicles, who is now living in the house of his friend Periplectomenus, next door to the captain. By breaking a passage through the party wall Palaestrio has enabled the lovers to meet secretly. Unfortunately another slave of the captain peers down through the skylight and perceives Philocomasium in the wrong house ; he has to be persuaded that the girl he has seen is really Philocomasium's twin sister, a feat which is achieved by the use of the secret passage and the girl's skilful performance in the double rôle. Finally Pyrgopolynices is induced to lose interest in Philocomasium by a report that his neighbour's wife is in love with him ; he allows Philocomasium to depart with a supposed ' ship's captain ' (really Pleusicles in nautical guise) who claims to have been sent by her mother, while the captain himself, in pursuance of his new intrigue, enters his neighbour's house, there to be seized and threatened with the barbarous punishment to which detected adulterers were liable. When his cowardice has been thoroughly exposed he receives a contemptuous pardon.

The brilliant portraits of the foolish captain, his cunning parasite and the genial old bachelor Periplectomenus, as well as the vigour of the play as a whole, compensate for certain improbabilities and weaknesses, such as the extraordinary ignorance on the captain's part as to his neighbour's domestic circumstances and the fact that the two main themes—the trick of the secret passage and the trick of the fictitious love-message—seem to have little to do with each other.

(6) *Mostellaria* (' The Ghost Story ').

Theopropides, an old gentleman of Athens, has been abroad on business for three years ; during his absence his son Philolaches lives a wild life under the direction of the slave Tranio, and has even borrowed from a money-lender in order to purchase the freedom of his mistress, the affectionate and faithful Philematium. A merry drinking-party of the lovers and their friends, Callidamates and his mistress Delphium, in front of the house is cut short by Tranio's arrival with news that he has seen Theopropides at the harbour. Tranio takes command, hurries the revellers indoors, locks the house and, when Theopropides arrives, scares him with a story that the house is haunted and has been abandoned. Matters are complicated by the arrival of the money-lender in search of his dues ; Tranio, hastily building lie on lie, pretends that Philolaches has borrowed money in order to purchase another house. What house ? Why, the house next door. Theopropides wishes to inspect the purchase ; the occupant appears ; Tranio manages to keep the conversation at cross-purposes during an amusing scene. Inevitably Theopropides finds out that he has been deceived ; Tranio, threatened with disaster, takes refuge just in time on the altar and there manages by native wit and impudence to hold his own until Callidamates appears and gets Theopropides to grant a general pardon.

The irrepressible and endlessly resourceful Tranio is perhaps the most delightful portrait in Latin comedy of the ' cunning slave '. The other portraits are all well drawn—the spendthrift young men, the tender Philematium, her worldly-wise old servant Scapha, the niggardly Theopropides, his more genial neighbour Simo, and the money-lender. The plot is one of the best-handled in Plautus.

(7) *Rudens* (' The Rope ').

An old Athenian gentleman named Daemones, whose daughter had been kidnapped in infancy, and who has lost his fortune through liberality, is living in humble exile in a lonely cottage on the African shore near Cyrene. His daughter, now called Palaestra, is in the power of the pimp Labrax, who has brought her to Cyrene ; there a young gentleman from Athens named Plesidippus has seen and fallen in love with her, and has even paid part of her purchase-money to Labrax. The pimp has tried to slip away with his slaves to Sicily, but is wrecked ; Palaestra and her maid come to shore near the cottage of Daemones and take refuge in the temple next door. Labrax also swims to shore and tries to seize the girls ; Daemones gives them protection, and Plesidippus arrives and drags Labrax off to be tried in Cyrene. Gripus, a slave of Daemones, fishes up a trunk containing (as he suspects) treasure ; the trunk belongs to Labrax, and inside are the toys of Palaestra's childhood, which proves that she is the daughter of Daemones, and can therefore marry Plesidippus.

The rural setting, the story of the storm, shipwreck and treasure-trove and the comparatively high moral tone of the play as a whole, make the *Rudens* one of the most refreshing examples of New Comedy. We may call it the most romantic play of Plautus, if this term is understood not to include any strong love-interest ; the treatment of the love-theme is indeed perfunctory.

Noteworthy features in the other plays of Plautus are the cynical studies in debauchery afforded by the *Bacchides* and the *Truculentus*, the vivid portrait of the pimp Ballio in the *Pseudolus* and, as a contrast, the moralizing tone of the *Trinummus*, which play also contains the most amusing exposure of a trickster in Plautus. The *Epidicus* (apparently one of its author's favourite plays) has a plot of remarkable complexity. In the *Asinaria* there is an effective scene in which a canny trader foils the plot of two swindlers ; the *Casina* (a very popular play) is exceptional in the riotous indecency of its concluding scenes ; the *Cistellaria* is unusually sentimental, a *comédie larmoyante* ; the *Curculio* has a striking opening scene, showing the lover calling on his mistress in the darkness of early morning. In the *Mercator* father and son are rivals in love ; this play is brilliant at times, yet curiously lacking in the usual Plautine touches. The *Persa* is remarkable in bringing a freeborn girl on the stage ; though she is only the daughter of a parasite, she has a dignity which contrasts sharply with the behaviour of the usual courtesan. The *Poenulus* contains a not unsympathetic portrait of a Carthaginian ; his remarks in Punic (or perhaps pseudo-Punic) * are ridiculously misinterpreted by a slave in a scene which must owe much to the Latin translator. The *Stichus*, one of the few plays known to be translated by Plautus from Menander, ends like the *Persa*, in a slaves' drinking-party. Finally the fragmentary *Vidularia* deals with the fortunes of a gentlemanly young castaway who is forced to hire himself out as a manual labourer.

* See p. 66 and note. For the pseudo-Indian of the Oxyrhynchus Farce cf. p. 156, and see New Chapter on Greek Literature, ii, pp. 215–222. A word supposed to be in Punic or some other African tongue is quoted in the pseudo-Plautine (?) *Caecus* : see Lindsay's Oxford Text, *Fragmenta*, line 45.

CHAPTER VIII

PLAUTUS : TREATMENT OF HIS ORIGINALS

LIKE MOST if not all of the other Latin dramatists, Plautus was not so much an original playwright as one who adapted Greek drama to Roman taste. We have no convincing evidence that he invented a single plot or character, or introduced into his originals any alterations which show constructive power. Scarcely one scene among several hundred can with certainty be ascribed to his independent authorship. His originality shows itself firstly in the fact that he limited himself to a single field, the translation of Greek New Comedy, secondly in his choice of plays for adaptation, thirdly in his intuitive perception both of what public taste required and of the limitations under which he must work ; but above all in his command of language and metre, of jest and metaphor, of rhetoric and repartee.

In limiting himself to one field of drama he set an example which was followed by nearly all subsequent dramatists. Both in width of interests and in power of innovation he was inferior to his contemporaries Naevius and Ennius ; he confined himself to comedy, not through lack of command of the tragic style (witness the noble rhetoric of his *Captiui*) but, presumably, because comedy was the field in which he thought he could win greatest success. If his work was governed by practical considerations (Horace accuses him[1] of being entirely mercenary), he seems at least to have taken some pride in his achievement ; he tells us[2] that he prided himself in his *Epidicus*, and Cicero makes Cato assert[3] that Plautus admired his *Pseudolus* and his *Truculentus*.* These favourite plays have certain qualities in common—a complicated plot, plenty of trickery, some remarkable turns of fortune, vigorous dialogue, metrical variety, heartiness, cynicism—qualities which are, indeed, common to most of his plays, and which, when combined, produce a result different from the extant work of any other

* A remark which (at least) tells us something of Cicero's tastes.

ancient dramatist.   How wide a choice of Greek originals he
enjoyed is outside our knowledge.   It is striking that he seems
to have taken so few plays from Menander—perhaps not more
than three out of the twenty-one, whereas with Terence the figure
is four out of six.   Liveliness of plot and abundance of farcical
situations seem to have been what Plautus sought, not that
interest in theme and in personality which attracted Terence
to Menander.   Scarcely a play of Plautus but contains at
least one scene of uproarious farce.   Something may be
learned of his tastes by observing the cases where he changed,
or is thought to have changed, the title of his original.   From
Philemon's somewhat moralistic ' Treasure ' (*Thesaurus*) he
translated his *Trinummus ;* the Latin title (if, indeed, due to
Plautus himself) shows that in his eyes the outstanding scene
was the encounter between the trickster (hired for ' three
nummi ') and the man whom he was impersonating.   The
Rudens (translated from an unknown play by Diphilus) has
many virtues in our eyes :—its refreshing, unusual setting by
the lonely African shore, its romantic story of shipwreck and
treasure trove, its satisfying conclusion—honesty rewarded,
child and parent restored to each other, love triumphant—
but the Latin title, ' The Rope ', indicates that for the inventor
of that title the central scene was the tug-of-war between
Trachalio and Gripus for the possession of the treasure.   The
Stichus was translated from one of two plays entitled ' The
Brothers ', by Menander.   It has been criticized on the ground
that its three parts have little to do with each other : part one,
the faithful wives ; part two, the disappointed parasite ; part
three, the slaves' drinking-party ; but whereas part one and
two have in common at least the inimitable Antipho, the Roman
writer's own taste seems indicated by the change of title ;
Stichus, the merry slave, does not appear until part three.

For a dramatist whose only object is to amuse the ground-
lings, an obvious resource is obscenity ; indeed, no comic
dramatist of antiquity found it easy to resist this temptation.
Terence's most successful bid for popularity, the *Eunuchus,*
contains the most artfully sexual scene [4] in Latin drama ; and
it is significant that the very play which we know to have been
revived soon after the death of Plautus, the *Casina,* is of all his
works the one which errs most grievously against decency.
There is, in fact, just enough obscenity in Plautus to make us

wonder why we do not find more. Apparently the police imposed no such absolute ban here as they did in the matter of personal slander and political satire. Of course views change from age to age as to what is or is not objectionable. The early editors of the Renaissance were shocked by such a play as the *Mercator*,* in which a father and son appear as rivals for the affections of a slave-girl ; to some modern readers such a situation appears merely a piquant variation of a stock theme of New Comedy, and some scenes of the play possess a grace and brilliance which seem to come straight from the Greek originals, untainted by coarseness of expression. But why are there not more scenes in Plautus like the concluding scenes of the *Casina,* so Italian in tone, so reminiscent of Ovid, Petronius and Apuleius ? The truth appears to be that on the topic of sex the Romans were highly sensitive, and public taste imposed its own limits. We must remember that the spectators included not only magistrates but women. That some at any rate among the Roman audience were not in favour of licence is suggested not only by the writer's conscious pride in the high moral tone of the *Captiui* [5]—' poets find few plays like this, showing good men becoming better '—but also in his care never to risk a jest which might sully the honour of a free-born woman.

All theories which ascribe to him independent power of plot-construction are based on hypothesis. One of the few alterations made by him of which we can be fairly certain is that, as Terence tells us,[6] in the *Commorientes* he omitted (or perhaps curtailed) one scene of his original, the *Synapothnescontes* of Diphilus. This omission Terence ascribes to Plautus' ' carelessness ', and his explanation may be accepted, if we interpret it as meaning that Plautus set no particular store on fidelity of translation—he took what he wanted and left what he did not want. The remark in the prologue of the *Casina* [7] that the young gentleman will not appear in the play, because Plautus has broken down the bridge by which he was to return home, may be merely a jesting way of saying that the plot (even of the Greek original) did not allow this character to appear. Of the expansion of certain scenes by the addition of stock comedian's ' patter ' there is, indeed, strong evidence. The monologue of the Property-manager in the *Curculio* [8] is

* See the edition by Professor Enk, i. p. 22 ff.

certainly an addition by Plautus or a later hand. It is a
description of Rome ; it has no relation to the plot , its effect
is merely to entertain. Possibly we should also ascribe to
Plautus the long Punic passages in the *Poenulus* [9] ; presumably
some of his audience had learned the language during the
war with Hannibal. That such enlargements might be
balanced by curtailment elsewhere is a not unreasonable
supposition (though there seems to have been no fixed length
for a play, and some are twice as long as others) ; in this way,
perhaps, we can explain the omission (or curtailment) of the
lively abduction-scene in the *Synapothnescontes*. But of remodelling of the plot there is no convincing evidence. Perhaps
the play which has been most often suspected is the *Stichus*,
and its three parts have often been felt to have little to do with
each other. But if Plautus drastically (and carelessly) re-
modelled the *Stichus*, how are we to explain the neatness with
which the rôles are made to dovetail into each other, so that a
cast of only three actors could perform the whole play ?

To ascribe to Plautus the credit for his plots and characters
may be justified only in the sense that it was he who chose and
translated the plays which possessed these plots and characters.
The dignified Alcumena, the absurd yet pathetic Euclio, made
miserable by his wealth, the noble and moving farewell scene
of the *Captiui*, the deft intrigue, droll situations and amusing
characters of the *Menaechmi*, *Miles Gloriosus* and *Mostellaria*—
all these have indeed been transmitted to world literature by
Plautus, but he was not their creator. Nevertheless it would
be quite wrong to think of him as a mere translator. However
closely he follows his originals, he could scarcely have avoided
infusing his versions with his own spirit. Without necessarily
attributing to him any structural alteration, we can admit that
on a congenial theme he let his pen run away with him,
regardless of ' the necessary business of the play '. The
dialogue between Sosia and his divine double, in the *Amphitruo*,
has surely been expanded by the Latin writer ; it is indeed the
longest scene in Plautus, and most of it is mere foolery—but
how Roman ! This quarrel between a street-bully and his
victim (*si rixa est ubi tu pulsas, ego uapulo tantum*) is as racy of the
streets of Rome as the famous scene in Juvenal's third satire.

What the Romans themselves ascribe to Plautus was
command of metre, dialogue and jest. When he died ' all his

measures beyond measure wept for him ', as his epitaph [10] runs.
For dialogue [11] he was ranked by Varro above all other Latin
comic dramatists, and Aelius Stilo said that, if the Muses were
to speak Latin, it would be the Latin of Plautus.   Horace
grudgingly admits that the Romans have been only too ready
to praise Plautus' *numeri* and *sales ;* his wit is put by Cicero on
a level with that of Attic Old Comedy ; Sidonius Apollinaris
regarded him as actually superior to the Greeks, and St.
Jerome used to console himself, after a night of weeping over
his own sins, by reading Plautus.[12]   It is hard to believe that
any one would turn to Menander for similar consolation.   Even
supposing that many of Plautus' jokes came from his originals,
we must admit that it is not difficult to spoil a good jest in the
telling.   The life and gaiety of his style could not have been
achieved by any ' obscura diligentia ' in translation.   And when
the jokes depend (as they so often do) on a pun, possible only in
Latin, or on some topical allusion which would have no
meaning outside Italy, we must agree that here the full credit
is to be given to the Latin writer.

The fragments of the earlier dramatists show nothing
approaching Plautus' variety of metres (though we must always
regret that time has spared so little of Naevius), nor do later
writers appear to have rivalled him in this respect.   In developing comedy on its musical side Plautus must have depended
to some extent on the development of instrumental talent
in Rome ; without setting too high the skill of Pellio, who
perhaps undertook the title-rôle of the *Epidicus* (apparently
not to Plautus' own satisfaction) or that of Marcipor, slave
of Oppius, who played the music for the *Stichus*, we may at
least agree that the technique of such performers was not
created in a day.   It is interesting to note that the metrical
effects are particularly rich in the plays which seem to have
been produced in Plautus' maturity or old age, while the
Mercator and *Asinaria*, which are unusually simple in metrical
structure, have for other reasons been thought to be early
works (see Duckworth, *N.R.C.*, pp. 54 f.).   The *Miles*,
which is also simple in metrical form, appears from the
reference to Naevius' imprisonment to be another of the early
works.   On the other hand the *Cistellaria*, which contains a
reference to the Hannibalic war as still going on (but apparently
drawing near its conclusion) shows a large range of metrical

effects. With the *Casina*, of unknown date but certainly displaying the author in characteristic vein, the variety has become prodigious.

The speed and power of Plautus' dialogue, and the purity of his style, were acknowledged by ancient critics ; nor do we depend on ancient testimony alone, for we have some twenty thousand lines of racy Latin, covering all the subjects within the sphere of broad comedy—buffoonery, conviviality, endearment, abuse, worldly wisdom and popular philosophy. What could be more effective[13] than to address an enemy as ' Dug from a dunghill ! ' (ex sterculino effosse) ? Where are the raptures of love better portrayed than in the words of Phaedromus ?

sibi sua habeant regna reges, sibi diuitias diuites,
sibi honores, sibi uirtutes, sibi pugnas, sibi proelia :
dum mi abstineant inuidere, sibi quisque habeant quod suom est.

> ' Gie me a cannie hour at e'en,
> My arms about my dearie O,
> An' warldly cares, an' warldly men
> May a' gang tapsalteerie O ! '

Such moments do not last long, and always in the background there is the cynical spectator to point out love's follies—for this is Latin comedy. Pseudolus, in the moment of his triumph, grows for a moment grave at the thought of the vanity of human wishes :

stulti haud scimus frustra ut simus, quom quod cupienter dari
petimus nobis, quasi quid in rem sit possimus noscere.
certa mittimus dum incerta petimus; atque hoc euenit
in labore atque in dolore, ut mors obrepat interim.

This is in the mood of the grave Roman satirist, with his eye on the sun-dial :

> dum serta, unguenta, puellas
> quaerimus, obrepit non intellecta senectus.*

The solemn note must have struck a responsive chord even in the hearts of that turbulent audience ; for mankind passes easily from one extreme of emotion to the other. This mixture of jest and gravity meets us elsewhere in popular Latin drama. But Pseudolus does not linger on the heights :

sed iam satis est philosophatum ! nimi' diu et longum loquor.

* Juv. ix. 128–9.

Everyone can recognize in Plautus the uis comica which Julius Caesar [14] found wanting in Terence; all the more striking, then, is the occasional recurrence of the serious note. Nor does this note always end in mockery. Something more than farce and cynicism was needed to win from Lessing [15] his tribute to the *Captiui* as ' the finest play that has ever been put on the stage '. The farewell of Tyndarus to the friend and master for whose sake he is going into deadly peril is of a quality which may move us, as it moves the honest Hegio, to admiring tears. And when the deception practised on the old man has been disclosed, and Tyndarus must pay the full penalty for his noble lie, he faces the prospect of death with a spirit worthy of a Roman legionary : [16]

> For if he break his word and not return,
> And I be fated in this land to die,
> Yet this my deed, when I am dead and gone,
> Will be for ever bright and memorable :
> That I from slavery, from foeman's might,
> Rescued my master, made him free once more
> To look upon his father and his home ;
> And, when no other hope nor help was his,
> To save my master's life, I gave—my own.

CHAPTER IX

THE GENERAL CHARACTER OF ROMAN TRAGEDY

THERE IS a widespread belief that tragedy was never popular at Rome. For this belief no better evidence is usually offered than a jest in the prologue of the *Amphitruo* [1] : ' I will tell you the plot of this tragedy. What ? Are you wrinkling your foreheads because I said it would be a tragedy ? ' The real reasons for the modern view are perhaps that only fragments of the tragedy of the Republican period have survived, and that the rhetorical style of these fragments makes little appeal to modern taste, especially when we compare them, as we sometimes can, with the originals by the great Greek masters. It must be remembered, however, that Roman tragedy continued to be performed for more than two hundred years, that the Romans regarded Ennius, Pacuvius and Accius as great tragic writers, that the tragedies of Ennius were sufficiently well known to the common people to induce Plautus to burlesque their style, that from the three leading writers alone over seventy titles have come down to us, that performances of tragedies in the time of Cicero were attended by eager crowds, some of whom knew the classics of the stage so well that at the first notes of the flute they could tell what performance was to follow, and that on one occasion, when an actor failed to take his cue, ' twelve hundred ' voices echoed the words ' mater, te appello '. In fact Graeco-Roman tragedy had at least as long a career on the Roman stage as any other form of literary drama, and its effect on the popular mind must have been far-reaching.

For the modern reader, however, Roman tragedy has little appeal. To begin with, it was almost wholly derivative. We have seen that the introduction of the native historical play proved a failure, only five or six fairly certain examples being recorded for the entire Republican period. In dealing with Greek tragedy Latin translators seem to have shown even less originality than in dealing with Greek comedy. Neither in tragedy nor in comedy have we any evidence that the Latin writers (apart from Terence) introduced structural changes ; they seem to have confined their alterations for the most part to sentiment and style.* In comedy they had the congenial task of infusing crude vigour into the somewhat languid Greek, and of scattering jests from a full sack. It is arguable that the plays of Plautus would prove better reading than their Greek originals, could we compare them. But the Roman tragic style was a poor equivalent for the style of Aeschylus or Euripides. Compared with the Greek, the Latin usually seems stiff, strained and unnatural. The Romans appreciated the very qualities which repel us. They enjoyed melodramatic effects, volleys of rhetoric, horrific plots and descriptions, flamboyant personalities, superhuman virtue, incredible vice. In another mood they were capable of laughing at these very things ; ut paratragoedat carnufex ² ! ' how the knave rants ! ' as a character of Plautus remarks. Our scraps of information on the behaviour of the crowd at performances of tragedy suggest that they were interested not so much in the essential dramatic qualities of the performance as in externals—impressive staging, violent utterance and action, lines which might be taken as topical, the arrival of distinguished spectators, and of course any mishap which might befall either the actors or any members of the audience. Yet in fairness we should remember that it is usually the exceptional which is recorded.

While we possess the names of over a dozen translators of Greek comedy, only five writers are certainly known to have composed tragedy for the stage. Terence's prologues suggest that the comic dramatist lived in a fiercely competitive world ; the careers of the writers of tragedy overlapped hardly at all. It seems that Livius was dead and Naevius was in disgrace by the time Ennius came to Rome, and Pacuvius was eighty years old when Accius made his first appearance. Livius and Naevius were certainly contemporaries, but Naevius' chief work was in comedy. Though Ennius and his nephew Pacuvius were producing tragedies at the same time, their relations may have been those of master and pupil rather than of rivals. It is obvious that Naevius, Plautus, Caecilius

* As for the modern theory that they combined different Greek originals, see the discussion of ' contaminatio ' in the chapter on Terence and Appendix K.

and Terence had, each in his own way, a special inclination
for comedy ; but what induced the tragic writers to take up
tragedy, except the need to earn a living in the only way open
to a writer—the stage—and the knowledge that they had no
comic talent ? Ennius (239–169 B.C.) [3] was a great poet and
personality, but it is hard to feel sure that he had any special
dramatic gift ; Pacuvius seems to have had a liking for complicated plots and dramatic discussion of philosophical problems,
and Accius had a noted turn for repartee. But the fact that
only fragments have survived from the tragedies of these writers
practically confines our discussion of their powers to points of
style. Criticisms by ancient commentators are sometimes helpful ; sometimes the choice of subjects indicated by the titles
is suggestive. In a few cases we have the Greek originals, or
fragments of them, and elsewhere our knowledge of Greek
mythology helps us to reconstruct the plots. The lines of
development of Republican tragedy may to some extent be
inferred from what tragedy became under the Empire. But
the often-cited evidence of vase-paintings, wall-paintings, etc.,
can seldom be shown to be relevant ; the mural decorators of
Pompeii probably derived their ideas of mythology from quite
other sources than Republican tragedy. If these illustrations
from imperial times are indeed taken from the stage, the
exaggerated stiffness of the figures and the dress may reflect
imperial rather than republican ideals. In imperial times
tragedy was something of a survival ; such tragedies as were
produced may have been the by now archaic plays of Pacuvius
and Accius, and the whole performance may have been
consciously artificial. In earlier times, when Roman tragedy
was still vital, the style of acting and of dress may have been
considerably more natural.

If we ask what was the essential character of Roman
tragedy, perhaps the answer should be that it was a harsh,
exaggerated yet not wilfully unfaithful imitation of its Greek
originals. Differences in detail will be noticed when we deal
with the individual writers.

ENNIUS

As if by official arrangement, there always appears to have
been one recognized writer of tragedy in Rome as long as

tragedy was still alive, and seldom more than one. The death of Andronicus and the disgrace of Naevius left the way clear for their successor, who, after completing his military service, arrived in Rome in 204 B.C. as a member of the suite of M. Porcius Cato. Quintus Ennius had a human weakness for talking about himself. Our biographical details are probably derived from his works, and for that reason fairly reliable. They show him to us as poor yet independent, proud of his native town and of his Roman citizenship, able to live on easy terms with the great, yet himself belonging to the workaday class of dramatists such as his fellow-lodger Caecilius and his nephew Pacuvius. Born in the year 239 at Rudiae, in the south of Italy, he prided himself on his knowledge of Greek, Latin and Oscan (the three languages, we may add, of ancient drama). From his arrival in Rome at the age of thirty-five he devoted himself to his many-sided literary activity. A man of versatile genius and broad human sympathies, an Italiot whose imagination was fired by the literature of Greece and the history of Rome, he brought into Latin literature and life a fresh impulse of Hellenism. Like Livius Andronicus he earned his living partly as a teacher and partly as a dramatist. Drama was only one of his literary activities. Though Terence refers to him together with Plautus and Naevius as one of those careless but gifted writers whom he preferred to his own laborious but dull contemporaries, it was as an epic poet rather than as a dramatist that he was honoured by later generations. He was apparently not regarded as the equal of either Pacuvius or Accius in tragedy, while in comedy Volcacius Sedigitus (see p. 117) puts him tenth, adding that even this honour is granted only in recognition of his early date ! We hear nothing elsewhere of Ennius as a writer of comedy, and possess of his comedies only two doubtful titles (*Cupuncula, Pancratiastes*) and three lines on stock topics.

The tragedies of Ennius undoubtedly had great influence, both as drama and as literature. We have twenty titles (*Achilles, Ajax, Alcumeo, Alexander, Andromacha, Andromeda, Athamas, Cresphontes, Erechtheus, Eumenides, Hectoris Lytra, Hecuba, Iphigenia, Medea Exul, Melanippa, Nemea, Phoenix, Telamo, Telephus, Thyestes*), with about four hundred lines ; we also have what some claim to be the titles of two praetextae, *Ambracia* and *Sabinae*, with a few lines.

The Hellenistic stage was dominated by the influence of Euripides, and in Euripides Ennius found a writer who appealed to his own questioning spirit and humanitarian sympathies. An ancient scholiast [4] tells us that Ennius took 'very many' tragedies from Euripides ; indeed more than half of his twenty titles have with greater or less probability been considered Euripidean.   In the *Hecuba, Iphigenia* and *Medea Exul* we can compare the Latin fragments with the complete originals. From Aeschylus he appears to have derived his *Eumenides ;* from Aristarchus, another fifth-century tragedian, his *Achilles* and some unspecified plays.   A remark of Cicero * has sometimes been strained to mean that Ennius took some of his plays direct from Homer.   This is utterly unlikely ; all our evidence goes to show that the original of each Latin tragedy or comedy was a Greek tragedy or comedy.

As to Ennius' methods of translation, we have two apparently contradictory statements by Cicero, who says in one place that the Roman tragedians (including Ennius and Pacuvius) translated ' ad uerbum ', ' word for word ', in another that Ennius, Pacuvius and Accius translated ' non uerba sed uim ', ' not the words but the sense '.†   These statements may perhaps be reconciled : the Roman tragedians followed their originals closely in *substance*, deviating only in choice of words.‡   The only evidence that Ennius allowed himself independence in more than style, sentiment and metre is provided by Gellius (19.10.11), who quotes a song of the chorus in his *Iphigenia* to which there is nothing corresponding in the original, Euripides' *Iphigenia in Aulide*.   In Euripides' play the chorus are a band of young married women of Chalcis who have come across the straits merely out of curiosity to see the Greek fleet.   Apart from singing occasional songs, songs which are sometimes long and difficult and have only indirect bearing on the story, they take practically no part in the play.   For some reason Ennius has, it seems, introduced a party of soldiers.   The canticum which he puts into their mouths reminds us of many passages

* *De Fin.* I. iii. 7 : ut ab Homero Ennius, Afranius a Menandro solet. Cicero is probably referring to Ennius' *Annales ;* in any case he is speaking of the insertion of occasional passages from a Greek author into an *original* Latin work.

† *De Fin.* I. ii. 4 ; *Acad.* I. iii. 10.

‡ Where Ennius translated Greek plays which have themselves been preserved complete, practically all the Latin fragments can be compared with their source in the Greek play.

of Plautine patter ; it is a short sermon on the theme of idleness, expressing the boredom of the soldiers (neque domi nunc
nos nec militiae sumus). Just so a Plautine slave will weary us
with a sermon on obedience or some such topic in a style which
suggests that the passage is entirely the work of the Latin writer.
If Ennius felt that the Euripidean chorus had no real connexion
with the plot and could safely be omitted, we may concede that
he showed some dramatic insight.   But he may merely have
been repelled by the difficulty of the Greek, or have thought
that his Roman audience would prefer a troop of soldiers to a
party of young women.   Nor can we be certain that he *did* drop
the Euripidean chorus ; the song of the soldiers may have been
added for its own sake.   In the canticum itself there is nothing
to suggest original dramatic power on his part.   In his *Medea
Exul* he evidently kept the Euripidean chorus of Corinthian
women.   The fact that Ennius translated Aeschylus' *Eumenides*
(the fragments can for the most part be referred to their origin
in the Greek play) makes us wonder whether he also translated the two other plays of the famous trilogy ;   it is hard,
however, to believe that, if he did so, the Romans would
have endured hearing the three plays produced one after the
other.   The *Eumenides* of Aeschylus forms a satisfactory story
in itself ;   the dramatic situation could, no doubt, have been
explained in a prologue.

In metre he took complete freedom.   Sometimes he keeps
the Greek metre, whether iambics (the opening lines of the
Medea, trochaics (the argument between Agamemnon and
Menelaus, *Iph.* iv.-vi.) or anapaests (the opening of the
Iphigenia) ; sometimes he turns iambics into trochaics (Medea's
altercation with Jason), and, in a still more emotional passage—
Medea's farewell to her children—he turns speech into what
is usually regarded as song :

> . . . saluete, optima corpora !
> cette manus uestras measque accipite !

On the other hand we find that a lyrical utterance of Euripides' chorus (*Med.* 1251 ff.) has been turned into trochaics.

In general, where we can set Ennius' Latin side by side
with the Greek, we find that the version is reasonably close.
He does not shrink from translating the boldest utterances of
Euripides, such as Medea's famous assertion that she would

rather fight three battles than bear one child. All the Roman
tragic writers seem to have indulged in sceptical outbursts ;
Euripides puts into Achilles' mouth (*Iph. A.* 955) a contemptuous reference to soothsayers ; Ennius expands the passage
into a more detailed attack on astrologers.

That Ennius was truly a poet is revealed in the dramatic
fragments as clearly as in the *Annales*. The opening lines of
the *Iphigenia*—a lyrical dialogue between Agamemnon and
an old man—conveys a sense of the majesty and mystery of
the starry sky not inferior to that of the Greek. Similar is
the feeling in a line preserved from the *Hecuba* :

> O magna templa caelitum, commixta stellis splendidis !

which perhaps corresponds to

> ὦ στεροπὰ Διός, ὦ σκοτία νύξ.

There is pathos in these lines of the *Alexander* which inspired
Virgil himself :

> O lux Troiae, germane Hector !
> quid ita . . . cum tuo lacerato corpore,
> miser, aut qui te sic tractauere nobis respectantibus ?

And Cicero (*Tusc.* 3.19.44) testifies to the moving power of
the lament in the *Andromacha* :

> O pater, o patria, o Priami domus,
> saeptum altisono cardine templum !

In general, however, the most characteristic quality of the
fragments of Ennius' tragedies, especially when compared
with the original Greek, is the heightening of the rhetorical
effect. All our evidence goes to show that Roman tragedy
was far more rhetorical than its Greek models. There are
times when rhetoric has its place : the altercation between
Agamemnon and Menelaus is an example (*Iph.* iv–vi). Whereas in Euripides we have

> ΑΓΑ.　τί δέ σε τἀμὰ δεῖ φυλάσσειν ; οὐκ ἀναισχύντου τόδε ;
> ΜΕ.　ὅτι τὸ βούλεσθαι μ' ἔκνιζε· σὸς δὲ δοῦλος οὐκ ἔφυν.
> ΑΓΑ.　οὐχὶ δεινά ; τὸν ἐμὸν οἰκεῖν οἶκον οὐκ ἐᾷς ἐμέ ;

in the Latin we have

> *Ag.*　quis homo te exsuperauit usquam gentium impudentia ?
> *Me.*　quis ted autem malitia ? . . . .

or again

> *Ag.* egone plectar, tu delinques : tu pecces, ego arguar?
>   pro malefactis Helena redeat, uirgo pereat innocens?
>   tua reconcilietur uxor, mea necetur filia?

Where the Greek simply shows us two angry men wrangling, the Latin seems to echo the skilled thrust and parry of a debate between two Roman advocates. This rhetorical effect is achieved by the familiar devices of alliteration and assonance, emphasis and repetition—often at the expense of simplicity and truth to nature. At times it can rise to grandeur —as in the oath of Achilles (*Ach.* ii) :

> per ego deum sublimas subices umidas,
> unde oritur imber sonitu saeuo et spiritu ;

or in *Thyest.* vii :

> aspice hoc sublime candens quem inuocant omnes Iouem

(cf. Eur. *inc.* 935);

but the force of Jason's words to Medea :

> ὡς Ἔρως σ᾽ ἠνάγκασε
> τόξοις ἀφύκτοις τοὐμὸν ἐκσῶσαι δέμας,

is not improved by the rhetorical jingle in

> tu me amoris magis quam honoris seruauisti gratia.

We are irritated by a Cassandra who begins a passionate outburst in this way :

> mater, optumarum multo mulier melior mulierum.

Roman pedantry and excessive preoccupation with the form of words shows itself in

> amicus certus in re incerta cernitur,[5]

a line thought well of by Cicero—who, when he champions Ennius, is partly an advocate who feels that he holds a brief for the earlier poets, partly a fellow-countryman who himself suffers from the same defects.

Rhetoric is more than a trick of style : it is an attitude to life. The writer who is excessively emphatic in words is apt to lay too much stress on immediate effect in thought and emotion. In Roman tragedy there is a tendency to over-statement ; crude effects are substituted for simplicity and naturalness. Ennius was a man of broad human sympathies, possessed of a genuine poetic talent ; but even he is not free from that straining after effect which was to become more and more marked in Roman tragedy. It must be conceded to the Roman tragedians that they were striving to create a worthy diction ; if the attempt is momentarily abandoned, the tone may become commonplace and sometimes, one might say, class-conscious [6] : compare

> ἡ δυσγένεια δ' ὡς ἔχει τι χρήσιμον·
> καὶ γὰρ δακρῦσαι ῥᾳδίως αὐτοῖς ἔχει
> ἅπαντά τ' εἰπεῖν· τῷ δὲ γενναίῳ φύσιν
> ἄνολβα ταῦτα

with

> plebes in hoc regi antistat loco : licet
> lacrumare plebi, regi honeste non licet.

This class-consciousness may also account for the extraordinary expansion of Euripides' phrase ' Corinthian women ' into

> quae Corinthum arcem altam habetis, matronae opulentae,
> optumates !

Perhaps we may sum up these criticisms by saying that Roman tragedy did not succeed in developing a style which was at once simple and dignified. That it did not do so is to be explained quite as much by popular taste in Rome as by the limitations of the writers of tragedy. The effects which to us seem forced may have appealed to the listeners for whom they were designed far more than would the artistic restraint of the Greek originals.

Cicero admired the tragedies of Ennius almost to adoration, was never tired of quoting from them and seems to assume that his audience knows them too. He tells us that the *Medea* was widely *read* [7] in his day. Other Romans seem not to have ranked Ennius as a dramatist quite as high as his great successors in tragedy, Pacuvius and Accius. That his plays were popular in his own day is shown by Plautus' burlesque (*Poen.* 1) and Terence's reference [8] ; how frequently they were acted in the late Republic we do not know.

CHAPTER X

PACUVIUS

WE ARE told that Marcus Pacuvius,[1] son of Ennius' sister, was born at Brundisium. At Rome he occupied himself with the writing of tragedy (some add satire) and with painting. He lived on terms of friendship with Laelius. He produced a play in his eightieth year (140 B.C.), one of the competitors in that year being Accius, fifty years his junior and his successor in tragedy. Later he retired to Tarentum, where he was visited by Accius, then on his way to Asia. Accius stayed with Pacuvius for a few days, and read his *Atreus* to the old dramatist. Pacuvius died towards the year 130 B.C. A well-known picture painted by him was preserved at the temple of Hercules in the Forum Boarium.

Such is the account we piece together from various sources of different authority. It was Accius himself, according to Cicero, who vouched for the fact that Pacuvius and he produced plays on the same occasion. The connexion with Brundisium is supported by the form of his name, which, according to philologists, is Oscan. (We notice that he uses the Oscan word *ungulus* for 'ring'.) The elder Pliny's reference to the existence (in early times) of a picture by him sounds reliable; but Pliny does not seem to have seen this picture himself, or to imply that it was extant in his own day. If Pliny is right in calling Pacuvius Ennius' nephew, then Jerome is wrong in saying that he was the son of Ennius' daughter—which, according to Jerome's own dates, would make Ennius a grandfather at the age of twenty. (Perhaps the discrepancy arose from the ambiguity of *nepos*, which sometimes means 'nephew', sometimes 'grandson'.) Pacuvius' friendship with Laelius may be a touch of fiction added by Cicero to lend human interest to what is itself a fictitious address 'On Friendship' put into the mouth of Laelius. Gellius' anecdote about Accius' visit to Pacuvius and their discussion of the tragedy of *Atreus* seems suspiciously like that other anecdote which shows Terence reading his *Andria* to the elderly Caecilius. As for the well known and rather impressive epitaph which Pacuvius is said to have composed and caused to be inscribed on his tomb, some suspect that (like the even better-known epitaphs of Naevius and Plautus) it is the work of Varro, in whose book ' On Poets ' Gellius found all three. Certainly Gellius does not mention having ever *seen* the tombs of any of these dramatists.

Pacuvius was the first Latin author to specialize in tragedy —if we may venture to disbelieve the evidence of Diomedes and Porphyrio that he wrote satire [2] also. We possess the titles of twelve tragedies—*Antiopa* (from Euripides), *Armorum Iudicium* (? from Aeschylus), *Atalanta*, *Chryses*, *Dulorestes* (i.e. ' Orestes as a Slave '), *Hermiona*, *Iliona*, *Medus*, *Niptra* (Sophocles), *Pentheus* (somewhat different in plot from Euripides' *Bacchae*), *Periboea* (Euripides' *Oeneus* ?), *Teucer* (Sophocles ?), and a praetexta, *Paulus*. The fragments amount to about four hundred lines.

For so long a career twelve tragedies may seem a small number. Perhaps he was a slow worker ; perhaps painting took up much of his time and supplied part of his livelihood. It is probable that he wrote with great care ; he was celebrated for his learning, and his language shows elaborate attention to sound. He was regarded [3] by Cicero, Horace and Quintilian as the leading Roman writer of tragedy, or second only to Accius, who is sometimes said to have surpassed him in force. Many of his plays enjoyed great popularity down to the end of the Republic.

To what did he owe his success ? His plays are lost, as well as their Greek originals, and we cannot now estimate the dramatic power of a tragedy of Pacuvius. He seems to have preferred plays with complicated plots (taken perhaps from post-Euripidean originals) and to have specialized in pathetic scenes. Possibly the most famous scene in Roman tragedy was the opening of his *Iliona*. Polydorus, youngest son of Priam, had been entrusted to the care of his sister Iliona, wife of Polymestor, king of Thrace. She brought him up secretly as her own son Deiphilus, pretending to her husband that Deiphilus was Polydorus. On the fall of Troy Polymestor, wishing to show his goodwill to the victors, murdered the supposed Polydorus—really his own son. The play opened as

III SCENE FROM COMEDY
Relief from Pompeii in Naples Museum

the ghost of the murdered boy rose to implore his sleeping mother for burial in tones which, as Cicero tells us,[4] moved the whole audience to tears. In the half-light of early morning the sleeping form of Iliona was ' discovered ' on the stage ; presently, out of the recess in the stage (the curtain-slot, it seems, according to the stage-practice of Cicero's day), the dismal figure of the ghost appeared. Unfortunately on one notorious occasion Fufius, the actor taking the part of Iliona, was really asleep, and failed to hear the appeal of his fellow-actor Catienus, who was taking the part of the ghost, until the whole theatre joined in the cry ' Mother, I call to thee '.

Another favourite scene occurred in the *Chryses*. Orestes and Pylades have been brought captive before Thoas ; he wishes to discover which of them is Orestes, and to punish him alone. The two captives vied with each other in generous rivalry, each claiming to be Orestes—a contest which at the first performance of the play brought the whole audience to their feet shouting their applause. (This is, at any rate, what Cicero makes Laelius say in the address ' On Friendship '.)[5]

In tragedy as in comedy the Roman crowd had a keen ear for what seemed a topical allusion. A canticum from the *Armorum Iudicium*[6] was declaimed at the funeral of Julius Caesar. One of its lines was particularly apposite : ' that I should have spared the men who were to murder me ! '

The pathetic rôles, such as that of Antiopa, gave Roman actors a chance of starring ; thus Cicero tells us that he has seen Rupilius,[7] who specialized in the part of Antiopa. The angry words of Telamo in the *Teucer* so inflamed the actor who spoke them that his eyes seemed to burn out of the mask. (Cic. *de Orat.* II. 46. 193).

It would appear from these references that Pacuvius paid attention to stage effects. His plays have those touches which we miss in Seneca. We can see[8] the actors entering :

atque eccum in ipso tempore ostentum senem !

We can see them eavesdropping on each other :

sermonem hic nostrum ex occulto clepsit, quantum intellego.

The stage-doors open audibly :

. . . quidnam autem hoc soniti est quod stridunt fores ?

4

So far we have been dealing with what Pacuvius derived from his Greek originals. It is of special interest to notice what modifications he introduced. As has already been said, the testimony of Cicero [9] is at first sight contradictory. In one passage he speaks of Pacuvius' *Antiopa* (and other Latin tragedies) as being translated ' word for word '. Elsewhere he tells us that Pacuvius, Ennius and Accius rendered ' not the words but the sense ' of their originals. It seems reasonable to infer that the Roman writers of tragedy kept fairly close (closer, perhaps, than the writers of comedy) to the general sense of the Greek* ; but that on occasion they would modify a passage for a special effect. Thus Cicero tells us [10] that in the final scene of the *Niptra* Pacuvius has actually improved on Sophocles. Sophocles allowed the mortally wounded Ulysses to express all his agony : Pacuvius makes him more restrained ; even his mild reference to his sufferings is rebuked by his stretcher-bearers, and he dies with the Stoic words :

> conqueri fortunam aduersam, non lamentari decet :
> id uiri est officium, fletus muliebri ingenio additus.

But in other passages, as might be expected, the Latin is more rhetorical and violent than the Greek. We have already mentioned the speech (which Cicero so much admired) in which the aged Telamo bitterly accuses Teucer of having deserted Ajax. The tone of Sophocles' play, to judge by the fragment (516.N) is here comparatively restrained. Pacuvius employs all the resources of his Latin to give a violent effect : note the sigmatism and alliteration of the lines :

> segregare abs te ausu's aut sine illo Salaminam ingredi,
> neque paternum aspectum es ueritus, quem aetate exacta indigem
> liberum lacerasti orbasti extinxti ?

This attention to sound-effect is equally marked in the ' foot-bath ' scene from which the *Niptra* took its title. The aged nurse is about to wash the feet of the stranger (really Ulysses) :

> cedo tuum pedem mi, lymphis flauis flauum ut puluerem
> manibus isdem quibus Vlixi saepe permulsi abluam
> lassitudinemque minuam manuum mollitudine,

---

* I see no reason to suppose that Pacuvius combined material from two or more originals. The fragment of his *Teucer*—patria est ubicumque est bene—is like Aristoph. *Plut.* 1151 ; but perhaps Aristophanes himself borrowed it from Pacuvius' original, or was quoting a popular saying.

lines which at least one Roman reader (Gellius)[11] thought
' delightful ' (iucundissimi).

This pictorial quality is further illustrated in a description
of the sailing of the Greek fleet from Troy, and the coming on
of the storm :

> flamma inter nubes coruscat, caelum tonitru contremit,
> grando mixta imbri largifico subita praecipitans cadit.

Whatever the Greek original may have been, it is the
Latin writer who is responsible for the Latin of such passages
as these. Pacuvius' style is often natural and moving :

> O flexanima atque omnium regina rerum oratio !

But he was criticized for weird compounds, as in the line :

> Nerei repandirostrum incuruiceruicum pecus,

' The upturnsnouted and roundcrooknecked herd of Nereus '
(Warmington's translation).[12] He seems to have had a liking for
philosophical discussions : his *Antiopa* included a debate
between Antiopa's sons Amphion and Zethus on the respective
merits of the artistic and the practical life. Cicero quotes [13] his
rendering of a passage in Euripides' *Chrysippus* on Heaven and
Earth as the universal parents of all life. The attack of soothsayers which Cicero quotes from the *Chryses* seems to me Roman
in feeling :

> For those who understand the speech of birds,
> And learn more wisdom from another's liver
> Than from their own, I vote one ought to hear
> Rather than heed them.

In the *Antiopa* Amphion sets the ' townsmen ' a riddle :
what is it that is

> Fourfooted beast, slow-stepping, haunting fields,
> Low set and rude and grim to gaze on, short
> In head, snaky in neck, and disembowelled,
> Without breath, yet with breathing sound endowed ?*

When they give it up, he replies in one word—' Shellback '

> (a pun on the two senses of testudo, ' tortoise ' and ' harp '
> —a pun which is also possible with the Greek χέλυς).

> * Warmington's translation

Perhaps these passages helped to earn Pacuvius his reputation for ' learning '.   But in a dramatist this quality may
degenerate into pedantry.   Even in the well-known lines
describing Heaven and Earth as the universal parents—lines
translated from the Greek, and supposed to be uttered by a
Greek—he must needs turn aside to remark that what the
Greeks call aether is called caelum by ' our people ', the
Romans.   Even Cicero displays uneasiness at lapses such as
this.   It is Cicero, too, who tells us that Pacuvius' Latinity [14]
was poor.

A later generation of readers turned away from Pacuvius ;
they found his style harsh, his pathos wearisome, and grew
somewhat tired even of his ' learning '.   But his popularity
on the stage for more than a century reflects credit both on
his dramatic power and on the ability of the Roman public
to appreciate a serious play.

CHAPTER XI

COMEDY AFTER THE DEATH OF PLAUTUS

THE PROLOGUE to Plautus' *Casina* refers expressly to a revival performance of the play after the author's death. The speaker remarks that wise judges will prefer old wine and old plays—especially as the contemporary comedies are worthless. In view of the general demand for the plays of Plautus, his company is therefore reviving the *Casina*, the première performance of which is still within the memory of the older members of his audience. 'At its first appearance the play surpassed all other plays; and yet at that time there were living a garland of poets (flos poetarum) who have now departed to the bourne where all must go.'

Of course the speaker of the prologue is bound to praise the wares that he has to sell. He is claiming special merit for the fact that he is offering not a new play but an old one. Terence, we notice, takes care to emphasize that *his* plays are new. In either case the object is to win the favour of the public. We have other evidence, however, that Plautus' plays were immensely popular after his death. The 'garland of poets' contemporary with Plautus must include Naevius; possibly also Ennius (though he seems not to have been very successful in comedy) and if Ennius, then presumably Caecilius too, as he is said to have died only a year after Ennius. But to add Terence to the flos poetarum would put the date of the *Casina* revival later than 160; this would presumably mean a gap of thirty years or more between the first and second performances of the play—and in that case perhaps the older members of the audience *might* have been able to see the première. If we prefer to include Terence, and perhaps Caecilius also, among the writers of the worthless new comedies, we may recall that both these dramatists had difficulty in winning a hearing for their plays.

The success of Plautus with the crowd had evidently left the public with an appetite for comedy, and at the same time set a standard for later dramatists which they found it hard to reach. We now have a world of keen competition between rival dramatists as well as rival troupes of actors. If we accept Festus' statement [1] that a guild for scribes and actors had been founded in Andronicus' day—the collegium poetarum—we can imagine that the dramatists who met there discussed their problems and the principles of their art. It was for them either to rival Plautus on his own field, or to find new ways to public favour. On their solution of this problem their livelihood would depend.

CAECILIUS

We are told by Jerome that Caecilius [2] was an Insubrian Gaul (some gave his birthplace as Milan) and by Gellius that he began his career in Rome as a slave. It is conceivable that he had been made captive in one of the wars which the Romans waged with the Insubrians about the years 222-219 B.C. ' Statius ', ' attendant ', was a name often given to slaves ; ' Caecilius ' would no doubt be the name which he adopted from his master on manumission. Looking again at Gellius, we may suspect that he is trying to *explain* the poet's possession of a slave-name ; brought to Rome as a slave, the poet was ' therefore ' called Statius. Perhaps the slavery is merely an inference from the name ; if so, it is not convincing ; not every one called Statius was or had been a slave. If there is anything in the story that Ennius, who prided himself on his Roman citizenship, shared lodgings with Caecilius, we may infer that Caecilius, like Ennius, was of citizen rank. It is only too probable that nothing was known in Jerome's day about his early career. Much more weight must be given to Terence's assertion [3] that Caecilius' early efforts as a playwright had met with opposition and disappointment, but that the actor-manager Ambivius Turpio had discerned his promise and, after some failures, had succeeded in winning public favour for his plays. A doubtful anecdote [4] brings him into direct contact with Terence, who is said to have been sent by the magistrates to read his first play, the *Andria*, to Caecilius, then the acknowledged master of comedy. The *Andria*, however, was not produced until 166, and Caecilius is said by Jerome to have died in 168, the year after the death of Ennius, and to have been buried near Janiculum.

We possess the titles of forty-two comedies : *Aethrio, Andrea, Androgynos, Asotus, Chalcia, Chrysion, Dardanus, Dauos, Demandati, Ephesio, Epicleros, Epistathmos, Epistula, Ex Hautu Hestos, Exul, Fallacia, Gamos, Harpazomene, Hymnis, Hypobolimaeus siue Sub-ditiuos, Hypobolimaeus Chaerestratus, Hypobolimaeus Rastraria, Hypobolimaeus Aeschinus, Imbrii, Karine, Meretrix, Nauclerus, Nothus Nicasio, Obolostates siue Faenerator, Pausimachus, Philumena, Plocium, Polumeni, Portitor, Progamos, Pugil, Symbolum, Synaristosae, Synephebi, Syracusii, Titthe, Triumphus.* The fragments amount to 280 lines or part of lines.

With Caecilius we come to a crucial point in the history of Latin comedy. Naevius and Plautus had treated their originals with considerable freedom, had Latinized the titles and had scattered allusions to Roman places and customs through the plays. Caecilius gives us no topical references, and even the titles of the plays are usually left in their Greek form. After his time Greek titles are invariable. Varro's assertion [5] that Caecilius excelled other comic writers in *plot* (*argumenta*) presumably means that he chose well-constructed originals. It appears that he was specially interested in Menander : sixteen of his titles are also found in the list of Menander's plays, Cicero speaks [6] of Caecilius and Terence as translators of Menander, and Gellius quotes a series of passages from Caecilius' *Plocium* for comparison with the original by Menander. Here again Caecilius stands half-way between Plautus, with only three certainly Menandrian plays in twenty-one, and Terence, with four Menandrian plays out of six. Menander's plays, if we may judge by what remains of them, were of a somewhat serious tone, and some evidence would suggest that Caecilius shared this quality. Horace says [7] that Caecilius was considered to be distinguished by moral earnestness (*grauitas*) ; Varro attributed to him emotional power ; Cicero quotes him in court to illustrate his own remarks on the relationship of fathers and sons. On the other hand Velleius finds in him a rich vein of Latin wit (dulces Latini leporis facetiae).

Fortunately we are enabled in his case, as in that of no other Latin comic writer, to set extensive passages of the Latin beside their Greek original. Gellius, wishing to illustrate his general view that Latin comedies, though well enough in themselves, were altogether inferior to their originals, takes

the *Plocium* as an example ; the Latin, he says, lags behind
the Greek of Menander in subtlety and truth to life, in delicacy
and style.

In the *Plocium* we have a familiar domestic situation.
Crobyle, a shrewish, suspicious, purse-proud wife, tyrannises
over her husband. The first passage quoted by Gellius from
Menander shows us the husband complaining to a friend.
What particularly galls him is that he has been forced to
dismiss a pretty servant-girl who has aroused Crobyle's
suspicions. Caecilius turns this passage from plain speech into
a canticum varying in metre from trochaic septenarius to
bacchiac and then to cretic. The main sense is unchanged ;
the expression is so different that we should not have recognized
the Latin as a translation of the Greek. The Latin writer has
thought out the whole situation for himself. Certainly his
version is coarse, but is it not lively and vigorous too ? Instead
of the rather too facile grace of the Greek we get a crude,
vivid energy, driving home its meaning with the hammer
blows of rhetoric. Roman literature excels in brief passages
of dramatic dialogue. Where Menander simply gives us the
husband's complaint, Caecilius' husband makes us hear the
nagging accents of Crobyle as well :

ita plorando orando instando atque obiurgando me optudit.

We have a vivid picture of her talking to her cronies, gloating
among them over her triumph :

quis uostrarum fuit integra aetatula
        quae hoc idem a uiro
impetrarit suo quod ego anus modo
effeci, paelice ut meum priuarem uirum ?

A reference (reminiscent of Plautus) to Crobyle's unpleasant
breath is inserted by Caecilius without the slightest justification
in the Greek. Gellius observes that Caecilius preferred to
raise a laugh instead of giving his characters only such words
as they might naturally have been expected to utter. Elsewhere
he remarks that Caecilius' additions are akin to the style of
the mime. (Cf. Volcacius Sedigitus : Caecilio palmam Statio
do *mimico*).

Gellius is speaking of Caecilius as typical of Latin dramatists
in general : they are all well enough, considered in themselves but their inferiority is at once apparent when they are

compared with their originals. We have other grounds for assuming that Plautus and Naevius departed widely from their originals ; besides altering speech to ' song ', they too introduced every kind of rhetorical device, and they missed no chance of raising a laugh, regardless of dramatic proprieties. It was perhaps this coarse, lively quality in Caecilius' work which seemed to Velleius typical of Latin wit. As for his reputed *grauitas*, Cicero's citation of an angry father's outburst may serve as an example :

> egone quid dicam ? quid uelim ? quae tu omnia
> tuis foedis factis facis ut nequiquam uelim.
> istam in uicinitatem te meretriciam
> cur contulisti ? cur inlecebris cognitis
> non . . . refugisti ?
> . . . cur alienam ullam mulierem
> nosti ? . . .
> > dide ac dissice,
> per me licebit . . .
> . . . si egebis, tibi dolebit, mihi sat est
> qui aetatis quod relicuom est oblectem meae.

Though the theme is a familiar one, the depth of feeling revealed in this outburst seems to exceed that of similar passages in Plautus and Terence.

We may wonder why Caecilius (the greatest Latin comic writer, according to Volcacius Sedigitus and perhaps to Cicero) met, like Terence, with opposition and public neglect at the outset of his career. Was there something new in his plays which at first repelled the public while attracting the discerning actor-manager Ambivius Turpio ? Such a new quality there certainly was in Terence's work : Terence, as I will try to show, was an artist with principles of his own, which he maintained although he knew they were not as yet fully appreciated by the ' populus studio stupidus '. We have no such evidence in the case of Caecilius. Though he does not seem to have introduced the topical references to Roman things so dear to Plautus—and so out-of-place in translated comedy —he was not above adding crude jokes of which Terence would have been ashamed. All we can say is that he left his titles for the most part in their Greek form, that he seems to have been something of a moralist, and that he was specially attracted by Menander. Menander was the most refined

4 *

author of New Comedy, but in his own day he was not the most successful on the stage. Whatever the new quality in Caecilius' work, the public seems eventually to have come to like it, even in his own lifetime (though we must never yield too credulous an ear to Terence, whose object in making this assertion is to persuade the public that in time they will like *his* plays too). If there really was in Caecilius a tendency to choose originals of a more serious type, in particular plays by Menander, and to avoid any topical references which would clash with the context, he had at least set foot on the road which was to lead to the more fully Hellenized palliata of his successors.

CHAPTER XII

TERENCE

TERENCE'S LITERARY methods were the subject of bitter criticism in his own day. He replied to his critics in his prologues, which themselves led to further controversy, not to be stilled by his early death. The conflicting statements of several later critics[1] were gathered together in the Life written by C. Suetonius Tranquillus (c. A.D. 69–140). This Life has come down to us prefixed to the commentary which bears the name of the fourth-century scholar Donatus (itself the work of several hands). In addition we have the didascaliae (notices of first and later productions) quoted in the manuscripts of the plays and in Donatus' commentary.

Suetonius tells us that Publius Terentius Afer was born at Carthage (about 185–4 B.C.) and came to Rome as the slave of the senator Terentius Lucanus (not otherwise known), who was so captivated by the boy's beauty and intelligence that he gave him a good education and set him free. He found an entry into the literary circle of the younger Scipio Africanus (185–129 B.C.) and C. Laelius (born about 186–5 B.C.). He was now a youth of medium height, slim build and dark complexion. When he offered his first play, the *Andria*, to the aediles, he was directed to show it to Caecilius. The elderly dramatist was at supper when his shabbily dressed visitor arrived. Terence was told to sit on a stool and begin to read. But on hearing the opening lines Caecilius invited him to take his place at table, and after supper heard the rest of the play with admiration. Terence was now embarked on his dramatic career, which was to bring him much disappointment as well as great and indeed unprecedented success. The *Eunuchus* won such applause that it had to be repeated on the same day (?), and earned its author the record fee of eight thousand sesterces. There was, however, a rumour that his plays were partly or wholly the work of his aristocratic friends ; and after he had produced six plays, while still in his twenty-fifth * year (160 B.C.), he left Rome, never to return. The reason for his voyage to Greece (or Asia) was given variously as the desire to escape from the slander of accepting help from others, shame because of his poverty, the wish for a holiday, or the desire to be more thoroughly acquainted with the ways and customs of the Greeks. Quintus Cosconius † said that he was drowned at sea while returning with 108 ‡ plays translated from Menander; others gave the place of his death as Stymphalus, in Arcadia,[2] or Leucadia, an island off the coast of Acarnania,§ the cause as illness or as grief at the loss of his advance luggage, including his new plays.

As Suetonius shows, many details in this story were disputed. Some tried to explain Terence's slavery by saying that he had been captured in war when a boy ; but Fenestella [3] (first century A.D.) pointed out the difficulties involved in this view. Who were the ' noble friends ' mentioned in the prologue to the *Adelphi* (quoted by Suetonius), and what were his relations with them, whether literary or personal ? The earliest authority quoted by Suetonius seems to be the bitter democrat Porcius Licinus (end of second century B.C.), who said that they were Scipio, Laelius and Furius Philus (sc. as consul 136 B.C.), ' the three leading nobles of that time ', and that Terence was their boy-favourite, whom they flattered, fed, enjoyed and then abandoned to destitution (sc. as aristocrats always do).[4] But Fenestella argued that Terence was older than Scipio and Laelius, while Santra (first century B.C.) held that they were too young to be spoken of as Terence speaks of his noble friends, and that more likely names were Sulpicius Gallus (a man of literary interests, and consul in 166, when the *Andria* was produced), Q. Fabius Labeo (consul in 183) and M. Popillius (consul in 173), the two latter being poets as well as ex-consuls. Even the precise statements of Suetonius that Terence left an estate of twenty iugera near the Temple of Mars on the Appian Way, and that his daughter

---

* Some inferior manuscripts read ' thirty-fifth ', which would put his birth in 195-4 B.C. This reading seems to be a deliberate alteration.

† A scholar of the first century B.C.

‡ Cum CVIII fabulis. Perhaps cum (CVM) was written a second time and mistaken for a numeral. Or the writer may have been thinking of some statement that Menander wrote precisely 108 plays.

§ Yet another version made him die at Ambracia : Comm. Lucani 5. 652 : malignos (Ambraciae portus) dixit quoniam est ibi Terentius mortuus.

married a Roman knight, are in contradiction with Porcius'
assertion that owing to his poverty he left no address at Rome—
not even a hired lodging—to which news of his death could
be brought.

Was Terence a Semite (as born in Carthage), or did he
belong to one of the Berber tribes ? The term Afer is sometimes applied to Carthaginians (e.g. Hor. *Odes*, 4.4.42),
sometimes to the native tribes in contrast to the Carthaginians
(e.g. Livy xxx.33.5) ; but it was also a cognomen in the
Domitian gens. An intelligent slave would probably have
better opportunities than a humble freeman for making the
acquaintance of the great. Caecilius' death is put by Jerome
in the year after the death of Ennius, i.e. in 168 B.C., in which
year Terence was seventeen. If the *Andria* was approved by
Caecilius, why did the aediles leave the honour of producing
it to their successors of 166 B.C. ? Or was it Caecilius' death
which left the way open for Terence ?

Personal though his prologues are, Terence names no
living person—not even himself. Accused of being aided
in his writing by noble friends, he retorts that there would be
no discredit in accepting help from men to whom the whole
State is indebted. Later writers may have had little to guide
them here except this ambiguous remark ; and their statements, though sometimes specific, do not agree with each
other. Memmius (praetor in 58 B.C.) asserted that Scipio
had written the plays ; Cicero (*ad Att.* 7.3.10) says that the
plays ' were thought to be written by C. Laelius because of
their elegance ' ; Nepos (see the Vita) reported ' on sure
authority ' that Laelius had on one occasion excused himself
for coming late to supper on the ground that he had been
composing *H.T.* 723 ff. ; Quintilian (10.1.99) refers cautiously to
the belief that the plays (because of their style) must have been
by Scipio. Grimal points out (*Le Siècle des Scipions*, p. 150) that no
plays were written by these noble persons *after* Terence's death.

Terence's voyage to the East is usually accepted as a fact ;
the motive for the voyage favoured by most scholars is that
Terence wished to improve his knowledge of Greece, and
acquire more Greek plays. (It is, however, somewhat dis-
turbing to find a modern biographer of Plautus sending *him*
on a similar student-voyage ' like Terence '.*) Whatever

* F. della Corte, *Da Sarsina a Roma*, pp. 47 f.

the motive for the voyage, all agree that he never returned.[5] Indeed the one inference which emerges clearly from the Life is that later Romans were deeply interested in Terence's career, and puzzled by its abrupt and mysterious close.

Can we ourselves hope to reconstruct the dramatic career of Terence from the prologues and the didascaliae? The authenticity of the prologues is unquestionable ; the very fact that they name no contemporaries is decisive against their having been the work of a forger. Their style is indeed somewhat forced and rhetorical, when compared with the style of the plays ; the explanation no doubt lies in the circumstances. Terence wrote the prologues against his will ; in them we find him defending himself against the attacks of the ' malicious old dramatist ' whose identity he indicates by saying that he is the translator of Menander's *Phasma* and *Thesaurus*. (As these translations survived, Roman scholars had no difficulty in supplying the name of Terence's enemy as Luscius Lanuvinus.)

The plays are generally arranged in the following order :

1. *Andria* (' Woman of Andros '), from the *Andria* by Menander, produced at the ludi Megalenses (April), 166 B.C.

2. *Hecyra* (' The Mother-in-law ') from the *Hecyra* by Apollodorus of Carystos, ludi Megalenses, 165 B.C. (a failure).

3. *Heautontimorumenos* (' The Self-Tormentor '), from Menander, ludi Megalenses, 163 B.C.

4. *Eunuchus* (' The Eunuch '), from the *Eunuchus* by Menander, ludi Megalenses, 161 B.C.

5. *Phormio*, from Apollodorus' *Epidikazomenos*, ludi Romani (September), 161 B.C.

6. *Adelphi* (' The Brothers ') from the second *Adelphi* by Menander, ludi funebres of Aemilius Paulus (father of the younger Scipio), 160 B.C.

7. *Hecyra*, second performance, ludi funebres of Aemilius Paulus, 160 B.C. (again a failure).

8. *Hecyra*, third and successful performance, perhaps ludi Romani, 160 B.C.

But according to some of our sources the *Adelphi* or the *Eunuchus* should be put second, the *Hecyra* fifth or sixth. It is evident that we must not be too ready to base a theory of Terence's development as an artist on the supposed chronology of his plays. But if internal evidence goes for anything, the *Adelphi* is the work of a practised hand ; and the record of its performance (with the *Hecyra*) at the funeral games of Aemilius Paulus is solid support for Terence's connexion with the family of Scipio. It is also agreed that the *Andria* was his first play, and that it was produced in 166 B.C.

All the plays have prologues ; the *Hecyra* has two, written for the second and third performances. (We have evidence in the Bembine didascalia that the *Hecyra* was produced without a prologue at the first (abortive) attempt.) All the prologues of Terence were written for delivery to an uncritical crowd, whose suspicions they were intended to allay for the moment so that an attentive hearing might be secured for the play which was to follow.

Up to now the main function of the prologue (at least as we find it in Euripides and Menander) had been to explain the dramatic situation ; Latin dramatists had also used the prologue to put the audience in a good humour. Terence dropped the explanatory prologue altogether. Evidently he thought that to make the situation reveal itself in the course of the dialogue was preferable to giving the audience a direct explanation. (What he did, or would have done, if his Greek original contained a prologue—especially a ' deferred ' prologue *—is not clear.) Here we have, perhaps for the first time, a Latin dramatist consciously setting before himself an artistic principle.† The other use of the prologue—to put the audience into a favourable humour—he would no doubt have abandoned also, had not the attacks of his enemies forced him to use his prologues for self-defence. He complains (*And.* 5) that they have compelled him to waste his energies in writing prologues.‡ He quotes a critic (*Phorm.* 13 ff.) as

* See page 160.

† There is perhaps some hint of a similar attitude in the prologues to the *Trinummus* and *Vidularia*. But more probably Plautus is thinking of the reactions of his audience (see p. 161) ; he is anxious to assure them that the play will begin without delay.

‡ The plural has caused some discussion, as this is presumably the only prologue that Terence has written so far. I regard it as a ' generalizing ' plural ; similarly I suspect that the ' enemies ' may number only one. Again in *H.T.* 17 ' many ' seems to mean merely ' two ', as in Donatus, *Eun.* praef. 11).

saying that but for their accusations he would not have had any material out of which to make prologues at all.

What these accusations were we can only infer from Terence's replies. The details of this literary controversy seem to have been soon forgotten. Donatus' commentary is composed merely of superficial inference from the very lines which he professes to explain. When the commentary quotes the Greek originals from which Terence drew, its evidence is trustworthy and precious ; other statements, though made in good faith and much more sensible than the remarks of later scholiasts, must be received with caution.

We gather from Terence's own words that he was accused of weakness of style (*Ph.* 4 f.), of accepting literary help from others, of entering on his profession as dramatist without proper preparation (*H.T.* 22 ff.), of stealing characters and passages from old Latin plays (*Eun.* 23 ff. ; *Ad.* 1–14), of ' spoiling ' or taking liberties with his Greek originals (*And.* 16 ; *H.T.* 17). Terence's style was indeed something new on the Roman stage. That he accepted literary help from his noble friends is perhaps unlikely, and even if true would have little relevance to our opinion of the plays as we have them ; we can understand, however, that tact would forbid him to give a direct rebuttal to this charge. The other two accusations, however spiteful, have this much basis in fact : Terence deliberately departed from his Greek originals. Earlier Latin dramatists had indeed translated with considerable freedom, as we have seen in the case of Caecilius. But Terence was the first, perhaps the only, Latin dramatist who deliberately tried to produce a Latin play which would be artistically superior to its Greek original. This he nowhere states, but it is implicit in much that he says. The *Andria* opens a new chapter in Latin literature.

Andria. The scene, as in all Terence's plays, is in Athens. The three houses shown on the stage are those of the old gentleman Simo (and his son Pamphilus), the girl Glycerium and the young gentleman Charinus. Simo wishes Pamphilus to marry Philumena, daughter of Chremes. But Pamphilus has secretly formed a liaison with Glycerium, a poor but modest girl who had recently come from Andros to Athens with her supposed sister Chrysis. Chrysis, after having been forced by poverty to become a courtesan, has now died.

In the opening scene Simo confides to his freedman Sosia the news that Chremes, hearing of the entanglement with Glycerium, has refused to give Philumena to Pamphilus (who was to have wedded her this very day) (line 102) ; however, Simo has not told Pamphilus of this, as he wishes to test his filial obedience. But Davus, Pamphilus' servant, who has divined that the wedding is off, advises Pamphilus to call Simo's bluff by professing his readiness to do what his father wishes. To complicate matters, Charinus is in love with Philumena, and privately begs Pamphilus to put the wedding off. But Simo now manages to talk Chremes round, and Pamphilus finds himself faced with immediate marriage to Philumena, while we listen to the cries of Glycerium as she lies in the pangs of childbirth. Davus redeems his blunder by getting Glycerium's bewildered maid, Mysis, to put the baby down in front of Simo's door just as Chremes arrives on the scene. Chremes' suspicions return with redoubled force, and he again withdraws his consent. Now a new character appears, Crito, Chrysis' cousin, looking for Glycerium, who, it turns out, is not the sister of Chrysis, but the lost daughter of Chremes. Accordingly Pamphilus may marry her, and in the final scene he promises Charinus that he will put in a good word for him with Chremes.

Donatus tells us that Terence has made certain alterations in translating Menander's *Andria*. Menander's play had opened with a monologue of the old man ; Terence has turned this into a dialogue by adding Sosia, who is a ' protatic ' character (ad *And.* 28)—that is, he will not appear again after this ' protasis ' or opening scene. Furthermore, Terence has added Charinus and his servant Byrria (ad *And.* 301), for these two ' are not in Menander '.

As has been said, the plot of the *Andria* turns on Simo's intention to marry Pamphilus to Philumena. Pamphilus has never even seen Philumena ; we find him wondering (line 250) whether she is a monster of ugliness, whose parents are trying to get rid of her. It is quite in keeping with New Comedy and with Greek life that marriage should be arranged between two young people who have never met. But Charinus, the young gentleman added to the play by Terence, is passionately in love with the young lady Philumena ; and his slave Byrria mentions her good looks and physical desirability

and assumes that this explains Pamphilus' apparent willing-
ness to marry her (lines 428–30). We are not told how Charinus
has made her acquaintance. Her father, though anxious to
find a husband for her, seems never to have heard of this
very eligible suitor (an incongruity which the author of the
spurious alternative ending tried to explain away). Apparently Terence has here introduced a situation foreign to what
we know of New Comedy, but presumably possible in Roman
life. He must, then, have invented Charinus, and with him
his slave Byrria—and this is the natural interpretation of
what Donatus says. The two characters have no influence
on the main plot, and the scenes in which they appear could
be altered without difficulty so as to eliminate them altogether.
But the *reason* for the introduction of Charinus may have been
not, as Donatus suggests, to supply Philumena (who never
appears on the stage) with a husband, but to provide an
interesting contrast in character and situation to Pamphilus.
The second love-plot is stated by Donatus (ad *And.* 977) to
be an addition made by Terence to Menander's *Andria* ;
he also tells us (ad *And.* 301) that each of Terence's plays
except the *Hecyra* contained two young men ; cf. Evanthius
De Fab. 3.9 (Donati Commentum i. p. 20 Wessner) : ' Terence
chose richer plots containing a double intrigue '.

These changes, then, and others as well, were made by
Terence when translating Menander's Ἀνδρία. He now
came up against the hostility of Luscius Lanuvinus, an elderly
and perhaps not very successful dramatist, who saw his livelihood threatened by this young protégé of the great. I find no
reason to believe that Luscius was actuated by any higher
motive than jealousy ; any slander which would put Terence
out of business was good enough for him. Luscius somehow
got to know that Terence had departed from his ostensible
original. There was indeed no law against this ; but Luscius
thought that by reporting Terence's procedure in as malicious
terms as he could find he might damage his reputation by that
most baffling of slanders, a half-truth. He accordingly began
to protest to all who would listen that Greek plays should not
be ' spoiled '. The word he used for ' spoil ' was ' contaminare '.

This charge put Terence in a dilemma. He felt that he
must reply to it, in order to secure a fair hearing for his play ;
accordingly he found himself forced to write a prologue.

Yet how was he to meet the charge in terms which the Roman crowd could understand ? They had been promised a version of a play by Menander ; he was now accused of intending to give them something different. Of what use would it be to embark on an explanation which, if honest, was bound to be technical and puzzling ? Some brief and intelligible reply was needed, which would make the changes he undoubtedly had made seem as innocent as possible.

What he says in the prologue is this. Menander wrote two plays, the Ἀνδρία and the Περινθία, alike in plot and differing merely in dialogue. The poet (Terence) has borrowed from the Περινθία what was suitable and has inserted it in his *Andria*. His enemies attack him for this, saying that plays should not be spoiled. Their charge shows their own ignorance ; in accusing Terence they are accusing Naevius, Plautus and Ennius, whose ' carelessness ' Terence professes that he would rather imitate than the ' dull carefulness ' of his critics.

Modern students, almost without exception, suppose that Terence has been accused of the very thing which he boasts of doing—namely, the borrowing of material from a second Greek play—and moreover that it is this procedure which he ascribes to Naevius, Plautus and Ennius. We are told that contaminare could mean ' to combine ' Greek plays ; that such combination was the established practice of the Roman dramatists ; that Terence was being accused of combining plays ; and that he defended himself by saying that he had in fact combined plays, thus following the ' careless ' example set by the great masters of the past, including Ennius, who had died only three years before the production of the *Andria*. This explanation breaks down at almost every step. The verb contaminare means ' spoil ' (see Appendix K) ; if Terence had been merely following established practice, where was the sting in saying that he had done so ? ; yet if this was in fact the charge, how could he hope to defend himself by admitting it ? and how could the combination of plays be equated with carelessness ?

Donatus gives us to understand that he read through the two Greek plays (in order, it would seem, to check what Terence says about them). Apart from the opening scene, he could find only two short passages in which they resembled

each other.* Apparently he failed altogether to find in
Terence's translation any passage which resembled anything
in the *Perinthia*. Donatus was naturally puzzled. Why,
he asks, should Terence accuse himself of doing something
which he has not done ? He can only suggest that the reference is to the opening scene. For here, though the wording
is ' almost identical ' in the two Greek plays, the scene is a
monologue in Menander's *Andria*, while in the *Perinthia* it
is a dialogue : the senex is talking to his wife.† Terence's
senex speaks to his freedman Sosia (who appears only in this
scene). Donatus seems to mean that Terence is indebted to
the *Perinthia* for the idea of using dialogue rather than
monologue. In substituting dialogue for monologue Terence
is no doubt aiming at greater dramatic effect ; similarly
in the *Eunuchus* he introduces Antipho in order that Chaerea
may be able to tell someone of his adventure instead of
soliloquizing, as in Menander.‡ But it is really unthinkable that
the conversation of patron and client was exactly like that of
husband and wife. The one example of borrowing which Donatus
claims to have discovered turns out to be no example at all.

Plainly Donatus was not satisfied. He read on, still
looking for passages borrowed from the *Perinthia*, and could
find none ; but near the end of the *Andria* (959–61) he found a
three-line illustration of general application which reminded him
not indeed of the *Perinthia*, but of a passage in a third play of
Menander, the *Eunuchus* (unfortunately he does not quote the
Greek), and he exclaims with what seems like relief, 'this is what
is meant by the remark that plays should not be contaminated'.§

* Prima scaena *Perinthiae* fere isdem uerbis quibus Andria scripta est ; cetera
dissimilia sunt exceptis duobus locis, altero ad uersus XI, altero ad XX, qui in
utraque fabula positi sunt.

† Sed quare ergo se onerat Terentius, cum possit uideri de una transtulisse ?
sic soluitur : quia conscius sibi est primam scaenam de *Perinthia* esse translatam,
ubi senex ita cum uxore loquitur, ut apud Terentium cum liberto. at in *Andria*
Menandri solus est senex.

‡ Ad *Eun.* 539 : bene inuenta persona est cui narret Chaerea, ne unus diu
loquatur, ut apud Menandrum.

§ Hanc sententiam totam Menandri de *Eunucho* transtulit. et hoc est quod
dicitur ' contaminari non decere fabulas '. Terence's lines may be translated:
' I think the gods eternal in the sense that their pleasures are all their own ; for
I too have won immortality, if no sorrow comes to mar this joy '. This is rather
remote from the supposed parallel, as reconstructed by Kock (190) from the
prose of Aristides i. 592 : ' The gods have not treated men as they treat themselves.
They, being immortal and lords of all, have pleasures for ever.' This is a complaint : Terence's lines express rapture.

Of course there may have been resemblances which
Donatus failed to notice. Two of our extant fragments oɪ
the *Perinthia* resemble passages in Terence's *Andria*.* These
would be verbal borrowings ; and verbal borrowings are
precisely what Terence seems to admit. But it appears from
Donatus' words that these borrowings were not very striking.
Many modern scholars hold that the added *characters*, Charinus
and Byrria, came from the *Perinthia*[6] ; and as we shall see
when we come to the prologue to the *Eunuchus*, Terence there
admits—indeed proclaims—that he has added two characters
to his *Eunuchus* from another Greek play.† But Charinus'
rôle is simply to be in love with the young lady whom the
principal lover (Pamphilus) is being forced to marry. Charinus
is dependent on Pamphilus : Pamphilus could do without
Charinus. Those who suppose that Charinus and Byrria
were taken from the *Perinthia* must further suppose that the
principal lover is also taken from the *Perinthia*. It is claimed
that there was a slave named Pyrrhias (= Byrria) in the
Perinthia. There is indeed a slave in the *Perinthia* whose name
apparently ends in -rias ; but he belongs to old Laches, and
we find him bringing faggots with which the intriguing slave
Daos is to be burned alive.‡
      The only other reference to this charge of ' spoiling '
Greek plays is in Terence's next prologue, that to the
Heautontimorumenos. Evidently his critics had not been silenced ;
their charge was now that he had ' spoiled many Greek plays
in making only a few Latin plays '. This charge may have
been based on his own words in the prologue to the *Andria* :
in effect his critics are saying ' when we accuse you of spoiling

* 397 K : ' The old hag never misses a goblet but drinks as it circles round '
(Allinson) might conceivably suit *And.* 229 ff., where the bibulous habits of the
midwife are mentioned ; and 398 K : ' The slave went in, carrying (two-pennyworth) of small boiled fishes ' (Allinson) might suit *And.* 368 f. : ' The slave was
carrying two-pennyworth of cabbage and small fishes for the old man's supper '.
      † Indeed a late scholiast (*Schol. Terentiana*, Schlee, p. 169, 1, quoted by
Thierfelder, ed. *Andria*, p. 23) states this : *Andria* continebat negotium Pamphili
et Glycerii, *Perinthia* negotium Charini et Philumenae . . . negotium Charini
et Philumenae transtulit. But this assertion may have been due to his misunderstanding of Donatus' words (Thierfelder, pp. 24 f.).
      ‡ Webster (*Studies in Menander*, p. 78) is one of those who believe that Charinus
and Byrria come from the *Perinthia*. It is interesting to note, however, that the
presence in the *Perinthia* of a slave of Laches whose name seems to end in -rias
is for Webster a positive embarrassment (p. 81). For others it is the only definite
evidence for the view which Webster shares. See the excellent remarks of Bignone,
Storia della letteratura latina, p. 425.

your Greek model, your reply is that you have spoiled not *one* model but *two* '. He replies that he does not deny what he has done ; that he will go on doing it, and that he has good example. Thus once more we seem to be faced with a dilemma : either the charge brought against Terence is pointless, or his defence consists of an admission of the charge.

If we cling to the common-sense view that ordinary Latin words probably have their ordinary meaning even in Terence, we may still agree that Terence is unlikely to have admitted that he had ' spoiled ' his Greek models. This was indeed the charge against him, but he only quotes it in Oratio Obliqua. His defence is not that he has spoiled Menander's plays, but that he is giving his hearers more Menander than he had promised. ' Carelessness ', again, cannot have seemed an admirable quality to him ; if he pretends to admire the ' careless ' dramatists of the past, he is being less than candid. Nor could ' carelessness ' have achieved the one type of alteration which he admits in his own case—the combining of two Greek plays. When Plautus omits a passage in a play which he is translating, Terence calls that ' carelessness ' (*Ad.* 14). The one thing in which Terence can honestly claim to resemble the old dramatists, as contrasted with the pedantic Luscius, is that they took liberties with their originals. Terence also intends to take liberties with *his* originals ; but the changes which *he* makes will be careful and artistic. When he taunts Luscius (*Eun.* 7 ff.) with ' turning good Greek plays into bad Latin plays by good translation and bad writing ', he implies that in his view ' good ' (i.e. close) translation is not enough.

Nevertheless the *Heauton Timorumenos* (' Self-Tormentor ') seems to be a straight translation from Menander (line 4 : ex integra Graeca integram comoediam).

The play opens with an evening scene (one of the finest scenes in Latin comedy). We see two old men, Chremes and Menedemus, walking home together from the ' country ' side-entrance (see p. 284). Chremes' questioning elicits from Menedemus a confession that he has been ' punishing himself' by heavy toil on his farm for having by harsh treatment driven his son Clinia to run away and enter military service abroad. Menedemus enters his house, and Chremes is about to enter his, when his son Clitipho comes out, and we

learn that he is sheltering Clinia, who has come back from
abroad.   Preparations are being made in Chremes' house
for supper ;   and presently there arrive two guests whom
Chremes does not expect : Bacchis, a courtesan, who is
Clitipho's extravagant mistress, and her friend Antiphila,
the modest girl whom Clinia loves.   The slave Syrus persuades
Bacchis to pose as Clinia's mistress, so as to deceive Chremes
into admitting her to his house.   A night passes ; next morning Chremes reports to Menedemus the presence of Clinia
and his mercenary mistress Bacchis.   Menedemus, overjoyed
to have Clinia back, is willing to endure all the extravagances
of Bacchis if he can keep his son at home.   There is much
mystification, but in due course Antiphila is discovered to be
the daughter of Chremes, and Chremes' self-importance is
deflated when he finds that Bacchis is the mistress, not of
Menedemus' son, but of his own.   The complications of the
plot are difficult to follow on the stage, or even in the study ;
but there is evidence that the play was produced more than
once, and we must applaud the public who could appreciate it.

Eunuchus.

The courtesan Thais has two lovers, Phaedria and the
braggart captain Thraso, who is attended by his parasite
Gnatho.   Thraso has offered to present Thais with a virtuous
and beautiful maiden, Pamphila, a foundling who had been
brought up with Thais but was afterwards sold by a miserly
uncle.   Phaedria intends to give Thais a eunuch, Dorio.
Phaedria's younger brother Chaerea sees Pamphila being
brought by Gnatho to Thais' house, is inflamed, and, at the
suggestion of the slave Parmeno, puts on the eunuch's clothes
and enters Thais' house while Thais is out at a party given
by Thraso.   A new character now appears, Chremes, a
cautious young gentleman who has received a mysterious
summons from Thais ; he is sent off to look for her at Thraso's
house.   Chaerea comes out of Thais' house and relates his
adventure to a friend, Antipho, who has come to look for him.
They go off in order that he may change his clothes at Antipho's
house.   Thais' maid returns from Thraso's house with the
news that Chremes' arrival there has provoked the soldier to a
storm of jealousy ; while the discovery that Pamphila has
been violated throws Thais' house into turmoil.   Presently

Chremes (slightly intoxicated) appears, soon followed by Thais ; she tells him that Pamphila is his sister, and that Thraso intends to carry the girl off by force. They defend the house against an assault by Thraso and his followers ; then Chaerea returns, learns that the girl whom he has out- raged is free-born, and promises to make what reparation he can by marrying her. Gnatho induces Phaedria to consent to an arrangement whereby he will share Thais with Thraso, and so in the end all parties are satisfied.

We gather from the prologue that, after the aediles had bought the play, a preliminary performance was given in their presence. Luscius Lanuvinus had contrived to see the play in manuscript, and was present at its performance. The play began. Suddenly he cried out that Terence was a thief : he had stolen two characters, the captain and the parasite, from an old Latin play, the *Colax*, translated from the Greek by Naevius and (? or) Plautus. There was no law of copyright in Rome ; still, the charge of theft was an ugly one. Terence's defence is that he took these characters not from the old Latin play (the very existence of which was unknown to him) but from its Greek original, the *Kolax* of Menander. And if one must not bring ' the same ' characters on the stage a second time, how is one to treat of the stock themes of comedy, or indeed to write a play at all ?

It seems that Terence agrees with his critics that he has added two characters from another play, which they have correctly identified. Yet this cannot be true : it must be either more or less than the truth. If by dramatic characters we mean the words that they utter, it is manifest that these are related to the context, and that to import into one play all the words uttered by a major character in another play would necessitate consequential changes in the new context. If we try to imagine the *Eunuchus* without the captain and parasite, it is plain that the plot would fall to pieces. Therefore Menander's *Eunuchus* cannot have been simply Terence's *Eunuchus* without the two added characters ; we must find others to take their places in the plot. Moreover, if Terence took over from the *Kolax* all the words uttered by the captain and the parasite, he must have taken over with them a large portion of the plot. There is quite a simple solution of this problem ; it is to suppose that Menander's *Eunuchus* had its

own captain and parasite, and that all that Terence did was
to add certain touches which characterized the captain and
parasite of Menander's *Kolax*. The entrance monologue of
Gnatho (232 ff.) and the dialogue of Thraso and Gnatho
(391 ff.) give us the touches which we want. Gnatho describes
himself in his monologue as a new kind of parasite, one who
attaches himself to would-be wits and plays upon their vanity ;
the soldier appears in the dialogue as just such a would-be
wit, who prides himself not on his exploits in war or love so
much as on his skill in repartee. But in the rest of the *Eunuchus*
Thraso seems to be very much the stock type of captain,
Gnatho the traditional parasite. So Terence's borrowings
from the *Kolax* are reduced to a few lines unconnected with
the plot of his *Eunuchus*. But why did he not explain all this
to his audience ? Because there was no time to go into such
technical matters ; what was needed was a brief and apparently intelligible reply to the charge, and that is what he
gave.*

In truth it would be easier to invent new characters than
to introduce them ready-made from another play. We are
assured by Donatus that Terence did in fact invent the
character of Antipho in order to convert Menander's monologue
into dialogue. The scene in which Chaerea describes how he
violated Pamphila was famous in antiquity [7], and is indeed of
considerable dramatic power ; but its effect is largely due to
its dialogue form. There is no reason to doubt Donatus'
evidence here ; yet many scholars will clutch at any theory
rather than concede so much original power to the Latin
poet.

There is one other passage in which Terence refers to the
changes which he has made in his Greek original. This
is in the prologue to his most famous play, the *Adelphi*. Demea
and Micio are two elderly brothers ; Micio is a genial bachelor,
Demea is the care-worn father of two sons, Aeschinus and
Ctesipho. Aeschinus has been adopted by his uncle, who
has given him every freedom, hoping by indulgence to win
his confidence ; Ctesipho has been kept under strict surveil-

---

* Webster, though a supporter of ' contamination ', concludes that Menander's
Eunuchus had its own captain and parasite (*Studies in Menander*, pp. 71–2). Grimal,
arguing equally logically in a different direction (*Le Siècle des Scipions*, pp. 153 ff.),
concludes that Terence has made profound alterations and interwoven the two
plots so closely that it is almost impossible for us to disentangle them.

lance by his cross-grained father. Thus the play strikes a
modern note by giving us a comparative study of two methods
of education. Neither system is successful ; both the young
men find sweethearts for themselves without consulting their
elders. Aeschinus, the stronger character, breaks into a
pimp's house and carries off the wench Bacchis in order to
hand her over to his timid brother, whose mistress she is ;
but his action is open to misconstruction, and news of it
distresses Pamphila, the poor but virtuous girl whom Aeschinus
loves. When Micio learns Aeschinus' secret, he consents
to Aeschinus' marriage with Pamphila ; but when Demea
discovers that he has been deceived by Ctesipho, he realizes
that his stern methods have been a failure, and turns the tables
on Micio by treating everyone liberally at his expense.

It would seem that in the Ἀδελφοὶ β of Menander the
carrying off of Bacchis by Aeschinus had been merely reported.
In Terence's play this happens on the stage. In the prologue
Terence tells us that Diphilus wrote a play called the
Συναποθνήσκοντες (translated by Plautus as the *Commorientes*)
in which a young man carries off a wench from a pimp ;
this passage had been omitted by Plautus owing to his ' carelessness ', and Terence has incorporated it in his *Adelphi*,
translating the Greek ' word for word '. He asks the public
to judge whether this is a theft, as his critics allege, or, as he
holds, the turning to good account of what Plautus had
neglected.

It appears that the accusations brought against Terence
were inspired not by artistic ideals but by spite. There is
little likelihood that Luscius had set before himself a new
and higher standard of fidelity to his original. Even Terence's
reference to Luscius' ' good translation ' may have been
introduced sarcastically, or as a mere antithesis to ' bad
writing '. Unacknowledged borrowing from various sources
was a frequent practice among ancient writers. Afranius
(see p. 131) tells us frankly that his supposedly ' native '
comedies contained material borrowed from whatever source
he thought suitable, whether Greek or Latin. Few Roman
dramatists would have felt qualms about inserting in their
plays, whether translations or original compositions, an effective line or passage which they had come across in their reading.
But this haphazard procedure was never recognized as a

specific method of literary composition. Of large-scale fusion of originals, of the combination of two Greek plots into one Latin plot, we have no examples, even in Terence.

He was, in a limited sense, an original dramatist forced by circumstances to pose as a mere translator. As a dramatist he could not afford to ignore the general public, but his opinion of their taste is revealed in his petulant reference to the 'populus studio stupidus' who left the *Hecyra* to see a rope-dancer. His admitted object is to write plays of a high artistic standard, sine uitiis (*H.T.* 30). Though he professes to admire and imitate the great careless masters of the past, we may be sure that his standards were very different from theirs. His repeated reference to Plautus' 'carelessness' in dealing with his originals is itself a criticism ; yet his boast that his own plays are 'faultless' suggests that, for him, mere translation of the Greek original is not enough.* Donatus frequently points out alterations introduced by Terence ; sometimes he enlivens a scene by turning monologue into dialogue, sometimes he makes his characters behave more naturally than in the Greek play (for example Micio, the comfortable old bachelor of the *Adelphi*, is allowed by Terence at least to protest before he is pushed into marriage), sometimes he adapts his original to Roman customs and feelings. Donatus' comments are supported by the evidence of the fragments preserved from the Greek originals. While toning down difficult allusions to peculiarly Greek institutions, Terence refuses to introduce anything specifically Roman or Italian. He adds no topical references, no allusions to contemporaries ; there is little word-play, little buffoonery ; the language is restrained ; the metrical effects are subdued. Reading Terence we find ourselves in a world which is neither characteristically Greek nor aggressively Italian, but independent of place and time.

Terence's great interest is humanity. The keynote of his dramatic technique is contrast of character. In the *Heauton-timorumenos*, the *Phormio* and the *Adelphi* we have contrasted

---

* He criticizes his rival Luscius Lanuvinus for making the defendant speak before the plaintiff in a trial-scene (*Eun.* 10-12). But Lanuvinus was presumably following Menander (*cf.* the trial-scene in the *Epitrepontes*). Terence's criticism implies that in Lanuvinus' place he would have altered Menander's arrangement and made the plaintiff speak first. We must not take too seriously what is probably a mere debating-point, but at least we can say that for Terence translation was not enough.

pairs of old as well as of young men. In the *Hecyra* we have a
study of two elderly couples. In the *Eunuchus* there is a double
love-plot. The addition of the abduction-scene in the *Adelphi*
may have been intended to bring into bold relief one side of
Aeschinus' character, as conceived by Terence. Donatus
tells us that in Menander's Εὐνοῦχος Chremes was a
'rustic'; in Terence's play he is effectively portrayed as a
timid creature, who has to be roused to action by the en-
couraging words of a courtesan ! Indeed one of the things
that struck ancient critics was the nobility of Terence's
courtesans.[8] In character-drawing, according to Varro,
Terence was first among Latin writers of comedy.

We have seen that Terence treated his originals with some
freedom. Exactly what liberties he took we cannot always
divine. There may have been more divergencies than those
mentioned by Donatus ; for that matter, Donatus occasionally
points out where Terence's text *agrees* with the Greek originals,
and it is impossible to suppose that Donatus has given all the
examples of such agreement. Apart from the addition of
characters in the *Andria* and the *Eunuchus* and the insertion of
a whole scene in the *Adelphi*, the changes made seem to have
been slight. One of Terence's objects may have been to extend
the use of surprise as an element in drama. Ancient drama,
on the whole, does not seem to have aimed at surprise effects ;
in tragedy the myths were already known * : in comedy, where
the plot was invented by the dramatist, the danger of puzzling
the audience had to be taken into account. Plautus, adapting
Greek plays for a Roman audience, often wearies us with the
pains he takes to explain each turn of the plot beforehand.
Terence expects more of his audience. Perhaps his total
avoidance of preliminary explanations of the plot (such as
Menander had thought necessary, at least in his *Perikeiromene*)
is connected with a desire to startle his audience, and even at
times to mystify them a little. The revelation of Chremes'
bigamy (in the *Phormio*), Pamphilus' discovery (in the *Hecyra*)
of what is really the matter with Philumena, the extraordinary
trick played by Davus (in the *Andria*) in making the unwitting
Mysis act the desired part much more effectively than she could
have done had he previously disclosed his intentions, Demea's
sudden abandonment of his previous way of life (in the *Adelphi*)

* Antiphanes, Ποίησις (Kock II. 191) ; but cf. Ar. *Poet.* 9.8.

and the success with which he turns the tables on Micio—these
scenes (which may indeed be purely Greek in origin, but are
unlike anything in Plautus) are not only 'dramatic' in our
sense of the word; well acted, they must have been excellent
'theatre'. Practical details of staging may sometimes be a
little obscure; the movements of characters are not made as
clear to us as they are by Plautus, who was above all things
a man of the theatre. In command of rhythm and metre,
in flow of language, in farcical power and animal spirits,
admittedly Plautus is the superior of Terence. Nevertheless it
would be altogether wrong to regard Terence as indifferent
to the applause of the crowd. He seems to be telling the truth
when he says (*And.* 3) that his aim from the start had been 'to
please the people'. What he would not do was to write
down to them. He could not but be influenced by the tone
of the society in which he moved, the phil-Hellenic Roman
aristocracy of the second century. The kingdoms of the
world seemed to lie at their feet; and some at least among
them tried to temper power with humanity, with sentiment.
Plautus had lived in the bleak yet bracing air of the struggle
with Hannibal. Though he admires courage, even religion and
virtue (as we see in his portrait of Alcumena), he is free from
sentimentality. He sees life like one of his own heroines (*Ps.*
343) :

> sine ornamentis, cum intestinis omnibus.

Menander's most famous and perhaps most melancholy line,
' he whom the gods love dies young ', reads in Plautus (*Bacch.*
816 f.) like a proverbial remark given a farcical setting.
Terence's most famous line is also presumably taken from
Menander (*H.T.* 77) :

> homo sum : humani nil a me alienum puto.

In Menander's play this remark may have been nothing more
than a characterizing touch indicating Chremes' inquisitive-
ness; but few readers of the line in Terence's play will take
it in so limited a sense. (See Duckworth, *N.R.C.* 304.)

In this deepening of sentiment I would find Terence's
chief claim to originality. The outlines may be less sharp
than in Menander; but there seems to be a gain in feeling.
To some extent we may agree with those who find in him the
herald of the new humanitas, the new urbanitas, which was

to refine, if not to ennoble, the harsh realities of Roman power.   Nowhere is this more evident than in the first scene he wrote, the opening scene of the *Andria*, which Cicero admired so much,* and which must have gained so much from being cast by Terence into dialogue form.   The art of Terence is like the beauty of Glycerium in her tears :

> et uoltu, Sosia,
> adeo modesto, adeo uenusto, ut nil supra !

' so modest, so winning of feature, that nothing could excel her ! '

Good manners, good feeling find their fitting expressions (43 f.) :

> istaec commemoratio
> quasi exprobratiost immemoris benefici.

' That reminder of a kindness you have done me amounts to a reproach of ingratitude.'   There are the memorable half-lines : ne quid nimis (61), a version, of course, of a Greek proverb, ' nothing too much ', but put in the mouth of the added character Sosia, and therefore presumably not from the Greek original ; and again the famous hinc illae lacrimae (126). Comedy is speaking now, not in the racy idiom of the market-place, hearty, cynical, uninhibited, but in the quiet, courteous phrases, the meaning silences, of the salon.   Life is a serious matter ; it cannot be successfully lived without tenderness as well as wisdom.   This may not be Christianity, as that word is understood in the north of Europe, but it is at least humane.

The dramatist was an artist, not a teacher ; yet many who saw the *Adelphi* may have felt that it had a message for them.   Here in Rome, where the spirit of old Cato was putting up a losing fight against the incoming Hellenism, they were looking at a play which depicted the results of two contrasted forms of education.   Yet even in this, his last play, Terence has added a scene of rougher quality, showing Aeschinus and his slave carrying off Bacchis regardless of the protests of Sannio, who is threatened in the traditional comic style with a ' smack on the jaw '.   So we see Terence trying to the last to carry with him both sections of the public, in spite of the widening gulf which would soon destroy the famous Roman unity admired by Polybius.

---

* *De Orat.* 2.80.325 ; *De Inu.* 1.19.27 and 1.23.33 ; *Pro Cael.* 25. 61 ; *De Off.* 2.69.

The study of Terence raises problems affecting our whole outlook on comedy and its relation to life. In dealing with these large themes it is easy to carry a sound argument too far, and in correcting the extreme views of others to be led ourselves into an opposite extreme. These are faults arising from the very nature of research. Ancient plays were not, I think, *pièces à thèse* : modern dissertations indubitably are. Is the *Adelphi* a picture of an actual situation in the Rome of the second century B.C. ? or alternatively in the Athens of the fourth century B.C. ? Is Demea Cato ? or is Micio Demetrius of Phalerum ? Either view is perhaps defensible ; but we can hardly hold *both*. Indeed the whole character of New (and Roman) Comedy seems to have been determined by the need to avoid offending the rulers of the State ; and political allusions subtle enough to escape the notice of authority would probably have been missed by most of the audience too. Is Terence a moral teacher ? or are his plays also examples of that 'immoral morality' which Mommsen (*Hist. of Rome*, Eng. Tr., ii. 428) found in Menander ? Should a dramatist show courtesans better than they are in real life (like Thais in the *Eunuchus* and Bacchis in the *Hecyra*) ? Is Plautus' pitiless cynicism a more honest and less dangerous guide ? Is Chaerea's rape of Pamphila presented with unnecessarily luscious detail ? Which play would do a young man more good, the *Eunuchus* or the *Truculentus* ?

What we must keep before us is the central fact that Plautus and Terence were both playwrights, and that as playwrights they must have shared the same aim—to please their public.* They are indeed different ; we are conscious of the difference, it might almost be said, in every line. Where they agree (and differ from their originals), the agreement may be regarded as due to their Roman background. According to Duckworth (*N.R.C.* 140) the one feature which their plays have in common is 'mental error, or misapprehension'. I would add that (in contrast to their Greek originals) they share the freer Roman outlook on sex, the Roman zest for life, the optimism inspired by Rome's victory. For all its fascination, New Comedy reflects a played-out world. In Latin comedy the element of enjoyment is more prominent. We must not exaggerate the difference between Plautus and Terence ; there is plenty of moralizing in Plautus (e.g. in the *Trinummus*

* See Appendix P.

and the *Captivi*), there is plenty of quiet humour in Terence (e.g. in the *Phormio* and the *Adelphi*) ; and both the moralizing and the humour are meant to be enjoyed. Plautus is farcical, exuberant, extravagant ; he aims at immediate effects : Terence is thoughtful ; his words are carefully chosen, his general design is more steadily kept in view. A Plautine character may say almost anything at any time : Terence's characters are more consistent, if less striking. Terence builds up his effects more carefully, and for that reason he is superior, I think, not only in surprise but also in irony.

Terence's appeal is to the reflective ; but this does not mean that his plays were a failure on the stage. To the end of the Republic, and even in imperial times, they were known to the theatre-going public ; Quintilian[9] seems to refer to contemporary performances of Terence's plays, and the illustrations in the manuscripts have been thought to suggest that their connexion with the stage reaches to even later times.

We may wonder why of all the Republican dramatists only Plautus and Terence have survived. The reason may be that later ages found them particularly good *reading*. Each in his own way was admitted to be a master of style. If Plautus was more amusing, Terence was more polished and more philosophic ; he was also easier to understand. The excellence of the manuscript tradition is evidence of his popularity in late antiquity and the Middle Ages. Few Latin authors are in less need of a commentator. Free from difficult expressions or topical allusions, written in the easy, graceful Latin of aristocratic Rome, his plays retain their attraction because they invest the themes of daily life with a certain nobility.

IV JUPITER AND MERCURY
Phlyax Vase-painting in the Vatican Museum

CHAPTER XIII

THE OTHER COMPOSERS OF PALLIATAE

THE ACTIVE world of contemporary comedy to which Terence's prologues introduce us has left little behind but the names of a few authors, some comments on their work, a few titles and a few fragments. In most cases we have nothing to guide us as to their date ; perhaps they were contemporaries of Caecilius or Terence, or came a little later in the second century B.C. TRABEA[1] is said to have had emotional power ; a fragment of an unnamed play shows us a lover in the full tide of joyful expectation : ' I will soothe Madam's palm with cash ! at a nod from me she will obey my wishes and desires ; I will come to the door and push it with one finger, it will open, all of a sudden Chrysis will see me. She will run to me, all eagerness to throw herself into my arms ; she will be mine ! Fortune herself does not know such fortune as mine '. Perhaps it is the same lover who later remarks in more reflective mood : ' I think that violent delight is a great source of folly '. ATILIUS[2] wrote a play called ' The Womanhater ', Misogynos ; he also seems to have gone in for tragedy, if it is the same Atilius who made a bad translation of Sophocles' Electra ; his style was harsh. AQUILIUS[3] wrote a Boeotia ; the passage preserved to us is a parasite's lament on the invention of the sundial, which has made his meals depend on the sun instead of on his own appetite. Varro considered the style of this passage proof that the play should be ascribed to Plautus. An attempt has been made to connect the passage with the introduction of the sundial into Rome, but of course it is in all probability translated from the Greek. LICINIUS IMBREX[4] wrote a Neaera from which we have two lines reminiscent of a passage in Plautus' Poenulus ; should we identify this writer with P. Licinius Tegula, who wrote a hymn in 200 B.C., on the ground that imbrex and tegula both mean ' tile ' ? JUVENTIUS[5] has left two or three lines as well as a title—Anagnorizomene ; VATRONIUS[6] seems to have written a comedy called Burra

(—Greek Pyrrha). VALERIUS[7] wrote a *Phormio*. We know a little more about LUSCIUS LANUVINUS,[8] the 'malevolent old poet' of Terence's prologues. As he was 'old' in 166 B.C., he must have been born about 210 B.C. or earlier. He translated from Menander the *Phasma* ('Ghost'), which told of a secret passage through a party wall used by a maiden whose appearance in the other house (her mother's) was at first taken to be that of a spectre by the young gentleman who lived there; on discovering his mistake he fell in love with and finally married her. The *Thesaurus* ('Treasure') told of a young spendthrift who, after running through his property, sent his servant to make an offering inside his father's tomb, as had been enjoined in his father's will. The field in which the tomb stood had passed into the hands of an avaricious old neighbour. In company with the slave this neighbour visited the tomb; there they found a treasure, which the avaricious neighbour promptly seized. The young man brought an action to recover the treasure; the neighbour, though defendant, is made to speak before the plaintiff—a point with which Terence taunts Lanuvinus. Terence also finds fault with Lanuvinus for introducing a 'running slave' who orders the public to make way for him, and for another scene in which a mad young man thinks that he sees a hind fleeing from dogs and imploring his protection. Lanuvinus' charges against Terence were that his style was thin, that he 'spoiled' (see pp. 98–102) his Greek originals, and that he was a novice, dependent on his noble friends, who had enabled him to enter on his literary career without proper preparation. These charges suggest the character and circumstances of Lanuvinus himself. Presumably he had passed through a long apprenticeship—possibly as an actor; he was not admitted to the society of the great, and disliked those who had this privilege; in fact he had a class-conscious, trade-unionist mentality. Some of Terence's charges against him seem unfair; the faults mentioned above, if faults, were presumably taken over from his Greek originals. Terence further accuses him of being 'a good translator and a bad writer' who has turned good originals into bad Latin plays because of his lack of style, and whose success on at least one occasion was due to the actors rather than to his own talents. Perhaps Lanuvinus translated his originals

fairly closely. He himself criticized Terence's style as ' thin '
and ' slight ', which may perhaps suggest that his own was
pompous and turgid ; the two extant lines support this view :

> Athenienses, bellum cum Rhodiensibus
> quod fuerit, quid ego hic praedicem ?

The bitterness of the dispute suggests that Lanuvinus
regarded Terence as a dangerous rival. On the one side we
have the old writer laboriously turning his originals into dull
Latin, on the other his young rival remodelling his originals on
novel principles so as to produce new plays written in the
choicest style.

The final name is TURPILIUS[9] (thirteen titles : *Boethuntes,
Canephorus, Demetrius, Demiurgus, Epiclerus, Hetaera, Lemniae,
Leucadia, Lindia, Paedium, Paraterusa,* * *Philopator, Thrasyleon ;* the
fragments amount to about 200 lines). We are told that
Turpilius died at an advanced age in 103 B.C. ; he must therefore have been born during the lifetime of Terence. It would
seem that the Hellenization of the palliata is now complete ; his
titles are all Greek, and his fragments contain nothing which
might not have been translated from the Greek.

We can follow the plot of the *Leucadia*[10] to some extent from
the remarks of Servius and the fragments. The original was
by Menander. Phaon was a poor and ugly boatman of Lesbos,
who plied for hire between the island and the mainland.
Venus entered his boat in the guise of an old woman ; he gave
her a free passage, and in return she gave him a box of oint-
ment ; when he rubbed himself with it, he became irresistibly
attractive to all the women whom he met. We see one of
these women, who has spurned her previous lover ; the lover
expresses his bitter feelings about the airs which the boatman
gives himself and about the shameless way in which the girl
makes love to him. Phaon scorns her advances, and she
determines to commit suicide by throwing herself from the top
of the Leucadian cliff into the sea. We see her standing in
terror on the cliffs, looking at the crags, listening to the waves,
appalled at the loneliness ; then, resolved on her desperate
act, she commits herself to the gods (excluding Venus) and the
winds and casts herself headlong. Her struggles in the sea are
observed by some one who bids his oarsmen row up ; we hear

* ' The Female Spy ', or ' We're very wide awake ', cf. *Theatre of Dionysus*, fig. 56.

her piteous request for a fire at which to dry herself ; apparently
she has recovered her senses, and perhaps she is reconciled to
her former lover.   Such a plot seems a refreshing change from
the usual urban setting of New Comedy ; how the play could
be staged without change of background is illustrated by the
Rudens.   Presumably the women of Lesbos enjoyed more
freedom than those of Athens.

Another play translated by Turpilius from Menander is the
' Heiress ' (*Epiclerus*).   A young man is being compelled by
his parents to marry a kinswoman who has been left an orphan
and heiress ; he bitterly resents his fate.   The opening lines
of Menander's play show him coming on the stage from his
sleepless couch to tell the story of his life.   Turpilius, after
the fashion of Terence, and possibly under the influence of the
opening scene of the *Curculio*, has converted this opening
monologue into a dialogue between the young man and his
slave : ' Pray tell me sir, where you are hurrying before daybreak with only one slave ? '   ' I cannot sleep indoors,
Stephanio.'   ' Why ? '   ' As usual, my troubles drive away
sleep and force me out of doors in the dead of night.'   The
Philopator dealt with a young man who ' loved his father '.
We gather that the heroine has been unfortunate, and hear her
(perhaps off-stage) lamenting her lot.   Somebody drops a
letter which some one else picks up, observed by a third party ;
hence, we may presume, comes the disclosure of some secret,
bringing the play to a happy conclusion.

Five of the thirteen titles suggest a Menandrian origin.
The later palliata seems to have maintained the interest in
Menander which appears in Caecilius and still more in Terence.
The tone of the fragments seems Menandrian ; there is a lack
of farcical or violent scenes, of rough jests, of inflated language ;
among Latin dramatists Turpilius seems to have been in the
line of Terence.   In metre we find plenty of trochaics, and
some cretics and bacchiacs.

Cicero speaks of a contemporary performance of Turpilius'
Demiurgus in which Roscius took part.   This reminds us that the
palliata lived on the stage long after the death of its last
composer.   Cicero refers [11] to Ballio, the pimp of Plautus'
Pseudolus, as a figure still familiar to the theatre-going public
in his own day.   Terence's didascaliae indicate revival performances of several of his plays.   We can thus see how

questionable is the current view that the public got tired of the foreign palliata and demanded something more native. Indeed its exotic flavour and avoidance of dangerous, topical references were among the chief attractions of the palliata ; in plot, moreover, native comedy was probably altogether inferior, even in the eyes of the Roman populace. Why the supply of composers for the palliata failed before that of any other type of drama is a difficult question ; but we may note that within little over a generation after the death of Turpilius the same fate seems to have overtaken all forms of literary tragedy and comedy, whether translated or original. The old classics were revived, but no new writers appeared. The explanation may be that the Greek quarry was thought to be exhausted, or that there had been a change in the social status of dramatic composers. We now have on the one hand the noble dilettante who writes plays for his own amusement and that of his friends, on the other hand the professional composer of subliterary theatrical pieces such as the mime. The feeling is growing up that connexion with the theatre, including even the writing of plays for public performance, is degrading. The composition, even the translation, of tragedy and comedy required a considerable standard of education, and those who possessed such a standard would now have felt that they were compromising their position by writing plays for the amusement of the general public.

NOTE ON VOLCACIUS SEDIGITUS [12] AND HIS LIST OF THE 'TEN BEST WRITERS OF COMEDY'.

About the end of the second century B.C. the writing of literary history had begun at Rome. Among the topics discussed were the dates of the dramatists and their respective merits ; one point in particular was the order in which the writers of palliatae should be placed with regard to quality. Volcacius Sedigitus drew up a list of the 'ten best writers of comedy' in these words :

> multos incertos certare hanc rem uidimus,
> palmam poetae comico cui deferant.
> eum meo iudicio errorem dissoluam tibi,
> ut, contra si quis sentiat, nil sentiat.
> Caecilio palmam Statio do*mimico*.
> Plautus secundus facile exsuperat ceteros.

dein Naevius qui*feruet*pretio in tertiost.
si erit quod quarto detur dabitur Licinio.
post insequi Licinium facio Atilium.
in sexto consequetur hos Terentius.
Turpilius septimum, Trabea octauum optinet.
nono loco esse facile facio Luscium.
decimum addo causa antiquitatis Ennium.

Too much importance should not be attached to what is manifestly
an individual opinion ; but Volcacius was not the only critic who
put Caecilius at the head of comic writers. We can understand
his putting Plautus and Naevius so high on the list (the description
of Naevius' fiery quality is uncertain : the Ms. read *seruet*) ; after
these three he does not seem to have cared very much how the other
writers should be arranged—' if there is to be a fourth place, it
will be given to Licinius '. It is surprising to find Terence only
sixth ; his only outstanding stage-success, however, was the
Eunuchus, and the qualities of his style may not have been appreciated
until a later age. Ennius was not regarded as an important comic
writer—if we can discount the testimony of Terence (*And.* 18-and
Terence may have been thinking of Ennius as a great and popular
writer who, among other things, wrote comedies). But in putting
Ennius *last* Volcacius seems to be expressing some particularly
personal view. It is true that, in date, Ennius lived earlier than
most of the writers here mentioned ; and the implication of
Volcacius' words is that he was earlier than all the writers *not*
mentioned ; apparently, then, Livius as a writer of comedy had
already been forgotten, or was actually supposed to be later than
Ennius. Donatus, indeed,[13] thought that Ennius was earlier than
Plautus.

CHAPTER XIV

ACCIUS

L. ACCIUS [1] is said to have been born in 170 B.C. Jerome's date agrees well enough with Accius' (Cic. *Brut.* 64.229) statement that he was fifty years younger than Pacuvius. There are independent records showing that the Accii were connected with Pisaurum, in Umbria. Jerome tells us that the poet's parents were ex-slaves ; whether this is true or not, there is evidence that the poet enjoyed the friendship of some of the highest men in Rome. During his long career he occupied himself with grammatical, theatrical and literary studies (Cicero, as a young man, discussed literature with him) and above all with tragedy ; his career was brilliant, and he was in old age the leading figure in the collegium poetarum. The stories about Accius bring before us a man of great energy and self-confidence ; in his character and industry, as well as in his style, there was a daemonic force. He appears to have been a hasty worker ; in his studies on literary history he was capable of gross mistakes, and even those who most admired his tragedies thought them inferior in learning and care to those of Pacuvius. We have the titles of over forty tragedies : *Achilles, Aegisthus, Agamemnonidae, Alcestis, Alcimeo, Alphesiboea, Amphitruo, Andromeda, Antenoridae, Antigone, Armorum Iudicium, Astyanax, Athamas, Atreus, Bacchae, Chrysippus, Clutemestra, Deiphobus, Diomedes, Epigoni, Epinausimache, Erigona, Eriphyla, Eurysaces, Hecuba, Hellenes, Io, Medea, Melanippus, Meleager, Minos* or *Minotaurus, Myrmidones, Neoptolemus, Nyctegresia, Oenomaus, Pelopidae, Persidae* (? = *Amphitruo*), *Philocteta, Phinidae, Phoenissae, Prometheus* (? = *Io*), *Stasiastae* or *Tropaeum Liberi, Telephus, Tereus, Thebais, Troades*) and two praetextae (*Aeneadae* or *Decius, Brutus*), with about seven hundred lines. The range of titles shows that he explored every field of tragedy—the Trojan, Theban and Pelopid cycles ; originals of the fifth century as well as later Greek tragedy, and

119

independent compositions on Roman historical themes. Unfortunately the fragments are all short and scattered, and cast only fitful gleams on his powers and methods as a dramatist. I have already mentioned the well-known anecdote which tells how, on his way to Asia, he visited Pacuvius, then living in retirement at Brundisium, and read him his new play, the *Atreus*. Pacuvius found the style impressive but harsh ; Accius replied that the best fruits required most time to mellow. We need not believe in the historical truth of this story (which reminds us of the equally suspicious account of the interview between Caecilius and Terence), but at least it shows that some of Accius' work was found crude by later generations ; indeed his outstanding quality was force, which might at times degenerate into violence. Cicero [2] calls him summus poeta, grauis et ingeniosus poeta ; from Horace and Quintilian we gather that though inferior to Pacuvius in learning he surpassed him in force and elevation, while sharing his impressive dignity of style, sentiment and characterization ; Velleius, who makes him the central figure of Roman tragedy, says that though less careful than Pacuvius he excelled him in energy (sanguis) ; Vitruvius speaks of the vivid picture of the author which his works brought to the reader ; Ovid bears tribute to his powerful rhetoric (animosi oris).

Preference for plots and treatment of a violent, melodramatic nature, majestic rhetoric, flamboyant character-drawing—these qualities seem characteristic of Roman tragedy in general, but are particularly marked in Accius. Another very Roman quality was his command of effective repartee, a command so evident in his dialogue that, according to Quintilian (5.13.43), he was asked why he had not made law his profession. More surprising is the power of pictorial description and the feeling for nature which his fragments occasionally display. The Roman dramatists, even if incapable of creating plots or characters on the large scale, seem at least to have thrown all their energies into visualizing and intensifying each scene as they came to it.

It is easy to show that Accius, like the other Roman tragic writers, was overfond of emphasis. We can compare some fragments of his *Phoenissae* with the original by Euripides. Tyrrell (*Lectures on Latin Poetry*, pp. 41–2) translates the opening lines of the Greek play thus :

> O sun, that through the fires of the firmament
> Cleavest thy way, and in thy golden car
> Launchest the flames from thy swift coursers' feet,
> Ill-starred the ray thou sheddest once on Thebes.

This is Tyrrell's rendering of Accius' version ;

> O sun, that in thy glistering chariot borne,
> With coursers swiftly galloping, dost unfold
> A sheet of gleaming flame and burning heat,
> Why with such baleful auguries and omens
> Adverse giv'st thou to Thebes thy baleful light ?

Similarly, while Eteocles' command to Polynices to leave the city is simply expressed in the Greek :

> Then get thee from these walls, or thou shalt die,

Accius might make us fancy that we see Cicero driving Catiline from Rome :

> egredere, exi, ecfer te, elimina urbe !

No doubt rhetoric is at times appropriate to the dramatic situation : what could be better than the famous retort of the tyrant Atreus — oderint dum metuant ! (a phrase apparently imitated from Ennius [3]). But the continual straining after rhetorical effect tends to eliminate all the delicate half-tones necessary to credible character-drawing and to leave us nothing but superhuman virtue and inhuman vice. Roman tragedy instinctively turned to horrific, melodramatic themes, such as the story of how Tereus violated Philomela and then cut her tongue out so that her sister should not know of the deed. There is force in Accius' picture of the lust-maddened barbarian (Ribb. 636–9) :

> Tereus indomito more atque animo barbaro
> conspexit eam ; hinc amore uecors flammeo
> depositus facinus pessimum ex dementia
> confingit.

Similarly Accius, like so many Roman dramatists, was attracted by the theme of how Atreus served up to Thyestes a meal of his son's flesh (Ribb. 220–2) :

> concoquit
> partem uapore flammae, ueribus in foco
> lacerta tribuit.

It is instructive to notice how Seneca, developing the innate vices of Roman rhetoric to their limit, works up his description of the same incident into a dozen ghoulish lines (*Thyestes* 760 ff.)

From the beginning Roman tragedy had tended to over-statement; with Accius this tendency has gone as far as it well can; with Seneca it goes further, and becomes absurd.

Splendid, flamboyant figures come before us as we read the lines of Accius. Atreus, the tyrant, introduces himself thus :

> en impero Argis, sceptra mihi liquit Pelops,
> qua ponto ab Helles atque ab Ionio mari
> urgetur Isthmos.* (Ribb. inc. inc. 104–6.)

The powerful retort of Ajax brings the speaker vividly before our eyes (Ribb. inc. inc. 61–3) :

> uidi te, Vlixes, saxo sternentem Hectora ;
> uidi tegentem clipeo classem Doricam ;
> ego tunc pudendam trepidus hortabar fugam.

That stoic quality in Ajax's character, which was so much appreciated by the Romans, is brought out by a famous line taken ultimately from the *Ajax* of Sophocles (156) :

> uirtute sis par, dispar fortunis patris.

Telephus displays similar stoicism (619–20) :

> nam si a me regnum atque opes
> eripere quiuit, at uirtutem non quiit.

We should, however, recognize that in Accius' rhetoric there is much genuine feeling. These are perhaps the words of Procne sorrowing over her mutilated sister (640–1) :

> O suauem linguae sonitum ! O dulcitas
> conspirantum animae !

We find a certain grave humanity and sympathy with mis-fortune (lines 187–8) :

> abducite intro ; nam mihi miseritudine
> commouit animum excelsa aspecti dignitas.

* It is not certain that these often-quoted lines are by Accius.

To his *Phoenissae*, indeed, Accius seems to have added a compassionate touch not to be found in Euripides' play—the care for the wounded (597–8) :

> obit nunc uasta moenia, omnis saucios
> conuisit, ut curentur diligentius.

In this compassion, this admiration for misfortune borne with dignity, there is a Virgilian quality—and we know that Virgil was a student of Accius, and borrowed from his *Clutemestra* some details of the storm in *Aeneid* i. There is a feeling for nature in the description of early morning in the *Oenomaus* (493–6) :

> . . . before the dawn had lit
> The earliest beams of day, when peasants rouse
> Their sleeping horned oxen to the plough,
> And split with the share the dewy steaming sod,
> And lift the ridges from the yielding soil.

The longest fragment is a well-known description in his *Medea* of the first ship, as seen by a peasant (391–402) :

> In from the sea the mighty monster glides :
> The billows hiss and roar ; in onward course
> It dashes down their blows 'mid foam and spray ;
> The eddies boil and bubble, while it moves
> Like some great storm-cloud torn from the sky
> Or towering crag by wind and tempest driven
> Or swollen water-spout, riding on high
> Above the tumult of the tossing waves.
> Or has the sea upturned its earthy bed,
> Or deep in Ocean's caverns, trident-armed,
> Has Neptune levered up some giant rock,
> Now poised between the billows and the heaven ?

Accius would hardly have been a Roman had he not possessed a strain of pedantry : Achilles quibbles as to whether his stubbornness should be called pertinacia or peruicacia (a verbal point which manifestly belongs to the Latin writer). Few writers seem more imbued with grauitas ; there is a manly note in

> non genus uirum ornat, generi uir fortis loco

(' The man's the gowd for a' that '). Looking through the fragments, we are struck with the frequency of the words uir, uirtus, and by the fact that women seem less prominent than in Ennius or Pacuvius.

When we turn from style to substance and dramatic structure, we are faced with the usual difficulty—the fragments are too short and scattered to permit of certain conclusions. Evidently Accius permitted himself some freedom in translation ; several of the fragments of his *Bacchae* and *Phoenissae* have nothing corresponding to them in the extant Greek originals by Euripides. We have no evidence of alteration in structure. The explanatory prologue would have been at least as necessary to the audience of Accius as to that of Euripides. Certain fragments of the *Bacchae* and *Phoenissae* come from the opening scenes, which themselves serve in the Greek as explanations of the dramatic situation. Servius tells us that the *Atreus* contained a genealogical chronicle ; this would naturally come in the prologue. We have another genealogical passage in *inc. fab.* 653 ff.

Accius, like all the Latin dramatists, took complete liberty with regard to metre ; fr. x of the *Phoenissae* shows that he has substituted recitative for the plain speech of Euripides, presumably because of the emotional character of this scene, in which Creon is told that he must sacrifice his son. That Accius' *Bacchae*, like its original, had a chorus of Bacchants is suggested by line 239 :

> agite modico gradu ! iacite tirsos leuis !

No passage in Euripides' play *quite* corresponds to this line in wording or in metre ; but the treatment of choral passages was probably a matter in which the Latin translators allowed themselves wide freedom. There are many passages in Accius' fragments which purport to be spoken by groups of people ; we have the plural titles (*Bacchae*, etc.) which in the Greek plays certainly indicated the chorus ; but for all such titles and passages the supposition of a spokesman with mute attendants, appearing on the stage when required, is perhaps an adequate explanation.

The staging of tragedy was presumably similar to that of comedy, except that the back-scene would be deemed to represent not the doors of private houses but a palace, a cave or whatever was appropriate. The palace door is mentioned (line 29). The cave of Philoctetes is shown, surrounded by a wilderness ; cf. line 557 :

contempla hanc sedem in qua ego nouem hiemes saxo stratus pertuli, and line 554 :

   quis tu es mortalis qui in deserta et tesqua te adportes loca ?

Even these lines were presumably spoken before the three-door
back-scene usual in comedy. Some would suppose that the
unwanted doors were screened from view, so that the central
door could represent the cave.* It is probable that, as in comedy,
the ' near distance ' lay on the spectators' right, the ' further
distance ' on their left ; line 318 (ab classe ad urbem tendunt)
suggests that we shall soon see the warriors as they make their
way from the ' harbour ' side of the stage to the ' town ' side.
The action may begin at dawn ; the stars wane in the growing
light (line 693). The arrival of a new character in the early
morning is indicated by some one standing on the stage (line
123) :

   sed quis hic est qui matutinum cursum huc celeranter rapit ?

A messenger arriving from a distance is bidden deliver his
report (line 499). The sound of the opening palace door
indicates that a new character is about to enter the stage
(line 29) :

                 sed ualuae resonunt regiae.

A speaker tells how he has overheard a conversation (line 281) ;
two characters come on the stage (i.e. into the ' open air ')
in order to converse without the danger of being overheard
(line 292). Some one remarks that it is unseemly to walk
quickly (line 24) ·

         celeri gradu gressum adcelerasse dedecet.

These and similar touches are the hallmark of the dramatist
who intends his plays to be produced on the stage. No doubt
Accius derived them from his originals ; at any rate they mark
out his tragedies as different in purpose from the closet-
dramas of Seneca.

ROMAN TRAGEDY AFTER ACCIUS

A contemporary of Accius and one of the first Romans of
the governing classes to try his hand at dramatic composition
was C. JULIUS CAESAR STRABO [4] (put to death in 87 B.C.).

                  * See p. 267 and note.

We have the titles of three plays : *Adrastus, Teuthras, Tecmesa ;* a late grammarian tells us, with what authority we do not know, that the author was particular to have the name ' Tecmesa ' so pronounced (i.e. not Tec*u*mesa) He was more celebrated as an orator ; Cicero tells us that his tragedies lacked power and that his style was too genial and witty to be strictly tragic. The three lines which have survived are not enough to enable us to judge his style for ourselves. He was a member of the collegium poetarum ; we hear that Accius refused to rise from his seat when Strabo entered, not out of disregard for Strabo's high position, but because of conscious superiority as a dramatist. We hear nothing further of Strabo as a tragic writer ; we have no reference to the performance of any of his plays, apart from the above-quoted remark of Marius Victorinus about his insistence on having ' Tecmesa ' pronounced in the Greek way *on the stage.* Cicero seems to think of him not as a practising dramatist but as a literary man, one of whose interests was the composition of tragedies. On the whole the impression we derive is that he was a dilettante in drama, though sufficiently interested in it to give his oratorical style a dramatic colouring. Similarly another orator-dramatist of about this time, or perhaps of the previous century, the Roman knight C. TITIUS,[5] is said by Cicero to have sacrificed strictly tragic style to display his wit. Indeed Afranius, the writer of togatae, made Titius one of his models. We have nothing left of Titius' tragedies, but a fragment of his oratory shows marked ability for social satire. Of POMPILIUS,[6] said to have been a pupil of Pacuvius, we have a single line, and of SANTRA,[7] perhaps to be identified with the grammarian, we have the title *Nuptiae Bacchi* (?) and about three lines. The strictly quantitative metre of these lines suggests that Santra belongs to a somewhat later period.

It seems to be true that after the death of Accius few or no more tragedies were written for the stage. The reason cannot have been merely lack of popular interest ; old tragedies continued to be performed down to the end of the Republic, and Aesopus, the tragic actor and friend of Cicero, enjoyed a great reputation. Perhaps the reason was a change in the attitude towards the writing of tragedy. On the one hand noble dilettanti were beginning to amuse themselves with the composition of tragedy ; on the other hand it was beginning to be felt that to write plays to be performed on the popular stage was scarcely a worthy occupation, at any rate for men of the class of these new noble writers. Perhaps there is a first hint of this new attitude towards practising dramatists in the liberty taken by a mime-performer [8] in mentioning Accius' name on the stage ; though Accius was successful in the action he brought against the offender, no Roman after Accius' day seems to have taken up the writing of tragedy as his profession. The Augustan age produced two famous tragedies, written (to judge by the fragments) in strictly quantitative metre, the *Thyestes* of Varius [9] and the *Medea* of Ovid ; we have the evidence of a scholiast that the *Thyestes* was produced at the games in celebration of Actium (possibly an exceptional occasion), but Ovid, later in life, protests [10] that he has never written for the stage, though some passages of his *Metamorphoses* seem to have been used as libretti for pantomime. The only respectable professional dramatist of any kind of whom we hear after the time of Accius is the mime-writer Laberius ; and his career was to show in melancholy fashion that it was now no longer possible to write for the stage and to retain one's dignity.

CHAPTER XV

NATIVE COMEDY: THE FABULA TOGATA

THE ROMANS had at all times an instinct for social and political satire. It was natural that this instinct should seek expression in their drama. Naevius, the first native-born Italian dramatist, though like Andronicus basing his comedies (so far as we know) on Greek originals, introduced a strong native flavour by references to such topical themes as the habits of guests from Praeneste and Lanuvium, or the picture of the Lares painted for the 'festival of the cross-roads' by the imported artist Theodotus. Naevius' tendency to introduce political themes and his attacks on certain nobles brought him to disaster, and future Latin dramatists took care not to offend in this way; but in Plautus we still find a strong Roman flavour of social satire and topical allusion. After Plautus' day there is a change; perhaps it was introduced by Caecilius, but by the time of Terence at latest the palliata seems to have renounced its old freedom to introduce topical allusions. Aesthetic questions were now being vigorously discussed, as the prologues of Terence indicate; fidelity in translation was felt to be important. It may be that the incongruity between a Greek setting and Roman allusions came to be regarded as objectionable. But in renouncing Roman topics the palliata left the field open for the rise of a new, native type of comedy, which would try to invent its own plots and find its characters in Italian life.

The known writers of the fabula togata or 'comedy in native dress' are Titinius, Afranius and Atta. Titinius is usually supposed to have been the pioneer. His date is not precisely known; he may have been a contemporary of Plautus, he may have been a successor of Terence. Afranius certainly wrote after the time of Terence, for whose loss he expresses regret; Velleius, in different passages, speaks of him as a contemporary of Pacuvius, Caecilius, Terence and Accius. Atta is said to have died in 77 B.C. When we compare these dates with those of the palliata, the last author of which was Turpilius, who died in 104 B.C., and when we further reflect that the classics of the palliata were still familiar to the theatre-going public in the days of Cicero, we may begin to feel doubtful about the modern view that the togata owed its origin to a public reaction from foreign comedy. The togata arose while the palliata was still in its heyday * ; so far from its driving the palliata off the stage, the two forms of comedy long existed side by side. Greek comedy was the more popular and important of the two, and much of its popularity was due to the very fact that it was exotic (and did not incur any danger of irritating native susceptibilities), but native comedy was at least more successful than native tragedy. The praetexta was never anything more than a parergon for writers of tragedy, and the total number of certain titles can almost be counted on the fingers of one hand. But the togata gave full-time employment for three writers, and has left to us about seventy titles.

The term togata could theoretically be applied to all drama not derived from Greek sources, but usually it was confined to comedy. The fate of Naevius warned its writers not to make fun of the governing classes in Rome ; consequently the togata finds its themes in the country towns of Italy,† or among the ordinary folk of no specified town. In this workaday world the ceremonial toga was not really the characteristic wear, and the term togata was hardly a happy description for the drama which dealt with the lives of such folk. Accordingly we find as a synonym for togata (in the sense of ' native comedy ') the term tabernaria, ' private-house comedy '. Tabernae in early Latin meant ' private houses ', in particular the houses of poor people, to which class most (though not all) of the characters of the togata belong.

Of Titinius[1] little is known. Varro praised the character-drawing (or moral tone ?) of Titinius, Terence and Atta ; if this order is to be taken as chronological (which is very doubtful), he must have been earlier than Terence. He has left us fifteen titles : *Barbatus* (' The Man with a Beard '),

---

* But I do not feel convinced by the view of some scholars (e.g. Warmington, *Old Latin* II. xv.) that togatæ were written by Naevius—far less by Donatus' statement (*Com.* iv. 5) that they were invented by Livius Andronicus !

† Cicero seems to use the term togati of the *Latins* (as contrasted with the Romans) : *De Orat.* iii. 11. 43. See Appendix D.

Caecus (' Blind '), *Fullonia* (' The Fullers '), *Gemina* (' The Twin Sister '), *Hortensius, Iurisperita* (' The Lady Lawyer '), *Priuigna* (' The Stepdaughter ') *Procilia, Psaltria siue Ferentinatis* (' The Music Girl, or the Girl of Ferentinum '), *Quintus, Setina* (' The Girl of Setia '), *Tibicina* (' The Flute-girl '), *Varus, Veliterna* (' The Girl of Velitrae '), and *Vlubrana* (' The Girl of Ulubrae '), with about one hundred and eighty lines. C. Quinctius Atta [2] is said by Jerome to have died at Rome in 77 B.C. and to have been buried at the second milestone on the Via Praenestina. Varro, as we have seen, thought highly of his character-drawing (or moral tone), and Fronto adds that he excelled in feminine conversation. We have from him eleven titles : *Aedilicia* (' The Aedile's Games '), *Aquae Caldae* (' Taking the Waters '), *Conciliatrix* (' The Match-maker ' or perhaps ' Procuress ') *Gratulatio* (' Well done ! '), *Lucubratio* (' Up by lamplight '), *Matertera* (' Auntie '), *Megalensia* (' The Games of the Great Mother '), *Satura* (' What you will '), *Socrus* (' Mother-in-law '), *Supplicatio* (' The Entreaty '), *Tiro Proficiscens* (' Off for his first campaign '), and about twenty lines. L. Afranius [3] seems to have been the most important writer of togatae. We have forty-four titles : *Abducta* (' Gretna Green '), *Aequales* (' Chums '), *Auctio* (' Going—going— gone ! '), *Augur* (' The Augur '), *Brundisinae* (' The Women of Brundisium '), *Bucco Adoptatus* (' The Clown's adoption '), *Cinerarius* (' The Hairdresser '), *Compitalia* (' The Crossroad Festival '), *Consobrini* (' Cousins '), *Crimen* (' The Accusation '), *Deditio* (' The Surrender '), *Depositum* (' Left on Trust '), *Diuortium* (' The Divorce '), *Emancipatus* (' The slave set free '), *Epistula* (' The Letter '), *Exceptus* (' Rescued from drowning '), *Fratriae* (' Sisters-in-law '), *Icta* (' She who gets slapped ' ?), *Incendium* (' Fire ! '), *Inimici* (' Enemies '), *Libertus* (' The Freedman '), *Mariti* (' Married Men '), *Materterae* (' Aunts '), *Megalensia, Omen* (' The Omen '), *Patelia* (' The Grain Goddess ' ?), *Pompa* (' The Procession '), *Priuignus* (' The Stepson '), *Prodigus* (' The Spendthrift '), *Proditus* (' Betrayed ') *Promus* (' The Butler '), *Prosa* (?), *Purgamentum* (' Trimmings '), *Repudiatus* (' The rejected Lover ' ?), *Sella* (' The Chair '), *Simulans* (' Not what he seemed to be '), *Sorores* (' The Sisters '), *Suspecta* (' The suspected daughter ' ?), *Talio* (' Tit for tat '), *Temerarius* (' Neck or Nothing '), *Thais, Titulus* (' The Inscription ' ?) *Virgo* (' The Maid '), *Vopiscus* (' The Twin that lived '), and over four hundred lines. Afranius, as he himself admits,[4] drew freely on the works of other dramatists, whether Greek or Roman ; he thought highly of Menander and Terence, and may have resembled them in some ways. Quintilian regrets to admit that Afranius made use of boy-love * as a dramatic theme, thereby (according to Quintilian) revealing his own character. To suppose that a dramatist's private life necessarily corresponds to that of any of his characters seems uncritical, but Quintilian's testimony that sodomy was employed as a dramatic motive by Afranius is supported by Ausonius.† Cicero speaks of Afranius' wit, and says that he modelled his style on that of the orator and tragedian C. Titius (whose date is itself, unfortunately, uncertain). It would appear not only that Afranius was a more gifted and fertile writer than Titinius or Atta (though not equal to them in moral tone ; but perhaps Varro also was thinking of his introduction of sodomy as a theme) but that he cast his net more widely than they in search of subjects.

Our main evidence, that of the titles and fragments, does not enable us to distinguish clearly between the work of these different writers of togatae, or to reconstruct with probability as much as a single plot. It would appear that a togata could be of some complexity. The *Vopiscus* of Afranius introduces the parents of the ' twin that lived ', a newly-married pair (scarcely to be identified with these parents), a husband whose wife has left him, a woman who feigns submission while really playing on the violence of a man's temper, a trusted parasite, a pampered slave, a door-keeper, a lady's maid. The *Fullonia* of Titinius shows us a wrangle between fullers and weavers, a wife who complains that her husband is squandering her dowry, and a philanderer who, in fear of capture by an angry husband, is about to commit himself (like brave Horatius) to the Tiber. Afranius' *Simulans* shows some one advising a man to ' feign ' anger with his son-in-law and pretend that he wishes to take his daughter home ; we see a father and mother quarrelling in the presence of their small child, some one angrily abusing a prodigal, a would-be peacemaker and a slave who is being turned out of doors. On the other hand we have a statement by a scholiast[5] that the cast of a togata, like that of an Atellana, was smaller than that of a palliata ;

* Antiphanes wrote a *Paederastes* and Diphilus a *Paederastae*.   † *Ep.* lxxix.

and on general grounds we should have suspected than an average togata would be both shorter and simpler than the borrowed type of comedy. No doubt in many cases the plot of a togata was modelled on that of a palliata, though its characters were necessarily taken from Italian life.

Sometimes at least there was a prologue ; in an unidentified play of Afranius the god Priapus [6] utters what appears to have been an explanatory prologue, while Afranius' defence of his literary methods, quoted from the *Compitalia*, presumably occurred in the prologue, which must therefore have been polemical in tone, after the fashion of Terence—whom Afranius admired. The play sometimes opened in the early morning (*Epistula* of Afranius, *Lucubratio* of Atta). There was probably no chorus ; Cicero's remarks (*Pro Sest.* 118) show that the ' troupe ', the ' actors ' and the ' singers ' were identical. Though on the occasion mentioned by Cicero the actors uttered in unison a denunciation of one of the characters, directing their gaze significantly to where Clodius sat in one of the front seats, this was evidently a ' put-up job '. The stage represented as usual a street in front of some houses (*Gratulatio, Epistula*) with the country lying on one side-entrance (*Diuortium*) and no doubt, the centre of the town in the other direction (*Hortensius*). The roof of the stage-building was perhaps used in Titinius' *Setina*. The usual tricks of eaves-dropping (*Priuignus*), of slaves swaggering along the street (*Pompa*), of doors opening, characters appearing precisely as their names happen to be mentioned, sounds of tumult ' within ', etc., all occur.

The stock plots of the palliata turn on peculiar features of Greek life, and would seem out of place in the togata. We are told by Donatus [7] that in the togata slaves were not allowed to be shown as cleverer than their masters ; this typical theme of the palliata had been made tolerable only by the exotic nature of that type of drama. Very different was the discipline which ruled in a Roman household. It would seem, then, that in the togata we must have none of those swindling slaves who extract money from their old masters in order to pay the expenses of their young masters' amours. Yet in Afranius' *Incendium* the old gentleman tells us, apparently in a prologue, that his son and his slave have laid a plot, presumably in order to swindle him. The wheels of the palliata were set in motion by love ;

yet we have seen how difficult it was for a respectable Athenian girl to appear in public. In Roman life this convention did not exist, at least to anything like the same extent ; young women of respectable class can appear in public, can meet eligible suitors, can accompany their fiancés on a social call. Hence all the devices whereby New Comedy succeeded in enabling girls to meet their future husbands—kidnapping, exposure of children, recognition-scenes, midnight festivals— seem unnecessary ; mere mercenary gallantries too, need no longer form the stuff of drama ; we find ourselves in an atmosphere of family life not unlike our own, where marriage is to some extent based on mutual attraction, and where relatives, female as well as male, express their opinion about a projected match. This does not mean that the togata could provide a true love-plot, or even give love as important a place as it occupies in New Comedy. Romance is impossible if the course of love can run smooth ; the authors of the togata, if they really desired to introduce a love-interest, would have to invent their own ways of preventing lovers from winning happiness too soon. There is no sign of a romantic interest in the fragments of Titinius' *Setina*, where the reluctant suitor doubts the wisdom of aspiring to a maiden of superior fortune, or in the family councils of the *Fratriae*, the calculation that a pretty girl will need less dowry and the hope for possible advantages in kind if she marries the confectioner. Indeed Afranius seems to be forced to resort to the themes of the palliata in order to secure a sentimental interest ; the heroine of his *Exceptus* is a Greek courtesan from Naples, her lover is for some reason induced to attempt suicide, and her tender reproaches reveal to him the depth of her love.

Another method of introducing a sentimental interest was the enforced separation of a happily married couple. In the *Diuortium* a father forces his daughters to leave their husbands, in the *Simulans* he is advised to follow a similar course, in the *Vopiscus* a husband seems to express his earnest but vain hope of inducing his wife to return home. These are all plays of Afranius. In general one would suspect that the togata was not sentimental but lively, amusing and satirical (though prone to occasional sententiousness). The opening scene of Afranius' *Epistula* shows some eager gallant or belated reveller, bare-headed and be-slippered, out of doors in the cold air of a winter's dawn ; the other fragments of this play give us glimpses of a drinking-party, of some one escaping from a street bully, of some one dressed up as a girl, of a girl who can hardly restrain her laughter while her mother storms in fury and of a general state of domestic turmoil. In other plays we hear of husbands trying to play the gallant—a stock theme in the palliata, it is true, but in the togata there is this curious difference : the erring husband chooses not the town but the country as the setting of his amours. Here, perhaps, we have a concession to Roman notions of propriety ; illicit gallantries must not be flaunted in the Roman forum. Afranius' introduction of the theme of sodomy is remarkable ; it shows that this type of drama was not fettered by the sexual conventions which the palliata had taken over from New Comedy. In the palliata, to borrow a phrase from the *Curculio*,* a man may love any one *except* ' maiden, wife or widow, youths or boys'; in other words love affairs can only occur between the hero and a courtesan or foreigner. In the togata not only do we have respectable alliances between social equals, but we find the darker themes of adultery, involving respectably born women, and of un-natural vice. What we should like to know is how a coherent plot was built up round such themes—but this is just what the fragments do not tell us. It is sad to have to admit that in the whole range of Latin drama we have no knowledge of the course of as much as one plot invented by a Latin writer.† Perhaps the togata did not contain a real plot (unless one borrowed from the palliata), but was merely a series of loosely-connected scenes taken from the everyday life of the streets, the shops, the private houses of Rome or the country towns ; if so, it may to some extent have resembled the old dramatic satura ; and indeed *Satura* is the title of one of Atta's pieces.

What the titles and fragments do show is that the togata depicted the life of ordinary Italian folk, especially of the lower classes. Titinius' *Fullonia* dealt with the fullers, a favourite butt for comedians—possibly because of the fact that one of the cleansing agents they employed was urine. One of the fullers complains ' We fullers have no rest, day or night ', while a weaver retorts ' But for our weaving you fullers would be out of work '. In Titinius' *Barbatus* an embroiderer throws up his job, leaving his needle and thread to his master and mistress.

* ll. 36–7.   † I am speaking of drama intended for the stage.

In Afranius' ' Butler ' we see two servant-maids wrangling ; in one of Titinius' plays a drunken servant-girl is detected in the act of stealing wool. People of higher rank occasionally appear—the heiress and the lisping dandy in Titinius' ' Girl of Setia ', the mistress of the house in his ' Twin Sister '. The personal names are usually typical Roman names, the local names those of country towns : Titinius wrote a ' Girl of Setia ', a ' Girl of Ferentinum ', a ' Girl of Velitrae ' ; Atta wrote about a spa called ' Aquae Caldae ' ; Afranius wrote ' The Ladies of Brundisium '. Yet titles such as *Megalensia* (Atta and Afranius), *Compitalia* (Afranius), which are the names of Roman festivals, and references to the Tiber or to the custom of throwing puppets into that river, would suggest that the writers of togatae, for all their prudence, could not altogether forgo the introduction of the capital. Afranius seems to have introduced Greek names at times ; one piece of his deals with a courtesan named Thais, another with a courtesan called Moschis ; he quotes a Greek proverb about how Amyclae fell through keeping silence ; and many of the familiar characters of the palliata appear, especially in Afranius—parasites and pimps, cooks and slaves and courtesans. Nevertheless the prevailing atmosphere, even in Afranius, is Italian. Titinius makes fun of the people of Ferentinum because of their craze for things Greek ; Numerius, a character of Afranius, laughs to scorn any Greek mannerism in conversation. Nothing can be more Roman than the contemptuous reference in Titinius' *Quintus* to people who speak Oscan or Volscian because of their ignorance of Latin.

The togata must have enjoyed some popularity, at least during the lifetime of its authors, for we have the titles of seventy pieces. Revivals at a later period are not often recorded ; the *Simulans* [8] was performed in Cicero's day (was its choice influenced by Clodius' enemies ?), the *Incendium* was staged in Nero's reign—but chiefly, we gather, in order to give a spectacular display of the fire ; actors were allowed to keep any property they could rescue from the burning buildings. We may suspect that the choice of old plays for revival was often dictated by motives which had no connexion with the dramatic merits of the play chosen. The purely literary togata continued to be written down to Juvenal's day (but perhaps Juvenal [9] was one of those who included under this

title all plays on native themes). Melissus,[10] a freedman of Maecenas, invented the trabeata, a special type of togata dealing
with middle-class life (the trabea was the characteristic wear
of the equites.)   One is reluctant to admit that Melissus can
have satirized the class to which his famous patron belonged;
perhaps the trabeata was akin to the praetexta, and dealt
kindly with the habits of Maecenas and his fellow-knights.
In any case, it was probably nothing more than a short-lived
literary curiosity.   For the survival of the togata on the stage
we have no evidence ; Suetonius refers [11] to an actor named
Stephanio, of the time of Augustus, who is called a togatarius—
but apparently what is meant by this term is that Stephanio
was the first to wear a toga when dancing in pantomime.

CHAPTER XVI

POPULAR FARCE: THE FABULA ATELLANA

IN TRAGEDY the Romans of the Republican period were content to adapt Greek originals ; for the Roman historical play seems to have had little importance. But in the restless search for new means of amusing the public, the Roman dramatists gave literary form to certain popular forms of farce, which had existed from early times as improvised performances but were now, perhaps for the first time, to be set down on paper and, in due course, published. Our information concerning the Atellana and the mime is fragmentary ; their importance in literature was probably small ; but we have reason to believe that in the life of the common people, from early times to the end of the Roman Empire, popular farce played a greater part than all the literary forms of Roman drama put together.

In antiquity, as in modern times, the Campanians had a reputation for jest and merriment. Horace has left us [1] an account of how two Campanian buffoons indulged in a sparring-match which was marked by high spirits, lively repartee and merciless personalities. At an early period there seems to have been developed in Campania a rustic farce which displayed certain traditional characters in ridiculous situations. The fabula Atellana is said by Diomedes [2] to have derived its name from a town of the Osci called Atella, where it had its origin. Atella was about nine miles from Capua, on the road to Naples; Oscan was an Italic dialect, akin to Latin, which was spoken by the population of the southern Apennines who, in the fifth and early fourth centuries, overran the greater part of southern Italy, including Campania. It would seem, therefore, that the Atellana was a form of entertainment popular among the Oscan-speaking people of Campania, ' including the inhabitants of Atella, and that the Romans, on becoming acquainted with it, called it either ' Oscan farce ' after the district as a whole, or ' Atellane ' after the town in that district—perhaps the town from which they had first derived their knowledge of it. (We may remember that the ' Fescenn-ine verses ' derived their name, according to one Roman theory, from the small Etruscan town Fescennium.)

One would certainly imagine that the ' Oscan farce ' must originally have been presented in the Oscan language. One of the stock characters in ' some Atellane plays ', the ' Grand-dad ' Pappus, is said by Varro [3] to have been called *Casnar* by the Osci. This implies that the Atellanae survived in Oscan in their original home after they had been introduced in Latin to Rome. Strabo, indeed, tells us that though the Oscan race had by his day died out, their dialect still survived among the Romans, and was used for the ' staging and miming of poems ' in a ' certain native festival '. But we have other evidence that the Oscan dialect was not intelligible to the ordinary Roman ; and it is difficult to believe that the Atellanes were ever performed at Rome—presumably for public entertainment— in an unintelligible tongue. Strabo may have been misled by the name ' Oscan farce ' into imagining that the farce was presented at Rome in Oscan ; or he may have misunderstood some reference to the peculiar Latinity of the literary Atellanes —which, judging by the fragments, was markedly rustic and crude. Juvenal uses the term Oscan (in its Greek form Opici) as ' barbarian ', ' vandal ', and Cicero's reference to the transactions of some town council in Campania as ' Oscan farces ' may also suggest that ' boorish ' is what the term meant to the Romans of his day. As for the name Atellana and the connexion of the farce with the town of Atella, we cannot now hope to know the facts. The explanations offered by Livy and Diomedes have the air of plausible guesses, based on nothing but the names ' Oscan farce' and 'Atellane play'. The modern theories are purely theoretical ; we have no evidence that Atella played any particular part in the development of the farce, or that the inhabitants of Atella were regarded as suitable butts for jest.* Nor can we tell how far Greek influence affected the development of the Atellana. Strabo's language shows that he thought of it as a kind of mime ; but the Romans seem to have drawn a sharp distinction between the Atellana and the mime,[4] and in its essential feature it differs from any Greek performance known to us.

* Mommsen, *History of Rome.* iv. 13.

This essential feature was the presence of certain traditional characters. No ancient writer has left us a list of these characters, but from the extant titles and fragments of the written Atellanae we collect the names of four or five : Maccus, Bucco, Pappus, and Dossennus, who is thought by some modern authorities to be identical with Manducus. All these characters seem to have had a certain family resemblance as coarse, greedy clowns, whose animal characteristics were such as might amuse a primitive and rustic audience, ever ready to laugh at gluttony and drunkenness, at horse-play and obscene jest. Attempts have been made to distinguish them more clearly from each other by arguments based on etymology. We know from Apuleius (*Apol.* 81) that Maccus and Bucco were fools ; Plautus also (*Bacc.* 1088) uses ' Bucco ' as a synonym for ' fool '. Does Maccus mean ' stupid ', or ' guzzler ' ? Aristophanes (*Eq.* 396) uses μακκοᾷ in the sense 'moon', 'be stupid'; and in the dialect of Sardinia the word *maccu* means ' stupid '. But the word *macco* was once used in Italian in the sense ' pap '.* If Bucco comes from *bucca* and means ' fat-cheeks ', does that indicate greed, or stupidity, or boastfulness ? Pappus is the Greek πάππος, ' grandfather ', a word used by Pollux in his list of comic masks—' first grand-father ', ' second grand-father ' and so on. We have quoted Varro's statement that ' in some Atellanae " old Pappus " is what the Oscans call " casnar " '. In the literary fragments Pappus appears as the Old Fool. Are we to derive the name ' Dossennus ' from ' *dorsum* ', and to conclude that Dossennus was a hunch-back ? There is not a scrap of evidence to support this view. That Dossennus was greedy appears from a line of Horace [5] concerning Plautus :

quantus sit Dossennus edacibus in parasitis,

' how monstrous a Dossennus Plautus appears among his gluttonous parasites ', which I take to mean ' what a super-glutton Plautus shows himself' (because of his eagerness to make money). In the belief that his name means ' hunch-back ', and that hunchbacks are popularly regarded as cunning, some scholars regard him as the Wise Fool, and press into service certain of the fragments to support this view. As

* See Walde, *Lat. et. Wört.* (1940), and Meyer-Lübke, *Röm. Et. Wört.* s.v. The difficulty is to find any historical connexion between the word meaning ' clown ' and the word meaning ' pap '.

for Manducus, Varro [6] tells us that his name comes from *mando*,
'chew': dictum mandier a mandendo, unde manducari, a
quo in Atellanis ad obsenum uocant Manducum.   Here
Müller emends ad obsenum to Dossennum, identifying these two
characters, but there is no other evidence for such an identification.   However that may be, Manducus is beyond doubt
the 'Chewer', an ogre with champing jaws.   A passage in
Plautus (*Rud.* 535–6) transports us from this world of theoriz-
ing into the unmistakable atmosphere of a popular festival at
Rome.   Labrax, his teeth chattering with cold, thinks of 'hiring
himself out as a Manducus at the games'.   Juvenal [7] gives us a
glimpse of a festival in some country town, with its grass-
grown theatre, and on the stage the 'traditional farce' with the
'hideous gaping mask' which makes the terrified youngster
seek refuge in his mother's arms.   Festus, explaining the word
'manducus', tells us that in ancient festivals, along with other
alarming and ludicrous figures, an ogre appeared with huge
jaws, gaping mouth and chattering teeth.   From the slang
manducare, 'champ the jaws' comes the Romance word for
'eat' (French manger).   The Atellane farce has indeed left
a record behind it in the languages of modern Europe.

These are the characters of whom we hear.   No doubt
they did not always appear together.   Pappus, according to
Varro's remark (quoted above), was seen in 'some Atellanae'
only.   Indeed we have no evidence that any two of them took
part in the same performance except one of the literary
fragments, which shows Dossennus as present in a piece
entitled 'Maccus the Maiden'.

Such stock rôles would, no doubt, require stock costumes
and masks.   Indeed without a mask it would not be possible
to represent Manducus' [8] huge champing jaws.   Festus tells us
that the Atellane performers were specially denoted by the
title *personati*,[9] as they were allowed always to wear their masks
on the stage, whereas other actors were compelled to lay theirs
aside.   Perhaps Festus is here (in somewhat confused language)
contrasting the Atellani with the only other comic actors widely
known in the imperial age, the unmasked performers of mime.
The use of the mask, rendering play of feature impossible, would
make expressive gesture all the more important; Juvenal
(vi. 72) refers to the 'gestures' of an Atellane actor, and
Tertullian (*De Spect.* 17) speaks of Atellani gesticulatores.

Atellane pieces were apparently of no great length ; they are referred to as Atellaniolae,[10] ' little Atellanes ', the number of characters in Atellanes, as in togatae, is said to have been ' rather small ', and their use as ' exodia ' or ' after-pieces ' would suggest that they corresponded in length to our ' curtain-raisers '. No doubt they were more or less impromptu performances until they received literary form in the days of Sulla. Nevertheless the Atellana had a plot containing surprising complications, tricae [11] Atellanae as they were called (our word ' intrigue ' is derived from this technical expression). But how could a short, impromptu performance have a complicated plot ? Indeed a figure like Manducus seems to have been more like an ogre in a dumb-show than a dramatic character. Some light is thrown on this problem by the titles and fragments, which show that a recurring motif was disguise and masquerade. ' Maccus the Maiden ' might quite quickly get into a complicated situation, reminiscent of the outrageous adventures of Chalinus dressed as a bride in that very Plautine comedy, the *Casina*. Even where there was no written dialogue, we may suppose that the actors had been coached in the outlines of the plot and were left to develop its humorous possibilities as the inspiration of the moment might suggest to them. They must often have fallen back on stock themes which would allow them to show off their command of ' patter '. Indeed much Plautine dialogue is of this nature. We learn that they were fond of introducing topical allusions, and of alternately propounding riddles [12] and trying to guess the answers. What did consistency of plot matter, so long as the crowd were amused ?

Livy's well-known summary [13] of Roman dramatic origins, however untrustworthy as history, can scarcely be ignored, especially when confirmed by other evidence, or when it deals with conditions prevailing in his own day. He tells us that the young citizens of Rome, when forced to abandon their amateur dramatics by professional competition after the time of Andronicus, revived the old Fescennine exchange of repartee ; this later received the name ' afterpiece ' and was blended with the Atellane play, a form of drama which was never allowed to get into professional hands. Hence in Livy's own day the Atellani retained citizen status and served in the army ' as if they had nothing to do with the stage ' (see p. 17). We may well doubt his ascription of amateur theatricals to third-century Rome ; indeed the passage already quoted from Plautus shows that the Manducus was paid for his services. In Livy's day the theatre was largely given over to the mimes, who were all ' infames '. Possibly the Atellani was regarded as superior to the mimes, in view of their long traditions. By Tacitus' [14] day this distinction seems to have disappeared. But from early times all who performed for the amusement of the public, whether ludii, histriones, Atellani or mimi, must surely have done so for pay.

The Atellana was well known to Plautus, who refers to Bucco and Manducus.[15] Whether or not we identify with Plautus the ' Maccus ' who wrote the *Asinaria* and the ' Maccus Titus ' who wrote the *Mercator*, we cannot help wondering whether this Maccus owed his name to having been an actor in Atellanes. The use of the Atellana as an exodium illustrates its popularity and its amusing character. Cicero, when dealing in his *De Oratore* [16] with the subject of jest, turns for examples to the Atellanae of Novius. When Paetus, Cicero's elegant friend, after mentioning a tragedy, the *Oenomaus*, turns to jest, Cicero's reply is ' after the tragedy you have introduced as exodium not, as was once the custom, an Atellana, but a mime '. Paetus' polished jesting evidently savours of the town, not the country, and is therefore compared not with the rustic Atellana but with the sophisticated mime. Nevertheless the Atellane survived in imperial times ; Juvenal [17] shows that it was still given as an exodium. The Roman grammarians compare it in this respect with the Greek satyric play, and like the satyric play it came to include not only rustic elements but burlesque of mythology.

In order to form a closer acquaintance with the Atellane of the late Republic we turn to the written Atellanes of Pomponius and Novius. But the assumption of literary form necessarily altered the character of this rustic farce ; Pomponius and Novius could not help being influenced by other forms of drama, and though they strove to retain the traditional characters and the traditional crudity of jest and language, the surviving titles and fragments remind us at times of the palliata, the togata, the burlesque and' the mime.

CHAPTER XVII

THE LITERARY ATELLANA

L. POMPONIUS [1] of Bononia, described by Velleius as the founder of the Atellana, is said by Jerome to have been active in 89 B.C. Novius, who is mentioned with equal respect, is quoted by Cicero in the *De Oratore*, [2] the dramatic date of which is 91 B.C. Evidently these two leading writers of Atellanae were thought of as contemporaries. At the beginning of the first century farce seems to gain at the expense of higher forms of drama ; from now on we hear of no writer who made a living out of the writing of tragedy or comedy for the stage. From Pomponius we have seventy titles, with fragments amounting to nearly two hundred lines or parts of lines ; from Novius we have forty-four titles with over a hundred lines of fragments. To distinguish between the styles of these two writers would seem impossible, so meagre is our information.

The large number of surviving titles supports our other evidence that the pieces themselves were comparatively short ; a pair of titles like ' Hog(g) Sick ' and ' Hog(g) Well ' suggests, indeed, that these two pieces were meant to be performed on the same occasion. The most obvious Atellane feature of the titles and fragments is the frequent reference to the stock characters. Maccus appears to be the most popular figure ; we have such titles as ' Maccus the Soldier ', ' Maccus the Inn-keeper ', ' Maccus the Maid ', ' Maccus the Exile ', ' The Twin Macci ' ; apparently ' Maccus ' alone was a title which could attract a crowd, as both Pomponius and Novius wrote plays with this title. We have also as titles ' Bucco the Gladiator ', ' Bucco adopted ', ' Pappus the Farmer ', ' The Bride of Pappus ', ' Pappus Defeated at the Poll ' (a title which attracted both authors), and ' The Two Dossenni '. Bucco, Pappus and Dossennus are also mentioned in the fragments, and a fragment of Pomponius' *Pictores* appears to mention Manducus (spelt *Manduco*) though perhaps only as an equivalent for ' glutton '. Other titles point to the maintenance of the primitive rustic atmosphere : ' The Pig ', ' The Sow ', ' Hog(g) Sick ', ' Hog(g) Well ', ' The Farmer ', ' The Wood-pile ', ' A-hoeing ', ' The Vine-gatherers ', ' The She-ass ', ' The She-goat '. Other titles, again, suggest the life of the town : ' All in White ', or ' the Candidate ', ' The Fullers ', ' The Inspector of Morals ', ' The Pimp '. Such characters might easily be imagined in any small town of Campania, and indeed some of the fragments remind us of the scribblings on the walls of Pompeii. Here, then, the Atellana approached the boundaries of the togata. Yet other titles remind us of the palliata and New Comedy : *Synephebi, Adelphi, Hetaera ;* a title like ' The Boy Favourite ' may suggest kinship with the Hellenized togata of Afranius or with the mime ; finally there are titles which point to burlesque of tragedy : ' The counterfeit Agamemnon ', *Marsyas, Phoenissae.*

It would seem that the earliest writers to give the Atellana a literary form, finding that the antics of Maccus and his fellows were not sufficient material in themselves, were forced to draw upon other sources. Nevertheless the traditional element was preserved, at least in some of these pieces. Maccus, in particular, appears in various situations, in which, we may be sure, he conducts himself with due crudity and absurdity. The fragments of ' Maccus the Soldier ' refer to gluttony. ' Maccus the Exile ' bids farewell to a door (presumably that of a host) in terms which seem to echo Plautus. In Plautus' *Mercator* [3] the young Charinus, before departing for a far land, takes tragic farewell of his father's door :

limen superum inferumque salue, simul autem uale !

So Maccus exclaims :

limen superum, quod mi misero saepe confregit caput ;
inferum autem, ubi ego omnino omnis digitos defregi meos:

' Lintel, whereon I have often banged my unlucky head, and threshold, where I have many a time broken all my toes '. That Maccus might be dressed up as a Maid is shown by the title *Maccus Virgo* ; and the feelings of some one who is deceived by such a trick are expressed in a surviving fragment of the *Macci Gemini* of Pomponius. In the ' Kalends of March ' of

Pomponius we find someone being coached in the art of adapting his voice to his woman's rôle.[4] Elsewhere we find characters disguising themselves by simply drawing their cloaks over their heads ; we recall the similar use of the ricinium or hood in the mime. We can imagine that ' Bucco the Gladiator ' was but a caricature of the Matador, so popular with women as well as with men :

> occidit taurum toruiter, me amore sauciauit.

' Bucco Adopted ' may deal with the theme ' If I were king ' ; sudden changes in fortune were a favourite mime-theme (modo egens, repente diues, as Cicero puts it [5] ; cf. Juv. x 602–8). Bucco's clownish wit appears when, on being asked to ' handle the job cleanly ', he replies, ' I have already washed by hands '. Such over-literal interpretations are a stock form of jest in comedy. The fragments do not allow us to determine the character of Bucco more closely.

Pappus is beyond doubt the Old Fool. In him, as the scarcely translatable title *Hirnea Pappi* shows, the disadvantages of old age were satirized with true Roman vigour. His defeat at an election was the theme of plays by both dramatists. Pomponius shows him being consoled by the suggestion that the crowd will alter their decisions later on ; in Novius' play some young man informs him with brutal candour that his electioneering will bring him not to the chair of office but to the coffin. It is no doubt Pappus who, when asked ' Why are you complaining, Dad ? ', replies drily ' Would you have me sing ? I'm condemned '. Pappus is no doubt the ' worthless old fellow ' of Pomponius' *Praeco Posterior*, whose young wife is to be induced by her stepson to leave him ; in spite of his early sacrifices at the temple of Venus (presumably for success in love), a clown brings him news of disaster. Pappus is naturally unfortunate as a husband ; his activities as a farmer are interrupted by the vivid account of his wife's misconduct (Pomponius' *Pappus Agricola*). The Romans seem to have taken particular pleasure in the exhibition of dotard passion ; Plautus makes full use of this theme, and perhaps our accounts of the latter days of Tiberius have been coloured by the Roman taste for this particular form of scandal. *Manducus* (in the form *Manduco*) occurs in Pomponius 112. It is not clear that any of our literary fragments refers to Manducus as a character,

6

but it can hardly be without significance that we find the writers of Atellanae using manduco for 'guzzler' and manducari for 'champ the jaws' (Pomp. 100). Dossennus was evidently greedy; in Pomponius' *Campani* some one proposes to distribute food to 'Dossennus and the fullers'.

In Novius' *Duo Dossenni* some one is called 'The terror of the winejar'. In Pomponius' *Philosophia* Dossennus is asked to say who stole the gold; his reply is that he expects to be rewarded for his information. In the *Maccus Virgo* he is seen behaving in a very unseemly way to one of the pupils in his school. Seneca[6] mentions an inscription commemorating his wisdom:

> hospes, resiste et sophiam Dossenni lege.

On these references to him as a detective, a schoolmaster and a wise man, coupled with the supposed meaning of his name— 'hunchback'—has been founded the theory that Dossennus was the Learned Man, Scholasticus, whose cunning was indicated by his hunch. But there is no necessary connexion, even on the stage, between cunning and deformity, and Dossennus' appearance as a schoolmaster may have been no more characteristic of him than Maccus' appearance as a Maid in the same play. It would appear, then, that we know nothing about Dossennus except that he was probably greedy. It is not possible to distinguish clearly between the different characters of the Atellanae. Pappus was elderly and Manducus was an ogre; all were greedy and clownish.

The rustic origins of the Atellana are further indicated in the homeliness of the language. A rustic defines wealth as 'a short-lived blessing, like Sardinian cheese'. The frequent references to bodily functions may recall Aristophanes, but contrast the Atellana with the plays of Plautus and Terence. Rustics in Atellanae referred to a scortum (lit. 'skin', i.e. 'whore') as 'a bit of skin' (pellicula); indeed this type of drama had a vocabulary of its own. The rustic character of the Atellana may have helped to suggest its use as an afterpiece, on the model of the Greek satyric drama, which also was rustic in tone. But by natural reaction the satyric drama seems to have communicated its element of mythological burlesque to the Atellana, as many of the titles indicate. The composers of this farce were not unduly scrupulous about preserving its native quality, provided they could amuse their patrons. All forms of light drama influenced each other. In the Atellana we meet familiar characters of New Comedy such as the parasite and the pompous quack-doctor ; elsewhere we find ourselves in the atmosphere of the togata ; but perhaps most frequently we are reminded of the mime, and indeed the Atellana must have tended to become a form of masked mime. The title of one piece, *Exodium*, reminds us of the use of Atellanae in general as ' after-pieces ' ; another title, *Satura* (if it does not mean ' The Fat Woman ') may suggest that this native farce was felt to be a ' Medley ' or ' What you will '. Novius' *Mortis et Vitae Iudicium* is curiously reminiscent of the (non-dramatic) *Satura* of Ennius which showed Mors and Vita engaged in debate.

Staging was probably modelled on the palliata. That the usual three houses were shown in the background is suggested by the fragment of the *Pictores* ' Here in the middle lives Pappus, a worthless old fellow '. The metres used in the fragments seem also to have been those of the palliata ; a grammarian[7] tells us that the jaunty and rather vulgar iambic septenarius was especially prominent in the Atellana. As contrasted with the palliata, the Atellana was vulgar, trivial, homely ; as contrasted with the mime, the Atellana was a masked, rustic performance. Even when its themes were mythological, we may suspect that the treatment was thoroughly Italian. It was sufficiently different from any other form of entertainment, and at the same time sufficiently amusing, to maintain itself even on the imperial stage. Of its history as a literary form subsequent to the days of Pomponius and Novius we know little. (The dictator Sulla[8] is said to have written ' satyric comedies ' in Latin ; these were scarcely intended for the theatre.) But Mummius[9] is said to have revived the Atellana after a long period of neglect ; we have a single title (*Riuinus*) and three short fragments of his Atellanae. Another writer, Aprissius (?), the form of whose very name is doubtful, has left us a single fragment. Perhaps these writers belong to the imperial period. The scantiness of the literary remains suggests that after the time of Pomponius and Novius the Atellane drama returned to a semi-improvised character. We have a few fragments of Atellane cantica[10] from the early empire, one of them in Greek. The cantica would naturally outlive the ordinary dialogue, which may have been little more than comedians' patter, puns, riddles and so forth (illa obscura quae Atellani e more captant, as Quintilian [11] puts it). These fragments further illustrate the perennial interest of the Atellana in politics, which led it even to indulge in veiled allusions to the emperor's private life. The occasional use of Greek may have been due to the desire to disguise, or give a special flavour to, these dangerous allusions ; * it can hardly have been frequently used, for Petronius' hero Trimalchio [12] speaks of the Atellana as something essentially Italian. In spite of all the extraneous influences which acted on it, this native, masked farce seems to have retained something of its primitive, rustic, Italian character. As a form of literature it seems to have been short-lived ; as a type of popular entertainment it enjoyed great popularity during the early empire, and perhaps formed part of the theatrical heritage which was handed on by the ancient world to the Middle Ages.†

* Of course Greek was widely understood in Rome—otherwise it would not have been used on the comic stage.

† Unfortunately the connexion with the Commedia dell' arte is incapable of proof. Croce (*Saggi sulla litteratura italiana del seicento*, pp. 219-220) refutes Dieterich : Zanni is probably not from Latin sannio but from Gianni, dim. of Giovanni. See Lea, *Ital. popular comedy*, i, 54, 225-9.

CHAPTER XVIII

THE MIME

OF ALL the forms of entertainment which come within our survey, the mime was at once the most primitive and the most permanent. In its earliest form it cannot be classed as drama at all. All over the ancient world there were jugglers, acrobats and public entertainers of all kinds, male and female, who displayed their skill in the market-place, at festivals or wherever and whenever they could secure patrons. Among these nameless mountebanks there were some with a special gift for mimicry. They could imitate with their voices the neighing of horses, etc. (Plato *Rep.* 396 b) ; they had still greater skill in gesture, an art which was carried to a high pitch in the ancient world and which involved the use of every limb—the mimi were akin to the acrobats—as well as of facial expression. We have been considering them so far as solo performers, but assistants were required when the chief mime wished to represent such everyday scenes as fruit-stealing or the arrival of a quack doctor. These were stock subjects for the deikelistai, little companies of players (probably masked) who were popular among the Dorian Greeks. We also hear of the autokabdaloi (' improvisers '), whose name reminds us that the performers of farce often depend a good deal on the inspiration of the moment. The social status of such performers was low, and their performance was of a simple kind. A rough platform served to raise them above the heads of the crowd ; for scenery a portable curtain was sufficient. The actors were concealed behind the curtain till their turn came ; then, parting the folds in the middle, they stepped into the public view. While they performed a colleague might be collecting coins from the spectators, as we see in a Roman wall-painting.* Xenophon [1] gives us a capital description of a performance by a boy and girl, the property of a Syracusan dancing-master, who by means of dance, gesture and words represented the love of Dionysus and Ariadne. This performance was given in a

* Reich, *Mimus*, p. 540.

private house as an amusement for the guests ; one of those present was Socrates. The girl was an acrobat as well as an actress, and had previously impressed the company by her skill in the sword-dance. Her dancing was, of course, accompanied by music. Their social class is shown by the dancing-master's admission that the boy was his concubine. Wide indeed was the gulf between such performers and the actors who, in dignified mask and costume, appeared in the theatre of Dionysus to perform the tragedies of Aeschylus. It is not certain that all low-class performers were always maskless ; the deikelistai are thought to have owed their name to their use of the deikelon, [2] or mask ; the phlyakes, supposed to have played low life scenes and burlesques in the towns of south Italy, are shown with masks (or grotesque features ?) as well as short body-garments and the phallus (or exaggerated genitals ?), a costume claimed to resemble that of Aristophanic comedy.* It is not easy to distinguish sharply between the various types of popular entertainers, but at least we may say that no respectable actor [3] would appear on the Greek stage *without* a mask. An element of indecency clung to the mime from the beginning ; its aim was mere amusement, the mimicus risus. The solo performer, who could mould his features as he pleased and suit his voice to the character he was representing, was a familiar figure at all periods ; the company performances would naturally tend to grow more elaborate with time. Hence we find the general division of mimes into Paegnia, a generic term but on the whole indicating performances of a slight, trivial character, and Hypotheses, or ' plots ', perhaps taken over from drama proper and rendered by the mimi in their own style. Another general division was into the spoken and sung mime.† But to be too precise about the classification of so primitive, popular and widespread a form of entertainment would be vain labour. Free from the shackles of social position, technical traditions and a written text, the mimi were a law to themselves.

The popularity of farce among the Dorian Greeks, who colonized much of Magna Graecia, meant that the mimi were well known in south Italy from an early period. Athenaeus (see [2]) tells us of a ' maskless ' actor named Cleon, who lived

---

* If we may assume that the vase-paintings do represent the performances of the phlyakes. But see p. 25, footnote, and *N. and S.*, iii. 2.

† This distinction is perhaps unreal : see ch. xxvi.

about 300 B.C. and was the best of the 'Italiot mimes'. Nor can such a type of entertainment have long remained confined to the Greek towns. Linguistic barriers were no hindrance to the art of gesture and facial expression ; the simple requirements of the troupes of strolling players—a rough platform on which to set up their curtain and a few costumes—required no elaborate outlay or preparations. The contacts of Rome with Hellenism which arose out of the Pyrrhic War and the struggle for Sicily meant that many Romans must have become familiar with the mime at a time when the literary drama of Rome had not yet begun its career. The growth of a slave population familiar with Greek provided the nucleus of an audience for the 'ludus Graecus'. Two years after the intro-duction of literary drama by Andronicus came the foundation of the festival of Flora,[4] a festival which either was from the beginning or became an important occasion for the performance of mimes ; the merry festival was riotously celebrated by the common folk, and licence went so far as to sanction the appear-ance of mime-actresses naked on the stage. We are told that in 212 B.C., at the first performance of the ludi Apollinares, there was a dance by an elderly mime named Pomponius.[5] Here, then, in the third century, was an actor who had already grown old in his profession. The influence of popular farce on the development of literary Latin comedy may have been considerable. Plautus' adaptations of Greek New Comedy contain much jesting, buffoonery and horseplay of a kind which he·can scarcely have found in his literary originals, but which would have been quite appropriate in the mime. His very name, 'Flat-foot', may perhaps suggest that he had him-self acted as a planipes or barefooted mime. His successor, Caecilius, seems to have displayed in his style something of the tone of mime. Volcacius [6] perhaps refers to him as mimicus (the reading is doubtful), and Gellius [7] complains that he introduced into his Greek originals nescio quae mimica—coarse jests, out of keeping with the context, and added merely to raise a laugh.

By this time the strolling companies of mimes were becoming familiar throughout the civilised world. A terracotta lamp [8] found in Athens shows us three mimologi who perform a hypothesis called 'The Mother-in-law', a title presumably taken from literary comedy. At its highest level, indeed, the hypothesis approached drama proper, from which it differed chiefly in its preoccupation with character-drawing and situation rather than with plot. But there still remained the solo performers, who prided themselves on their skill in impersonation. The epitaph of one of them, Vitalis,[9] boasts of his skill in moulding his features and his voice to suit his part whether male or female. Perhaps our earliest Latin record of a mimus is the epitaph of Protogenes,[10] slave of Clulius, which was found near the town of Amiternum :

> Protogenes Clouli suauei heicei situst mimus,
> plourima que fecit populo soueis gaudia nuges.

Buecheler thinks the epitaph not much later than the time of Ennius. Protogenes was evidently a slave of Greek origin who amused the crowd with his ' merry trifles ' ; presumably he was a solo performer of paegnia. From the age of Sulla, or perhaps later, comes the epitaph found at Rome which commemorates Eucharis, slave and later freedwoman of Licinia. Eucharis [11] was a mime actress who had just been reaching renown when she was cut down by death at the age of fourteen. The epitaph tells us of the grief of the girl's father at the early death of this little maiden, beloved by her parents and her mistress, and so skilled in her profession that it seemed that the Muses themselves had taught her. She had recently danced at games given by the ' nobles ', and she is described as the first actress to have appeared on the ' Greek stage '. It seems probable, however, that women took part in the mime from the beginning, even in Italy, and from the second century B.C. we have a farewell poem addressed by Antipater of Sidon to the actress Antiodemis [12] on her departure for Rome.

Genuine drama demanded a free atmosphere ; the mime could and did maintain itself even in the courts of despots. We find that the dictator Sulla was fond of the mime, and that one of his friends was the lysiode* Metrobius.[13] About this time farce seems to have gained at the expense of higher drama ; the Atellane performance now rises for a while above the literary horizon, soon to be followed by the mime. On the whole, however, the mime remained sub-literary. We can picture these small companies of strolling players, men, women and children, travelling from town to town like gypsies, setting up their simple stage and curtain in some market-place and giving

---

* The lysiode played female characters but wore male attire.

their show. Chief among them was the leading actor or actress (archimimus,[14] archimima), to whom the rest were little more than foils. Improvisation was probably the rule. The arch-mime would perhaps begin by announcing the title, or even summarizing the plot (habebant suum auctorem qui, antequam mimum agerent, fabulam pronuntiaret, as Isidore [15] tells us) ; he was almost continuously on the stage, and he kept the dialogue so much under his control that ' the second actor in the mime ' was a phrase denoting one who, as we should say, ' played second fiddle '. The actor secundarum partium took such rôles as the clown or fool ; one of his methods of raising laughter was probably to take the words of the archimimus in too literal a sense—an old trick even in Plautus' day. The distinctive costume was the ricinium,[16] apparently a square hood which could either be thrown back or drawn forward so as to conceal the head, the centunculus, a patch-work jacket, tights and the phallus [17] ; the head was shaven, the feet were bare. It is not to be supposed, however, that all the characters in the performance were so attired. The elegant philanderer of whom Ovid speaks must have been dressed as a man of fashion, and a beautiful actress would appear in the most attractive and expensive clothes. The size of companies was perhaps not so large as it later became ; three mimologi are shown on the Attic lamp (they presumably had a female colleague to act the title-rôle of the mother-in-law), and Ovid[18] speaks of a cast of three—the peccant wife, the foolish old husband and the foppish lover.

The plots were simple, the dénouements often abrupt. A stock theme was the appearance of some one in a novel situation —a poor man suddenly become rich, for example (modo egens, repente diues, as Cicero [19] puts it). Juvenal,[20] when speaking of foundlings adopted into great houses, is reminded of the mime.* The riches might not last, and the ex-millionaire might have to disguise himself in his cloak and hurry off the stage. Abrupt endings[21] were natural in these short, improvised pieces ; Cicero pointedly contrasts the mime in this respect with the regular

---

* We may remember how Augustus,[22] on his death-bed, asked the bystanders whether he had played the ' mime of life ' in fitting fashion. Was he thinking of his extraordinary elevation to supreme power, of the dominating yet lonely part which he had played, of the fact that circumstances had forced him to adopt a pose, or of the unsatisfactory, inartistic and even farcical form which real life often takes—mimus, non fabula, not a play but a mime ?

drama, telling us how, when the plot had reached a deadlock, some character would make his escape, the scabillarii would sound the signal for 'curtain', and the aulaeum would rise from the floor to conceal the stage from view. Another form of curtain which was perhaps more particularly associated with the mime was the siparium, possibly a portable curtain behind which the actors awaited their cue. Diomedes gives as a possible (but surely unlikely) explanation of the term planipes [23] the fact (if it is a fact) that originally the actors of mime stood not on the raised stage but on the level of the orchestra, where they set up their outfit and performed their piece. A corrupt passage of Festus [24] seems to mean that the mimes performed in the orchestra while the stage was being set for a new play. Diomedes and Festus appear to be thinking in terms of the Greek theatre, which had a large orchestra, suitable for interludes. Apuleius describes how in the theatre of Corinth, after a preliminary dance (presumably given in the orchestra), the great aulaeum was raised, the siparia were folded up, and a most elaborate scene was disclosed. By Apuleius' day it appears that the drop-curtain had come to be operated as in our modern theatres (see Appendix E). In Cicero's time the mimi had evidently performed on the stage, like all other performers in a Roman theatre. Apparently the curtain, whatever its form, was of more importance to the mime than to other forms of drama.

Short, amusing, topical, utterly unrestrained by any considerations of technique or decency, yet capable of adopting on occasion the most sententious style, the mime came nearer than any other form of drama to the real tastes of the Roman populace. It would be difficult to describe in more detail so formless or rather Protean a type of composition; but some further light may be derived from a study of the literary fragments.

THE LITERARY MIME

The first Latin writer to give the mime written form was Decimus Laberius [25] (b. 106 B.C.), a Roman knight of high standing and character. Needless to say, he did not choose to act in his own mimes; his position in society was so established that he was able to refuse Clodius' request for a mime with the taunt that all the demagogue could do to punish him would be to

send him for a short period of exile in Dyrrhacium (a reference
to Cicero's recent banishment). Bitter indeed was the blow to
his pride, when, in his sixtieth year, he was forced by Caesar [26]
to appear on the stage as a competitor with a young mime-
writer and actor, the ex-slave Publilius Syrus. We still possess
the dignified and manly prologue which Laberius uttered on
this occasion, with its significant warning to the dictator
himself :

> Many he needs must fear whom many fear.

Caesar awarded the prize to Syrus ; to Laberius he gave half
a million sesterces and a gold ring, thereby signifying the res-
toration of equestrian rank which Laberius had forfeited by
appearing in a mime. Nevertheless his fellow-knights failed to
make room for him when he tried to resume his seat as a
spectator. Cicero called mockingly from the seats of the
senators ' I would make room for you, were I not so short of
room myself' (an allusion to Caesar's packing of the senate) ;
whereupon Laberius replied with considerable presence of
mind ' It is surprising that you are short of room, for you usually
sit upon two seats at the same time ! ' In the prologue of his
next mime he included a dignified allusion to the transience of
a dramatist's popularity. A year or two later, in 43, he died
at Puteoli.

We have forty-two titles and about one hundred and forty
lines or parts of lines. The contrast between the long extract
from a single prologue and the meagre remnants of the mimes
themselves has been thought to indicate that only the prologue
of a mime was fully written out, while the rest of the piece was
to some extent improvised. The titles are partly Greek (*Cacomnemon, Necyomantia, Ephebus*) but mostly in Latin ; some are
reminiscent of the palliata (*Aulularia*), rather more of the togata
(*Aquae Caldae, Compitalia, Fullo, Saturnalia, Staminariae*). *Anna
Perenna* may have been a mythological burlesque, akin to the
Rhinthonica. The mime, considered as a type of drama, is
so formless that it is hard to say what a typical mime-title would
be; as we hear, however, of dogs which performed in mimes,[27] it
is interesting to find titles like *Catularius* and *Scylax*, while *Cen-
tonarius* reminds us of the mime-clown's traditional motley, the
centunculus. *Paupertas* may suggest some sort of debate between
the personified figures of Poverty and Riches ; we remember

Novius' title *Mortis et Vitae Iudicium.* *Gemelli,* ' The Twins ',
suggests a favourite New Comedy subject, mistaken identity ;
but as the mimes are supposed to have been usually maskless, it
is hard to see how the necessary resemblance was obtained
between two actors ; perhaps ' The Twins ' are Castor and
Pollux, and the play a burlesque. The titles ' Ram ', ' Bull ',
' Twins ', ' Crab ', ' Virgin ', suggest that Laberius wrote a
whole set of pieces named after the signs of the zodiac—one
would infer that such pieces must have been short.

There is evidence in the fragments that these mimes were
indecent in subject and language and that they dealt with the
traditional mime-theme, adultery (for which Laberius seems
to have invented a set of technical terms, moechimonium,
adulterio, adulteritas) and unnatural vice. A line in the
' Needle-woman ' (' our mistress loves her stepson to distrac-
tion ') suggests some such plot as that of the Oxyrhynchus Mime,
including perhaps an attempt to get rid of the unwanted
husband by poison ; we have three references to drowsiness or
sleeping-draughts (3, 10, 86) which perhaps point to the
felonious administration of drugs. The guilty stepmother may
have been detected in time ; perhaps she is betrayed by the
stepson, who remarks ' I see your wife, my stepmother, being
stoned by the people '. Another mime-theme, the utterance of
an outlandish tongue or gibberish (such as the pseudo-Indian of
the Oxyrhynchus Farce, see p. 62), may appear in the remark ' I
didn't realize that you spoke Moorish '. The typical mime-
theme of stupidity may have been prominent in ' The Man with
a bad Memory ', with its fragment ' This is that dolt who came
to me from Africa two months ago '. The traditional fondness
of the mime for topical allusions of the most biting kind is
illustrated by a reference to some plunderer of his province
(such as Verres), an allusion to Caesar's creation of Market-
overseers and his supposed plan to legalize bigamy, and a line
in the famous prologue · ' Roman citizens ! we are losing our
liberties ! ' The homely style of some passages is illustrated in
the regrets expressed by some one for having come out of his
cottage or shop (taberna) in the rain. The fuller, treading the
clothes in the tank, is compared to a Balearic crane. Philosophers are always fair game for the comedian ; we have
scoffing references to the Cynics and Pythagoreans. Did the
Ephebus contain a scene in heaven, where the gods discuss the

destiny of Rome ?   Apparently Jupiter is asked to curb the
lust and licence of the gens togata ;   perhaps it is Juno who
declares with bitterness that the gods have bestowed on the
gens togata their wide empire.   A striking passage of the *Restio*,
perhaps from the prologue, sets forth the feelings of a rich and
miserly father who sees his riches being squandered by his son.
' The philosopher Democritus of Abdera set a shield to catch
the sun's rays in order to dazzle and blind his own eyes and
prevent himself from seeing the good fortune of wicked citizens.
So I too wish to make the gleam of money blind the end of my
days, in order not to see my worthless son in luxury.'

We still find the Latin comic genius pursuing the pun in
such lines as :

> delenimenta
> ad amorem deliramenta, ueneficia autem beneficia
> sunt.

There is a Plautine ring in

> non mammosa, non annosa, non bibosa, non procax.

We are told, indeed, that Laberius took liberties with the
language, used forms of doubtful Latinity and made slang
fashionable (e.g. manuarius for ' thief ') (Gell. 16.7).

Horace [28] admits Laberius' farcical power, but says that this
is not enough in itself to entitle his pieces to admiration as
' fine poems '.   The fragments are all written in the usual
metres of stage declamation ;   of ' lyrical ' metres (so-called)
there is only the slightest trace.

The successful rival of Laberius, Publilius Syrus,[29] was, as
his name implies, a slave from Syria, gifted with the wit for
which Syrians were noted.   His qualities of mind as well as his
grace of body won for him freedom, education and patronage.
He made his fame as a writer and actor of mimes in the provincial towns of Italy ;   then, coming to Rome for the ludi
Caesaris of 46 or 45, he challenged his rivals to extempore
performance, and was victorious over them all, including
Laberius.   The high place in Caesar's favour of the ex-slave
mime-writer once more illustrates the liking of despots for the
entertainments of the common people.   As we should expect
in the case of pieces which seem to have been largely extempore,
very little is left of Syrus' mimes.   There are two doubtful
titles, two not very enlightening fragments and a passage

sixteen lines long denouncing the extravagance of the Romans, which is quoted by Trimalchio (Petr. 55.5) as the work of Syrus, but is usually thought now to be an imitation of Syrus' style composed by Petronius himself; most surprising of all, we have a vast collection of moral sayings and epigrams attributed to Syrus; many of them must be genuine. Their high ethical standard surprised Seneca,[30] who observes that they are worthy of tragedy rather than mime. Evidently the Romans liked a graver element to be included even in the outrageous foolery of the mime; such lines as

O uitam misero longam, felici breuem !

show that Syrus had more in him than mimicae ineptiae and jests aimed at the gallery (uerba ad summam caueam spectantia), and we are told that these very epigrams were capable of bringing down the house (non uides quemadmodum theatra consonent quotiens aliqua dicta sunt quae publice adgnoscimus et consensu uera esse testamur ?).

With Laberius and Syrus we have come down to the very end of the Republic. All the forms of drama known to the Republican stage have now been described. In accordance with the general plan of this work, I will now try to give some account of how these plays were produced and staged, relying for information where possible on the text of the plays themselves.

CHAPTER XIX

THE LATIN PROLOGUES AND THEIR VALUE AS EVIDENCE FOR THEATRICAL CONDITIONS

ALL THE plays of Terence and most of the plays of Plautus are introduced by prologues. The prologues of Terence are the author's replies to the attacks of his enemies ; clearly, therefore, they are written by Terence himself, and they reflect the conditions of his own day. The origin of the Plautine prologues is not so clear. The prologue to the *Casina* specifically refers to a revival performance of the play some time after the death of Plautus, but still within the lifetime of some who had seen the play when it was first produced. Evidently this prologue is, at least in part, post-Plautine, and equally evidently the post-Plautine part at least is not translated from a Greek original but is of Latin origin. The two-line prologue to the *Pseudolus* ('You had better get up and stretch your legs ; a long Plautine play is coming on the stage ') also seems to be post-Plautine. The speaker of the prologue to the *Menaechmi* remarks 'I bring you Plautus—on my tongue, not in my hand '. Would Plautus have referred to himself quite in these terms ? Hardly any Plautine prologues can be positively said to contain a contemporary reference which must have been written by Plautus himself. (But see *Cist.* 197-202). I think, however, that even where we may suspect the presence of post-Plautine insertions, such insertions should still be ascribed, like the *Casina* prologue, to a period not long after the death of Plautus. They are presumably the work of producers—for who but a producer would have had either the opportunity or the motive for tampering with the text ? They belong therefore to a period when the theatre was active and before the text had been established by editors for the benefit of a reading public. They are thus good evidence for the theatre of the second century. On the other hand some parts of some prologues may conceivably be translated from the Greek—presumably by Plautus himself. But references to

theatrical conditions can scarcely have been taken over from
the Greek original. Descriptions of the actual conditions in the
Greek theatre would not have been appropriate to the Roman
theatre ; and no sane dramatist would have taken over
descriptive passages of such a kind (supposing he found
them in his original) without modifying and adapting them
to the conditions of his own day.

We have very little direct evidence concerning the prologues of Greek New Comedy. We know that gods sometimes
appeared to give the audience necessary information about the
dramatic situation. The *Perikeiromene* of Menander contained
a prologue of this kind, spoken by the goddess Misapprehension,
of which part is preserved. The tone of this unique fragment
is matter of fact ; the goddess appears to take it for granted
that the spectators are interested in the play, and she makes no
attempt to enliven her narrative with jokes, appeals, promises
or topical allusions of any kind. This is a ' deferred ' prologue,
spoken, that is, not at the beginning of the play but after some
scenes have already been performed. It is quite as sober in
tone as the explanatory prologues of Euripides. We have also
some slight references in Middle and New Comedy [1] to literary
topics—and one or two of these seem to occur in prologues ;
indeed, they deal with the use of the explanatory prologue and
kindred matters. The prologues of Plautus and Terence are
quite different from what we know of the Greek prologues.
The difference is that between information and propaganda.
The Latin writers are not able to assume that their audience is
interested in the play. Their prologues are designed above all
things to secure a hearing for the play.

The Plautine prologues have a genial air. The speaker
takes his audience as he finds them. His object is to give them
what they like. The prologues of Terence are earnest, dis-
trustful, plaintive. Terence wishes to give the audience what
they ought to like. It is hard to say which writer gives us the
more dismal impression of the Roman public.

The purely informative prologue would not have done, it
seems, for the Roman audience. The dramatist had to win
their attention at the very beginning. But how ? That was
the problem. An appeal for silence, a joke, a promise that the
play will be amusing, a topical allusion might be successful.
Alternatively it might be better to have no prologue but begin

the play right away with a lively or impressive scene. A possible compromise is to give the needed information in a 'deferred' prologue, such as that spoken by the goddess Auxilium in the *Cistellaria*, which is factual enough to be considered a direct translation from the Greek. When Plautus does give information at the beginning of the play, we notice that he sometimes promises to be brief :

> nunc argumentum accipite atque animum aduortite ;
> quam potero in uerba conferam paucissuma (*Men.* 5, 6).

So too *As.* 8, *Trin.* 4-5. Evidently the dramatist was in a dilemma. If he gave too much information the audience might get bored. If he gave too little they might get confused. He may have felt that it was only by being discursive, by interjecting comedians' patter and by tricks of all kinds, that he could hold the attention of his audience while imparting the necessary information. He had to consider tactics rather than strategy.

For the Romans the theatre was essentially a place of entertainment ; what they expected of comedy was that it should amuse them. The theatre had to compete with other forms of entertainment such as rope-dancing. Failure to make an immediate impression might result in empty benches, as the two prologues to Terence's *Hecyra* show. Faced by such a possibility, the dramatist is compelled to cry his wares :

> inest lepos ludusque in hac comoedia ;
> ridicula res est !

(*As.* 13-4). Such promises were intended to secure the necessary silence and attention :

> ita huic facietis fabulae silentium,

(*Amph.* 15 ; so too *Capt.* 54, *Poen.* 3).

The Plautine prologues were meant to amuse, and should not always be taken literally. For instance we can hardly assume that the comic injunctions issued to married ladies, nurses and courtesans were intended to be obeyed ; but they do at least imply that women were present among the audience. The prologues of Terence were not meant to amuse, but sometimes, perhaps, they were meant to mislead.

DEVELOPMENT OF THE DRAMATIC FESTIVALS IN ROME

All dramatic performances in Rome were given as part of some festival. From the beginning the festivals were associated with the State religion, and they always retained an official air. Apart from festivals intended for a particular occasion (such as funeral games) all ludi were under the charge of magistrates ; expenses were defrayed by the State, the presiding magistrates, or other wealthy individuals, and entry was free for the whole population. The ludi scenici, or public festivals which included dramatic performances, were :

Title	In honour of	Instituted	Made scenic	Magistrates : Date	Duration under Empire
1 Romani	Jupiter	? 6th cent.	364 B.C.	Cur. aediles 15 Sept.	4-19 Sept.
2 Florales	Flora	238 (made annual 173)	?	Cur. aediles 28 April	28 April- 3 May
3 Plebei	Jupiter	? 220	By 200	Pleb. aediles 15 Nov.	4-17 Nov.
4 Apollinares	Apollo	212	By 169	Praet. urb. 13 July	6-13 July
5 Megalensia	Gt. Mother	204	By 194	Cur. aediles 4 April	4-10 April

The festivals included other amusements—circus races, gladiatorial fights, beast-fights, wrestling, boxing, rope-dancing etc ; sometimes these rival attractions were taking place simultaneously with the dramatic performance. The place of performance varied ; races were naturally given in the circus ; in the days before Rome had a permanent theatre, plays would be shown in an improvised theatre, erected, perhaps, near the temple of the god in whose honour the festival was given. There were also special games, such as the ludi uotiui given at the inauguration of some public building, games in celebration of a triumph or other happy event, and funeral games in honour of some deceased nobleman. Like the regular ludi, these special ludi continued to grow more lengthy and magnificent ; by the end of the Republic and still more under the Empire there were frequent occasions during the summer months on which the public could see dramatic performances. In the winter, from late November to March, open air performances were necessarily suspended ; Juvenal[2] tells us that then the devotees of the theatre had to be content with private theatricals.

While all ludi aimed at winning public favour, and those who gave the games taxed their resources more and more extravagantly to secure this result, State supervision kept the freedom of the performers within certain bounds. The fact that so large a part of the electorate were assembled had a political significance. They were worth entertaining because they had votes ; but any attempt to use the theatre for a political demonstration was watched with a jealous eye. The comparative decency of Latin comedy (as distinct from farce and mime) may perhaps be attributed to the official character of the games; but at the merry Florales,[3] as we have seen, licence went so far as to allow the mime-actresses to appear naked.

This is a general account of the festivals of the Republic. In the time of Plautus things were on a simpler scale. Kurrelmeyer calculates that in 240 B.C. there was probably only one day in the year for plays ; by 214 this had increased to four days of the Ludi Romani. From 200 we can add at least one day of the Ludi Plebei, and from 191 at least one of the Ludi Megalenses (didascaliae to *Stichus* and *Pseudolus*). ' Before 200 B.C. therefore there is no definite evidence that there were more than four days on which the public games included ludi scaenici, though by 190 B.C. the number may have been increased to seven or eight.' (Kurrelmeyer, *Economy of Actors in Plautus*, p. 7). More than one play may have been produced in the same day (*Pseud.* prol.), but still the opportunities for dramatists and actors were very limited—and it is not easy to see how the actors earned their living during the 51 weeks when they were not acting. Perhaps they took part in Atellane farces, mimes and the like. Plautus himself may have done so, if the explanation of his name as indicating that he was planis pedibus is to be connected with planipes, ' flatfoot ' or ' barefoot ', the mime (see p. 47). Maccus, the author of the *Mercator* and *Asinaria*, according to the prologues, bears the name of one of the stock Atellane roles. The actors—and playwrights—of early Rome seem to have earned a meagre livelihood by entertaining the public and serving the great as opportunity offered—by dancing, singing, clowning, by writing lampoons or panegyrics, as their talents and their training allowed.

CHAPTER XX

THE ORGANIZATION OF THE ROMAN THEATRE

IN THE interval between the writing of a play and its appearance on the stage there is much to be done. On the organization of the early Roman theatre we have little information ; Plautus is almost silent, Terence is evasive, and the later writers may not have known the facts. Between the impecunious dramatist who wanted to sell his play, the general public who wanted to be amused at some one else's expense, and the ambitious magistrate who was willing to supplement the State grant (lucar) out of his own resources, an essential link was the producer and actor-manager. Such a man was Ambivius Turpio, the producer of Terence's plays. He bought the plays at his own expense (pretio emptas meo, *Hec.* 57) * though hoping no doubt to recoup himself with the money paid him by the magistrates (*Eun.* 20). In a prologue written for him by Terence (*Hec.* 14 ff), he claims to have encouraged Caecilius by bringing out his plays in spite of the unfavourable attitude of the public. He must have been the elderly actor who spoke the prologue to the *H.T.* He has a tone of dignity and authority as a man who is conscious of having befriended struggling dramatists, one who has not aimed at mere profit but has even incurred financial risks in fostering talent for the benefit of the public.

We do not know what sort of bargains the producer struck with the dramatist on the one hand and the magistrates on the other. The common-sense view seems to be that the dramatist sold his manuscript outright to the producer, who acquired thereby the right to perform the play as often as he liked and found practicable. If we are to take *Bacch.* 214–5 at its face value, Plautus must have quarrelled with Pellio after selling the *Epidicus*. ' Though I am as fond of the *Epidicus* as of my own self, I cannot bear seeing it if Pellio is taking the (leading)

---

* But see Clift (*Latin Pseudepigrapha*, p. 42) who takes these words to mean ' bought ' (sc. by the aediles) ' at my own price '.

part.' This suggests that revival performances of Plautus' plays were given in his own lifetime, but that he had no control over them. Terence evidently kept on better terms with Ambivius Turpio. After each of the two failures of the *Hecyra* the manuscript was returned to the author, who added on each occasion a prologue. The first of these prologues, after mentioning how the opening performance was ruined by the counter-attraction of the rope-dancer, adds ' Now the play is as good as new, and the dramatist did not wish to produce it again in order to sell it again '. Like all of Terence's personal utterances, this cryptic remark is presumably a reply to an accusation. I imagine that rumour had said ' He is trying to revive his old play merely to pocket a second fee '. Such a charge would indeed carry with it the absurd implication that failure might be more profitable than success. Terence briefly answers ' That is *not* my reason '. The true reason was that neither Terence nor Ambivius Turpio was willing to sit down under defeat ; moreover Terence was proud of the *Hecyra*, and meant to persist until he secured it a fair hearing.

The manuscript of a play presumably remained the property of the producer until he sold or bequeathed it to some other producer. It owed its preservation to its commercial value. Some plays, it is true, were preserved which had little value to a producer—for example the archaic plays of Andronicus.[1] The prologues of Terence had no commercial value, but they were preserved as part of the precious manuscript.

Plautus does not trouble to mention that his plays are new ; Terence takes care to point out that *his* plays have not been seen before. It may be that by Terence's day producers had grown over-fond of reviving the plays which they already possessed, and for the use of which they had no need to fee an author. The post-Plautine prologue to the *Casina* actually claims that plays, like wine, are all the better for being old— for the new plays are worthless. This is making a virtue of necessity, or at least economy. A new play meant a fee to the writer. Suetonius tells us that Terence's [2] *Eunuchus* won for its author the unprecedented sum of 8000 sesterces, and that this payment was recorded on the title page of the manuscript. The other fees received by Terence must therefore have been smaller. In six years he produced six plays ; his income must have been meagre compared with the half-million sesterces earned annually by the actor Roscius[3] in the next century. Terence says[4] that failure would mean starvation for him. Though drama offered almost the only means of earning a living by one's pen, it can hardly have yielded a fortune.

Ambivius Turpio was responsible not only for the purchase of the play from the author but also for its performance ; he acted with the other members of his company. These functions may sometimes have been divided ; the prologue to the *Asinaria* (line 3) speaks of the grex or troupe of actors, the domini or ' masters ' of the troupe, and the conductores or persons who ' undertook ' the contract to produce the play. We hear occasionally of the choragus or property-manager, who hired the costumes to the actors ; in the *Curculio*[5] Plautus brings him on the stage to express his uneasiness about the prospect of recovering his property.

The actors are usually called histriones ; another word is cantores, as all actors had to be able to declaim. They were organized into a troupe (grex, caterua). It is commonly said that all actors were slaves, or at best freedmen. This is true of professional actors in imperial times, but we have some evidence that the acting profession had not always been so despised. Livy (see p. 17) speaks of a time when the young citizens of Rome had thought it no shame to act in public, and of how Andronicus, ' like all (the dramatists) of his day ' had acted in his own plays. What truth there is in these remarks we do not know. It seems clear that Ambivius Turpio was a man of some consequence, while in Cicero's day the comic actor Roscius was the friend of Cicero ; Sulla made him a knight, and Cicero thought him worthy to be a senator. That Roscius[6] began as a slave is a probably wrong inference from Pliny *N.H.* vii. 128. He made a large fortune by his acting, he was a teacher of his art and wrote a book about it. His contemporary, the tragic actor Aesopus, left a fortune of twenty million sesterces. Evidently the profession of acting was not in itself a bar to social advancement ; a sharp contrast is presented by the mime. Laberius, as we have said, felt disgraced when compelled by Julius Caesar to perform in one of his own mimes (domum reuortor mimus) : by his appearance on the stage he forfeited his equestrian status, which was restored to him after the performance by the Dictator.

Nevertheless the social status of the average actor in tragedy or comedy was probably not high. The very fact that actors were organized in a troupe under a dominus suggests something not far removed from slave status. Of course they enjoyed a far pleasanter lot than the degraded slaves of an Italian plantation ; indeed when we consider on how few occasions in the year plays could be performed, we may feel that actors needed some master or patron to maintain them, or that they made a living as public entertainers, dancers, singers, etc.* The epilogue to the *Cistellaria* tells the audience that the actors are retiring to take off their costumes ; then those who have acted well will get a drink, those who have acted badly will be thrashed. This is perhaps a joke, but we cannot easily imagine such a remark being made in the theatre of Dionysus. The increasing vulgarity of the Roman audience must have tended to degrade the status of those who performed to amuse that audience. Polybius [7] tells us that in 167 B.C. the eminent Greek musicians assembled on the stage found that the readiest way to please the crowd was to indulge in a mimic battle.

It is often said that in Rome companies were larger than in Greece. There seems to be no evidence for this except the remarks of late grammarians,[8] who may have been thinking of the crowds brought on the stage in shows of the late Republic and the Empire. The Roman stage-tradition was derived from the Greek ; in Greece the number of trained actors was kept small. The Greek use of masks and the limitation of the number of characters who may speak in any one scene made it possible for a company of three or four to divide between them a considerable number of parts, thereby securing economy and efficiency. How far the Roman actors followed the Greek custom of each taking more than one part we cannot tell ;† all we can say is that the Latin plays are so constructed that a company of five trained actors (aided on occasion by mutes) could perform almost any scene in Latin comedy.

Competition between different companies was keen ; every member in each team was therefore on his mettle. We have references [9] to prizes awarded to companies or individual

* Cf. *Rudens* 535.

† There was certainly *some* doubling on the Roman stage ; cf. ibo, alius nunc fieri uolo. (*Poen.* 126). The *positive* Greek evidence for doubling is slight (*D.F.* 139).

actors, and indeed to unfair canvassing by actors for such prizes. We hear of how they stationed their supporters throughout the theatre with instructions to applaud at the right moment, of solicitation in person or by letter, and even of attempts to bribe the magistrates.

Crassus Diues,[10] curule aedile in 211 B.C., is said to have been the first to present gold and silver crowns. That good acting might give a bad play undeserved success is suggested by Terence (*Phor.* 9, 10) ; Plautus remarks that bad acting may spoil a good play (*Bacch.* 214–5).

A musical element was present in all Greek and Roman drama. Greek New Comedy had reduced this element, but not removed it (it occurs in Menander's dialogue, as well as in the choral dances), and on the Latin stage it was increased to a degree which we may find hard to realize. The greater part of most Latin plays was declaimed to musical accompaniment. The musician had two pipes, each about twenty inches long, bound to his mouth by a bandage round his head, so as to leave his hands free to work the stops. The pipes were called pares if they were of the same length and impares if one was longer than the other. With one, it is supposed, the musician played the air, with the other an accompaniment.* Such pipes have been found at Pompeii, and we have illustrations showing the musician standing among the actors on the stage and accompanying their words. Of all the wealth of metres which we find in the plays of Plautus only one—the six-foot iambic line—is employed for plain speech without musical accompaniment.† And so in the *Stichus* of Plautus, when the slaves are holding a drinking-party and decide to give the musician a drink too, the metre changes to six-foot iambics for seven lines (762–8) while the tibicen is drinking. A prefatory note in the oldest manuscript tells us that the music for the *Stichus* was ' made ' by Marcipor, slave of Oppius. Perhaps he was both composer and performer. Flaccus, slave of Claudius, ' made ' the music for Terence's plays. The tibicen must have had considerable powers of memory ; each leading ' part,' it would appear, had its

* This view is rejected by the *Oxford Classical Dictionary* (*s.v. Music*, 9, ii.) : ' if . . . there was some device . . . to allow the pipes to speak separately, the two instruments may have combined to produce a more extended scale.'

† It should perhaps be added that the Romans did not distinguish as sharply as we do between speech and song ; see chapter xxvi.

traditional music, and as soon as the tibicen struck up the overture, connoisseurs knew what character was to appear.*

It is commonly said that on the Roman stage trained vocalists were employed to sing the cantica or songs, while the actor accompanied the words in dumb show. This seems to have arisen from confusion in Livy's account [11] between the pantomime and drama proper. To try to divide the spoken parts from the sung parts in this way would make Latin comedy, as we have it, unstageable. We must suppose either that the actors were unable to ' sing ' (in which case they must have remained silent throughout the greater part of the play) or that they were able to ' sing ' (in which case they had no need of the vocalists). To suppose that the vocalists sang from behind the scenes is inconsistent with the account in Livy, our sole authority on this matter.

We hear incidentally in the prologues of various servants of the theatre. The crier (praeco) may sometimes have been called on to ask for silence at the commencement of a performance (*Poen.* 11). The dissignator (*Poen.* 19–20) showed people to their seats. The conquistores (*Amph.* 65) saw that order was kept—but perhaps this was not a regular office. There must have been stage carpenters, stage-hands, cleaners and the like, who could probably don mask and costume and take a ' mute ' part at a pinch. In the course of time men were needed to work the curtain ; to these the signal was given when time-keepers known as scabillarii † tapped their specially designed wooden shoes on the floor.

A more exalted official of the late Republic was the censor of plays. In earlier times it may be that the magistrates who sponsored the performance were left to satisfy themselves that the play to be shown contained nothing offensive. The prologue to the *Eunuchus* tells us of a preliminary performance given in the presence of the magistrates and of certain other interested persons such as Terence's rival, Luscius Lanuvinus. While there is nothing in this passage to indicate that a preliminary performance was in any way an unusual expedient, we have no other reference to such an arrangement. Perhaps the continual criticism of Terence's methods had induced the

---

* Cic. *Acad.* II. 20, primo inflatu tibicinis Antiopam esse aiunt, aut Andromacham, cum id nos ne suspicemur quidem. But is the reference to drama, or to some early form of pantomime ?

† See the illustration in *Daremberg et Saglio*.

magistrates on this occasion to demand an opportunity to see the play before it was shown to the public.

It is not easy to say whether any notice of a forthcoming performance was given to the public. In later times notices were displayed giving an account of the various attractions to be provided at the games. Some of Plautus' prologues seem to take it for granted that the public do not know the name of the play they are going to see or of its Greek author or Latin adaptor. Terence, on the contrary, does not find it necessary to give his name in his prologues. In the prologue to the *H.T.*, after announcing the title, he says that he would add his own name and that of the Greek writer but for the fact that they are already known to most of the audience. Indeed it would appear that there had been only too much public discussion before the appearance of each of Terence's plays. Whatever previous notice had been given, it could not be taken for granted that every member of the audience had seen it. I have already referred to Cicero's remark that the opening bars of the musical overture indicated to connoisseurs the name of the character represented. This implies that neither connoisseurs nor the general public had previously known what character was to appear. What is certain is that in Imperial times prospective theatregoers in Pompeii were informed by notices painted in public places that if they went to the games on a certain date they would find awnings * to shield them from the sun and showers [12] of perfumed water to temper the sultry air. Similarly, while it seems plain from the prologues of Plautus that there were no programmes to help the spectators to follow the play, Ovid speaks of programmes [13] as being available at circus races and gladiatorial shows, and of how skilful use of the programme might enable a young gentleman to ingratiate himself with the girl sitting in the next seat. But we have no evidence that programmes were ever used in the theatre. In Imperial times there were theatre-tickets indicating where the holder was to sit ;† probably these were held by certain privileged spectators. Reservation of seats [14] for senators and (later) equites had been a practice from Republican times onwards, and seems to have caused much ill-feeling among the under-privileged.

* Lucretius (iv. 75–83) mentions the magnificent coloured *vela* spread over the whole theatre, which, by excluding the glare of the sun, added to the effect of the decorated stage.   † See page 175 and Bieber, *Theater*, figs. 455–7.

CHAPTER XXI

SEATS IN THE ROMAN THEATRE

LET US now imagine ourselves present at a performance in the time of Plautus or Terence, and look about us in the theatre. The theatre consisted of two main parts, the scaena and the cauea, the scaena for the actors, the cauea for the spectators. Let us take the cauea first and ask ourselves what sort of accommodation was provided for the spectators, and what can be known about the spectators themselves.

A difficulty meets us at the outset. Were seats provided for the spectators? Ritschl denied this on the authority of a passage in Tacitus (*Ann.* xiv. 20), and consequently regarded all references in the prologues to seats as proof that these prologues could not have been written before the year 145 B.C. Ritschl's view is now generally abandoned. (See Appendix A).

We may consider at this point a number of references in Livy[1] to seats in the first half of the second century B.C. In 194 special seats were, according to Livy, assigned to the senators. In 179 the consul Lepidus ordered the construction of a ' theatre and stage ' near the temple of Apollo (theatrum et proscenium ad Apollinis) ; here the word theatrum denotes, as in Greek, the auditorium—what the Romans called the cauea. In 174 the censors undertook the construction of a stage which was to be of use to magistrates giving shows in the future (scaenam aedilibus praetoribusque praebendam), but this again seems to have been only a temporary structure. In 155 a stone theatre was planned and its building begun near the Palatine, but Puritanical opposition, led by the consul Publius Cornelius Nasica, not only secured the destruction of this theatre but prevented for some time the customary erection of tiers of seats for the spectators, who were therefore forced to stand (Livy *Epit.* xlviii). No permanent stone theatre was erected until the building of the theatre of Pompey in 55 B.C. In the light of these records we can perhaps understand why Tacitus[2] makes the diehards of Nero's day claim that in the good old days, before the building of Pompey's theatre, both the stage and the seating had been mere temporary structures, and that at an earlier period still the spectators had been compelled to remain standing ' lest, if they were allowed to sit, they should spend whole days idling in the theatre '.

The Roman theatre had from an early period drawn upon itself the suspicions of respectable citizens. We can see an attempt to placate this Puritanical opposition in the prologue and epilogue to the *Captiui*. In the eyes of such opponents of the theatre the occasional erection of a temporary structure, to be demolished after the games were over, was one thing : the building of a permanent stone theatre quite another. The project of building the Theatre Royal in Bristol in the year 1764 was opposed by the Quakers and Methodists, who feared that it would ' diffuse an habit of idleness, indolence and debauchery throughout this once industrious city'. But there can be no doubt that seating, of however limited a character, was provided for the public of Plautus and Terence.

NOTE ON CURIO'S REVOLVING THEATRES

The elder Pliny (*N.H.* 36, §§ 116–120) gives a circumstantial account of the two wooden theatres built back to back by C. Curio in 50 B.C., which at a given moment revolved *on their axes* (while the spectators still occupied their seats) so as to meet along the diameter in the form of an amphitheatre. This account, rejected by P. W. (s.v. *amphitheatrum*), seems to me to involve a geometrical impossibility, as well as engineering problems which would baffle the twentieth century. Unfortunately its rejection casts some doubt on Pliny's previous description (§§ 114–5) of the theatre of Scaurus, with its three-storied scene-building and its 80,000 seats. As for Pliny's reference (35, § 23) to the scena erected by Claudius Pulcher (? the aedile of 99 B.C.), so realistically painted in perspective that ravens thought the painted tiles were real, its chief value is to confirm our other evidence that by ' scene-painting ' was meant merely the decoration of the scene-building. Cf. Val. Max. 2, 4, 6, and see below, p. 275.

CHAPTER XXII

THE SPECTATORS

ALL CLASSES went to the theatre. The show was given by the magistrates. Livy speaks of special places being reserved after 194 B.C. for the senators. The prologue to the *Poenulus* contains injunctions to married ladies (matronae), nurses with their infant charges, prostitutes, slaves (who are forbidden to occupy seats), lackeys (pedisequi), attendants on the magistrate (lictores). That women were present is stated by Terence also (*Hec.* 35).* Admission to the theatre was free ; the theatre tickets of Imperial times (which indicated where the holders were to sit) were probably as yet unknown. A tumultuous crowd of every age and condition and of both sexes poured into the theatre in search of fun and excitement, shouting to each other, laughing, quarrelling, fighting for seats. The State, which kept so jealous an ear for what was said on the stage, seems to have made little or no attempt to control the behaviour of the audience. The ushers (dissignatores) may have done something to maintain order ; but the playwright and the actors knew that it rested on their joint efforts to secure a hearing for the play, for no one else would come to their assistance.

In the modern theatre we pay for admission, and have a natural inducement to get our money's worth. We enter a building, and forget the outside world. Artificial lighting concentrates our eyes and our thoughts on the stage. It was quite otherwise in the early Roman theatre. The spectators might become aware that there were rival attractions close at hand. The first performance of the *Hecyra* failed because the public were more interested in a rope-dancer and a pair of boxers. The second, after a promising start, was broken up by a rumour that a gladiatorial display was about to take place.

* Vitruvius (V. iii. 1) tells us that ' at the play citizens with their wives and children remain seated in their enjoyment."

Apart from the reservation of special places for the senators after 194 B.C., the rule seems to have been first come, first served. The front seats* would naturally fill up soonest. Even after the play had begun the ushers might still be escorting late arrivals to their places (*Poen.* 19-20). People at the back had difficulty in hearing (*Capt.* 11-14). In one prologue a gentleman at the back is invited to walk up nearer to the stage. In another prostitutes are cautioned not to seat themselves on the stage itself (*Poen.* 17-18). Ladies are warned not to chatter ; nurses must not bring squalling children to the theatre. There must have been considerable bustle and confusion, particularly at the beginning. The actors had to make themselves heard over this din, and it is not surprising to find the speaker of a prologue declaring that he will not burst his lungs for any one (*Capt.* 14). Once the play was fairly started the actors might hope that the spectators would at any rate keep still. Indeed it may have been difficult to leave one's seat till the end of the performance. Hunger and thirst affected audiences then as now, but no provision for refreshment seems to have existed in the theatre. The audience are bluntly told (*Poen.* 6-10, 30-1) that there is nothing to satisfy their appetite except the play itself. Outside the theatre vendors of eatables plied their trade during the festival ; the lackeys are advised (*Poen.* 40-3) to make a dash to a neighbouring cookshop while the cakes are still hot. In the Greek theatres, we are told, vendors of refreshments[1] made the rounds of the auditorium during the performance ; apparently this was not the custom in Republican Rome. Quintilian tells us[2] that Augustus was shocked to see a knight drinking in the theatre, and sent a messenger to him to say ' When I want a drink, I go home '. ' Yes,' replied the knight, ' but the Emperor is not afraid of losing his place.' Decorum was probably less strict in the back seats. A play could probably be got through in a couple of hours ; those who wished might then make their escape before the next performance began.

Even after the days of Plautus and Terence, it seems that the actors had no light task in confronting so motley an audience. Public attention was fickle[3] ; the spectators were as much interested in each other as in the play. The arrival

---

* Except those (if any) which were reserved for privileged persons such as senators.

of an important public personage in the front seats, a remark
on the stage which might seem to be a topical allusion, a
mishap of any kind, might take their thoughts off the play.
Nevertheless we have evidence that the Roman audiences
were capable of following a scene with close attention. The
generous contest between Orestes and Pylades,[4] each trying
at the risk of his own life to save the other, brought the whole
theatre to their feet in enthusiasm. The very existence of
plays like the *Captivi* suggests that we should not too readily
despise the public for whose entertainment they were written.

Graeco-Roman Theatre Tickets (see *D.F.* pp. 272-5)

CHAPTER XXIII

THE STAGE AND THE ACTORS' HOUSE

OUR NOTIONS of the appearance of the Plautine stage are derived to some extent from the still visible remains of the imperial theatres, the extant illustrations dating from imperial times, and the description written by Vitruvius in the time of Augustus. Such information may be misleading. There is nothing more certain than that the imperial theatre was ornate, there is nothing more likely than that the Plautine theatre was simple. From the evidence of the plays I will endeavour to describe the simplest arrangement which would permit these plays to be staged.

The essential feature of the Roman theatre from the earliest times was the wooden stage; Plautus calls it [1] scaena or pro-scaenium,* and the Latin for ' dramatic festival ' is ludi scaenici. It was probably not more than five feet high, but may even in the days of Plautus have been of considerable length and some depth.† Between the stage and the foremost tier of seats lay a flat space, corresponding roughly to the Greek orchestra or ' dancing-place ' and called orchestra by later generations of Romans, but not normally used by Roman performers; here some movable seats were sometimes set for distinguished spectators. From the orchestra a short flight of steps led up to the stage; this flight of steps would have been convenient for any member of the public who wished to appear on the stage (like the prostitutes who are forbidden to do so in *Poen.* 17–8), but it does not seem to have been used by the actors in the performance of a play.

Behind the stage stood the actors' house or dressing-room, the front wall of which formed the permanent back-scene. At either end the stage was enclosed by the projecting wings of the actors' house. The front wall of the house was pierced

---

* Scaena can mean (1) scene-building, (2) stage, (3) a picture, whether on the stage (e.g. one of the panels displayed on the periacti) or not.
† This is the usual view, but in considering the evidence of the plays we should remember that actors can make surprising use of even a small stage.

V POET (MENANDER?) AND COMIC MUSE
CHOOSING THE MASKS (?)
Relief in the Lateran Museum

by three doorways containing folding-doors (normally kept closed). At either end of the stage an open passage or side-entrance led into the projecting wing (Vitruvius calls it uersura)[2] of the house. Thus actors had five means of communication between the stage and the dressing-room: the three doorways in the back-scene and the two side-entrances.

The doors must have been solidly constructed, for they had to stand a good deal of hard knocking. Apart from the doors, the back-scene seems to have been a blank wooden wall. The house was of modest height, and had a practicable roof. (There was as yet no roof over the stage). In *Amph.* 1008 Mercury announces his intention of climbing on to the roof from inside the house in order to drive Amphitruo from the door by emptying pots on his head.

The only object permanently to be seen on the stage was the altar, which figures in so many plays. There was probably as yet no scenery and no attempt to adapt the setting for any particular play or scene of a play. There was no drop-curtain; the back-scene, such as it was, lay permanently open to view.*

Our only evidence on these matters is the text of the plays —that is, the words which the dramatists put into the mouths of their characters. We have no direct evidence as to how these plays were actually staged. The responsibility for the staging and production belonged not to the dramatist but to the actor-manager. The dramatist was acquainted with the general conditions of the contemporary stage; but we have no evidence that he instructed the actor-manager as to how particular plays, or scenes in plays, were to be shown. It seems to me fallacious to argue from a particular reference in a play that there was something unusual in the way in which that play was actually staged—whether at the first production or at a revival performance. The actor-manager no doubt had his own ideas—which may not have been those of the dramatist, or of other managers. All that we can hope to establish is the general conditions necessary for the production of our Latin plays—which do not contain (and perhaps never did contain) any stage-directions other than what is implied by the words put into the mouths of the characters.

* See Appendix E. Vitruvius (V. v. 7) remarks that musicians would turn towards the stage-doors when they wished to obtain 'superior tonus.' Evidently the doors were still of wood in his day, though the rest of the scene-building was now built of stone.

THE CONVENTIONS AND PRACTICES OF
ROMAN STAGECRAFT

Roman drama owed what success it achieved not to the craft of the scene-painter but to the art of the dramatist and actor. That art was exercised according to the conventions of the ancient theatre, conventions accepted almost unconsciously by the contemporary audience, yet puzzling and surprising to the reader of another age and country. All drama rests upon convention of some kind. It is absurd that people should discuss their most intimate concerns within hearing of the public; yet without this convention drama would be impossible. Convention enables the imagination to redeem material deficiencies; yet a certain amount of realism in dress, scenery and properties has often been found helpful. When we attempt to use the Latin plays as evidence for the way in which they were staged, we have frequently to ask ourselves whether the passage we are considering is an instance of convention or of realism. The fact that an actor mentions some object as present may sometimes be evidence that that object was actually shown on the stage; at other times we know that the object was not and could not be shown to the eye, and therefore had to be suggested to the imagination by words and gestures. The entry of an actor carrying a lamp may serve to indicate that it is early morning; the lamp is real, the darkness is indicated by the actor's actions and words.

The modern convention which enables our theatre-going audience to see into the interior of a house would have startled the Greeks and Romans. Their basic convention was quite different. The stage represented for them an open street, or some other open place; they were the general public assembled on the other side of the street or in the open country, and looking at the buildings which fronted on the street or open space. Every scene, in order to be shown on the stage, had to be thought of as taking place in the open air. In Mediterranean countries much does take place in the open which in our latitude would occur indoors; but the real and sufficient reason for staging a banquet, a toilet-scene or a confidential conversation on the street was that otherwise such a scene could not be staged at all.

The expedients to which the dramatists are forced to

resort by this convention are evidence of the validity of the convention itself. If it is necessary to disclose what is supposed to be taking place within the house, a character on the stage may be asked to peep inside the door and report what he sees (*Bacch.* 833 ff.). The spectators can never look through those doors with their own eyes. The test case is the banquet in the *Asinaria*. The party begins indoors (ll. 745, 809-10), but at 828 the revellers appear ; are we to understand that, as the Loeb editor would have it, the doors are opened and they are shown just inside ? Admittedly this would make it easier to understand why Artemona, who comes out of her own house at line 851, does not see them till the Parasite points them out to her at line 880. But this solution raises more difficulties than it removes, and the evidence of the text is against it. Lines 828-9 (omitted by the Loeb editor, following Leo) show the party coming out and the slaves setting tables for them. Artemona's failure to see them at first is to be explained not by the presence of any physical obstacle but by the convention that the actor does not see what the dramatist does not want him to see ; in other words, she takes care not to look in their direction. Her dramatic irruption on the party would lose its effect if we supposed it to take place within the actors' house ; the wrangle between husband and wife must have occurred on the open stage. At line 940-1 Artemona carries her husband off, and the two remaining members of the party go into Philaenium's house.

Our modern stage convention enables us to look for a while into the interior of a house, which at the end of the scene will be hidden from us by the drop curtain. The ancient stage, which represented the open street, lay, like the street, permanently open to view. The plays of Plautus are so constructed as to make it clear that no drop curtain was used or known. Each play begins with an empty stage ; characters come from their houses or from one of the side-entrances, usually explaining in their opening words who they are, whence they have come and whither they are going. At the end of the play some pretext is made for getting the characters off the stage, but before they go one of them informs the audience that the play is over and asks for their applause. There is no such thing as an opening or final tableau ; and at the end of the play the stage is empty and set for the beginning of the next play. If in the course of the play some object has to be brought on the stage for a particular scene, we presently see it being taken away again when it has served its purpose. Of this we have a striking example in the *Mercator* : when the cook has set down his dishes at the door and walked off in high annoyance, the unhappy husband has to ask his wife to have the now detested dishes taken inside, lamely remarking that they will improve the family meal. (ll. 800–2.)

The absence of a curtain implies the absence of special scenery for any one play or scene in a play. The opening scenes of the *Rudens* present us with a picture of a wild landscape, covered with rocks, full of caves, overgrown with rushes. If we suppose that these features were actually depicted on the stage, then we have to face the dilemma that either they remained on the stage throughout the rest of the play (in which they are entirely ignored) or that they were bodily removed under the eyes of the spectators during the course of the play. It is much more likely that the references to the natural surroundings were addressed to the imagination, and that the efforts of the two girls to find each other (220–243) are frustrated for so long by nothing but the fact that they take care not to look in the right direction. It would, no doubt, as Dr. Pickard-Cambridge has suggested to me (cf. his *Theatre of Dionysus*, p. 68), have been a simple matter for the stage-carpenter to contrive a suitable setting for a particular occasion ; but such a setting would have been a positive embarrassment when the occasion for it was over. Yet how could it be removed ? The same considerations seem to apply to the setting of a play as a whole. That play succeeded play with the same permanent background seems to be indicated by *Pseud.* 1, 2, and *Men.* 72–6. Such as it was, therefore, the scenery probably remained unchanged from play to play.

Reduced to the barest terms, the permanent scenery consisted of the plain wall at the back with its three doors, the two projecting wings with the side-entrances, the flat roof of the actors' house, and on the stage itself an altar. The roof is actually used in the *Amphitruo* (1008 and frag. iv–vi) and would seem to be mentioned in *M.G.* 156 ff. and *Rud.* 85 ff. ; the five entrances were in constant use. The three doors at the back could represent one, two, or three separate houses *; perhaps the side-entrance on the right of the spectators was supposed to lead to the near distance, that on the left to the more remote distance. Thus if the action were laid in town the right-hand side-entrance might lead to the town centre, that on the left to the country and harbour. In the *Rudens* the setting is a lonely spot near the African sea-shore; in the background are the cottage of Daemones and the temple of Venus, represented by two of the three doors; the side-entrance on the right would lead to the beach near by, that on the left to the town and harbour of Cyrene. In *Amph.* 333, set in the city of Thebes, Sosia is speaking as he enters from the harbour, i.e. from the spectators' left; Mercury, facing the audience, says 'some one is speaking on my right'. Other relevant passages are *Men.* 555, *Rud.* 156, *And.* 734. The significance of the stage-doors and the side-entrances in any particular play is usually made clear in the prologue and in the remarks of the characters.†

In the normal way any one entering or leaving any of the ' houses' or making his way between the town centre on one side and the harbour or country on the other must appear on the stage. When for some reason the dramatist wishes to move a character from one of these places to another without bringing him on to the stage he falls back on another convention, the use of the angiportus (or angiportum).

The word angiportus means ' street', and can be used even of the street represented by the stage. Its special significance in drama is to denote the back-street supposed to run behind the houses which face on to the stage, connecting them by means of their back-doors and gardens with each other and also with the town, harbour and country. The angiportus is not shown and could not be shown to the eye; its use is exceptional, and receives express mention; it is a device which enables the dramatist to escape at times from the general rule that a character who leaves the stage by a particular door or wing must return by the same door or wing.‡

In order to make the plot easily intelligible to the spectators

* That unwanted doors were temporarily concealed by a curtain is conceivable, but unproved. In the *H.T.*³ the third door is used once, and only once, in the play. That the Greek dramatists sometimes used a two-door setting which the Latin dramatists have altered to a three-door setting is altogether unlikely; see Appendix G. † See Appendix B. In *Rud.* 156, *And.* 734, I have to suppose that the speaker has turned slightly away from the spectators.

‡ See Appendix C.

(and incidentally to help the actors when rehearsing the play) it is usual for each entrance on the stage to be announced before- hand. These announcements, which are part of the dialogue, serve as stage-directions, and were probably meant to give a waiting actor his cue. The general custom that a character already on the stage shall warn the audience that some one else is about to appear leads to some interesting results. That a character standing on the stage, which represents a street, should be able to see farther up and down the street than the spectators can see, and so should be able to perceive some one approaching from the town-centre or harbour before they can do so, is quite natural ; but it would not seem so natural for him to announce that some one is coming out of one of the house-doors, which faces the audience and is behind his back. This difficulty is got over by making the opening door creak and so draw the actor's attention. Like the whole of the actor's technique, this device is of Greek origin. Sometimes the Greek dramatist describes the person coming out from the house as ' striking ' the door (*i.e.* in the act of opening it). This phrase, misunderstood in late antiquity, gave rise to the absurd notion that the early Greeks knocked on doors not only when they wanted to go in but also when they were coming out.*

A grand principle of the stage was that a character saw and heard only what the dramatist meant him to see and hear. We are familiar with the situation in which one character spies on another and overhears his words while himself remaining (at least temporarily) unobserved. Both actors are on the stage, in full view of the spectators. There is no physical object on the stage behind which the eavesdropper can take shelter. He usually secures his temporary invisibility merely by standing at the back of the stage, and he is always liable to be detected as soon as the other actor allows himself to look in the right direction. This is absurd, perhaps, but no more absurd than that other convention of the ancient stage, the ' aside ', audible to thousands of spectators, yet inaudible, or only partly audible, to a character standing only a few yards from the speaker.

When we reflect on the fact that all the actors † wore masks

* See Appendix G.
† Excluding, perhaps, the speaker of the prologue when appearing in his own person.

and that a very large part of their lines was not spoken but declaimed to the accompaniment of the flute-player, we realize that the Roman style of acting must have differed widely from the naturalistic, conversational style of our own day. Our actors talk to each other ; the Roman actors declaimed to the audience. They stood, where possible, well to the front of the stage ; they faced the audience, they kept their eyes on the audience, they aimed above all things at making their words carry even to the farthest seats.* If an actor entered from a house-door he usually walked to the front of the stage, looking neither to his left nor to his right. This made it easy for others already on the stage to step back and observe him. A character coming in from a side-entrance would also address himself to the audience and turn as best he could towards them while making his way to the middle of the stage. It is thus not surprising if for some time he fails to notice the presence of other characters on the stage. To face the audience was very necessary if one's words were to carry to the back of the large, open-air theatre. The art of the actor lay not in naturalism or in mimicry but in clear utterance conveying the appropriate emotion and supported by appropriate gesture.[4] It seems probable that the actor made no attempt to alter his voice according to whether he was taking the part of a gentleman or a slave, a man or a woman (but see p. 145). In the same way the dramatist makes all his characters talk the same kind of Latin. The art of gesture, on the other hand, was carried in ancient times to a height which we can scarcely comprehend. When we try to imagine a scene from a Roman play, we must picture to ourselves the masked actors, their gestures, their carefully plotted movements on the stage, their voices raised in rhythmical declamation, while the flute-player stepped up now to one, now to another,† playing the accompaniment for each actor in turn. When we consider how widely the style of Roman acting must have differed from our own and how misleading Roman writers often are on this subject, we realize how dangerous it is to use our own notions of fitness as a guide to the practice of the Roman stage.

* Vitruvius (V. iii. 4) points out how important it is that the *case-endings* of words should be audible even in the " gods ". Of course I do not mean that an actor was *never* allowed to turn away from the spectators. See p. 181, note †.

† Cic. *Pro Mur.* 12, 26.

CHAPTER XXIV

COSTUMES AND MASKS *

IN THIS chapter my object is (1) to describe the costumes worn by actors in Republican times, (2) to show how these costumes were turned to account by the dramatists. The evidence used will be that of the extant plays and fragments. It is usual to supplement this evidence by reference to the statements of Pollux, Donatus and other late writers and to Campanian reliefs, wall-paintings, terra-cottas and the illustrations in certain medieval manuscripts of Terence. Unfortunately all of this material is of doubtful value, interesting when it is supported by the evidence of the plays, but otherwise only too likely to give a wrong impression.

Costume on the Roman stage evidently varied according to the type of drama, for it was used as the basis of classification of the different types of drama. Our complete plays belong to what Donatus (*De Com.* vi §§ 1 and 6) calls the palliata, comedy in which the characteristic dress was the pallium or Greek mantle of everyday wear. The Roman actors of the palliata, like the Greek actors of New Comedy, wore the ordinary Greek dress of contemporary life, with certain modifications which will be described. I shall begin by summarising the essential features of ordinary Greek dress, most of which are mentioned in the plays.

The undergarment was the Ionic chiton (Latin tunica), a linen or woollen shirt with holes for the neck and arms. Sometimes it had sleeves. It was drawn on over the head, and fastened with a girdle by which it could be tucked up if necessary. Sometimes the chiton was the only garment. But it was usual to wear outside the chiton the himation (Latin pallium), a woollen wrap, rectangular in shape, which was drawn round the body and adjusted in various ways. It was usually fastened with a clasp over one shoulder. Sometimes the pallium was the only garment. As the ordinary pallium

* See Appendices D and I, and Pickard-Cambridge, *Dramatic Festivals*, pp. 175–238.

was somewhat cumbrous, we find that where freedom of movement was required the pallium was not worn, or was worn in a special way. Workmen might wear the tunic alone. Others might wear outside the tunic the *chlamys*, a kind of light-weight pallium, often gay in colour (like our blazer).

Footwear for town (ἐμβάδες) was normally light : sandals (ὑποδήματα, soleae ; sometimes the Romans used the word crepidae, from the Greek κρηπίς), and slippers (called by the Romans *socci*). The sandal was fastened with thongs and bands ; the soccus had no fastenings.

The head was normally uncovered. But Greek workmen wore caps of felt (πῖλοι) or leather (κυναῖ). The broad-brimmed hat (petasos, causea) came with the chlamys from Thessaly, the two forming part of the characteristic costume of Athenian youths when serving in the cavalry. The petasos had a band which fastened it round the head, and a strap under the chin which could be used by the wearer to let the hat hang down his back. The Roman cap (pilleus) was similar to the conical πῖλος ; it was in particular the head-wear of newly emancipated slaves. The petasos was sometimes worn by Roman invalids or valetudinarians, as for example Augustus ; Caligula[1] sanctioned its use in the theatre as a protection against the sun.

Greek women, also, wore suitable sandals, chiton and himation (the Latin word for a woman's cloak is palla). As in real life, both in Athens and in Rome, there was no distinctive garb for slaves ; some town slaves might wear much the same clothes as their masters, others went barefoot.* Rustics, whether slave or free, might wear goatskins.

No doubt in real life there was much greater variety than would appear from this summary. Aristophanes mentions many kinds of garments and of footwear of which we hear nothing in New Comedy. No doubt, again, practical considerations would enforce simplicity of wardrobe on the actors of this cosmopolitan form of drama. We are often, indeed, asked to believe that custom prescribed a particular costume for every age and profession. Thus Donatus (i. 29–30) dealing with stage practice, tells us ' Old men in comedy are dressed in white, as that is said to be the oldest style ; young men wear garments which contrast with each other in colour.

* But not, I think, in the palliata ; see p. 188.

7*

Slaves in comedy wear a short garb, either because of the
poverty of early times or to allow of free movement. Parasites
wear their mantles wrapped ' (presumably in some special
way). ' White is the colour for a cheerful character ; a man in
trouble wears shabby clothes. Purple (purpureus) is the colour
for the rich, red (puniceus) for the poor. A Captain wears
a purple chlamys ; girls are dressed in foreign style. A pimp
wears a costume of variegated hue ; a harlot is given a yellow
mantle to indicate her avarice. Trailing robes (syrmata)
are worn by characters in grief to show their neglect of personal appearance.' Pollux, on the other hand (iv. 119 ff.)
says that young men wear a red or dark purple mantle, pimps
a ' dyed ' (presumably brightly dyed) tunic and ' flowery '
(presumably gay) mantle (as did the courtesans at Syracuse,
according to Phylarchus [2]), that young men wear white linen,
heiresses white (tunics) with a fringe, old women ' apple-
coloured ' (perhaps ' quince-yellow ') or sky-blue clothes,
except for the priestesses, who wear white ; bawds a bright red
ribbon round the head. We have also Pollux's detailed
description of forty-four masks used in comedy (nine for
old men, eleven for young men, seven for slaves, three for old
women, five for young women, seven for courtesans and two
for servant-maids). It is customary for modern writers
to say that as soon as a character appeared on the stage the
spectators knew from his appearance a good deal about
him : ' par elles ' (the colours) ' en même temps que par les
masques, le public était souvent instruit sur le champ de
l'âge, de la condition, du caractère même des personnages
qui entraient en scène. Cette convention avait passé dans
la comoedia palliata des Romains.' (Navarre, *Le Théâtre
grec*, pp. 225–6).

   I follow Navarre in holding that the Roman stage-
convention was based on the Greek—even with regard to the
use of masks. The actor's mask covered the whole head
(Gellius v. 7) and the hair belonging to a mask was coloured
to suit the part. Thus in general the elderly would appear
grey-haired, or in some cases partly bald ; the young would
usually have dark hair ; most slaves would have red hair.
Women's hair would look quite different from that of men.
But even these statements must be accepted with some reserve,
in view of the evidence of the plays.

Let us consider the practical necessities of the stage. As performance was continuous, actors had to be able to change their costumes in a very short time (sometimes within six lines).* Costumes, especially elaborate costumes, were expensive. The natural tendency would be to reduce the property manager's outfit to a limited number of costumes of as few types and as simple style as possible. Masks on the other hand were probably cheap. They had to be well differentiated from each other, for it was the mask which gave each character its identity. As in real life, so on the stage, one character would be known from another not by the clothes he wore but by his features. But if we were to enforce on the property-manager the rules laid down by Pollux and Donatus, we should greatly increase the extent and cost of the outfit. Moreover these writers are not in agreement with each other, or even with themselves. Old men, we are told by Donatus, are dressed in white ; but white is also the colour for a cheerful character. What is an old man to wear when he is not cheerful ? Even if we dismiss these minor questions, the main fact remains that Donatus and Pollux, as well as the ancient artists, were thinking in visual terms. But in the plays we get the impression that the appeal was not to the eye but to the ear and the imagination of the public.[3] When a new character appears, we are told in plain language who he is. It is only in special circumstances that stress is laid on his costume. Men dressed somewhat differently from women ; slaves of the rougher type, and some foreigners, were dressed to suit their part.; otherwise one would gather from the plays that all characters wore much the same clothes, a tunic, a pallium and (presumably) a pair of slippers or sandals. In fact costume is comparatively unimportant in New Comedy. But we are more aware of it in Plautus than in Terence or Menander.

Plautus, as a native of Italy, is conscious that his characters are dressed like Greeks, Graeci palliati (*Curc.* 288), in contrast to the spectators, who wear the toga (*Amph.* 68). He also realizes that the actor's costume costs money (*Curc.* 464–6 ; *Pers.* 157–160 ; *Trin.* 857–9 ; *Pseud.* 1184–6 ; *Amph.* 85), particularly when it is out of the ordinary. Little is said of footwear. Slaves wear slippers (*Epid.* 725 ; *Trin.* 720) like

* Kurrelmeyer, *Economy of actors in Plautus*, p. 19.

free men (*Heaut.* 124). Young men and women wear sandals, which they order to be removed when they are about to recline on a couch (*Most.* 384 ; *Truc.* 478, 631). On one occasion special sandals are worn as part of a foreign-looking disguise (*Pers.* 464). Perhaps we should conclude that 'slippers' and 'sandals' mean much the same thing, or that, if they were different, the normal wear was slippers. Indeed the soccus became a synonym for comedy of this kind (as contrasted with the high boot or cothurnus of tragedy, or with the barefooted mime). No character is said to be barefooted, or to have any footwear other than slippers or sandals. Though the tunic and the mantle are often mentioned, there is little evidence that one tunic or one pallium differed from another. A woman's palla differed from a man's pallium (*Men.* 191–2, cf. Aristophanes *Eccles.*) and a man may be disguised in woman's clothes (*Cas.* 769–70). A bridegroom wears white clothes (*Cas.* 767–8). Old men are evidently recognizable as such at sight—but this may be a matter of the mask and gait and not of the costume. The chlamys is worn instead of the pallium by soldiers, some travellers and some foreigners. The tunic is sometimes allowed to trail by women (and innkeepers). (*Po.* 1298–1303). There is a jesting reference to a sleeved tunic (*Ps.* 738).

We must allow for the fact that this is comedy, and that a dramatist may sometimes think fit to make fun of what is really the established convention, whether in dress or in anything else. The general impression I derive is that costume was more or less the same for all characters, that the profession of a character was sometimes indicated by such attributes as the cook's knife, the fisherman's hooks and line or his net, the soldier's sword and so on, and that it was the mask which gave the character his individuality within the play as a person of a particular age and temperament.* Costume becomes important when it is used to disguise a character. The disguise is usually outlandish: a character puts on a chlamys and a travelling hat and pretends to be a foreigner. He cannot change his mask, for the mask *is* the character. Therefore, if he wishes to deceive some one who knows him,

---

* The courtesan can pose as a respectable woman by merely altering her head-dress and her gait (*M.G.* 791–2, 872). (Apparently, then, it *was* possible to alter the appearance of the hair which went with the mask). In the fabula togata she would need a long robe as well (see p. 192, *n.*).

he must alter his appearance by wearing a patch over one or both eyes. The spectators will of course penetrate his disguise —for they must be able to recognize him. His victim will be deceived, because the dramatist so ordains it. (*Pers.* 155–6 ; *M.G.* 1177–81 ; *Ps.* 735 ; *Trin.* 771, 851 ; *Curc.* 392–5, 461–5, 505, 543–5).

The dramatist uses costume for his purposes ; he is not the slave of convention. Since the two Menaechmi must appear alike, the traveller from Syracuse is dressed just like his brother who appears from his own house. In the *Amphitruo* both Amphitruo and his slave Sosia wear hats, as having just arrived from abroad. But so do their divine doubles, Jupiter and Mercury, who are pretending to be leaving for abroad (142–6), but in fact do not leave. The writer of this prologue has considered a problem of staging : in the case of doubles, how are the spectators to know one from the other ? The solution here is that each of the gods will wear a distinguishing mark attached to, or under, his hat. Hence, we may suppose, the need for hats—which are actually worn by Sosia and Mercury in the opening scene, but are never mentioned again. Indeed Mercury must have removed his hat before he can think of putting on a garland (999). In fact there is no need for the hats or the distinguishing marks : Sosia and Mercury, when they meet in the opening scene, speak in character, and nobody could mistake one for the other. Besides, Sosia carries a lantern. The two Menaechmi are supposed to be exactly alike ; yet it is impossible to mistake one for the other. Each makes his identity clear by his words ; each enters and leaves by his own side-entrance ; the stolen palla which one or the other carries in turn helps further to identify him.

In the *Casina* (769, 814 ff.) a man dresses up as a girl. Apparently the 'bride's' breast is padded realistically (848) ; she does not speak, and we can imagine that her ' face ' was hidden by the bridal veil, worn in Greek as well as in Roman weddings.

The plot of the *Captiui* turns on the exchange of identity between master and slave. According to the prologue (37) Philocrates and Tyndarus have changed clothes ; but this is not in keeping with the text of the play ; for when Aristophontes meets and recognizes Tyndarus (541) he expresses no surprise at Tyndarus' clothes ; from which it would seem that neither Philocrates nor Tyndarus had worn a dress which was indicative of their status. It would further seem that neither wore a mask which was distinctively that of a slave. Hegio takes Philocrates to be the slave ; yet we know that he is really the gentleman ; besides, he will later appear (922) in his true character, and the spectators must be able to recognize his features. His appearance is described (647–8); we at once notice that he has red hair—like all the slaves whose hair is described in comedy. Evidently, then, red hair was not confined to slaves. Tyndarus cannot wear a slave-mask either ; for Hegio takes him for the master, and we know that he is really Hegio's son. Menaechmus of Epidamnus, when rescued by his brother's slave, addresses him simply as ' young man ' (1021–5). Some slaves dress like dandies (e.g. Tranio in the opening scene of the *Mostellaria*). There is a difference between one slave and another, no doubt ; Tranio is more elegant than Grumio, Trachalio is superior socially to Sceparnio or Gripus. But we have no evidence that on the stage, any more than in real life, it was possible to tell a slave at sight from a freeman. (Cf. *Pseud.* 610, where Harpax says to Pseudolus ' are you a free man or a slave ? ' also *Amph.* 343.)

The stress laid on such properties as the cook's knife, or the soldier's sword, itself suggests that the clothes worn were not in themselves indicative of profession. It is said by Pollux[4] that the parasite carried an oil flask and scraper as a professional badge. This is perhaps merely an inference from the plays ; the parasite is the poorest creature on earth ; all he has are the indispensable articles of toilet—but perhaps he keeps them at home. On the stage all he has—all he can pledge in a wager—is his pallium * (and presumably tunic and slippers).

In the prologue to the *Amphitruo* (116–7) Mercury refers to his ' slave's get-up ', ' seruile schema '. We cannot tell what in his appearance was particularly slave-like ; he wears tunic and cloak, travelling hat and beard. Perhaps all he means by ' seruile schema ' is ' in human guise ' (instead of appearing in divine form). So common is the wearing of the pallium with town-slaves that they have a special way of wrapping it round their necks when in a hurry.

* *Curc.* 355 ; *St.* 230.

We have thus reached the surprising conclusion that costume may have played comparatively little part in helping the spectators to follow a play. The costumes were not particularly distinctive. The mask distinguished the individual as such, but did not reveal his profession or status. It is taken for granted ; Plautus seldom or never draws attention to its use. Of course the references to facial expression in Latin as in Greek plays must not be taken to mean that the actor's own features were visible. Change of expression was impossible. Quintilian [5] indeed tells us of a mask with one cheerful and one serious eye, which enables the wearer to display to the spectators a different appearance according to the needs of the play. Such devices seem difficult to reconcile with the needs of the real stage. It is far better to suppose that language referring to change of feature is addressed to the imagination of the spectators, aided by the gestures of the actor.

STAGE COSTUME IN FORMS OF DRAMA OTHER THAN THE PALLIATA

Here we no longer have complete plays to help us, and the fragments throw little light on the subject. In tragedy translated from the Greek the actors wear Greek dress ; Varro used the term palliata of derivative tragedy as well as comedy. We nowhere find derivative tragedy distinguished from derivative comedy by the *dress* of the actors ; what we do find is that the high boot worn by Roman tragic actors (the Romans called it cothurnus) [2] is used as a synonym for tragedy, just as soccus is used to denote comedy. The Greeks did not use κόθορνος in this sense ; with them the cothurnus was worn by women (Ar. *Frogs* 47, 557; *Lys.* 657) and hunters. We have no compelling reason to believe that Greek tragic actors wore any exaggerated footwear; the high tragic boot, as well as the use of the word cothurnus to denote it, may have been of Italian origin. Horace uses cothurnus of 'tragedy'. But it seems unlikely that the Republican actors wore boots with the thick soles indicated (above the pegs) on the ivory statuette from Rieti. Perhaps we should picture the actors of Ennius' day as wearing a somewhat rich form of contemporary Greek dress ; Plautus (*Capt.* 61-2) indicates that the outfit for comedy was not adequate for the presentation of tragedy.

In native drama native dress was the rule ; on this point the Romans were sensitive. The toga would therefore be worn with appropriate Roman footwear both in native comedy and in historical drama ; both were included, according to Diomedes, under the title togata. But the characteristic purple-striped toga worn by Roman magistrates was used specifically to distinguish the historical play, fabula praetexta or praetextata, from native comedy as well as other forms of drama. The meagre fragments of the praetexta tell us nothing about costume ; in the togata we have references to the toga in *Tit.* 25, 44, to special patrician shoes (116), to the perfumed tunic and toga of some dandy (138), to ' white togas and dirty tunics ' (167-8), to some one found out-of-doors in sandals (which a Roman would have regarded as indoor wear, suitable for banquets) ; see *Afr.* 105. It seems clear, therefore, that the wear for actors in native comedy was toga, tunic and shoes.*

The fabula Atellana and the mime had each its own distinctive style. The Atellana was characterized by traditional masks ; we meet a bald fisherman (*Pomp.* 119) and a bald messenger (135). Masks are mentioned (*Nov.* 2). The mime was characterized by the bare feet of the typical performer. Laberius refers to the ' toga-wearing race ' (43, 45). He mentions a tunic (61).

Such is the meagre evidence which I have been able to glean from the fragments. It may be that these varieties of drama did not permanently adhere to the traditional costumes, but that they all tended to influence each other, in costume as well as in literary form.

THE USE OF MASKS[7] ON THE ROMAN STAGE

Greek drama was always a masked performance. The advantages of the use of masks are that it enables a small company to represent a considerable number of characters ; that the less important parts can thus be as well rendered as the leading rôles ; that the exaggeration inherent in mask-design enables spectators even at a distance to distinguish the

---

* Afranius (133-4) indicates that courtesans normally wore a short dress, although for safety's sake they might sometimes assume the stola of the Roman matrona.

features of the character represented ; that women's parts can
be taken by men ; that the appearance of characters can be
made to correspond with the requirements of the play ; above
all, perhaps, that the identity of the actor is concealed. The
Roman acting tradition was derived from the Greek. Nevertheless we are told by a late grammarian,[8] Diomedes, that at
first wigs, not masks, were used on the Roman stage ; masks,
he says, were introduced by Roscius to hide his squint. Donatus
names as the first ' masked actors ' Cincius Faliscus in comedy
and Minucius Prothymus in tragedy. Perhaps Donatus is
using the word personati simply as ' actors ' (of course in masks),
and his meaning is that these were the first Roman actors.
At any rate it is evident that Diomedes and Donatus are not
in agreement. Cicero, speaking of the importance of an
orator's play of features, speaks approvingly of those elder
contemporaries who ' did not speak very highly even of Roscius
when he had his mask on '. Again Cicero may be using
personatus as synonymous with ' actor ', his meaning being
that the orator necessarily has an advantage in the eyes of
good judges over even the best of actors, because his features
are visible. Possibly this very passage of Cicero was the source
of Diomedes' statement. It is the custom nowadays to accept
Diomedes' evidence, thus denying the use of masks to the
Roman stage in the time of Plautus and Terence. Further
evidence is sought in the references to facial expression which
occur in Latin comedy, e.g. *Adelphi* 643 ' he has blushed ; all
is well '.* But we find similar references in Greek drama, which
was certainly performed by masked actors. Terence uses
persona in the applied sense of ' character in a play ' (*Eun.*
26, 32, 35). If the original sense of persona was ' mask '
(possibly connected with the masked figure Phersu who appears
in some Etruscan paintings) we cannot explain Terence's
applied use except on the assumption that Terence was familiar
with the use of the mask to indicate the actor's rôle. The
mask was traditional in the fabula Atellana, and must have
been familiar to the Romans even before the introduction of
Greek drama in translation. It is hard to see why in adapting
Greek drama they should have denied themselves so useful a
device. Naevius is said by Festus to have written a comedy

---

* Of course the actor could not blush at will. The simple explanation of this
and similar passages is to be found in the use of gesture.

entitled *Personata* (? personata fabula), and Plautus' fond-ness for the theme of identity of appearance itself suggests that he took the mask for granted. He uses the word persolla, diminutive of persona (*Curc.* 192), in the sense of ' ugly face '. The frequent descriptions of the appearance of characters—including their faces—are more likely to have been descriptions of masks than of the actual features of members of the company. (See Appendix I.)

COSTUME OF PROLOGUE

To judge from *Hec.* 9, orator ad uos uenio ornatu prologi, it might seem that there was a special costume for the speaker of the prologue. Nevertheless this prologue is spoken by Ambivius Turpio in his own character ; he reminds the audience of how he had assisted Caecilius, and of his two failures to get a hearing for the *Hecyra*. It would therefore seem that he is not wearing a mask. We must compare with this line *Poen.* 123, 126. In the second of these lines the Prologue tells the spectators that he must now leave them in order to become ' a different character ', that is, to change his costume and take a part in the play. In line 123 he has said ' I will go and put on my costume ', which suggests that at the moment he is speaking in his own character, without a mask. A special prologue-mask would seem quite inappropriate for the speaker of any of Terence's prologues, and also, probably, for the *Asinaria, Captiui, Casina, Menaechmi, Poenulus, Pseudolus, Trucu-lentus*, and *Vidularia*. But when the prologue is spoken by one of the characters in the play, he will naturally wear the costume and mask of his part. In the *Mercator*, for example, the hero himself introduces the play to us. In the *Rudens*, again, the prologue is spoken by the god Arcturus, who apparently wears a ' bright star '. The deferred prologue is always put into the mouth of a character in the play or some other fictitious person, such as ' Help ' or ' Misapprehension '. The weight of evidence seems to be against the view that there was a special costume for the Prologue as such. In all probability he wore (if not the toga) the usual tunic, pallium and slippers, but *no mask ;* and was therefore recognizable at once as speaking in his own person and on behalf of the dramatist. Apparently, then, in *Hec.* 9 Ambivius Turpio is explaining that he comes on the stage without a mask, in the usual style of the Prologue, to make a special plea. There is thus no reason to suppose that he was carrying an olive branch[9]—a suggestion put forward on a very doubtful interpretation of an illustration to the *Adelphi*, in which it is perhaps intended to show the speaker as carrying a cypress branch, since the play had been produced (as the artist could read in the didascalia) at the funeral games for L. Aemilius Paulus.

NOTE ON POLLUX'S LIST OF MASKS

If we may judge by the evidence of works of art, as well as by Pollux's list, mask-design was formal : it was not realistic. That is why I think it dangerous to use our modern notions of realism in order to connect a particular mask with a particular character in extant drama. *Either* actual stage-usage was more flexible than is usually allowed, *or* dramatists were indifferent to our anxiety that the masks should harmonize with the personality.

CHAPTER XXV

THE ROMAN ORIGIN OF THE LAW OF FIVE ACTS

THE INTRODUCTION of the five-act law, and of act-division itself, into Renaissance drama was due to the desire to obey classical precept and example. Horace had laid it down for all time that a play should have five acts if it was to be a success. Moreover the plays of Terence had been divided according to this principle by Roman editors, and so came down in five-act form to the modern world. It would seem natural to suppose that the law was based upon the practice of classical dramatists. Yet until the discovery of the *Dyscolus* in 1959 the most careful researches of modern scholars had been unable to discover clear evidence of five-act division in any Greek play which has reached us complete, or in the plays of Plautus or Terence. Consequently some have held that the law was a mere invention of theorists, whether of Hellenistic or of Roman times. The discovery in 1905 and later of considerable portions of Menander's text of the stage direction χοροῦ, ' a performance by the chorus ', in these almost non-choral plays seemed clearly to divide them into acts ; and though the evidence did not show how many such choral interludes occured in any one play, it was argued that there were at least three of them in the *Epitrepontes*. Further researches might well be expected to demonstrate the existence of a fourth interlude in this particular play, and in other plays as well ; and all agreed that a play with four interludes must necessarily contain five acts. An earlier event of some importance was the appearance in 1884 of Prou's paper 'Les théâtres d'automates en Grèce',[1] in which he drew the attention of scholars to the account given by Hero of Alexandria of the Nauplios-show, with its five scenes, and claimed it as a five-act play of Hellenistic times. The importance of this new evidence was that it seemed to confirm in some measure the statements of Donatus and Evanthius. From them we gather (a) that each play of Terence should be divided into five acts ; (b) that this five-act arrangement was not introduced by Terence, who tried in fact to eliminate act-division altogether ; (c) that Varro found acts not only in Terence but also apud Graecos ipsos ; (d) that the Greek dramatists divided acts by means of the chorus ; (e) that Menander, when he suppressed the chorus, still ' left a place for it '.* All these statements seemed now to be capable of explanation. Menander had removed the chorus from taking part in the action of the play ; he had, however, marked in his manuscript places where it was to appear and perform an interlude. These interludes divided each play of Menander (and perhaps of New Comedy in general) into five sections—what the Romans called *actus*. Terence, by omitting the interludes, had eliminated the outward sign of act-division. The task of the Roman scholars was therefore to restore this division into five acts. And though they do not seem to have carried out this task very successfully, at any rate we may assume that the Latin plays were translated from five-act originals, and all that we have to do is to find where those choral interludes occurred which separated the acts from each other.

This reasoning was not universally accepted. The negative view is expressed with admirable sense and humour by Michaut.† But a positive theory has a tactical advantage over scepticism. Research in Menander is now largely a matter of arranging the scanty remains of each play according to the five-act law. Now it is one thing to divide into acts a play which has survived complete ; such a procedure, whether justified or not, at least leaves the text unchanged. But Menander's text is largely a matter of conjecture ; and the kind of conjectures put forward will be materially affected according to whether their author accepts or rejects the five-act law.

In 1940 there appeared Weissinger's ' *Study of Act Divisions in Classical Drama* ' (Iowa Studies, no. ix). Weissinger believed, as most scholars do, that the law was of Greek origin—that is to say that it had at any rate been formulated by critics of the Alexandrian if not of an earlier age. He had, however, to confess that it cannot be shown to hold good

* Compare with the present view the remark of Körte in 1900 (*Neue Jahrb. für das Klass. Alt.* V. 88) : was sich der brave Euanthius mit den Worten *ut choros tollerent locum eis relinquentes* gedacht hat, weiss ich nicht, vermutlich gar nichts.
† *Comédie romaine*, i. 184–196.

either for fifth-century tragedy, or for Old Comedy, or for Menander, or for Plautus and Terence. 'It is likely' (page 60) 'that the five-act convention was becoming established in Menander's day, but it is unsafe to conclude from the scanty evidence that the rule had already become *de rigueur*.'

While hoping for further evidence, we may with profit examine our assumptions. One of the merits of Weissinger's work is that he forces us to consider certain fundamental questions which have too long been disregarded. The first concerns the meaning of ' act '. Our notions of what it implies are based partly on the usage of the modern theatre, partly on our reading of plays, particularly, it may be, the plays of Shakespeare. In our theatres the curtain falls at the end of each act ; the lights are switched on in the body of the theatre, and the disciplined spectators are free to leave the theatre for a stated time. For those who choose to remain in their seats a light musical interlude is usually provided. Meanwhile, behind the curtain, the scenery is prepared for the next act. At the end of the interval the lights are switched off in the body of the theatre, the curtain rises, and the attention of all is concentrated on the brilliantly lighted stage.

In other words, modern developments have made act-division highly convenient both for the spectators and for the management. The dramatist, too, finds that he can turn act-division to account by employing it to denote lapse of time. Our modern convention is that the dramatic time covered by a scene does not greatly exceed the actual time it takes to perform. But the action of the play as a whole may be supposed to occupy several years. This is made possible by the existence of pauses between the acts, and the value we conventionally give to these pauses. The realistic nature of our scene-painting and the use of programmes have helped to establish in our minds an association between the interval and a change of place and time.

Conditions and conventions were very different when act-division first appeared in our drama. The Elizabethan theatre had neither drop-curtain nor realistic scenery nor any of those modern devices which have made act-division so convenient for us. The introduction of act-division was due not to its intrinsic value but to respect for classical tradition, as embodied in the precepts of Horace and Donatus and the five-act division imposed by Roman editors on the plays of Terence. The native English tradition was continuous performance ; 'acts and scenes', to quote Sir Edmund Chambers (*Elizabethan Stage*, iii. 199) 'which are the outward form of a method of construction derived from the academic analysis of Latin comedy and tragedy, make their appearance, with other notes of neo-classical influence, in the court tragedies, in translated plays, and in a few others belonging to the same *milieu* of scholarship '. No scheme of act-division other than the five-act scheme was recognized (cf. Hunter, *Review of English Studies*, vol. II, 1926, p. 295). In other words act-division in Elizabethan drama was not a natural development ; it was directly due to respect for Roman precept and example ; and where observed in theatrical practice it necessitated act-pauses. The word 'act' is defined by Cotgrave (1611) as a ' pause in a Comedy or Tragedy ', and we have the same sense in a post-Shakespearian stage-direction in the Folio of the ' Midsummer Night's Dream,' at the end of Act III —' they sleep all the acte '. These pauses had to be filled up with interludes—dumb-shows, musical effects, or, as in Ben Jonson's *Catiline*, reflective utterances of the Chorus.

It should be realized that the act-pauses were not at first used to indicate change of scene or lapse of time. The native tradition had left the dramatist free to suppose his scene changed as often as he pleased—a freedom which Sidney satirizes in his remarks on *Gorboduc*. The classical influence brought into fashion not only the five-act rule but also the unities of place and time, as we see them in Ben Jonson's plays. Undoubtedly Shakespeare allows changes in place and lapse of time—but then it is not certain that Shakespeare observed act- and scene-division. All that Professor Dover Wilson will grant (*Rev. of English Studies*, vol. III, 1927, p. 395) is ' that the company and the audience found a short break convenient in the middle of a long play like *Hamlet*. But such a break had no structural significance ; might occur at any point in the play where the stage was left clear ; and was a mere matter of theatrical convenience.' It would seem, then, that Shakespeare did not use a pause in performance to convey the sense of lapse of time—even of so long a lapse of time as the sixteen years' interval in *The Winter's Tale*, where he brings Time himself on the stage to give the informa-

tion in plain English to the audience.   Of course Shakespeare
knew of the five-act law, and knew that some of his fellow-
dramatists observed it.   If he, then, knowing the act-pause
as a fact in the contemporary theatre, did not use it to convey
the sense of lapse of time, he cannot have seen any necessary
connexion between the act-pause and the lapse of dramatic
time.   Later dramatists, while retaining the classical act-
pauses, abandoned the classical unities ;   consequently they
were able to employ the act-pauses in the way with which we
are familiar.   But if Granville Barker and Dover Wilson are
right, it would be a complete fallacy to use the changes of
place and time which Shakespeare allows as evidence that he
intended his plays to be divided into acts.

The question before us is whether act-division was observed
by any dramatist of classical antiquity ;   this question cannot
be answered if we are not clear in our own minds as to what
we mean by ' act '.   Though there is some variation in modern
definitions of the term, it seems to be agreed that the act
must be followed by a definite and perceptible pause in performance.   While this pause may be, and usually is, occupied
with an interlude of some kind, this interlude must not advance
the action of the play :   indeed the spectators must know
beyond doubt that the interlude is *not* an essential part of the
play.   Moreover each act should be an artistic unity in itself,
forming a clearly defined part of the action of the play as a
whole.   It is thus plain that ' act ' has a theatrical as well as a
dramatic significance.   When Kuiper (*Grieksche Origineelen*,
p. 257) says ' we find for the Greek *Andria* five distinct chapters,
corresponding to the five acts :   (1) Exposition ;   (2) Apparent
Success ;   (3) Frustration of Simo's scheme ;   (4) Recognition ;
(5) Dénouement ', he is evidently thinking of the ' act ' as a
dramatic entity, capable of definition in literary terms.   But
if there were no outward and objective indication of where
each of these ' chapters ' ended and the next began, how could
the spectators be expected to appreciate the artistic unity of
each act, or even to know when it was complete ?   Therefore,
even on literary grounds, the act-pause is essential to the act.
This is nowhere denied ;   indeed it is generally taken for
granted, even by students of Greek drama.   Thus Maidment
(' The later Comic Chorus ', *C.Q.* 1935, vol. XXIX, p. 15)
says that ' the *Heauton* definitely demands four pauses.'   That

is to say, if the *Heauton* were being produced at the present day, we should feel that four pauses were appropriate. Were such pauses in fact observed in the practice of the Greek or Roman theatre ? If we cannot answer this question in the affirmative, then we must admit that the *modern* sense of the term ' act ' was unknown in the ancient world.

I doubt if any one seriously believes, or has ever believed, that the performance of a Greek play was broken at regular intervals by blank pauses. We know that—at least in the fifth century—it was the custom to produce several plays in one day. Compared with modern standards, Greek plays were short. At the end of each play there was necessarily a break, which would give to the spectators the breathing-space which we find necessary in the modern theatre, and which is afforded to us by the break between acts. Within the bounds of each individual play continuous performance was the rule. Acted and choral portions alternated, but both were equally part of the play. This is indeed admitted on all sides ; nevertheless an attempt has been made to find the germ of act-division present in the separation of the acted portions from one another by the choral odes, and the use of μέρος to denote each separate ' part ' which was performed by the actors. Here we must guard against the common confusion between genuine Greek and Graeco-Roman evidence. When Marcus Aurelius (xii. 36) speaks of τὰ πέντε μέρη as necessary to form a complete play, we may presume that he is using ' part ' as the nearest Greek he can find to translate the Latin ' actus '.* To go back to undoubtedly Greek sources, it is clear that μέρος could mean for Aristotle or his interpolator (*Poet.* 1450*a*, 1452*b*) not ' act ' but ' constituent part ' or ' member ' ; thus, quantitatively considered, the ' members ' were prologue, episode, exodos and choral song (the last-named including parodos and stasimon). On the other hand there is evidence that, when it was necessary to refer the reader to a particular passage in a play, the play could be regarded as divided into Part One, Part Two and so on. Aristophanes (*Frogs* 1119-20) speaks of the prologue as the ' first part ' of a tragedy, and the scholiast ad loc. seems to be merely echoing his words when he comments ὁ γὰρ πρόλογος μέρος πρῶτον τῆς τραγῳδίας. Great importance is attached by Leo (*Pl. Forsch.*, 2nd ed.

* Cf. Freté, *La Structure dramatique des comédies de Plaute*, p. 9.

p. 230) to a passage in the hypothesis to the *Andromache* in which the speech of Hermione is said to occur ἐν τῷ δευτέρῳ μέρει, 'in the second part'. This speech actually occurs immediately after the parodos, that is to say, at the beginning of the first episode. As the *Andromache* has a prologue, it seems clear that the prologue is here regarded as the 'first part', the first episode as the 'second part'. The ancient *Life* of Aeschylus says that in the *Niobe* the heroine sits silent 'until the third part'. These are, I believe, the only examples of this use of μέρος which can be cited from the pre-Roman period. Arrian (Teubner ed., 1. 24. 15) reports Epictetus as saying that some king in tragedy, when things go wrong with him, cries out 'about the third or fourth part' certain words which actually occur in the exodos of the *Oedipus Rex* (a play containing a prologue and four episodes, as well as the exodos). Epictetus, like Marcus Aurelius, may have been thinking in terms of Horace's five-act rule. What the three pre-Roman passages suggest is that, for the purposes of reference, the choral odes were regarded as dividing the play into parts; thus the prologue would be Part One, the first episode Part Two, and so on. Weissinger (p. 16) argues that the parodos forms part of the second μέρος, as against Flickinger, who put it in the first μέρος. I venture to suggest that the parodos and the stasima were not regarded as belonging to the μέρη but as forming the boundaries between the μέρη. (If it were desired to refer to a particular ode, a ready-made nomenclature was available—the 'parodos', the 'first stasimon' and so on). Evidently Greek scholars made use of the obvious fact that the choral odes divided the acted portion of a play into sections, which they called 'parts'. But μέρος, as used for this purpose, may not have conveyed any of the theatrical implications associated with the word 'act'.

The essential characteristic of act-division is the pause in performance. The choral odes of fifth-century drama could not be regarded as pauses in the performance: on the contrary they were a vital element in the performance. But in time the importance of the chorus declined. In Menander's plays it seems to have been confined to occasional appearances in which it danced and perhaps sang; but its songs have not been recorded. The general view is that these appearances were so unconnected with the action of the play that they had the effect of breaking up that action into chapters, each of which was a unity in itself. The appearance of the chorus, in other words, was not part of the play : it was a signal that for the time being the action was suspended. While the chorus was dancing, the spectators were experiencing that sense of pause which we derive from act-division. The dramatist composed his play with these pauses in mind : he used them to give that sense of lapse of dramatic time which is given by the act-pause in modern drama.

This theory may have derived support from the traditional belief in the high Hellenistic stage on which the actors stood, twelve feet above the orchestra in which the chorus performed ' interludes between the successive acts '. (Haigh, *Attic Theatre*, 3rd. ed. by Pickard-Cambridge, p. 128). But Dr. Pickard-Cambridge later abandoned his belief in the raised stage, even for the Hellenistic theatre (*Theatre of Dionysus*, 1946, p. 165). The view that the Menandrian chorus never took any part in the action seems to me incapable of proof. It is generally supposed (cf. Maidment, *l.c.*, p. 20) that the guests who enter the house of Chaerestratus (*Epitr.* 195–201 Capps) are the chorus of the play, whose appearance at this point is indicated by the direction χοροῦ. A few lines later Habrotonon hurries out of the house ' remonstrating with one and another of the revellers who try to detain her ' (Allinson). The chorus have a relationship to one of the characters of the play ; they enter his house as his guests ; they accost one of the actors, and are addressed by her. How can it be claimed that the appearance of such a chorus is not part of the play, but is an interlude between two acts of the play ?

To suppose that the chorus could be regarded in this light is to suppose that a revolutionary change had occurred in the position of the chorus. Instead of being part of the play (albeit a part of diminishing importance) it had become extraneous to the play (and thereby assumed a new importance in the sense that it now divided the play into separate episodes). Yet it is generally agreed that in some Hellenistic plays, if not in those of Menander, the chorus still took part in the action. And the old tragedies were still produced, displaying the chorus as an integral part of the play. Can we be certain that the contemporaries of Menander held two radically different views of the function of the chorus ? [2]

In fact we know very little about the Menandrian chorus. We do not even know whether, once it had made its appearance, it remained within view for the rest of the play, or withdrew as soon as it had performed the dance or sung the song required of it. Körte inclines to the second view (article on ' Neue Komödie ' in *P.W.* xi, 1266 ff.). This chorus of revellers is commonly asserted to be a return to the κῶμος or ' revel ' out of which Old Comedy sprang. This assumption would perhaps afford a basis for the other assumption that the Menandrian chorus had become so external to the action that it could be felt, and in fact was felt, to divide that action into sections. But how does this square with the theory that New Comedy is more closely akin to the later tragedy than it is to Old Comedy ?—a theory which is necessary if we are to link the Roman references to actus-division in *tragedy* with the structure of New Comedy.

The chorus was the original element in Greek drama, the stuff out of which was developed the acted part (at least in tragedy). As long as we can trace the history of Greek drama, the chorus was retained. In Elizabethan drama, on the other hand, the chorus was something external and alien to the native tradition ; it was inserted by classicizing dramatists to divide the play into acts. Is there not all the difference in the world between the stage-direction ' Chorus : Music ' in Ben Jonson's *Sejanus* and the direction χοροῦ in Menander ? Flickinger (*Class. Phil.*, vii, 1912, page 33-4) suggests that ' in Agathon's Mss. there were gaps indicated between the acts. In actual performance suitable odes were thrown in (ἐμβόλιμα).' The trouble is that we have no evidence for these ' gaps ' except the existence of the odes. Would there have been gaps if there was no chorus ?

Nevertheless it is mainly on these supposed ' interludes ' that the case for five-act division in Menander is founded. This should logically mean that there were four such interludes in each play of Menander. That is how Legrand understood the matter ; the five-act law was for him a four-interlude law. If, therefore, we had the complete text of Menander, we should expect to find the stage-direction χοροῦ occurring exactly four times in every play. But apart from the *Dyscolus* the largest number of occurrences of χοροῦ so far assigned to any one play is three, in the *Epitrepontes* (Maidment, page 17). And, as

Conrad points out (*Technique of continuous action in Roman Comedy*, page 9) ' even if one or several plays of Menander are discovered to be divided into five acts, it would still remain uncertain whether all, or any large number, of the writers of New Comedy were rigidly bound by a law of five acts or not '.

The argument from the proved occurrences of χοροῦ to the five-act law is so obviously a non-sequitur that it is in many cases tacitly abandoned.* The editors of Menander profess to discover act-division even where the word χοροῦ is not known to have occurred, or is even believed not to have occurred. Thus Capps can say in his introduction to the *Perikeiromene* (*Four Plays of Menander*, page 144) : ' according to the divisions of the play adopted in this edition, the chorus makes its appearance after the second act and does not furnish an entertainment between the third and fourth acts.' But if there was no interlude at the end of the third act, how would Menander's audience have known that the third act had ended? Allinson and Capps suppose Act I of the same play to finish with Agnoia's speech. At this point the text is preserved complete, and there is no trace of a χοροῦ between this and the following scene (cf. Maidment, page 17). On the *Hero* Capps (page 6) remarks ' it is noteworthy that no chorus is mentioned in the list ' (of characters). ' Possibly the entertainment provided between the acts was of too informal a character to be dignified by the name " chorus ".' In other words Capps is prepared to make act-division quite independent of the appearance of a chorus. Weissinger, on the other hand, bases act-division on the use of χοροῦ (page 54), and consequently has to conclude (page 61) that ' not more than a possibility exists that the plays of Menander uniformly had five acts '.

If we grant, as we must, that ' acts ' have no reality unless there is some external mark of division between them, and if we have no evidence that the chorus appeared four times in any play of New Comedy, then we must either abandon our belief in the five-act law or suggest some other mark of division than a ' choral interlude '. Körte's article (referred to above) suggests that on occasion the flute-player supplied an inter-lude. For this there is no evidence at all in Greek drama,† and only one example in Latin comedy, with which I shall deal

---

* See Appendix O.

† Aristophanes, *Birds* 220, gives the stage-direction (αὐλεῖ), ' the note of the flute is heard '. This is not an interlude but an integral part of the action.

presently.* Are we to understand that the flute-player supplied all the interludes in some plays, the chorus all the interludes in other plays, or that there were plays in which the interludes were supplied partly by the chorus, partly by the flute-player—but that, however achieved, the interludes always amounted to four ? Such suppositions may be justified if there is independent evidence of a five-act division in New Comedy ; but belief in such a division cannot properly be based on the known occurrences of χοροῦ in Menander.

This is where Hero's account (see p. 196) of the Nauplios puppet-show, with its five episodes, seems particularly relevant. Prou's learning and enthusiasm convinced Legrand, Leo and others that here at last we have a Greek drama with five acts and four act-pauses. Hero's interest in the puppet-show is purely that of an engineer. Having dealt with the ὑπάγοντα αὐτόματα, ' movable puppet-shows ' which were mounted on a movable platform, lay permanently open to view, and consequently could present only a single scene, he turns to the στατὰ αὐτόματα, or stationary puppet-show. This seems to have been a box mounted on a pillar. The box had folding doors, which, when opened, revealed movable figures seen against a painted background. I give a somewhat abbreviated version of Hero's description (Prou, page 207 ff.) :

The problem is to make the puppet-show (pinax) open of its own accord and reveal the figures inside in motion befitting the theme of the story ; then the pinax is to close automatically and after a short interval to open again, revealing other figures, some or all of which are if possible to be in movement. This process is to be repeated several times (πλεονάκις). The arrangement employed by the early designers was simple. When the pinax was opened, there appeared in it a painted head. This moved its eyes, raising and lowering them repeatedly. The pinax was shut and then opened again ; the head had disappeared, but painted figures were seen arranged in accordance with some story (εἰς τινα μῦθον διεσκευασμένα). The pinax would shut and open once more, revealing another arrangement (διάθεσις) of figures to complete the tale. There were thus only three different movements : that of the doors, that of the eyes and that of the curtains.

* pp. 202–3.

But in our time designers have introduced interesting tales into their puppet-shows, and have made use of many and varied movements. As I promised, I will describe one show which seemed to me to be the best. The story set forth in it was that of Nauplios. This is how it was divided up (τὰ δὲ κατὰ μέρος εἶχεν οὕτως) :

At the beginning the pinax opened and displayed twelve painted figures, arranged in three rows. These represented some of the Greeks preparing their ships and getting ready to launch them. These figures moved, some sawing, some chopping. . . . They made a loud noise, as in real life. After a sufficient time had elapsed, the doors shut and opened again, and there was a new arrangement (διάθεσις). It showed the ships being launched by the Greeks. The doors again shut and opened, and nothing was visible in the pinax except sky and sea. Presently the ships were seen sailing by. . . . Again the pinax shut and opened. There were now no ships to be seen, but Nauplios was there brandishing his torch and Athene standing beside him. A flame burned above the pinax. . . . Again it shut and opened, revealing the wreck of the fleet and Ajax swimming in the sea. A mechanism in the top of the pinax was raised, there was a peal of thunder, a lightning flash fell on Ajax, and his figure vanished. The pinax closed, and the story was ended."

Prou's treatment of this passage is coloured by his view that the puppet-show was a form of drama. Weil (*Journal des Savants*, July 1882, p. 418) pointed out that only the fourth scene was suited for dramatic treatment. 'Les conditions du spectacle dramatique et du spectacle mécanique sont trop différentes.' I must add that the terms employed by Hero are not reminiscent of the stage. He speaks of a πίναξ, not a θέατρον; he calls each separate scene a διάθεσις or 'arrangement' (but see *D.F.* 153, n. 3). Leo (Pl. Forsch, p. 230), claims that Hero uses μέρος in the sense 'act'—quoting the words ἵνα μηδὲν τῶν προειρημένων . . . μέρος τοῦ πίνακος φαίνηται. The passage in question (149 β : Prou, p. 239) deals with the need for care that the mechanism described shall not ' be visible in the front *part* of the pinax '.*

I can find in Hero's account only one reference to the

---

*. Was Leo thinking of the occurrence of μέρος in the passage quoted above (τὰ δὲ . . .) ?

theatre : when he comes to suggest how the effect of thunder may be given (141 γ : Prou, p. 209) he describes how similar effects are produced ἐν τοῖς θεάτροις.

That there were five scenes in this particular show seems to be fortuitous. The earlier show referred to had three scenes, and nowhere in this connexion does Hero stress or indeed mention the number five. The closing and opening of the doors and the episodic nature of the show were essential if a story was to be told at all in this medium. In fact, so far from the Nauplios-show supporting the case for the five-act law in drama, the only link with drama which Weil could find in it was precisely the fact that it has five parts. This would be interesting if there was any independent evidence that the number five played some part in the construction of the drama of Hero's day. But no such evidence exists. And if we can base any opinion on the earlier development of drama, the tendency was to move away from five as the normal number of μέρη. I quote Weissinger (without accepting all his figures) : ' It is true that all of Aeschylus' extant plays have five such sections except the two which have no prologues. But in Sophocles only one (*Philoctetes*) has five, three have six and three have seven. In Euripides only one (*Troades*) has five, fifteen have six, and one (*Medea*) has seven '.

Nevertheless it is assumed by most scholars that the five-act law found expression in Hellenistic theory : that this was probably one of the things which Horace derived from Neoptolemus of Parium and included in the *Ars Poetica* (congessit praecepta Neoptolemi τοῦ Παριανοῦ de arte poetica non quidem omnia sed eminentissima, as Porphyrio tells us). Assuming that this is so, how do we suppose Neoptolemus to have framed the rule ? Not, surely, that all plays *had* five μέρη ; for the number of μέρη depended not on theory but on the actual number of choral odes and on the presence or absence of a prologue. That all plays *ought* to have five μέρη ? In that case Neoptolemus was perhaps upholding the practice of Aeschylus as against that of Euripides and Sophocles. This is hypothetical, but it would be even more hypothetical to suppose that Neoptolemus was referring to the practice of dramatists of his day, and that they had returned in this respect to the arrangement favoured by Aeschylus. What we have failed to find is any *Greek* evidence that the Greeks recognized

VI   STREET MUSICIANS
Mosaic by Dioskorides, from Pompeii

the five-act law, or act-division of any kind, either in practice or in theory. The case for the law rests on Latin evidence alone.

For the practice of the Latin dramatists we have the evidence of the plays. We have also some conflicting statements by the grammarians. Evanthius tells us (*Donatus*, Teubner ed., i. 18) that the Latin comic dramatists ' did not even leave a place for the chorus ', thus obscuring the act-division, as he adds. Donatus (i. 266) says that Terence ran all five acts into one (uult poeta noster omnes quinque actus uelut unum fieri). Furthermore, Donatus' rule for restoring the act-divisions (i. 38) is to look for empty-stage intervals at which it is possible to assume a performance by the chorus or the flute-player ; and as he complains of the difficulty of this procedure, it seems that the Latin text offered him no clear guidance. The implication is that Donatus' text of Terence contained no mention of choral odes or interludes. So too Diomedes (iii. 14) : Latinae igitur comoediae chorum non habent. (Kaibel, *Com. Graec.* fr. i. 61). But in the *Liber Glossarum* (Kaibel, *Com. Graec.* fr. i. 72) we read aput Romanos quoque Plautus comoediae choros exemplo Graecorum inseruit. (*Corp. gloss.* v. 181. 7, *de com. Graec.* 72 K.). It is difficult to suppose that the writer of this remark had seen a text of Plautus containing stage-directions corresponding to χοροῦ. Consequently it is generally supposed that the reference is to such passages as the ' song ' of the fishermen in the *Rudens* (290–305), or the presence of the aduocati in the *Poenulus* (504–816)—both presumably taken over from the Greek original. Schanz (*Röm. Lit.-Gesch.* i. 131) further refers us to *Bacch.* 107, *Heaut.* 170, where there is no mention of a chorus in our texts, but traces are supposed to remain of a chorus in the original. Others refer us to such purely Roman insertions as *Curc.* 462–486 (description of Rome by the property-manager). The Oxford editors of Terence actually insert the stage-direction (*Saltatio Conuiuarum*) after *Heaut.* 170, referring us in a footnote to Skutsch's article in *Hermes*, vol. xlvii (1912). The suggestion put forward by Skutsch (and independently by Flickinger, *Class. Phil.* vii. 24–34, also in 1912) was that in *Menander's* play the chorus had entered at this point. This suggestion seems to raise more difficulties than it solves (cf. Jachmann, *Plautinisches und Attisches*, pp. 245 ff., and Drexler, *Hermes* lxxiii (1938) p. 65 ff.)* ; but in any case it

* See *Hermathena* lxxiv (1949) pp. 26–38.

referred to Menander's play, not to Terence's adaptation, and for the Oxford editors of Terence to insert a choral interlude into the middle of a scene is a liberty which calls forth a protest from Jachmann (p. 245, note 1) and Weissinger (p. 64).

There may conceivably be traces in the Latin plays of the appearance of the chorus in the Greek originals. But if act-division can ever be proved on internal arguments alone, then any such arguments based on the structure of the Latin play are presumably valid in the first place for the performance of the Latin play and only indirectly for the performance of the Greek play. The suggestion has been made that we should postulate intervals and interludes to obviate awkward encounters between characters leaving and characters entering the stage. Several examples are cited by Miss Johnston (*Exits and Entrances in Roman Comedy*, 1933, pages 106–119), who suggests that a brief interlude by the flute-player might allow one actor to get away before another entered. It may be so, though, as Harsh remarks (*C.W.* 1935, page 163), 'It is not an assumption which can definitely be proved correct'. Miss Clifford, on the other hand (*Dramatic Technique and the Originality of Terence, C.J.* 26, pages 605–618), regards these awkward encounters in the wings as proof of the clumsiness with which Terence adapted his originals. But surely we may suppose that the stage was on occasion left vacant for a few seconds, in order to allow one character to depart before another entered, or to give a solitary actor time to enter a house and return. (Harsh cites *Aul.* 627, *As.* 809, and from Greek drama *Eccles.* 513 and *Alc.* 861).

Far more important is the view that intervals must be assumed to allow for action off stage. In default of external evidence the case for intervals can be founded only on the text of the plays and our own sense of what is fitting. The question arises whether we can assume that the theatrical convention of the Greeks and Romans was in this respect like our own. In modern practice, while there is no limit on the dramatic time occupied by the play as a whole, the dramatic time covered by each separate scene, as has already been said, does not greatly exceed the time which the scene takes to perform. The difference between the total time of action and the two or three hours of performance is covered by the intervals, which can represent any desired period. In ancient drama the total dramatic time (if we may use so modern a phrase) was as a rule limited to one day; but the dramatist was free within that limit to give any time-value he liked to any scene or choral ode. There was, therefore, no dramatic need for intervals of the kind familiar to us; and indeed it is generally held that in fifth-century drama at least there were no such intervals. Some of the most striking lapses of time, and all the changes of place, occur when the chorus is not present. In *Eumenides* 234 the chorus of Furies is driven off the stage; in the very next line we find that we have been transported from Delphi to Athens. Even if we assume a pause in the performance here, it cannot have been occupied by a choral ode; for the chorus are absent. The parabasis of the *Lysistrata* ends at line 705; between 705 and 706 five days are supposed to elapse (cf. line 881). Here Weissinger actually suggests that the chorus was removed for some minutes ' to make the break more decisive through the external device of a completely empty stage ' (page 38). At all events it must be admitted that the gap in time here is not covered by a choral *interlude ;* but few will accept Weissinger's suggestion that the chorus *left* the theatre merely to give the sense that time was elapsing.

Nevertheless it is assumed that in New Comedy pauses in performances were employed to give the effect of a lapse of time. Let us at least be clear whether we are discussing the Latin plays or their Greek originals, and whether we are postulating blank intervals or interludes. For blank intervals in the performance of a play by Menander there is no evidence; for interludes there is the evidence of the χοροῦ passages, which is usually regarded as decisive. Even Conrad (page 71) after making out a strong case for continuous performance in the case of the Latin plays, can say ' there still remain a small minority of vacant stages which everybody must admit furnish reasonable grounds for the view that there were some essential pauses in the action, at least in the Greek original, and possibly even in the Latin adaptation. The most striking are a few vacant stages which separate the withdrawal and re-appearance of the same character or group of characters. Now it is always proper to use this small number of cases as evidence of χοροῦ in the Greek original '.

The argument appears to be that the Greeks would have

found continuous performance intolerable in these cases, although the Latin translator may not have felt the difficulty. But if continuous performance can be assumed in *Eum.* 234–5 and similar cases, and if the Roman audience would tolerate it in the cases Conrad has in mind, do we know enough about Menander to be certain that he would have inserted χοροῦ in those cases? The argument assumes, too, that in these passages the Roman translator made no other change than to omit χοροῦ. If he introduced other alterations, then we cannot use his text as evidence for the structure of the Greek play.

We are on firmer ground when we use the Latin plays as evidence for the practice of the Roman theatre. Were there blank intervals, deliberately employed for this purpose? The most striking instance of lapse of time is *Heaut.* 409–10. At 409 the guests go indoors for supper. At 410 Menedemus appears from next door and remarks ' the dawn is breaking '. It is difficult to assume that Menander had here brought on a chorus of revellers going to the party; for the party is already complete. (Flickinger supposes a chorus of ancillae here and a chorus of conuiuae at 171 (*C.P.* vii. 28)). As for the Latin play, does it help to assume a blank interval of perhaps five minutes, or a solo by the flute-player? Let us consider the prologues of Plautus and Terence, so different in style, and yet so alike in their anxiety to induce the spectators to give the play a hearing. Is it likely that once the play was under way the Latin dramatist would deliberately bring the performance to a dead stop, merely to convey the sense of lapse of time? Let us consider, in particular, the brief prologue to the *Pseudolus* : ' You had better get up and stretch your loins ; a long play by Plautus is coming on the stage '.*
Surely this implies (*a*) that play followed play, (*b*) that once a play had begun the spectators would have no break until it was ended. To assume that the flute-player was required to give a solo at such passages as *Heaut.* 409–10 is to assume (*a*) that the dramatist brought the action to a stop ; (*b*) that, realizing the danger of such a course, he then tried to bridge the gap by a flute-solo. Is it not simpler to suppose that there was no pause?

The only known example of a flute solo in Latin drama (*Ps.* 573*a*) is the exception which proves the rule. Pseudolus,

---

* So, too, the last line of the *Epidicus*.

left alone on the stage, suddenly announces that he will enter the house to think out a plan ; he promises the spectators that he will not be long absent, and that in the meantime the flute-player will entertain them. He then, evidently, goes indoors, and presumably the flute-player does strike up an air, for when Pseudolus reappears at the next line of the play the metre has changed from the rhythm of speech to that of 'song '.

Here, beyond doubt, is a break in the action of the play. It is occupied by an interlude. But that interlude does *not* indicate the lapse of any dramatic time. Nothing happens while Pseudolus is off the stage * ; he claims indeed to have formed his plan, but we never hear what the plan is, and a new turn of events makes it unnecessary. My explanation of this unique passage is founded on the quite exceptional circumstances. Pseudolus' rôle is very heavy. The dramatist wishes to give him a break in the longest continuous spell of duty to be found in Latin comedy (lines 1–766). Therefore, as soon as Pseudolus is alone on the stage, he makes a transparent excuse and retires, assuring the audience that he will soon return and that they will not be without entertainment during his absence. Plainly the dramatist thought that this expedient, however necessary here, involved some risk, and that may be why we find no other instance of it in our extant plays.

In default of other evidence, act-division is based on the occurrence of empty-stage breaks. Unfortunately their number varies from two (in the *Mostellaria* and *Andria*) to ten (in the *Rudens* and *Adelphi*). If act-division is to be identified with empty-stage break, then only two or three of Plautus' plays and perhaps none of Terence's obey the five-act rule. Attempts are often made to distinguish the breaks which con-- stitute act-division from those which do not, the usual criterion being the lapse of dramatic time. Even if the critics were agreed on this matter (and they are not), it is difficult to see how they can introduce five-act division into plays which have less than four breaks. In truth the evidence of the Latin plays (in the form in which they have come down to us) is

* Freté (*Structure dramatique des Comédies de Plaute*, p. 12) has noticed that the play gains nothing from Pseudolus' absence (rien n'empêchait Pseudolus de rester en scène pour imaginer sa fourberie).

overwhelmingly against the validity of the five-act law so far as the Roman theatre is concerned.

The fact remains that the Romans bequeathed to us the five-act law. To be more exact, Horace said that a play should have five ' actus '. The word actus means ' performance ' by the ' actores '. When Terence says (*Hec.* 39) primo actu placeo, he means ' the beginning of the performance was successful '. (Similarly, in *Ad.* 9, in prima fabula means ' in the beginning of the play '.) But if the performance of the actors should be broken up into sections by something not performed by the actors, then each of these *sections* would itself be an actus. Accordingly Horace, when instructing Roman literary men on the composition of choral tragedy, says that if a play is to be successful it must have five acts and no more than five. In other words Horace is recommending that a play should be neither too short nor too long ; a prologue, three episodes and an exodos, separated by choral odes relevant to the plot, will be about right.

Horace's principle of act-division was the choral ode : the chorus, he says (*A.P.* 194–5) is not to sing ' between the acts ' except on themes relevant to the plot. It is plain that Horace is not concerned with how to divide up a non-choral play into acts ; still less is he to be taken as affirming that every play ever written necessarily consists of five acts.

A passage of Cicero (*Q.F.* 1.1.16.46) has sometimes been taken to imply that he regarded the third act as the climax of a play. ' Let this third year of your command,' he says, ' like a third act, seem to have been the most finished and splendid of all.' I think that no emphasis is to be placed here on the word ' third ' where it is applied to ' act ' : if we translate ' let this third year—a third *act* as it were—be the best. . .' we interpret his meaning correctly.* (Cicero speaks elsewhere of the ' fourth act ' of Verres' wickedness, *Verr.* ii. 16. 18.)

One of Cicero's friends, the antiquarian, Varro, was especially interested in act-division. According to Donatus (ii. p. 192) Varro said that we must not be surprised to find the acts in the *Hecyra* and other plays unequal in the number of lines and scenes, since act-division depended on subject-matter, not on equality of length, and that this was true not

* Cf. Freté, op. cit., p. 9.

only of the Latin writers but of the Greeks themselves. This passage comes immediately after Donatus' proposed division of the *Hecyra* into five acts. Let us grant for argument's sake that this five-act division of Terence's plays goes back to Varro. It certainly does not go back to Greek sources ; what Greek would have concerned himself with Terence ? Varro, who died in 27 B.C., cannot have read the *Ars Poetica* ; but Horace may have read Varro or Varro's Roman authority. Two things are involved : the practical rule that five acts are the right amount for a play, and the academic theory that any play, even if non-choral, can be analysed into five acts. It is just conceivable, as has been remarked above, that Neoptolemus of Parium had said that the best Greek plays consisted of five μέρη, but it is inconceivable that he had said that all plays consisted of five μέρη, if he meant by that a prologue, three episodes and an exodos, for such a statement would be contrary to known fact.

The attempt to analyse each play of Terence into five *actus* was evidently the work not of Greek but of Roman scholars. There is an obvious contradiction involved in the attempt to divide a play which is admitted to be non-choral into parts the separate existence of which depends on choral interludes. Indeed Evanthius tells us that the omission of the choral interludes by the Latin comic dramatists has made it difficult to discern the five-act division in their plays (Donatus i. 18 W. : postremo ne locum quidem reliquerunt, quod Latini fecerunt comici, unde apud illos dirimere actus quinquepartitos difficile est). Elsewhere (i. 38) a suggestion is made for solving this problem : we must look out for empty-stage intervals at which an interlude by the chorus or the flute-player may be postulated. In another passage (i. 266) Donatus explains that Terence ran all five acts of the *Eunuchus* into one for fear the bored spectators might take the opportunity afforded by act-intervals to leave the theatre. Nevertheless the *Eunuchus*, like other plays, must have its five acts, which the Greek dramatists divided by means of the chorus (hoc etiam ut cetera huiusmodi poemata quinque actus habeat necesse est choris diuisos a Graecis poetis).

It is on these passages that the case for the five-act law depends. The argument may be put thus : the Greek dramatists observed five-act division, depending on choral interludes.

Terence, translating these five-act choral Greek plays, omitted the chorus and so obscured the act-division—that is to say, the act-division of the Greek originals, which in them was clearly indicated by choral songs, or the stage direction χοροῦ. The argument implies that, apart from omitting these choral odes or stage-directions, Terence kept the structure of the Greek original as he found it ; for of course if he had altered the structure of his Greek original, Donatus would have had no right to introduce the act-division of the Greek original into Terence's adaptation. It implies too, that the Roman scholars had the Greek originals in front of them and were able to compare them with Terence's adaptations. (We have other evidence that this was the case—Donatus often refers to the words of the Greek original).*

But if the only difference introduced by Terence was to omit the choral songs or directions for interludes which were clearly indicated in the text of the Greek plays, why was the task of restoring the five-act division of these Greek plays so difficult for the Roman scholars of a later day ? All they had to do, ex hypothesi, was to note where the indications of act-division occurred in the Greek text and to insert act-division at corresponding places in the Latin text. They did nothing of the kind. The suggestions that Donatus gives for establishing act-division and the difficulty which he and his predecessors admittedly found in establishing it alike imply that comparison of the Latin with the Greek text afforded no solution of the problem. Indeed Donatus nowhere says that the Greek originals of Terence were divided into five acts.† All that is clear from his remarks is that Roman scholars found ' actus ' in Greek plays ; and what they meant by ' actus ' is clear from the words choris diuisos a Graecis poetis. ' Old Comedy ', according to Evanthius (i. 18) ' was at first purely choral ; gradually actors came to be added and five-act division was the result. Then the gradual disappearance of the chorus resulted in New Comedy, in which not only is there no regular chorus, but there is no place left for choral interludes. For after spectators began to be difficult to please and formed the

---

* This seems to invalidate Professor Webster's suggestion to me that Donatus relied on summaries of Menander such as the περιοχαί of Homerus Sellios, on which see Körte, Berl. Phil. Woch. xxxviii. 787 f.

† Apuleius' reference (Florida 16) to the third act of a play of Philemon seems —like the whole anecdote—to be a Roman invention.

habit of leaving the theatre when the actors withdrew and left the singers to continue the play, the poets were compelled first to remove the chorus, merely leaving room for them (in the text). This was the practice of Menander, a practice which is to be explained as has been indicated, and not on the hypotheses put forward by other writers. Finally the dramatists did not even leave room (in their text) for the chorus, and this was the method followed by the Latin comic dramatists, so that it is difficult to recognize the five-act division in their plays.'

Considered as an account of the development of Greek drama, the remarks of Evanthius and Donatus involve absurdities which, as Michaut says (I. 191), would do honour to a professional humorist. Another contradiction is presented when we come to the theory that comedy (excluding the prologue) consists of protasis, epitasis and catastrophe, of which *protasis* is defined as primus actus initiumque dramatis (i. 22, cf. i. 27). The scholars of the Renaissance did their best to reconcile the two theories, five-act and three-part, but I agree with Leo (*Pl. Forsch.* p. 232) that the two are mutually exclusive. To judge by the terminology, the division into protasis, epitasis and catastrophe is Greek. The five-act theory seems to be nothing but the product of Roman pedantry, based ultimately on Horace's practical hint—possibly itself derived from some remark of Varro. If we are to look for a Greek origin for Horace's law, it can only have been some statement such as ' the number of episodes in a tragedy should be three ' (or ' the number of choral songs should be four ') ; and if any Greek writer ever framed such a rule (a supposition for which there is no jot of evidence), he can only have justified it by adding some such words as ' in accordance with the practice of Aeschylus, not of Euripides '.

Continuous performance, which is the negation of act-division, was the rule for ancient drama from Aeschylus to Terence. It is usual to cite Seneca as a dramatist who obeyed Horace's law. If by this is meant merely that the number of choral songs in a play of Seneca is commonly four, the argument is perhaps sound ; but it must be pointed out that in five cases he has merely taken over the structure of his model. In the *Octavia* there are five odes, and in the *Phoenissae* there are none. The very most that can be said of Seneca is that he shows a marked preference for four as the number of the choral odes in a

8*

play. He does not number off the divisions of the play as
' Act One,' ' Act Two ', any more than did the Greek
dramatists. His odes are often relevant to the plot, and cannot
be regarded merely as entertainment designed to fill an interval.
But what puts Seneca out of court is that in all probability his
plays were designed not for performance but for reading by
a single reciter. No doubt the structure of his plays had much
to do with the introduction of the five-act law into modern
stage-usage ; but Seneca himself was not concerned with
stage-usage. There was no act-division, there were no acts,
in his plays, because those plays were not meant to be acted.*

* See Appendix P.

CHAPTER XXVI

MUSIC AND METRE

THE COMEDIES of Plautus have been compared to such works as *The Beggar's Opera* or the light operas of Gilbert and Sullivan.* Such comparisons, however stimulating, are apt to mislead. Latin comedy was indeed written in various metres, most of which were intended to be accompanied by the music of the pipes (tibiæ) ; the actors evidently illustrated their words with gesture and sometimes with dance ; but the essential element of all opera is song. To us the difference between song and speech is obvious ; but it is by no means clear that this difference was recognized by the Romans or the Greeks.

Our ancient sources of evidence, however discordant in other ways, agree that a Latin comedy (excluding the prologue) consisted of two elements, diuerbium (or deuerbium) and canticum ; and that these two taken together make up the whole of a play except the choral part—which, we are told in the same connexion,† did not exist in Latin comedy. Naturally we assume that canticum means 'song', and consequently that diuerbium means 'speech'. This is the obvious sense to attach to the terms as used by Livy in his famous account (VII. ii) of how, when Andronicus' voice gave way as the result of taking too many encores, he employed a boy to sing, standing in front of the piper, while he himself, freed from the necessity of using his voice, was able to concentrate on miming the canticum with appropriate gestures. This was, according to Livy, the origin of the custom whereby the actors merely mimed the sung part (ad manum cantari) and confined their vocal powers to the delivery of the diuerbia. Perhaps Livy is here thinking of some form of theatrical performance of his own day in which there was a clear distinction between

---

* See Lindsay, *Early Latin Verse*, p. 263, and ' Plautus and the Beggar's Opera ', *C.R.* 37 (1923), p. 67.
† Diomedes, G.L.K. i. 491. 24.

the rôles of the actor and the vocalist or chorus ; we know, for
example, that the performance of the pantomime was assisted
by vocalists (Lucian *De Salt.* 64). It may be, indeed, that the
attempt to find a historical explanation of this is the origin of
the anecdote concerning Andronicus. At all events it seems
clear that Livy regarded the canticum as something which
required a special vocal effort, greater than what was needed
for the diuerbium. Diomedes, however, tells us * that the
diuerbia are those parts of comedy in which two or more
persons converse, whereas in a canticum only one person must
be present (or, if there is a second character, he must merely
overhear the other and must not converse with him). In other
words, for Diomedes canticum means ' monologue ', diuerbium
' dialogue ' ; which is a perfectly clear distinction, but quite
different from that between ' song ' and ' speech '. Elsewhere †
Diomedes recognizes the connexion of canticum with cano ;
contrasting Greek with Latin plays (drama, ' action ', with
fabula, from fari, ' speak '), he adds ' for in Latin plays there
are more cantica which are sung ' (plura sunt cantica quae
canuntur). If he means by this ' more cantica than there are
in the Greek plays ', it is not easy to follow him ; the cantica,
so far as we can tell, were a Roman innovation.‡ But we cannot
reconcile Livy and Diomedes by supposing that all monologues
were sung, all dialogues spoken ; for there can be no doubt
that many monologues were spoken.

At the head of certain scenes in some of the manuscripts of
Plautus occur the letters DV or C. We are told by Donatus
(*Adelphi*, praef. i. 7) that DV, placed after the names of the
characters at the head of a scene, represents diuerbium, and
it may be inferred that C stands for canticum. In general, DV
appears over scenes written in iambic senarii (whether dialogues or monologues), C over scenes in other metres (whether
monologues or dialogues).§ We are told (*de com.* p. 30 W.)
that the actors spoke the diuerbia, and that the cantica were
set to music composed not by the poet but by a musician
(diuerbia histriones pronuntiabant, cantica uero temperabantur

---

* G.L.K. i. 491, 24.   † ib. 490.

‡ Whatever the origin of the metres—whether in Greek tragedy, or in New
Comedy, or in Alexandrian or Italiot mime—the distinctive feature of the Latin
cantica is the use of metrical variety to produce dramatic effects.

§ Two scenes in senarii—*Pers.* IV. vi, *Trin.* IV. iv—seem to have the mark C ;
two—possibly three—scenes in trochaic septenarii—*Capt.* III i, *Cas.* IV. iii and
perhaps *Epid.* I. ii.—are apparently marked DV. See Lindsay, E.L.V., pp. 273, 283.

modis non a poeta sed a perito artis musicae factis). Donatus (*Adelph.* praef. p. 4 W.) says that some cantica were marked MMC (presumably mutatis modis canticum) because they were sung with frequent changes of music (saepe mutatis per scaenam modis cantata). In his prefaces to the other plays he echoes these remarks, but without adding any very precise information ; e.g. ad *Phorm.* p. 346 W.—diuerbiis quoque facetissimis et gestum desiderantibus scaenicum et suauissimis ornata canticis fuit. These verbal echoes, this lack of clarity, may tempt us to doubt whether Donatus or Diomedes attached any definite meaning to the words they were using.

When we examine the metres used by Plautus, we find great variety. Less than half of his work is in iambic senarii ; a great part of the remainder is in trochaic septenarii and iambic septenarii and octonarii, while the numerous other metres (trochaic octonarii, anapaests, cretics, bacchiacs, etc.) are grouped together in all sorts of ways, though no one of them is kept up for long. In the whole of Plautus there are about 1300 iambic septenarii and 400 iambic octonarii ; trochaic octonarii are few and scattered, while trochaic septenarii run into thousands. It is generally agreed that the passages in senarii were diuerbia, intended to be spoken, and that the cretics, bacchiacs, etc., were cantica and were meant for song. But what of the long scenes in septenarii and iambic octonarii ? It has been suggested that they were delivered in something between ordinary speech and song, a kind of recitative or chant to musical accompaniment. It is even claimed that we know the Greek name for this form of utterance—παρακαταλογή. By means of somewhat tenuous arguments based partly on Greek, partly on Latin evidence, we arrive at the conclusion that there were three kinds of dramatic non-choral utterance used alike on the Greek and on the Roman stage—speech, song and recitative. But the Roman writers speak of only two— diuerbium and canticum*. Was recitative included by them under diuerbium or under canticum ? Were there two kinds of diuerbium—speech and recitative—or two kinds of canticum —recitative and song ? Was MMC the special mark of the true songs—and if so, must a true song have 'frequent changes of music' and presumably of metre? Or was one of the three forms of delivery left without a Latin name—and, if so, which one ?

* See Haigh, *Attic Theatre*, pp. 266-71 ; *D.F.*, p. 155, n. 3.

It is generally agreed that the passages in iambic senarii
were meant for utterance without accompaniment, and that
all the other metres were meant to be accompanied by the
pipes. The senarius is no doubt modelled (with a difference)
on the Greek iambic trimeter, the normal vehicle of dialogue
in Greek drama. Aristotle (*Poet.* iv) tells us that of all metres
the iambic is the best adapted to represent speech (λεκτικόν),
and that it was therefore employed when speech or dialogue
(λέξις) was introduced into tragedy. He also says (*ib.* vi)
that some effects in drama are produced by metre alone,
others by music (μέλος) ; and we infer that there was at least
one metre without musical accompaniment. Lucian (*De Salt.*
27) satirizes an extravagant tragic actor who at times ' goes
about singing the iambics ', which seems to imply that they
were not meant to be sung. Cicero (*Orat.* lv. 183–4) speaks
of the senarii of the Latin comic poets as scarcely distinguishable
from ordinary prose ; and as he refers in the same passage to
bacchiac verses which are accompanied by the pipes, the
implication is that the iambic verses are not so accompanied.
We must, of course, be careful not to confuse Greek and Roman
practice, or early and late evidence. But with regard to the
practice of the Roman stage in Plautus' day we have a striking
piece of evidence in *Stichus* 758 ff. Up to this point the metre
of the scene—a merry slaves' drinking-party—has been trochaic
septenarius. At 758 the piper is invited to pluck his pipes from
his mouth and have a drink. To allow for his drinking, the
metre changes for seven lines to iambic senarius. Then he is
told to puff out his cheeks and play a new tune in return for his
draught of old wine. As he begins to play, the metre changes
from senarii to an iambic octonarius followed by iambic
septenarii, etc. Evidently* the actors dance :

Sang.   qui Ionicus aut cinaedicust, qui hoc tale facere possiet ?
            (*iamb. oct.*)
St.   si istoc me uorsu uiceris, alio me prouocato.
            (*iamb. sept.*)
Sang.   fac tu hoc modo.
St.   at tu hoc modo.
Sang.   babae !
St.   tatae !
Sang.   papae !
St.   pax !   (*iamb. sept.*)

* Cf. *E.L.V.* p. 262.

Sang. nunc pariter ambo. omnis uoco cinaedos contra.
          (*uers. Reizianus*)
          satis esse nobis non magis potis quam fungo imber.
          (*uers. Reiz.*)
St.   intro hinc abeamus nunciam : saltatum satis pro uinost.
          (*iamb. sept.*)
          uos, spectatores, plaudite atque ite ad uos comissatum.
          (*iamb. sept.*)

We can almost see the actors dancing as they utter these lines. Evidently the septenarii, like all the other metres except the senarii, were accompanied by the pipes. Moreover we have the express statement of Cicero (*Tusc.* I. xliv. 107) that the actor was accompanied by the pipe when delivering a passage of trochaic septenarii (cum tam bonos septenarios fundat ad tibiam). The lines quoted are

neu relliquias sic meas siris, denudatis ossibus,
taetra sanie delibutas foede diuexarier.

The question still remains : was there a difference in the method of utterance between the senarii and the other metres ? Furthermore, was there a difference between the way in which some metres were uttered to musical accompaniment and the way in which other metres were uttered to musical accompaniment ? When Cicero (*Tusc.* I. xliv. 106), after quoting some iambic octonarii, says haec pressis et flebilibus modis, qui totis theatris maestitiam inferant, concinuntur, ' these lines are sung to so subdued and mournful a melody as to draw tears from the whole audience ', does he mean that they were sung as we understand song ? And, if so, do these octonarii differ in the method of utterance from any other of the metres intended for accompaniment ?

Of Roman music we know very little. We have, however, some information about the music of the Greeks, who no doubt influenced the Romans in this as in the other arts. As Monro points out (*The Modes of Ancient Greek Music*, 1894, p. 113), ' several indications combine to make it probable that singing and speaking were not so widely separated from each other in Greek as in the modern languages with which we are most familiar.' As Greek was in the fifth century B.C. spoken with a predominantly pitch or musical accent, Greek speech was more like music than ours. Aristoxenus, a pupil of Aristotle, points out (Monro, p. 115) that ' there are two movements of the voice, not properly discriminated by any previous writer : namely, the *continuous*, which is the movement characteristic of speaking, and the *discrete* or that which proceeds by intervals, the movement of singing. In the latter the voice remains for a certain time in one note, and then passes by a definite interval to another. In the former it is continually gliding by imperceptible degrees from higher to lower or the reverse.' Nicomachus (first century A.D. or later) says (*Enchiridion*, p. 4) that ' if the notes and intervals of the speaking voice are allowed to be separate and distinct, the form of utterance becomes singing.' So long as the accent remained predominantly musical, it is difficult to see how it could have been ignored in utterance ; in other words, it is difficult to suppose that the natural pitch of the syllable was violated so that the voice might agree with the instrument. But when the pitch accent began to give way to a stress accent, the difference between speech and song might become more obvious. Aristides Quintilianus (between the second and fourth century A.D.) ' recognizes a third or intermediate movement of the voice, that which is employed in the recitation of poetry ' (Monro, p. 116). It is by no means clear that such a distinction could have been made in the fifth century B.C. The view that ' recitative ' was employed in Greek drama is really founded not on any precise and positive evidence but rather on the fact that the Greeks do not seem to differentiate clearly between ' speech ' and ' song '.* So far indeed as the evidence goes, it may be said that there were not *three* distinct forms of dramatic delivery but only *one*, a form of speech more musical than our speech but not at all corresponding to our idea of song.

According to most English scholars, the Romans had ·from early times a predominantly stress accent. They would therefore, presumably, have been more predisposed than the Greeks to recognize a distinction between speech and song. Nevertheless, like the Greeks, they seem frequently to confuse these terms. So Horace (*Odes* IV, xii. 10) talks of ' speaking a song ' (dicere carmen), and Ovid claims that his elegiacs were ' sung all over Rome ', totam cantata per urbem (*Trist.* IV, x. 59). We scarcely notice this confusion of terms, so familiar has it become. No doubt there are other references in Latin literature

---

* So Aristotle (*Poet.* xii) defines the πάροδος as ἡ πρώτη λέξις ὅλου χοροῦ, ' the first *speech* of the whole chorus '.

to 'speech' and 'song' which show that a distinction was sometimes made ; but if the terms were so often confused in the Augustan age and later, we can hardly assume that the modern distinction between 'speech' and 'song' was actually observed in theatrical practice in the time of Plautus.

We are dealing not with a verbal distinction but with a real problem. A possible clue may be afforded by the dramatic uses to which the different metres are put. We find that senarii are used invariably in prologues, and that the verse, if not already in senarii, tends to change to that metre when documents are being read aloud (*Asin.* 751 ff., *Bacch.* 997 ff., *Curc.* 429 ff.) ; when an oath is being dictated (*Rud.* 1338) ; when the speakers are recounting dreams (*Curc.* 246, *Merc.* 225, *Rud.* 593) ; in a scene of quiet persuasion (*Amph.* 882) ; after a display of insanity (*Men.* 872) ; where a serious piece of business has to be transacted (*Cist.* 747, *Curc.* 635). Septenarii, usually trochaic, are normal in epilogues and concluding scenes, and are very commonly used in lively, bustling scenes. Iambic octonarii have a slower movement ; Lindsay calls them the metre of soliloquy,* and we can see how suitable they are to represent the timorous gait of Sosia through the dark streets :

> qui me alter est audacior homo aut qui confidentior,
> iuuentutis mores qui sciam, qui hoc noctis solus ambulem ? †

Cretics, bacchiacs and other 'lyric' metres are often used to depict terror or some other intense emotion. We may take as an example of dramatic crescendo the first three scenes in the 'Third Act' of the *Rudens*. At line 593 Daemones appears alone and relates his dream ; he speaks in senarii. At line 615 Trachalio hurries out of the temple, bawling for help in somewhat burlesque style ; the metre is trochaic septenarius. At line 664 the terror-stricken girls appear ; their despair finds its natural expression in cretics. But elsewhere the 'lyric' metres (cretics, bacchiacs, etc.) are used with comic effect. Moreover many spirited scenes are in senarii : cf. *Rud.* 780 ff., 839 ff. Indeed an effective heightening of tension is created by the change from septenarii to senarii in *Rud.* 450, where (after a scene of badinage) the music stops abruptly as Ampelisca catches sight of the hated Labrax. There is no more dramatic scene in Plautus than *Capt.* 659 ff., where the

---

* *E.L.V.* 277.   † *Amph.* 153 f.

change from hurrying trochaic septenarii to business-like senarii effectively reflects the change in Hegio's mood from bewilderment to resolve.   In these and other cases the sudden silence of the accompaniment creates an atmosphere in which, as we might say, 'one could hear a pin drop'.   Plautus' choice of metre is in general decided not (as in Greek drama) by tradition but by the mood of the moment and the love of variety for its own sake.   Certain metres are almost inevitable ; we take it for granted that a hurrying messenger will speak in septenarii (cf. *Capt.* 768, *Curc.* 280, *Most.* 348, *Trin.* 1008), while a sedate traveller arriving from abroad will use senarii (*Men.* 226, *Most.* 431, *St.* 402).   But sometimes it is not so much the choice of metre as the change itself which is dramatic.   In *Rudens* 413 Ampelisca, speaking in iambic septenarii, knocks at a strange door :

heus, ecquis in uillast ? ecquis hoc recludit ? ecquis prodit ?

The door bursts open and the angry Sceparnio appears with an explosive trochaic line :

quis est qui nostris tam proterue foribus facit iniuriam ?

Here the dramatic effect depends on abruptness ; it is unlikely that there was a pause while the piper changed to the new rhythm.   In other words the piper had to take his cue from the actors' words ; his part was altogether subordinate to theirs.

A totally different effect is achieved in *Curc.* 158 f., where again the metre changes to trochaic septenarius as the door opens stealthily at the husky whisper of the old duenna :

placide egredere et sonitum prohibe forium et strepitum cardinum, ne quae hic agimus eru' percipiat fieri, mea Planesium.

The bacchiac, which in *Rud.* 259 ff. represents the dignified entry of the priestess, is used in *Men.* 753 ff to portray the futile effort of the old man to mend his pace :

ut aetas mea est atque ut hoc usu' facto est,
gradum proferam, progrediri properabo.

It is evident that Plautus was keenly interested in metre and rhythm, and that he used them for dramatic effect in a way which can scarcely be paralleled in Greek literature.   Compared with him Terence is uninspired.   But all the Roman dramatists, to the best of their ability, freely employed metrical variety to bring out the theatrical effects at which they aimed.   All drama was in metre ; the value of the accompaniment was to emphasize the metre. But to argue from the presence of the accompaniment that certain scenes were sung presents us with a formidable dilemma. Song, in our sense of the word, demands a special vocal and mental effort ; while the actor is singing everything else—gesture, dance, etc.—must take second place ; for the time being the action of the play is held up. Now it is practically certain that all the metres in a Latin play except the senarii were meant to be accompanied. But these metres, taken together, occupy the greater part of each play. It is difficult to suppose that they were all meant for song. Therefore most critics strive to distinguish the true songs from the mass of recitative. But any attempt to do so must be arbitrary ; Latin writers do not hint at such a distinction, and we have to fall back on our own sense of what is fitting.

Perhaps the most plausible example of song in Plautus is the eight-line serenade in cretics which Phaedromus addresses to the bolts of the door which shuts him from his mistress (*Curc.* 147–54). He has asked his slave ' Shall I go up to the door and sing a serenade ? ' and the slave replies, ' I won't say no or yes, seeing that your character is so changed.' Then Phaedromus begins :

> Bolts, ah, bolts, I greet you gladly ;
>   Take my love and hear my plea,
> Hear my prayer, my supplication,
>   Fairest bolts, ah, favour me.
> Change to foreign dancers for me,
>   Spring, I pray you, spring on high,
> Send a wretched man his dear love,
>   Love that drains his life-blood dry.
> Look ! they sleep, those bolts most base
>   Will not budge to do me grace !
>   (Nixon's translation.)

If the *Curculio* were being presented on the modern stage, this ' serenade ' would undoubtedly be sung. So ineradicable is our habit of attributing to antiquity our own outlook that we do not stop to enquire whether in fact the Roman actor used for these lines a form of utterance different from what he had used for the preceding dialogue.

That Plautus knew the charm and power of instrumental music is indicated in several passages. In the *Casina,* as the supposed 'bride' is being brought out of doors, the waiting bridegroom calls on the piper to 'fill the whole street with the sweet marriage tune', and together with Lysimachus he cries 'hymen hymenaee o hymen!' In *St.* 761-2 the piper is bidden 'hurry up and play us some charming sweet wanton air to make us tingle to our finger-tips.' Pseudolus, leaving the stage for a minute or two, promises the spectators that during his brief absence they will be entertained by the piper (573 *a*).

Nevertheless it is very doubtful whether we can regard the serenade in the *Curculio* as a song in our sense of the word. The word occentare (which I have translated 'sing a serenade') cannot be pressed too far ; Plautus himself uses the word elsewhere (*Pers.* 569) of the uproar made by a party of angry revellers before they burst into a house.* The serenade is indeed marked out from its immediate context by the cretic metre ; nevertheless that context is itself in metres usually considered 'lyrical' ; the preceding dialogue between Phae-dromus and his slave (138-46) is in anapaests, the following few lines are in glyconics and dochmiacs, and one of them seems meant not for song but for whisper :

> st, tace, tace !—taceo hercle equidem.—sentio sonitum.

The content of the serenade is not particularly lyrical ; the effect is comical rather than sentimental. I cannot discover any markedly lyrical quality in the so-called 'lyrical' passages in Plautus. He seems to me to reach his highest note in the trochaic septenarius. There is no passage more like a drinking-song in tone than *St.* 729 ff. :

> haec facetiast, amare inter se riualis duos,
> uno cantharo potare, unum scortum ducere.
> hoc memorabilest : ego tu sum, tu es ego, unanimi sumus ;
> unam amicam amamus ambo, mecum ubi est, tecum est tamen ;
> tecum ubi autem est, mecum ibi autemst ; neuter neutri inuidet.

On the modern stage these lines would readily lend themselves to song. Yet so far as the metre is concerned they are in no way different from the rest of this long, lively scene of dialogue in trochaic septenarii. Nowhere does Plautus come nearer to the spirit of a modern love-song than in *Curc.* 178-80 :

> sibi sua habeant regna reges, sibi diuitias diuites,
> sibi honores, sibi uirtutes, sibi pugnas, sibi proelia :
> dum mi abstineant inuidere, sibi quisque habeant quod suom est.

---

* *Merc.* 408 (occentent ostium) might be taken in either sense. See p. 40.

These lines again form merely part of a long scene of dialogue in the same metre. By way of contrast, what specially lyrical quality can any one find in the bacchiacs with which Eunomia admonishes her brother (*Aul.* 120 ff.) :

> uelim te arbitrari med haec uerba, frater, . . . ?

The one point clearly established is that Plautus relied on the piper to accompany all metres except the iambic senarii. What music the piper would supply was probably left to him. He was not a composer but an instrumentalist ; the didascaliae give his name after that of the chief actor, and he seems to have been a slave (' Marcipor, the slave of Oppius ', ' Flaccus, the slave of Claudius '). No doubt he had at his command a number of simple phrases and chose whichever of them seemed best suited to the metre of the scene. His art, such as it was, was entirely ancillary to that of the actors. At the rehearsals he would presumably have become familiar with the play. The letters C and DV (if we may suppose that they were written in the author's manuscript, which was also no doubt the actors' book) would make clear at the beginning of each scene whether it was to be accompanied or not. Plautus was an artist in rhythm, and he well knew how much the rhythm of his lines depended on accompaniment if it was to have its full effect. Cicero (*Orat.* lv. 183–4) tells us that, but for the presence of the piper, even some bacchiac verses in tragedy would seem like prose :

> quaenam te esse dicam ? qui tarda in senectute . . .
> quae, nisi cum tibicen accessit, orationi sunt solutae simillima.

We distinguish between ' song ' and instrumental accompaniment ; for the Greeks and Romans this was almost impossible. The word cantare is used of the instrument : cf. tibicinam cantantem (*Most.* 934). The word canticum meant ' utterance to musical accompaniment ' without any implication that the utterance, considered vocally, was anything more than rhythmical speech. Cicero (*Sest.* 118) uses the words cantores, histriones and actores of the same persons. But in the same passage (122) he refers to some lines in septenarii as having been *spoken* by the actor (illa quem ad modum dixit); and as he applies the verb ' agere ' to the actor's rendering alike of the septenarii and of the anapaests, he seems to imply that the style of utterance was not markedly different. Plautus (*Pseud.* 366) makes Ballio address his critics as cantores probos ! meaning not ' how sweetly you sing ! ' but ' what lungs you have ! ' So canto and cano are used by the dramatists of any loud utterance—e.g. the crowing of a cock (*M.G.* 690)—or droning repetition (*Tr.* 287, *Ph.* 495). Whatever the metre, the words are said to be ' spoken ' (dico or loquor) : so after a passage in cretics and other metres uttered by Sosia the listening Mercury remarks (*Amph.* 248) :

> nunquam etiam quicquam adhuc uerborum est prolocutus perperam.

In *Cas.* 166 Myrrhina, after beginning a speech which is partly in anapaests, partly in cretics, asks ' ecquis haec quae loquor audit ? ' It seems unlikely that *Cas.* 213 was meant to be sung, though the metre is glyconic :

> st ! tace !—quid est ?—em !—quis est quem uides ?—uir eccum it.

We have plenty of evidence that Roman as well as Greek actors were expected to have *loud* voices ; the all-important thing was to make themselves audible. Terence's actor-manager, Ambivius Turpio, complains of the strain put on the actor's strength by his violent efforts and loud *shouting* :

> clamore summo cum labore maxumo (*H.T.* 40).

There is no reference in the plays to any one's powers of singing, as distinct from speaking, and no mention of a special vocalist. The lyrical metres are distributed among all the characters : thus in the *Casina* Pardalisca, Olympio and Lysidamus are all on the stage together, each speaking for the most part in lyrical metres (814–54) ; then Myrrhina, Pardalisca and Cleostrata (855–73) ; then Olympio, Cleostrata and Myrrhina (874–936). If cretics, bacchiacs or any other metres denote ' song ', then Plautus must have taken for granted that the actors would all be able to sing. A single vocalist could not have undertaken the singing of all the cantica, no matter how narrowly we try to define the term.

Beyond all doubt Plautine comedy is drama, not opera. Nevertheless it had a musical element. In some measure Plautus here resembles Shakespeare. Each wrote at a time when the spirit of the language was struggling to assert itself against quantitative metres imported from abroad, or from classical tradition. Each wrote verses intended for musical accompaniment, which he expected others to supply. That there was music and song in Elizabethan drama was in part due to the classical tradition ; poets since the days of Homer had been said to ' sing ' their verses, and no one stopped to ask what the Greeks had meant by ' song.'* The Elizabethan age itself was pre-eminently an age of song. This was made possible by unique musical and cultural conditions ; there was a close relation between poets and musicians, and a general love of music and poetry. The essential difference between the Plautine cantica and Shakespeare's songs may be made more plain when we consider that Shakespeare's songs (1) are short ; (2) are easily distinguishable from their context ; (3) are composed in stanzas, intended to be sung to a repeated air ; (4) are lyrical not only in form but in sentiment ; (5) though often of great dramatic importance,† nevertheless do not advance the action in quite the same way as does the dialogue ; (6) are assigned to a particular character, obviously because his part was meant to be taken by an actor with a good voice ; (7) are usually referred to in the context in terms which indicate specifically that they were sung. ' A mellifluous voice, as I am true knight ! ' ' My voice is ragged ; I know I cannot please you.' ' Truly, young gentleman, though there was no great matter in the ditty, yet the note was very untunable.'[1] ' The cantica of Plautus satisfy none of these conditions. If the term includes all passages accompanied by music, they occupy the greater part of each play. If we exclude the septenarii, the other metres are so mingled that it is impossible to isolate the so-called ' songs '. No one has succeeded in discovering any trace of ' strophic ' composition in Plautus.‡

---

* See Bruce Pattison, *Music and Poetry of the English Renaissance*, p. 20–1. Perhaps the music which Homer played on his lyre was not unlike the music played by the Norman minstrels (ib. p. 24) : ' a little snatch of melody served for a single line and was repeated throughout the composition. This sounds terribly tedious to us, but the attention of the audience was no doubt concentrated on the story.' There is much uncertainty as between declamation and song : the O.E. expression ' singan and secgan '—' sing and say '—suggests that Epic ' came to be declaimed '.

† See Noble, *Shakespeare's Use of Song*, p. 12.

‡ Even Crusius, who believes that he has proved the existence of Responsion (in his sense of the term), has to admit that ' syllabic responsion scarcely exists in Plautus ' (*Die Responsion in den Plautinischen Cantica*, 1929, p. 2). The true explanation for the frequent examples of symmetry in Plautus has been pointed out by Lindsay (*Early Latin Verse*, p. 113) : ' he likes to make a reply the exact counterpart of a question . . . stroke is exactly matched by counter-stroke, cut by parry . . . This is a feature of all lively comedy, English as well as Latin.'

The passages in cretics, etc., are no whit more lyrical than certain passages in the septenarii. The normal action of the play is carried on as freely in one metre as in another,* although when audibility is specially important the accompaniment stops altogether and the metre becomes the senarius. Cretic and bacchiac passages are distributed as freely as any others among the characters. There is no specific reference to song, the musical use of the human voice, in Plautus, and it is conceivable that in his day the very idea of ' song ' (in our sense of the word) did not exist.

The much-debated question as to the origin of the cantica would seem to be largely unreal. Whatever metrical hints the Latin dramatists gathered from external sources, their use of the metres is characteristically Roman. Professor Fraenkel has rightly exorcized the phantom of ' Hellenistic opera ' conjured up by the imagination of Leo and Wilamowitz (*Plautinisches im Plautus*, p. 333). Unfortunately he himself clings to the view that Plautine comedy is distinguished from its Greek originals by its ' interchange of spoken and sung scenes ' (*ib.* p. 323). If by ' song ' we mean rhythmic declamation supported by instrumental accompaniment, two-thirds of Plautus is song ; if the term implies that the vocalist keeps to a definite tune, there is no song in Plautus. His achievement was to exploit the dramatic possibilities of rhythm as no writer before or after him has done. The nameless poet who composed his epitaph showed sound judgment when he made Laughter and Rhythm the chief mourners at the dramatist's grave.

* Duckworth (N.R.C. 371 n.) says, ' This is not true of the many monodies which are used expressly for the expression of emotions or for moralizing '. That may be because they are monodies.

CHAPTER XXVII

EPILOGUE : DRAMA UNDER THE EMPIRE

THE THEATRE was a characteristic part of Roman life and civilization. Consequently under the Empire we find Roman theatres, great or small, springing up in every province. When we ask what kinds of performances took place in these buildings, the answer is doubtful and disappointing. Such information as we possess suggests that the entertainment normally provided in the imperial theatres consisted of trivial or degrading performances, whether mime, recitation, pantomime or even gladiatorial combat.

The establishment of the Empire helped to confirm certain tendencies which had already become visible in Republican drama, and also to create others. Long before the end of the Republic the supply of new plays for the stage had practically ceased. The Augustan age gave birth to two famous tragedies, Varius' *Thyestes*[1] and Ovid's *Medea* (almost certainly these were original works, not translations). According to one scholiast[2] the *Thyestes* was produced at the games in celebration of the victory of Actium ; if this information is accurate, it appears to be our last record of the performance of a new Latin play. Otherwise such few performances of literary tragedy or comedy as are recorded are revivals of old plays. For example Seneca (*ep.* 80) seems to speak of a contemporary performance of Accius' *Atreus*. Yet the inevitable change in literary style would make the works of the Republican tragedians seem more and more archaic as time went on. For Quintilian Pacuvius and Accius are the rude pioneers of Roman tragedy, which culminates in writers like Ovid. But as Ovid himself,[3] long after the publication of the *Medea*, protests that he never was so depraved as to write for the stage, it would appear that Quintilian is here thinking of tragedy simply as a literary form, not as something intended for performance. Something of the spirit of tragedy may have survived in the dramatic recitations ; Nero, we are told, ' sang ' Orestes the Matricide,

Oedipus Blinded, Hercules Mad. These seem to have been cantica depicting certain scenes of tragic character ; sometimes the words were Greek. The vogue of these recitations, such as it was, itself suggests that tragedy proper was no longer familiar on the stage. Far more important was the pantomime,[4] introduced in 22 B.C. by Pylades and Bathyllus. This typically Roman performance (the Greeks called it the ' Italian dance ') stood at the opposite extreme to the dramatic recitation ; the central figure was the masked dancer, who performed scenes in dumbshow, while appropriate words were sung by a chorus. Lucian's lively account shows that the themes were taken from mythology—for example the love of Ares and Aphrodite and the snare set for the guilty pair by the injured husband Hephaestus. The libretto sung by the chorus was specially written for the performance. The writing of such libretti was a lucrative if degrading occupation which attracted even such poets as Lucan and Statius.[5] The performance took place on the stage ; some believe that elaborate scenery (illustrated, perhaps, in the Pompeian wall-paintings) formed the background.* Some passages in ancient authors would suggest, it is true, that the pantomime was regarded as drama, whether tragic, comic or satyric ; but in reality it seems to have been something quite new and unconnected with drama proper. The modern view that tragedy was decomposed, so to speak, into the dramatic recitations and the pantomimic dances is altogether artificial. The most obvious link of the pantomime with drama was the stage setting ; its themes, taken from mythology, might naturally be tragic ; at its highest level it may have appealed to that section of the public who would in other circumstances have been interested in tragedy ; but our evidence is that the essential attraction of pantomime was the supple, artistic, expressive, passionate, sometimes exquisitely lascivious movements[6] of the dancer—and what has such a performance to do with true tragedy ?

Occasional attempts are made by modern writers to show that the tragedies attributed to Seneca were intended for performance on the stage. They happen to be the only complete Latin tragedies which we possess, and their interest as literature would be greatly increased if we could regard them

---

* The usual view ; but there is no evidence to support it. See Purser's article on *Pantomimus* (Smith's *Dictionary of Antiquities*, ii. 334–6).[7]

as genuine drama.   But if anything is clear about Roman drama as a whole, it is that no one wrote for the stage except to make money.   This is true even of Republican times, when the theatre was still fairly respectable ; under the Empire the Romans of the literary class regarded the theatre with something like horror.   It is incredible that Seneca, one of the richest men in Rome and a man who openly admits [8] his distaste for close contact with the common people or their amusements, should have composed plays intended to win the favour of the general public.   The dramatist who writes for the stage must take into account not only the tastes of his audience but the requirements of the stage ; and the internal evidence of the Senecan plays shows that the author has not visualized the actions of his characters.   The usual technique of bringing characters on or taking them off is ignored.   We often realize that a person is conceived as present only by the fact that a speech is put into his mouth.   We cannot tell when he leaves the stage except by the fact that no more words are attributed or addressed to him.   A long speech is attributed to Clytaemnestra (*Agam.* 108–124) ; yet it appears from the remarks of the other person present (126) that Clytaemnestra has been silent ; the speech must therefore represent her *thoughts*.   Things happen which could not have taken place on the classical (or indeed any) stage : Hercules shoots his wife and children ; afterwards he tries to commit suicide by shooting himself with his own bow and arrow ; the fragments of corpses are pieced together, etc.   If at times the author seems vaguely conscious of a stage, the explanation is that though his plays are original works, he is using as his models Greek plays, which were of course intended for performance. There is no evidence that Seneca (or whoever the author was) was imitating the old Latin tragedies ; the Senecan tragedies are simply artificial imitations of Greek tragedy, worked up in the style of the Silver Age, and they are meant to be read or declaimed, not to be acted.*

The *Octauia,* our sole extant example of the Roman historical play, is generally thought to have been composed by some unknown author shortly after the death of Nero, to which event there is a ' prophetic ' reference circumstantial enough to indicate knowledge of the facts.   While in style less brilliant and somewhat more natural than the tragedies of

* See Appendix P.

Seneca, it is equally regardless of stage requirements. The plot is based on the facts of history, but is worked up on the model of Greek tragedy. That Octavia, Nero's innocent and unfortunate wife, should have a nurse in whom to confide is perhaps admissible ; but that his hardened mistress Poppaea should also be assigned a nurse is more than we can stand. It is doubtful whether there is any connexion between this piece and the old Republican praetextae, which celebrated the achievements of Roman consuls in battle. The *Octauia* is a purely literary and artificial treatment of recent history on the lines of Greek tragedy.

Even in Republican days the Roman government had been very sensitive to political allusions, however veiled or even unintentional, if uttered on the stage. Under the Empire such allusions might bring appalling consequences to the author and the actor concerned. The tragedies of Seneca as well as the *Octauia* present absolute rulers in an odious light—a consideration which makes it still less likely that they were composed for production in the presence of the general public (including the Emperor himself) during the reign of Claudius, Nero or Vespasian. For although the occasional revival of an old tragedy, such as Accius' *Atreus*, might be sanctioned (and our evidence suggests that such revivals were infrequent), and although a spice of political allusion, however dangerous, was in the very nature of the mime, the composition and performance of new tragedies which might rouse popular feeling against the imperial system was another matter.

It is highly unlikely that any of the tragedies which have come down to us from the Empire was ever performed until the Renaissance. *Then* their influence was all-important, and went far to determine the nature of modern drama. In A.D. 1551–2 Seneca's *Troades* was performed at Trinity College, Cambridge. The Elizabethan audiences, almost as inured to scenes of blood as the Romans, liked the Senecan blend of moralizing and melodrama. Juliet's Nurse, the Ghost in *Hamlet*, the Tyrant as portrayed in *Richard the Third*, are figures which owe something to Seneca. Fortunately for the world, the Elizabethan drama was the product of many other factors as well as the influence of Senecan classical tragedy.

The position of comedy under the Empire was no better than that of tragedy. The very word comoedus is used of a slave who reads extracts from comedy as an entertainment for guests at dinner. Purely literary comedies were composed : Pliny tells us[9] that he has heard Vergilius Romanus ' reading to a few listeners ' his imitation of Old Greek Comedy (which included a flattering reference to Pliny himself). Vergilius had also written imitations of New Comedy, which Pliny compares in excellence to the works of Plautus and Terence.* Quintilian, in his reference to Latin comedy, mentions no composer later than Terence ; nevertheless he refers to contemporary actors of comedy, who wore masks, played the stock rôles of the palliata, and were so moved by their own acting as to be seen in tears after they had removed their masks. Apparently, then, there were still performances of genuine high comedy ; but what were the comedies so performed ? Immediately after his mention[10] of the contemporary comic actors Demetrius and Stratocles, Quintilian quotes a passage of comedy to illustrate his meaning —and the quotation is from Terence. This suggests that the comedies performed in the Imperial theatres were the old classics. Such revivals were probably exceptional ; Pliny speaks of comedy, as well as tragedy, as suitable for declamation; the performances which he mentions are mimes and panto- mimes. Juvenal speaks[11] of togatae as still being written in his day—but apparently only for recitation. The only togata which we know to have been performed under the Empire is the *Incendium* of Afranius,[12] and this was revived merely in order to give a spectacular display of a stage fire. If the palliatae and togatae written under the Empire were as oblivious of stage needs as are the tragedies of Seneca, we can understand that theatrical managers, if they wished to produce a comedy, were forced to draw on the Republican classics.

If we can judge by the history of Greece and Rome, a certain measure of public freedom is necessary to the production of true drama. It was difficult for the Romans of the Empire to feel any sense of corporate freedom or responsibility, or even to take pride in the greatness of the universal Empire ; patriot- ism is impossible in a State which fills the world. In such circumstances men's interests were confined to themselves, their own affairs and the trivial interests and follies of everyday

* Cf. the epitaph (CIL. ix. 1164) of M. Pomponius Bassulus (second century A.D.) : ' lest I should live a life of bestial sloth, I translated some dainty plays of Menander, and composed some new plays myself'.

life.   Under foreign domination the Greeks had indeed produced New Comedy ; the Romans, overwhelmed under their
own Empire, gave themselves up to a merely sensual existence.
In their theatres pantomime took the place of tragedy, while
comedy gave way to farce.   Since the sole aim was to tickle the
jaded palate of the public, producers not only lavished all the
resources of wealth and technique on their extravagant
productions, but also descended to the lowest depths of the
disgusting and the obscene.   Even Livy regarded the theatre
of his day as a danger to public morals and the existence of
the State ;   soon sexual [13] displays were visibly presented on
the stage, and stage ' executions ' [14] were carried out in reality
(by substituting for the actor a condemned criminal).   While
we must always bear in mind that it is usually the exceptional
and the extreme which is recorded, and that much of our
information comes from sources hostile to the stage, the
cumulative weight of testimony makes it clear that the dramatic
standards of the Empire were altogether below those of the days
when such plays as the *Captiui* and the *Adelphi* were written
and produced for the amusement of the people.

The fabula Atellana [15] maintained its place on the stages of
the first century A.D., both in Rome and in the provincial
theatres.   It was still a masked performance, given as an
' after-piece ' ; it still had a rustic flavour, and it still brought
on the stage the familiar figures of Maccus, Bucco, Pappus,
Manducus and Dossennus ; its performers were still fond of
quips, riddles and topical allusions ; their status, whatever it
had been in Livy's day, seems now to be no better than that
of the other theatrical performers, whether slaves or freedmen.
Tacitus speaks with contempt of the enormous vogue and the
degraded morality of the Atellana in the time of Tiberius.
We hear occasionally of Greek cantica and of mythological
themes, but on the whole the Atellana seems to have preserved
its Italian, country-town flavour.   The wealthy freedman
Trimalchio,[16] so proud of his humble Italian origin that he
compelled his flute-player to play only Latin airs, also insisted
that the troupe of ' comedians ' which he had bought should
perform only Atellane plays.   We hear practically nothing of
literary Atellanae, or of the authors of such Atellanae as were
performed on the stage.   Perhaps after the time of Pomponius
and Novius this type of farce had returned to its sub-literary,

semi-improvised form. No doubt in the course of time it grew more and more like the mime, though the use of masks must always, one would imagine, have been a characteristic feature. After the end of the first century A.D. we hear no more of the fabula Atellana.

The composition of purely literary mimes was one of the amusements of dilettanti ; belle componis mimos, as Martial remarks[17] to one of these writers. Perhaps these literary mimes were mimiambi, such as were written by Pliny's versatile friend,[18] Vergilius Romanus, character studies intended for recital, modelled on the mimiambi of Herondas. The mime intended for performance on the stage remained sub-literary, un-metrical and largely impromptu. The term, as in earlier times, includes any ' imitative ' piece from sheer mimicry to playlets introducing several characters and containing several scenes.

No Latin mimes have survived ; we have, however, an acting edition of a Greek mime[19] preserved from the second century after Christ, containing six or seven short scenes. The action takes place in front of a house (the door of which could conveniently be represented by the opening in the curtain through which the performers make their appearance). The beginning of the mime is lost. The opening words show us the archimima or ' leading lady ' in the character of a faithless wife, trying to seduce Aesopus, one of her slaves. He is in love with a fellow-slave, Apollonia, and rejects his mistress's advances. She then orders the lovers to be taken away and left to die. A later scene shows the ' body ' of Aesopus being brought in ; the other slaves pretend that he has thrown himself from a height (actually they have drugged him for his own safety) ; his mistress mourns his death, but soon consoles herself with the company of another slave, Malacus, with whom she conspires to poison her husband, whose ' body ' is presently brought in. Now comes the turning-point. The old man gets up and denounces his guilty wife and Malacus ; they are led off to punishment, while Aesopus and Apollonia are found to be alive and well, and all ends happily.

The dialogue is in prose ; probably the actors—or at least the archimima, who has by far the most important rôle—felt free to expand it at will. The sordid theme and the startlingly indecent language seem to be characteristic of the mime in general. (See Appendix L.)

In indecency the mime reached incredible depths. Not only was adultery a stock theme : the Emperor Heliogabalus ordered its realistic performance on the stage. It was natural that the Christian church[20] should set itself against the mime, and equally natural that the actors should retaliate by mocking Christian sacraments, much to the delight of the crowd. Gradually the church won the upper hand. In the fifth century all performers of mime were excommunicated. In the sixth century Justinian closed the theatres. Yet the mime lived on. Its simple requirements—a stage and a curtain—could be supplied in any public place or private house, and in such settings it continued to entertain audiences who were now nominally Christian. Though forced to drop its burlesque of the sacraments, it still scandalized the Fathers by its indecency and the immorality of its performers. Yet, as one of the last strongholds of paganism, the mime did not lack defenders. About A.D. 500 the sophist Choricius of Gaza wrote his apology for actors (i.e. performers of mime), while the mime-actress Theodora, whose ' strip-tease ' acts had delighted the public of Byzantium, succeeded in captivating the affections of Justinian himself, and was elevated to the imperial throne.

How far the mime survived the fall of ancient civilization is a doubtful point. So simple and elemental a type of performance might arise independently in many ages and countries. Yet it is hard to feel confident that the classical mime ever wholly ceased to be. Certainly the Middle Ages had their mimes. In its latest phase the classical mime was the last representative of classical drama ; its strolling performers, ' birds of passage '[21] as a Greek poet calls them, had taken over all that was left of a great tradition. Somehow or other they may have handed on their craft to their successors of the Dark and Middle Ages. When the darkness clears away we see a new drama arising. Perhaps its performers were historically linked with the strolling companies of classical times. However that may be, the re-birth of classical literature was to ensure that the new drama would grow to its full stature under the shadow of the drama of Rome.

VII   THE ROMAN THEATRE, ORANGE

APPENDIX A

SEATS IN THE GREEK AND ROMAN THEATRES

(*Classical Review*, Vol. liii. pp. 51–5.)

THERE are several passages in ancient authors * which, taken together, seem to imply that the spectators of Roman drama during its productive period were forced to stand. This view was readily accepted by nineteenth-century scholars, eager to find as many differences as possible between Greek and Roman practice ; it is, of course, incompatible with the frequent references to a seated audience in the prologues of Plautus' plays ; † such references were therefore regarded as proof that the prologues themselves were post-Plautine.‡ We may, indeed, agree that a prologue is the part of a play which is most liable to modification at the hands of later producers ; § and with the prologues we might be willing also to sacrifice the concluding words of the *Truculentus* :

> spectatores, bene ualete, plaudite atque *exsurgite.*

There are other references to seats, however, within the body of the plays (*Aul.* 719, *Curc.* 644-7, *Poen.* 1224) ; and these passages set us a pretty dilemma : are we to regard them as examples of somewhat mechanical translation from the Greek, or as post-Plautine insertions ?

The supposed evidence against the existence of seats seems to imply further that the spectators were forced to stand not merely from lack of accommodation but because of decrees designed to check luxury and idleness.‖ Such legislation must have been singularly unpopular with the theatre-goers who had to remain on their feet throughout long plays, the actors and playwrights who were handicapped by the discomfort thus inflicted on their public, and even the magistrates who gave the shows in order to win the favour of the electorate. Every one present would, of course, be aware that in Greek theatres no farther away than Pompeii seating accommodation was provided for all. In *Poen.* 1224 a character remarks ' in pauca confer : sitiunt qui sedent ', ' Cut it short : the

---

* Given in P.-W., s.v. *theatrum.*

† *Amph.* 65 ; *Capt.* 12 ; *Poen.* 10 ; *Pseud.* 1.

‡ This view is still upheld, e.g. by Wight Duff, *Literary History of Rome to the Close of the Golden Age,* 1927, p. 157.

§ Cf. the prologue to the *Casina,* which refers expressly to a revival performance.

‖ Cf. Tac. *Ann.* xiv. 20 : stantem populum spectauisse, ne, si consideret theatro, dies totos ignauia continuaret.

stalls are thirsty '.   Is this, perhaps, an example of mechanical
translation from the Greek ?   But how irritated would a *standing*
audience be at such a reference to the (comparatively trifling)
discomforts of a *seated* audience !   How tactless the dramatist who
would allow such a reference to remain !   This line must, therefore,
be a post-Plautine insertion (in spite of its Plautine ring) ;   we may
admit that jokes of this kind might well be added by an interpolator.
But it is not so easy to explain away *Aul.* 718-9 :

> quid est ? quid ridetis ? noui omnes, scio fures esse hic complures,
> qui uestitu et creta occultant sese atque sedent quasi sint frugi.

' Eh, what's that ?   What are you grinning for ?   I know you, the whole
lot of you !   I know there are thieves here, plenty of 'em, that cover themselves up in dapper clothes and sit still as if they were honest men ! ' *

Here Euclio, robbed of his gold, is addressing the audience—
and he refers to them as seated.   Jesting references to the knavishness
of the audience may, of course be paralleled in Greek (e.g. *Frogs*,
274-6), and it would be natural to assume that Plautus is here
translating his original ;   but we cannot suppose that the lines
quoted were addressed to a *standing* audience ;   they cannot, therefore, be an example of mechanical translation from the Greek,† but
must ex hypothesi be another post-Plautine insertion.   But I now
wish to draw attention to a remarkable passage in the *Curculio*
(643-7) :

> THER. nutrix quae fuit ?   PLAN. Archestrata.
>   ea me spectatum tulerat per Dionysia.
>   postquam illo uentum est, iam, ut me conlocauerat,
>   exoritur uentus turbo, spectacla ibi ruunt,
>   ego pertimesco.   ibi me nescio quis arripit . . .

These lines occur in the vital ἀναγνώρισις or ' recognition ' scene.
The heroine is explaining how she was kidnapped in her infancy.
Her nurse had taken her to the show at the Dionysiac festival.
' We had scarcely arrived, and I been put in my place, when a
perfect hurricane arose ;   the seats caved in—I was so terrified !
Then some one or other seized me. . . .'   (Nixon's translation.)
So far as I know, the authenticity of these lines has not been questioned ;   in fact, they form an appropriate and almost essential
part of an essential scene.   There can be no reason, therefore, for
doubting that they are from the hand of Plautus himself.   From
this it would seem to follow that even in Plautus' times the word
spectac(u)la had acquired the sense ' seats for spectators ' in which

---

* Nixon's translation.
   † Especially in view of the apparent reference to togas, togae cretatae,—which
seem to have been worn as early as the fifth century (Livy IV. xxv. 13).

we find it regularly used in Classical and Silver Latin.* Moreover, as the scene described is Greek in detail, and as the passage would have been as essential to the Greek original as to the Latin translation, it would seem to follow that Plautus is here translating from the Greek.

The scene of the *Curculio* is in Epidaurus (line 341) ; the kidnapping of the heroine, however, must have occurred somewhere else.† Of the Greek original of the *Curculio* we know nothing ; but as Athens was the birthplace and focus of New Comedy,‡ it is natural to suppose that this play also was written and first produced at Athens, and further, that the heroine should herself be regarded as Athenian by birth (like Palaestra in the *Rudens*). The kidnapping would, therefore, have occurred during the festival of Dionysus in Athens. I know of no evidence that special seats were erected for the spectators of the processions on such occasions ; the natural assumption is that the kidnapping occurred in the theatre.§ Apparently, then, we are to understand that the spectators' seats in the Athenian theatre collapsed in a storm. That this incident had actually occurred, and within the memory of the spectators who first saw the original of the *Curculio*, is suggested by Therapontigonus' remark (line 651) : ' memini istanc turbam fieri '.

To justify this conclusion, I must now endeavour to show (1) that the word spectacla in the passage quoted can only mean ' spectators' seats ' ; (2) that, even in the time of New Comedy, there were still, in the Athenian theatre, seats capable of being blown down by a storm—in other words, wooden seats supported on scaffolding.

Two passages in Suetonius show clearly that spectacula can be used of the part of an amphitheatre occupied by the spectators (*Cal.* 35 : ' hunc spectaculis detractum repente et in harenam deductum Thraeci comparauit ' ; *Dom.* 10 : ' patrem familias quod Thraecem murmilloni parem, munerario imparem dixerat, detractum spectaculis in harenam canibus obiecit'‖). The references here would presumably be to the tiers of *stone* seats : but that spectacula can also mean ' grand stands ' is indicated by Tac. *Ann.* XIV. 13 : ' exstructos, qua incederet, spectaculorum gradus, quo modo triumphi uisuntur ' ; and that the ' gods ' in the amphitheatre occupied such wooden stands is suggested by Suet. *Aug.* 44,

---

* Cic. *Pro. Sest.* 124 ; Livy I. xxxv. 8 ; Ovid *Met.* x. 668 ; Tac. *Ann. xiv.* 13 ; Suet. *Calig.* 35, *Dom.* 10.

† Kidnapped children are always taken to another town : see *Captivi, Menaechmi, Poenulus, Rudens*.

‡ Half of Plautus' plays are staged at Athens.

§ The vexed question whether women were admitted to the Athenian theatre would seem to be settled, for the late fourth century at least, by this very passage.

‖ The pater familias would presumably be sitting (within earshot of the emperor) in one of the rows of stone seats which formed the lower two maeniana of the Flavian Amphitheatre.

where we are told that, to allay a panic, the emperor left his place and *sat* in that part of the building which seemed threatened with collapse.* That the occupants of the spectacula normally sat even in the time of Cicero is shown by *Pro Sest.* 124 : ' maximum uero populi Romani iudicium uniuersi *consessu* gladiatorio declaratum est . . . in hunc *consessum* P. Sestius . . . uenit . . . tantus est ex omnibus spectaculis . . . plausus excitatus . . .' Finally we have a description in Livy of the ' grand stands ' of the primitive Circus (I. xxxv 8) : ' tum primum circo, qui nunc maximus dicitur, designatus locus est. loca diuisa patribus equitibusque ubi spectacula sibi quisque facerent ; fori appellati ; spectauere furcis duodenos ab terra spectacula alta sustinentibus pedes '. Evidently the Fathers stood—or (perhaps more probably) sat— on platforms twelve feet high, which were supported by forked poles.

Not only can spectacula mean ' seats at a show ' : it is the only precise word for such seats (though we find subsellia, scamna, sedilia, used for the ' seats ', ' benches ', or ' rows '). The usual meaning of the word [1] is ' show ', ' spectacle ', its only other sense is ' seats ' (or ' stands ') for the spectators of a show ; nowhere does it mean ' stage scenery '. In the *Curculio* passage it cannot bear its primary meaning : how could the ' show ' be blown down by the wind ? Evidently something collapsed and thereby spread panic among the spectators ; what could this have been unless the seats or scaffolding on which they sat or stood ? We should also consider the words ' ut me conlocauerat ', which surely describe how the nurse set the little girl on a seat. The only reason for resisting this argument is that we seem to have proved too much ; in trying to show that the Roman spectators sat on wooden seats, we seem to have shown that the Greek spectators sat on wooden seats too.

We are so accustomed to picture the audience of Sophocles sitting on rows of stone seats that we find it hard to realize that the evidence is against such a view. Even Haigh, after proving to his own satisfaction (*Attic Theatre*, pp. 83-6) that the seats in the theatre of Dionysus were not of stone but of wood until long after the end of the fifth century, is apt to forget his conclusions and slip back to the earlier view. I doubt the relevance of the archaeological evidence ; while Puchstein tries to date the stone seats as far back as the last years of the fifth century, Dörpfeld, supported by Haigh, assigns them to a date not earlier than the middle of the fourth century ; and Haigh suggests that they owe their origin to the reconstruction of Lycurgus, who was minister of finance between 338 and 326. The inscriptions on the seats seem to belong to the age of Hadrian. I turn to the literary evidence.

The only word I can find in fifth-century Greek for ' seats in the

* cum consternatum ruinae metu populum retinere . . . nullo modo posset, transiit e loco suo atque in ea parte consedit quae suspecta maxime erat.

theatre' is ἰκρία (ἴκρια).* The general sense of this word appears to be 'planking resting on uprights'; thus in Homer it denotes 'decks'; in Herodotus v. 16 it is used of the platforms of lake-dwellers (ἰκρία ἐπὶ σταυρῶν ὑψηλῶν ἐζευγμένα ἐν μέσῃ ἕστηκε τῇ λίμνῃ). Sometimes in mediaeval authors it seems to be used of upright poles; nowhere have I found it used to denote an object made of any material other than wood. Of its use for 'seats in the theatre' we have two fifth-century examples :

Ar. *Thesm.* 395 :

> ὥστ' εὐθὺς εἰσιόντες ἀπὸ τῶν ἰκρίων
> ὑποβλέπουσ' ἡμᾶς

(of the men coming home to their wives from the theatre) ;

Cratin. *Incert.* 53 (Meineke) :

> χαῖρ', ὦ μέγ' ἀχρειόγελως ὅμιλε ταῖς ἐπίβδαις,
> τῆς ἡμετέρας σοφίας κριτὴς ἄριστε πάντων·
> εὐδαίμον' ἔτικτέ σε μήτηρ ἰκρίων ψόφησιν

(where the poet is addressing the Athenian audience, who delight in the 'clatter of the benches', spectaculorum strepitu, as Meineke translates it).

I have found no other word in Greek drama for 'spectators' seats' (as opposed to the 'seats of honour' of the πρόεδροι).

For further information about these theatrical ἰκρία we must turn with due caution to the mediaeval lexicographers :

Photius (ninth cent.), s.v. ἰκρία : τά ἐν τῇ ἀγορᾷ ἀφ' ὧν ἐθεῶντο τοὺς Διονυσιακοὺς ἀγῶνας πρὶν ἢ κατασκευασθῆναι τὸ ἐν Διονύσου θέατρον.

Suidas (c. 1100 A.D. ?), s.v. ἰκρία : ὀρθὰ ξύλα . . . καὶ τὰ τῶν θεάτρων . . . ἐπὶ ξύλων γὰρ ἐκάθηντο. πρὶν γένηται τὸ θέατρον, ξύλα ἐδέσμευον καὶ οὕτως ἐθεώρουν. Ἀριστοφάνης Θεσμοφοριαζούσαις κ.τ.λ. (as already quoted.)

Id. s.v. Αἰσχύλος: . . . φυγὼν δὲ εἰς Σικελίαν διὰ τὸ πεσεῖν τὰ ἰκρία ἐπιδεικνυμένου αὐτοῦ . . .

Id. s.v. Πρατίνας : . . . ἀντηγωνίζετο δὲ Αἰσχύλῳ . . . ἐπὶ τῆς ὁ ὀλυμπιάδος . . . ἐπιδεικνυμένου δὲ τούτου συνέβη τὰ ἰκρία, ἐφ' ὧν ἑστήκεσαν οἱ θεαταί, πεσεῖν, καὶ ἐκ τούτου θέατρου ᾠκοδομήθη Ἀθηναίοις.

Gramm. Bekker. Anecd. p. 354, 25, s.v. αἰγείρου θέα : Ἀθήνησιν αἴγειρος ἦν, ἧς πλησίον τὰ ἰκρία ἐπήγνυντο εἰς τὴν θέαν πρὸ τοῦ θεάτρου γενέσθαι. οὕτω Κρατῖνος.

Suidas, etc., s.v. ἀπ' αἰγείρου θέα : ἡ ἀπὸ τῶν ἐσχάτων· αἴγειρος γὰρ ἐπάνω ἦν τοῦ θεάτρου, ἀφ' ἧς οἱ μὴ ἔχοντες τόπον ἐθεώρουν.

See also Hesychius, s.v.

Haigh's explanation of these conflicting statements is, briefly, that at the beginning of the fifth century the Athenian audience sat on wooden benches rising in tiers óne above the other, and resting

* πρῶτον ξύλον seems to be used only of the front bench at the Pnyx or in the courthouse.

on wooden supports ; that these ἰκρία collapsed during a performance in 499 B.C. ; that the Athenians then built, not stone seats,
but an earth embankment to support the wooden seats, which were
still used : this earth embankment took the place of the ' " ikria "
or wooden supports on which the seats had previously rested ' ;
that, finally, the stone seats were constructed towards the end of
the fourth century. This is a desperate attempt to reconcile the
statements of Suidas with Dörpfeld's discovery that ' the earth
foundations of the present auditorium . . . consist of two layers.
The upper one belongs to the fourth century, as is shown by the
fragments of pottery embedded in it ; the lower one is proved by
similar evidence to be not later than the fifth '. But Haigh's view
that the ἰκρία (which he wrongly takes to mean the *supports* of the
seats) were done away with soon after 499 is contradicted by the
passages I have quoted from Cratinus and Aristophanes, which
speak of ἰκρία as still in use much later. So prominent a feature
of the theatre were they in 410 that ' to come from the ἰκρία ' is
used for ' to come from the theatre '. That they were still made of
wood is indicated, I think, by the phrase of Cratinus ' the rattle of
the benches ' ; stone seats would make but little ψόφησις. We
may compare Pollux's remark s.v. πτερνοκοπεῖν : τὸ μέντοι τὰ ἐδώλια
ταῖς πτέρναις κατακρούειν πτ. ἔλεγον· ἐποίουν δὲ τοῦτο ὁπότε τινὰ ἐκβάλοιεν.
Haigh explains : ' The Athenians had also a peculiar custom of
marking their disapproval of a performance by kicking with the
heels of their sandals against the front of the stone benches on which
they were sitting '. Not so peculiar a custom, if the benches were
of wood ! Haigh has wantonly inserted the word ' stone ', against
his own theory and against common sense as well.

We notice that Suidas in one place says that the spectators
stood on the ἰκρία and in another that they *sat* on them. Some of
our ' grand stands ' at football grounds do not allow the occupants
to sit ; they merely give elevation. These are, of course, intended
for less wealthy folk. Perhaps we should picture the highest and
most remote ἰκρία as being of this uncomfortable type. That the
general public sat, at least by the time of Aristophanes, is indicated
by *Av.* 793-6, where the birds suggest that if one of the spectators
should espy in the part of the theatre reserved for members of the
βουλή the husband of the lady with whom he is carrying on an
intrigue, a pair of wings would enable the lover to visit his mistress
and then resume his seat in the theatre (αὖθις αὖ καθέζετο).
About the end of the fourth century we find several references to a
seated audience : cf. Heges. *Adelph.* 29 :

πολλοὺς ἐγὼ σφόδρ' οἶδα τῶν καθημένων.

But the evidence suggests that the audience during the fifth and
early fourth century were accommodated on tiers of wooden
scaffolding which itself rested on an artificial earth bank ; most of

them sat, but the less fortunate people on the topmost tiers had to stand ; others, again, were perched on trees. If we add to our picture the itinerant vendors of wine and edibles (Philoch. ap. Ath. p. 464E : παρὰ δὲ τὸν ἀγῶνα πάντα οἶνος αὐτοῖς ᾠνοχοεῖτο καὶ τραγήματα παρεφέρετο) and the din of the wooden benches, we have a scene reminiscent of Derby Day.

The evidence points to the reconstruction of the theatre as the result of a collapse of the scaffolding. I suggest that this is a correct view, but that the date of this particular accident (there may have been many like it) and of the consequent reconstruction has been placed far too early. The only large-scale reconstruction of which we know was the building of stone seats, perhaps towards the end of the fourth century. The original of the *Curculio* may well have been produced about this time, and the reference to a collapse of seats may have been a reference to a real event.

There is therefore nothing, it would appear, to prevent our supposing that *Curc.* 644-7 was translated by Plautus from his Greek original. If we grant, then, that the word for ' seats at a show ' was already established in Latin at that time, it becomes more than ever difficult to resist the conclusion that the plays of Plautus were written for presentation before a seated audience.

It is now becoming recognized that the *external* evidence against seats in the time of Plautus is weaker than was supposed, and the whole argument based on such supposed evidence is demolished by the latest Pauly-Wissowa, s.v. *theatrum*.* Perhaps the *internal* evidence cited in this article will serve to drive a nail in the coffin of Ritschl's theory and help to re-establish confidence in the prologues of Plautus as coming, in the main, from his own pen.

* Pauly-Wissowa does not explain how the curious belief arose that the Roman authorities, while officially arranging for theatrical performances, should for puritanical reasons have forbidden the spectators to sit. I suggest (1) that the wooden scaffolding or benches of Plautus' day left no visible trace for future ages to contemplate ; (2) that some race-conscious Roman antiquarian, rather hurt at finding imposing tiers of stone seats in the theatres of *Greek* towns, tried to explain the absence of similar remains in Rome in a way which would flatter his countrymen's pride in the mos maiorum.

APPENDIX B

SIDE-ENTRANCES AND ΠΕΡΙΑΚΤΟΙ IN THE HELLENISTIC THEATRE

(*Classical Quarterly*, Vol. xxxii. pp. 205–10.)

THE greatest confusion prevails among modern writers as to the use of the side-entrances in New Comedy and its Latin derivatives. The statements on this subject made by editors and others, whether confident or hesitating, differ widely from one another, and are seldom supported by any real consideration of the ancient evidence. In 1933 Professor Mary Johnston published a careful treatise, entitled *Exits and Entrances in Roman Comedy* (W. F. Humphrey Press, New York), in which she discussed the internal evidence afforded by the Latin plays, and came to the conclusion (page 151) that ' on the stage of the Roman theatre the side-entrance to the right of the spectators was used for entrances and exits of characters from and to the city and the forum, and that the side-entrance to the left of the spectators was used for entrances and exits of characters moving from and to the port and foreign parts, and, probably, from and to the country as well '. With regard to Greek usage, Professor Johnston was content to accept the orthodox view ' that the side-entrance (parodos) at the spectators' right led to the harbour or the market-place and that at their left into the country, since the scene was regularly placed in Athens and since these were the actual topographical relationships in the Athenian theatre ' (Flickinger, page 208). Her conclusion, therefore, involved a discrepancy between Greek and Roman usage as far as the harbour was concerned.

The possibility of such a discrepancy has been admitted by other writers (e.g. Flickinger, page 234) ; but it raises certain difficulties. At line 461 of the *Captiui* Ergasilus enters on the empty stage. He has come from the forum (cf. lines 478 and 490) and is on his way to the harbour (line 496), in which direction he departs after line 497 (cf. lines 768 ff.). He had no intention of calling on Hegio, whose offer of a cena aspera he regards merely as a last resource. The only pretext for his appearance upon the stage must therefore be that he has to cross it in order to get from the forum to the harbour. This is perfectly natural if Professor Johnston is right as to the *Roman* convention. But how are we to visualize Ergasilus' movements in the Greek original of the play ? Had Ergasilus some errand at Hegio's house, all reference to which has been suppressed by Plautus ? Or is the whole scene an insertion by Plautus ?

If our solution of every difficulty in Plautus is to take the traditional form of assuming that he has tampered with his original in some way, we shall inevitably involve ourselves in a hopeless tangle of subjective argument. Yet either of the alternatives suggested seems preferable to assuming that, in the Greek play, the parasite walked on, delivered his monologue, and then walked off *by the same side-entrance.*

The Roman dramatists must have taken over their use of the side-entrances from Greek sources ; not merely literary sources, but the usage of the Hellenistic theatres of Magna Graecia. Why, then, should they have heaped up difficulties for themselves by modifying Greek convention in one vital point ? Few will accept the view of Fensterbusch (*Philol.* LXXI, 1926) and Kelley Rees (*A.J.P.* 32, 1911, page 400) that *Roman* topography had something to do with the matter. Are we really so certain as to what Greek usage was ?

The relevant passages in ancient authors appear to be :

(*a*) Vitruvius, V. vi. § 8 :—ipsae autem scenae suas habeant rationes explicatas ita uti mediae ualuae ornatus habeant aulae regiae ; dextra ac sinistra hospitalia ; secundum autem spatia ad ornatus comparata, quae loca Graeci περιάκτους dicunt ab eo quod machinae sunt in eis locis uersatiles trigonae, habentes singulae tres species ornationis, quae cum aut fabularum mutationes sunt futurae, seu deorum aduentus cum tonitribus repentinis, uersentur mutentque speciem ornationis in frontes ; secundum ea loca uersurae sunt procurrentes, quae efficiunt una a foro altera a peregre aditus in scenam.

(*b*) Pollux, IV. xix. §§ 125-7 :—παρ' ἑκάτερα δὲ τῶν δύο θυρῶν τῶν περὶ τὴν μέσην ἄλλαι δύο ἂν εἶεν, μία ἑκατέρωθεν, πρὸς ἃς αἱ περίακτοι συμπεπήγασιν, ἡ μὲν δεξιὰ τὰ ἔξω πόλεως δηλοῦσα, ἡ δ' ἀριστερὰ τὰ ἐκ πόλεως, μάλιστα τὰ ἐκ λιμένος. καὶ θεούς τε θαλαττίους ἐπάγει, καὶ πάνθ' ὅσα ἐπαχθέστερα ὄντα ἡ μηχανὴ φέρειν ἀδυνατεῖ. εἰ δ' ἐπιστραφεῖεν αἱ περίακτοι, ἡ δεξιὰ μὲν ἀμείβει τόπον, ἀμφότεραι δὲ χώραν ὑπαλλάττουσιν. τῶν μέντοι παρόδων ἡ μὲν δεξιὰ ἀγρόθεν ἢ ἐκ λιμένος ἢ ἐκ πόλεως ἄγει· οἱ δὲ ἀλλαχόθεν πεζοὶ ἀφικνούμενοι κατὰ τὴν ἑτέραν εἰσίασιν.

Pollux further tells us that the keraunoskopeion was a ' high periactus ' (§ 130) ; he couples it with the bronteion or, ' thunder-maker ' ; immediately afterwards he describes the theologeion (on which the gods manifest themselves) and states that the καταβλήματα were painted curtains or boards which were ' dropped ' (κατεβάλλετο) on the periacti, and showed such views as a mountain, a river or the sea, or whatever else might be suitable to the play (§ 131).

There is also a passage in the *Vita Aristophanis* (quoted by Haigh, *A.T.*, page 194, note) to the effect that, if the *chorus* entered ' as from the city ', it used the ' left ' ἁψίς : if from the country, the right.

I can find no reference to any other authoritative texts on the

9*

subject of side entrances, or for that matter on the nature and use of the periacti.   The passage in the *Vita* deals, of course, with the entry of the chorus into the orchestra by means of the orchestral πάροδοι.   I am assuming * that there was a stage in the Hellenistic as in the Roman theatre, and that it is to this stage that Pollux and Vitruvius are referring ; but the author of the *Vita* may fairly be quoted as evidence for the view that on·the stage, as in the orchestra, the town and country entrances were opposite to each other.   But any fair-minded reader of Haigh's note, referred to above, will agree that the expressions ' right ' and ' left ' in both Pollux and the *Vita* cannot be understood without further evidence. Such evidence does not exist, so far as the Hellenistic theatre is concerned.   The confident statements made by modern writers about the influence of the topography of Athens on the growth of the convention which we are discussing are entirely in the air.†

The origins of a dramatic convention should be sought in dramatic, not in topographical, conditions.   The scene of most New Comedy plays was a street—usually in Athens ; characters very frequently come on from the forum or go off towards the forum ; the harbour is mentioned rather less frequently ; still less frequently is reference made to the country.   Professor Johnston calculates (pp. 38 ff.) that, of the twenty-six Latin plays, twenty-four are set in town ; of these five require forum, harbour and country ; thirteen require forum and harbour only ; three require forum and country only ; in three plays of Plautus only the forum (town) is actually required (but these three plays are (*a*) the *Asinaria*, in which ' the entrances are confused, and the movements of the characters cannot be followed satisfactorily ' ; (*b*) the *Casina*, in which frequent reference is made to the country, though no one actually goes there ; (*c*) the *Persa*, in which some pretence is made of using the harbour entrance) ; only two plays, the *Rudens* and the *Heauton*, are set in the country.   If we assume that the harbour lies in the same direction as the forum, we leave the opposite entrance unused in some two-thirds of the plays.   If, on the contrary, we follow Professor Johnston in opposing the forum to both country and harbour, we shall find that both side-entrances are used, actually or in appearance, in all the plays with a city setting, with the exception of the *Asinaria*.   But in the plays with a country setting circumstances may be quite different.   It is clear that in the

* But Dr. Pickard-Cambridge has now abandoned his early belief in the raised stage, even for Menander's theatre (*Theatre of Dionysus*, 1946, p. 165).   I accept his view, which in no way affects my argument.

† They seem to me founded on fallacy.   I do not believe a theatrical audience is so conscious of topography as the theory implies.   And if the Greeks were, how can we explain the fact that New Comedy was produced in various theatres all over the Greek world, with quite different topographical settings ?   Or that, as this article shows, the convention varied according to where the play was supposed to take place ?

Rudens both the town and harbour of Cyrene are thought of as lying in the same direction ; on the opposite side is the beach. In the *Heauton* the town as a whole lies on one side ; there is no specific mention of the open country, which we may presume lies on the opposite side, but it can well be imagined that when Clitipho is sent off for a walk (line 590) in order to get him out of the way, it is towards the open country that he directs his footsteps.

If we now turn to the remains of Menander's plays we find a higher percentage of country settings. The scene of the *Hero* is a country district near Athens ; we hear that a party of hunters will arrive from the town (Fr. Sabb., Capps, page 21) ; we are also led to expect that Laches will arrive from Lemnos (line 65), presumably via the Piraeus and the town. 'Town' and 'harbour' would, in such circumstances, naturally be thought of as lying in the same direction ; on the opposite side would be the open country, the farms of neighbours, etc. The *Epitrepontes* is also set in the country near Athens ; we get the general impression that 'town' and 'country' lie on opposite sides ; there is no use made of the 'harbour'. The scene of the *Perikeiromene* is a street in Corinth ; opposition of market-place and country gives a natural setting ; there is no mention of the 'harbour'. The scene of the *Samia* is given by Capps as a street in Athens ; the use of the forum entrance is probably indicated in line 69—ἐκ τῆς [ἀγορᾶς] ; there is no mention of either harbour or country. The *Gorgias* seems to be set in the town (cf. line 79) ; Davus comes in from the country (Allinson, line 32).

So far the results of our inquiry are meagre. But in the *Citharistes* we have evidence of a more interesting nature.

Moschion, while on a visit to Ephesus, had seen the procession of freeborn maidens bringing offerings to 'Diana of the Ephesians', and had fallen in love with one of them, daughter of Phanias, a harp-player, who lived next door to his father Laches in Athens. It seems that Moschion has now married this lady ; when the play opens he has just returned to Athens, and is expecting his wife by another ship. This ship has not yet arrived. The opening scene, as given by Allinson, shows Moschion (?) on his way from the harbour to the market-place, talking to a friend, and followed by slaves carrying luggage. He has sent a messenger to summon his father from the country. He is very worried that his bride's ship has not yet arrived, and is pouring his troubles into the sympathetic ear of his friend, and proposes to finish the story as they go together to the market-place. As he passes his father's house he issues a hasty order to his slaves : 'Let someone take these things into the house out of sight as quickly as possible'. Moschion and the friend depart for the market-place ; Laches enters from the country. He is mystified at the summons he has received from his son. He is going to look for Moschion indoors ; if the lad is not there, he will

go on to seek him at the market-place.   Laches goes into his house ;
Moschion returns from the market-place, wondering whether his
father has yet arrived.   Laches appears : Moschion greets him
with warmth, and embarks on the story of his love affair.

In this summary I have followed Allinson's reconstruction
closely (cf. also Sudhaus) ; if he is right, then we have a setting
which can only be visualized on the assumption that the harbour
entrance was opposite to the market-place entrance.   Otherwise
how can we account for Moschion's appearance on the stage, in
front of his father's house, when hurrying from the harbour to the
agora ?   It is true that the harbour is not mentioned in the extant
fragments of the scene ; but the young man's reference to his
anxiety at his wife's having failed to arrive and his fear lest some
misfortune has befallen her at sea, coupled with his order to the
slaves, seems to make it clear that he himself has only just arrived
from abroad, and has not yet entered his father's house.

I have failed to find any evidence in the remaining fragments of
Menander.   I now turn to the statements of Vitruvius and Pollux,
quoted above.   The concise words of Vitruvius ' una a foro altera
a peregre ' agree with the view I have expressed, so far as they go ;
the trouble is that Vitruvius has not given us enough detail.   Pollux
tells us that the ' right-hand parodos ' leads ' from the country or
the harbour or the city '.   This cannot be right ; emendation,
however, is impossible without assuming the answer to the very
question which we are discussing.   In each of the passages quoted
we find the side-entrances closely connected with the periacti.
Combining the statements of Vitruvius and Pollux, we find that
these devices were revolving three-sided stands, set one at either
end of the permanent back-scene, between the side-doors and the
side-entrances.   Each of the three sides of a periactus displayed a
different scene.   The right-hand periactus, according to Pollux,
showed ' the region outside the city ', the left-hand ' the things
from the city, especially the things from the harbour ' : it also
introduced sea-gods, and whatever was too heavy for the $\mu\eta\chi\alpha\nu\dot\eta$.
To revolve the right-hand periactus alone indicated a change of
$\tau\delta\pi\sigma\varsigma$, to revolve both periacti a change of $\chi\acute\omega\rho\alpha$.   Vitruvius, on the
other hand, tells us that the revolution of the periacti denoted
either a change of play or the arrival of a deity, accompanied by
sudden peals of thunder.

None of the descriptions which I have read in modern works
(including the 1934 and 1937 P.W.) makes any real attempt to
deal with this curious and apparently contradictory evidence ;
even the sober Haigh (A.T., pages 197-9) is both inadequate and
fanciful.   All writers seem to agree in regarding the periacti as
appliances for changing scenery, ' the only appliances for changing
scenery that are mentioned by the ancient Greek writers ' (Haigh).
But New Comedy does not appear to have allowed for any change

of setting within the course of any one play. There is no evidence
for such a change either in Plautus, or in Terence, or in the
fragments of Menander. From the beginning to the end of any one
play the audience were confronted with the usual three-door
back-scene. And what would such a back-scene have to do with
the καταβλήματα which Pollux says were placed on the periacti,
showing a mountain, a river, or the sea? How artificial, too,
would be the ' curious conventional custom ' (Haigh) whereby *one*
periactus was turned to denote a ' slight ' change of scene—' merely
from one part of the same district to another ', whereas ' when the
action was transferred to an entirely new district, then both the
periacti were turned round, and the scenery was changed at each
end '. Such an account can have been penned only by a writer
who was thinking chiefly in terms of fifth-century drama. We can
understand Haigh's conclusion that ' it must have been chiefly in
the intervals between successive plays that the periacti were employed ' ; in fact Vitruvius has told us that they *were* so used (cum
fabularum mutationes sunt futurae). But the periacti seem by their
nature to have been designed for *rapid* alteration. And what of
Vitruvius' other remark that they denoted the arrival of gods, and
of Pollux's reference to the introduction of sea-gods ' and objects too
heavy for the mechané ' ? ' It is possible that, of the two sides of the
periaktos which were out of sight of the audience, one contained a
small ledge or balcony, on which the sea-god took his stand. As
the machine rolled round, he would come suddenly into view '
(Haigh).

Let us look again at Vitruvius and Pollux. We observe :—

(*a*) that both writers refer to the periacti in close connexion
with their accounts of the side-entrances ;

(*b*) that both writers speak of ' arrivals '—deorum aduentus,
θεούς . . . θαλαττίους ἐπάγει—as in some way connected with the
use of the periacti ; with which evidence we may couple the ἐκ
of Pollux—' the things *from* the city ', ' the things *from* the harbour ;

(*c*) that Pollux's description of the scenes shown on the periacti—
' the region outside the city ', ' the things from the city ', ' the
things from the harbour '—is strongly reminiscent of the use of the
side-entrances to denote arrivals from or departures to ' country ',
' town ' and ' harbour ' ;

and when we further remember that, while there were only
two side-entrances, there were *three* conventional significations to be
shared between them, we shall, I think, be forced to the conclusion
that the function of the periacti was to indicate to the audience the
conventional significance to be attached to the side-entrances at
any given moment in the play.

Let us suppose that the scene is the usual street in Athens. At
the back are the usual three doors, denoting three houses, or two
houses and a temple or the like. The significance of these doorways

will be made clear to the audience (a) in the prologue, if there is
one ; (b) by frequent references in the course of the play.   Moreover these doorways in the back-scene will retain their significance
unaltered throughout the course of the play.   On either hand are
the side-entrances.   Their function differs from play to play ; it may
be altered more than once within a play.   To avoid the necessity of
issuing frequent reminders to the audience, use is made of the
periacti, set close to the side-entrances ; one may present a view of
the market, the opposite one a rural scene (a river, a mountain,
etc.).   An arrival from abroad is anxiously expected ; suddenly
one of the periacti swings round, presenting to the audience a
picture of the sea, the harbour, a ship, a dolphin or the like.   This
is a change of τόπος.   The play has ended ; another, with an
entirely fresh setting, perhaps in a foreign town, is to be brought on.
It will still require the three doorways ; but a revolution of both
the periacti will give these doorways the appropriate framework ;
this is a mutatio fabulae, a change of χώρα.   A deity is to manifest
himself, with appropriate thunder and lightning.   Above the stage
is set the ' high periactus ', also called the ' flash ' (περίακτος ὑψηλή,
κεραυνοσκοπεῖον) ; on one, two or all of its sides (we may
suppose), a fiery streak is painted on a dark background.   The
' high periactus ' turns—or perhaps whirls ; the βροντεῖον, or
' thunderer ', rattles, and the deity appears by the celestial side-
entrance, the μηχανή or θεολογεῖον.   Such an entry we may
suppose was made by Jupiter at the end of the Amphitruo :—

strepitus, crepitus, sonitus, tonitrus : ut subito, ut prope, ut ualide tonuit !
      (line 1062) ;

      ardere censui aedis, ita tum confulgebant (line 1067) ;

and finally :—

sed quid hoc ?   quam ualide tonuit !   di, obsecro uestram fidem ! (1130)

and the god appears in majesty, delivers his decree, and departs
whence he came (ego in caelum migro, line 1143).   A sea-god,
however, cannot well appear from the sky ; to herald *his* arrival
one of the side periacti will revolve to show a view of the sea, and
the god will walk in by the neighbouring side-entrance.   Groups
of deities, collectively too heavy for the μηχανή, will enter in some
such way ; ghosts and infernal deities will appear as it were from
the depths of Hades ; the varieties of the detachable καταβλήματα
are unlimited.

      I have made no attempt to interpret the terms ' right ' and
' left ' as used by Pollux.   On any view his account is confused, and
he is drawing on different and imperfectly understood authorities.
Professor Johnston's independent study of the Latin plays has led
her to put the ' forum ' entrance to the spectators' right, the

'harbour' and 'country' entrances to the spectators' left.* The only qualification I would add is that this arrangement should be limited to plays with a 'town' setting ; a setting in the country may well have necessitated placing the harbour in the same direction as the town, as is, in fact, the case in the *Rudens*, and perhaps in the *Hero* ; our arrangement of the *Rudens* will depend on our interpretation of ad dexteram in line 156 and again in line 254. What I am most concerned with is to show that, so far from there being any discrepancy between Greek and Roman practice, there is every reason to suppose that the Romans adopted unchanged the use of the side-entrances which they found prevailing in the theatres of Magna Graecia.

* This goes well with Pollux's statement that it was the 'right-hand' periactus (i.e. that to the spectators' left) which indicated 'the things outside the city,' and which also was revolved to show a change of 'place'. The other periactus, displaying a view of the city-centre, would not need to be turned so frequently. See Pickard-Cambridge, *Theatre of Dionysus*, pp. 234 ff.

APPENDIX C

THE ANGIPORTUM AND ROMAN DRAMA

(*Hermathena*, Vol. xxviii. pp. 88-99.)

THE word angiportum is commonly taken to mean ' alley ', or even ' blind alley ', ' cul-de-sac '. As to its use on the Roman stage, the conventional view is given by Professor Mary Johnston (*Exits and Entrances in Roman Comedy*, 1933, page 15) :—' An alley or passage (angiportum) was supposed to lead back from the street between two houses '. But Mr. P. W. Harsh (*Classical Philology*, vol. xxxii, No. 1, pages 45 ff.) argues that ' alley ' is a misleading translation ; that the word simply means ' street ', and may be used in comedy even of the street upon which the houses front (*Pseud.* 961), though elsewhere it is ' sometimes a more secretive place than the stage itself ', and is ' apparently thought of as running behind the houses portrayed on stage ', and that even in Terence, *Adelphi* 578, the sense ' cul-de-sac ' is entirely dependent on the additional words non peruium. The discrepancy between these views seems to justify some attempt to review the evidence so far as stage usage is concerned.

The usual word in comedy for the street on which the houses front is platea, of which Harsh lists ten examples ; uia is also used ' in a general way for the thoroughfare on which the characters stand (cf. *Cas.* 856 ; *St.* 606, etc.) '. In *Ps.* 1234-5 we find uia apparently opposed to angiporta ; Ballio, leaving for the forum, remarks to the spectators :

> nunc ne exspectetis dum hac domum redeam uia ;
> ita res gestast : angiporta haec certum est consectarier.

Ballio does not, in fact, appear again, and we must suppose that he returned to his house by the back entrance. Here, th n, angiportum would be the back street upon which the back en.rance opened ; the plural may be used merely as an equivalent of the singular, or may include the other streets through which Ballio would pass on his way from the forum to the back of his house. Perhaps, however, *uia* depends on the addition of *hac* for its meaning here, and would not by itself bear the same meaning as platea. To quote Harsh (page 49, note 10) : ' uia is also used in a general way for the thoroughfare on which the characters stand (cf. *Cas.* 856 ; *Stich.* 606, etc.) '. Turning to the passages here cited, we find :

> acceptae bene et commode eximus intus
> ludos uisere huc in uiam nuptialis (*Cas.* 855-6)

' After our nice, enjoyable entertainment inside, here we are out on the street to watch the wedding games ' (Nixon's translation). Here uia means ' the open street ', as opposed to the privacy of indoors.

GE. non tu scis quam—ecflictentur homines noctu hic in uia?
PAM. tanto pluris qui defendant ire aduorsum iussero (*St.* 606–7).

Here, again, there is a demonstrative to make the meaning of uia clear, and the general sense is, as before, ' in public ', ' in the open street ', as opposed to the *safety* of indoors.

The passages cited by Harsh for the use of platea (apart from *Bac.* 632,* where it is merely a proposed emendation) are :

ne quis in hac platea negoti conferat quicquam sui (*Capt.* 795).
suaui cantu concelebra omnem hanc plateam hymenaeo mi (*Cas.* 799).
          parasitum tuom
uideo currentem ellum usque in platea ultima (*Cur.* 277–8).
sterilis hinc prospectus usque ad ultumamst plateam probe (*Mil.* 690).
sed quis hic est qui in plateam ingreditur . . .? (Trin. 840).
sed quis hic est qui huc in plateam cursuram incipit ? (*Trin.* 1006).
in hac habitasse platea dictumst Chrysidem (*An.* 796).
illa se(se) interea commodum huc aduorterat
in hanc nostram plateam (*Eun.* 343–4).
si te in platea offendero hoc post unquam . . . (*Eun.* 1064).
sed hic quis est senex quem uideo in ultima platea ? . . . (*Phor.* 215).

In all these passages the sense is ' *this* street ', and there is no suggestion of a contrast with ' indoors '. Nor is platea here used in the sense of ' way ' or ' means of getting to any particular place '. All the examples of uia cited in Lodge's *Lexicon Plautinum* would seem to come under one of these three heads—(1) ' in public ', (2) ' way ', (3) ' highroad ' : cf. *Cas.* 675 : de uia in semitam degredere. It would appear, then, that uia and platea are not interchangeable terms so far as comedy is concerned.

A fairly general view of the typical stage setting is that the two side doors (hospitalia) represent the entrances of two houses, while the central door (ualuae regiae) is the entrance to an ' alley ' separating the two houses, and would, as such, presumably stand open during the whole of the play. There are obvious objections to such an arrangement. Why should the principal door be assigned so secondary a function ? If it remains open, would not the spectators be able to see inside, and, if so, what would they see ? The interior of the greenroom ? A blank wall ? If the door is usually shut, we have the absurdity of an actor being forced to open it in order to enter an alley. Nowhere is there any reference to the opening of a door on such an occasion.

We seem forced to suppose that the door stood permanently open

* Here I differ entirely from Dalman.

during the course of a play requiring such a setting as we are discussing, and that, a few feet inside, a screen stood displaying a view of an alley. Actors who were supposed to leave the platea by means of the angiportum would enter the doorway, step behind the screen, and so disappear from the view of the audience. If this was the arrangement adopted, we still have to ask ourselves :

(a) What happened when (as in the *Pseudolus*) the setting included *three* houses as well as an angiportum (cf. line 1235) ?

(b) Why is the angiportum, in fact, so seldom used, and for so limited a range of services ? To quote Professor Mary Johnston (*Exits and Entrances*, page 37) : ' No entrances are made through an angiportum at any time, so far as our material shows. In most passages where the angiportum is referred to at all it is mentioned in accounting for movements of the characters when they are unseen and off the stage, if it is not convenient to bring them on the stage '.

(c) Why is there no reference to this use of the central doorway in Vitruvius or Pollux ?

(d) Where is the ' alley ' supposed to lead ? What is its relation to the garden which is occasionally mentioned in connexion with it ? (Cf. *As.* 741-2 ; *Most.* 1044-5).

(e) Why should angiportum be translated ' alley ' in certain passages, when elsewhere it clearly means ' street '—often, it is true, with a suggestion of secrecy, but still ' street ' and not ' alley ' ?

For the relation of the angiportum to the hortus and the posticum, or ' back-door ', certain passages in the *Mostellaria* are of particular importance. In line 928 Theopropides sends Tranio to the country. Tranio, as he departs, remarks to the audience :

> nunc ego me illac per posticum ad congerrones conferam.

As Theopropides remains on the stage after Tranio's departure, it is difficult to suppose that Tranio, instead of leaving the stage by the ' country ' side-entrance, should slip back to the central door and so into the angiportum. To execute such a manœuvre under the eyes of his master would have been disastrous. We must think of him as actually going off the stage by the ' country ' side-entrance. His next appearance is at line 1041. He tells us (lines 1043-6) :

> nam erus me postquam rus misit, filium ut suom arcesserem,
> abii illac per angiportum ad hortum nostrum clanculum,
> ostium quod in angiportu est horti, patefeci fores,
> eaque eduxi omnem legionem, et maris et feminas.

This is how the present writer would arrange the stage setting :

angiportum		ostium horti hortus posticum	angiportum
L. (rus)	House of Simo	House of Theopropides	R. (forum

Tranio goes off the stage at line 932 by the left-hand side-entrance, but by voice and gesture informs the audience that he intends to make his way round to the 'back door'. He sets forth his movements in more detail in lines 1043-6. He made his way from the side-entrance to the street which ran at the back of the two houses, entered from this back street the garden behind Theopropides' house by means of the garden gate, got into the house of Theopropides by the back-door, and was then able to remove the occupants through the back-door, the garden, the garden gate, and so into the back street, and off to the forum, if that is where they ultimately go. At line 1041 Tranio enters by one of the side-entrances—perhaps R, as it seems more natural to imagine that Philolaches and his friends would go to the town than to the country or harbour. Line 1076 would seem to imply that by this time Tranio was standing near the 'country' side-entrance ; in reply to Theopropides' question he remarks that the country-folk are on their way to town, and that Philolaches will shortly arrive. This would mean that during his monologue (1041-1062) he has crossed the stage. Where does he hide when Theopropides appears (line 1064) ? In the left-hand side-entrance ? This would seem to be the only retreat available, if we abolish the ' alleyway', and would make his entry at line 1075 quite natural.*

These conclusions may be tested with reference to the other plays which make use of the back-entrance.

(1) *As.* 740-3 : ARG. Leonida, curre, opsecro, patrem huc orato ut ueniat.
                 LE. iam dudum est intus. ARG. hac quidem non uenit.
                 LE. angiporto
                 illac per hortum circum iit clam, ne quis se uideret
                 huc ire familiarium : ne uxor resciscat metuit.

The scene of the play is a street in front of the houses of Demaenetus and Cleaereta. At line 126 Demaenetus left for the forum. At line 545 Leonidas and Libanus enter from the forum, where they have met Demaenetus. The slaves talk to each other until Argyrippus and Philaenium come out of Cleaereta's house (line 585). All four characters have since been on the stage. It would, therefore, have been impossible for Demaenetus to make his way from the forum and across the stage to the front-door of Cleaereta's house without being seen by Argyrippus. When informed by Leonidas that Demaenetus has, in fact, found his way into Cleaereta's house, Argyrippus naturally replies : ' He certainly didn't come this way '. Leonidas explains that the old gentleman, afraid of being seen by any of the servants, who might tell his wife, has ' stolen round that way by the back street and through the garden '.

* I now hold that there were *no* hiding-places on the stage. Tranio simply steps back, and Theopropides is obliging enough not to see him. But see pp. 263 f. on the *Phormio*, where there is express reference to the side-entrance.

At line 830 we are shown Demaenetus in front or coming out of Cleaereta's house. The stage setting will, therefore, be :

	a n g i p o r t u m	a n g i p o r t u m
		hortus
L.	House of Demaenetus	House of Cl. R. (forum)

There is nothing to show the relative position of the two houses, but clearly Demaenetus did not enter the ' alley ' from the stage.

> (2) *Cas.* 613–4 : abi et aliud cura, ego iam per hortum iussero
> meam istuc transire uxorem ad uxorem tuam.—

We may arrange the setting in this way :

(angiportum)	(ostium)	(ostium)	(angiportum)
	hortus Lysidami	hortus Alcesimi	
	(posticum)	(posticum)	
L. (*rus*)	House of Lys.	House of Alc.	R. (forum)

The two gardens would, of course, be separated by a roughly built wall (maceria). There may be a gate in this wall, but as the evidence of other passages rather suggests that there was usually no such gate, it seems safer to suppose that Alcesimus would send Myrrhina through their own garden and into the *angiportum* and so round to the garden of Lysidamus. In fact the mention of the garden implies the existence of an angiportum, and though there is no express reference to an angiportum in the play, its existence would make the movements of the bridal procession much more intelligible. At 815-6 the procession comes out of Lysidamus' house, ostensibly on its way to the country, though Lysidamus' real object is, of course, to escort the ' bride ' to Alcesimus' house, which has been cleared of occupants. To enter by the front-door in full view of Lysidamus' own house would be a risky proceeding, and there is no reference to any such entry. Clearly, the procession leaves by the ' country ' side-entrance, and we are to think of them as making their way round by the angiportum and garden into the back of the house. At 875 Olympio, the ' bridegroom ', rushes out on the stage from the front-door of Alcesimus' house.

> (3) *Ep.* 660-1 : Ep. Thesprio, exi istac per hortum, adfer domum
> auxilium mihi,
> magnast res.

Epidicus, shouting at the door of Chaeribulus' house, bids his fellow-slave Thesprio go ' out through the garden there ' and so ' home ' to the house of their master, Periphanes.

> (4) *Merc.* 1007 : illac per hortum nos domum transibimus.

Eutychus has just invited Demipho indoors, and adds that Demipho's son is inside. Demipho accepts the invitation, and remarks that he and his son will go home ' that way, through the garden '.

(In other words, the spectators must not expect to see them re-appear ; the play is at an end).

(5) *Pers.* 444-6 : Tox. abi istac trauorsis angiportis ad forum ;
eadem istaec facito mulier ad me transeat
per hortum. Do. iam hic faxo aderit. Tox.   at ne
propalam.

Dordalus is to enter his house (istac) and thence to make his way by ' cross-streets ' to the forum, where he will have the money tested which Toxilus has handed him as payment for Lemniselenis ; at the same time (eadem) he is to send Lemniselenis through the garden into the house of Toxilus' master, thus avoiding publicity. At line 448 Dordalus departs ; he returns at line 470, apparently by the *forum* side-entrance ; in other words, he must have sent Lemniselenis into the house of Toxilus' master *before* he went to the banker's. The dramatist thus avoids having to bring Lemniselenis on the stage at this point.

(5*a*) *Pers.* 678-9 : Tox. per angiportum rursum te ad me recipito
illac per hortum.

Sagaristio is to pretend that he is a foreigner ; after entrapping the unfortunate Dordalus he is to complete the deception by departing through the left-hand side-entrance, as though on his way back to the harbour. Cf. lines 676-7 :

ubi argentum ab hoc acceperis,
simulato quasi eas prosum in nauem.

Once off the stage, he is to slip round by the *angiportum* into the garden and so rejoin Toxilus indoors. This plan is carried out ; Sagaristio departs for the harbour at line 710, and reappears (line 763) from inside the house of Toxilus' master ; he is accompanying Lemniselenis.

(6) *Stichus* 431-2 :   amicam ego habeo Stephanium hinc ex proxumo,
tui fratris ancillam.
  „   437 :   iam hercle ego per hortum ad amicam transibo
meam . . .
  „   449-52 :   . . . est etiam hic ostium
aliud posticum nostrarum harunc aedium :
(posticam partem magis utuntur aedium)
ea ibo opsonatum, eadem referam opsonium :
per hortum utroque commeatus continet.

The stage-setting is perhaps as follows :

	(angiportum)	(angiportum)	
	hortus	hortus	
	ostium posticum		
L.	House of Epignomus	House of Pamphilippus	House of Antipho R.

There is no specific reference to the *angiportum*, but its presence is necessary to enable Stichus to make his way from the garden of Epignomus' house to market and back to the house of Pamphilippus, from the front-door of which he appears at line 641. There is another reference to the garden entrance at line 614, where Pamphilippus declares that he will use it in order to make his way to Epignomus' house for supper. Stephanium must also make frequent use of it, as she is cooking in both houses. We are left in some doubt as to whether there is direct communication between the two gardens.

> (7) *Pseud.* 960–2 : Simia, pretending to be entering from the harbour, remarks :
>
> habui numerum sedulo ; hoc est sextum a porta proxumum
> angiportum, in id angiportum me deuorti iusserat ;
> quotumas aedis dixerit, id ego admodum incertum scio.

And at line 971, addressing Ballio, he asks :

> ecquem in angiporto hoc hominem tu nouisti ?

In these passages angiportum is used of the street on which the houses *front*. Ballio's house is situated, not in an ' alley ', but beside the houses of Simo and Callipho. Pseudolus, entering from the forum (line 905) with Simia, indicates Ballio's house with the words (line 952) tertium hoc˙est.

> (8) *Truc.* 303–4 : quid maceria illa ait in horto quae est, quae in noctes singulas
> latere fit minor, qua isto ad uos damni permensust uiam ?
>
> „ 248–9 : sed is clam patrem etiam hac nocte illa per hortum transiluit ad nos.

Strabax has been paying nightly visits to Phronesium, climbing over the wall which separates the gardens of the two houses. Either, therefore, there was no gate in this wall, or if there was a gate it was kept locked at night, and Strabax was not trusted with a key.

> (9) *Phor.* 891–2 : sed hinc concedam in angiportum hoc proxumum :
> inde hisce ostendam me, ubi erunt egressi foras.

Here we are probably to understand that Phormio steps into the right-hand side-entrance.* At 898 he shows himself, declaring loudly his intention of looking for Demipho. Thus this passage, which might at first sight be thought to support the ' conventional ' theory that the angiportum was an ' alley ' between two houses, and

---

* Not simply as a hiding-place, but in order that Demipho and Chremes may presently see him coming on to the stage from this side-entrance.

could be entered from the stage, really disproves it ; Phormio's entry from such an alley might arouse the suspicions of Demipho and Chremes, whereas they would find it quite natural that he should enter from the ' forum ' side-entrance, presuming that he is coming from his lodging, where Demipho would expect him to have been since he last saw him (line 440).

We may reconstruct the setting of the *Phormio* as follows (v. Johnston, *Exits and Entrances*, page 32) :

	(angiportum)		(angiportum)	
	(hortus)	(hortus)	(hortus)	
L.	Demipho's House	Chremes' House	Dorio's House	R.

At line 314 Demipho, having ordered Geta to fetch Phormio and Phaedria to fetch Antipho, enters his house, announcing that he will pay his devotions to the household gods and thence (inde) make his way to the forum and bring some friends back with him for the interview with Phormio. Phaedria starts obediently in the right direction, but slips into Dorio's house (line 310) as soon as Demipho's back is turned. Geta goes off to fetch Phormio (line 310) and reappears with him at line 315. At line 346 they see Demipho approaching from the forum. Clearly he must have left his house by the hortus and angiportum, as he has not reappeared on the stage. A gesture at the word inde would make his intention clear to the spectators. No doubt the explanation of lines 829–30 is similar ; here Phormio refers to a visit to Dorio's house which he has just made, though in fact we have not seen him enter it ; he must have made his entry and departure by the back.

It would appear from our study of the *Phormio* that the side-entrances can be used as temporary hiding-places, but also that the term angiportum can be used of the streets into which they lead. Nor is this surprising, for in *Pseud.* 960, 961, 971, as we have seen, angiportum is used of the platea itself.

(10) *Adelphi* 908–9 : atque hanc in horto maceriam iube dirui
quantum potest : hac transfer : unam fac domum.

This passage seems to prove that the gardens of two adjoining houses should be thought of as separated by a single wall, through which there is no gateway ; else why should Aeschinus have to pull the wall down in order to convey his bride from one house to the other ? Still less is there any room for an angiportum between the two gardens.

It appears abundantly clear that the ' alley ' of which editors so often speak could have had neither place nor function on the Roman stage. The only means of entry and exit were the house-doors and the side-entrances.[2]

APPENDIX D

CREPIDATA, PALLIATA, TABERNARIA, TOGATA

(Classical Review, Vol. liii. pp. 166–8.)

THE Roman classification of the different kinds of drama according to the characteristic dress or footwear used by the actors seems to have grown up haphazard and never to have achieved a satisfactory or agreed form. The loci classici are Diomedes (Keil, *Gram. Lat.* i), pages 489-91 ; Evanthius, *De Fabula*, ch. iv ; Donatus, *De Comoedia*, ch. vi, §§ 1 and 5 ; Donatus on *Ad.* 7 (for Evanthius and Donatus see Wessner's Teubner edition) ; Lydus, *De Mag.* i. 40. In these passages attempts are made to classify drama ; some of the technical terms employed are used, somewhat more casually, by other writers such as Horace (*A.P.* 288) ; a comparison of all such passages shows that the Romans themselves differed as to the meaning of certain terms which our literary histories are apt to employ with perhaps unjustified assurance.

Diomedes tells us that at first togata was a general term, including (apparently) all forms of drama not translated from the Greek. The corresponding term for all forms of drama derived from Greek sources he gives as palliata, quoting Varro : Graecas fabulas ab habitu aeque palliatas Varro ait nominari. Diomedes admits that a communis error has grown up of limiting togata to one form of native comedy, namely tabernaria, so that people speak of the togatae of Afranius, while even Horace, he regrets to say, contrasts togatae with praetextae. Diomedes himself uses palliata to include tragedy, comedy, satyric drama and mime, while under togata he includes praetextata, tabernaria, Atellana, planipedia. The word palliata occurs in two passages, viz. Donatus, *De Com.* vi, §§ 1 and 6 ; in both these passages it is used in its modern sense of Latin adaptations of Greek comedy. Evanthius, who is concerned with native Latin drama, and Lydus, who is classifying tragedy, have no occasion to use the word ; but it is surprising to find that Donatus on *Ad.* 7, in his attempt at a complete classification of drama, does not mention palliata : his list here is tragedy, comedy, togata, tabernaria, praetextata, crepidata, Atellana, μῖμος, Rhinthonica. As it is inconceivable that Donatus, in his commentary on Terence, should have left out of consideration the very form of drama which Terence composed, we must suppose that one of the nine terms in this list can bear the meaning, ' Latin adaptation of Greek comedy '. So far, then, against two uses of palliata in the modern sense, we have one where

it means something different and one where some other word takes
its place. What is this other word ? If we suppose that Donatus
includes under ' comedy ' not only Greek originals but Latin
adaptations from them, how are we to explain his distinction
between tragedy and crepidata? Lydus, loc. cit., tells us τέμνεται
(ἡ τραγῳδία) εἰς κρηπιδᾶταν καὶ πραιτεξτᾶταν· ὧν ἡ μὲν κρηπιδᾶτα ἑλληνικὰς
ἔχει ὑποθέσεις, ἡ δὲ πραιτεξτᾶτα ῥωμαϊκάς. Crepidata would then mean
Latin adaptations of Greek tragedy—and this is the sense in which
most modern writers use the word ; but it cannot be the sense in
which Donatus uses it, if the text and logic of his note on *Ad.* 7
are sound. Apparently, then, the only two ancient writers who
use the word crepidata use it in different senses.

In view of this conflict among our authorities, perhaps we should
consider the words palliata and crepidata themselves. Drama was
classified according to characteristic dress and footwear, and the
pallium was recognized as the characteristic Greek dress even in
Plautus' day (*Curc.* 288). The crepida (κρηπίς) was a kind of Greek
open shoe or sandal ; Gellius (xiii. 21. 5) gives crepidula as a Greek
equivalent of solea, a half-shoe (quibus plantarum calces tantum
infimae teguntur). The numerous illustrations in Daremberg and
Saglio show the great difference between this sandal and the high
boot which became for the Romans the symbol of tragedy under
the title cothurnus. There is plenty of evidence that the Romans
associated the pallium and crepida as typical Greek wear (Livy,
xxix. 19. 12, cum pallio crepidisque inambulare in gymnasio ;
Suet. *Tib.* 13, redegit se, deposito patrio habitu, ad pallium et
crepidas ; Cicero, *Pro Rab. Post.* 25-7, speaks of the pallium,
chlamys, crepida, and soccus as typically Greek—crepida and
soccus seem to mean much the same thing in this passage). The
crepida was an everyday type of shoe, such as might be worn by
slaves (Cic. *In Pis.* 38, ' crepidatus, ueste seruili '). Finally, as we
see from Plautus, *Pers.* 464, ' hanc hospitam autem crepidula ut
graphice decet ! ', the crepida was worn in comedy.

The essential point about the pallium and crepida is their association as typical Greek wear. ' Fabula palliata ' and ' fabula
crepidata ' should therefore be synonyms denoting Latin drama of
Greek origin. Varro, followed by Diomedes, used palliata as an
inclusive term for all such derivative drama ; more generally,
however (as Diomedes admits), the term was confined to derivative
comedy. There may have been a similar variation with regard to
the meaning of crepidata. When Lydus uses it of tragedy derived
from Greek sources the emphasis is on *Greek* rather than on *tragedy ;*
he might just as well have used palliata (in its Varronian sense).
Normally, however, the associations of the crepida and the pallium
are with everyday life, and so with comedy ; and, though Sophocles
is said (*Vita*, ch. 4) to have introduced white κρηπῖδες into tragedy,
no Roman could have used crepida as synonymous with cothurnus

to denote tragedy *as opposed to comedy*. The normal term for the footwear of the comedian is soccus ; but where it was desired to emphasize the Greek origin of a form of Latin comedy, the word crepidata would have been exactly in place. The word missing from Donatus' list is therefore some word specifically denoting Latin tragedy derived from Greek sources ; and he may have left it out for the very good reason that no such word existed.

As for togata and tabernaria, we have seen that Diomedes uses togata to include native drama of all kinds, while protesting against the communis error which identified it with tabernaria, the correct term for the work of Afranius and Atta. We may agree with Diomedes to this extent, that togata was not a very happy term for these native comedies depicting humble life in country towns (where, as Juvenal tells us, nobody wore the toga except as a shroud). A word denoting the dress of humble folk might have been more in place—perhaps tunicata (cf. Horace's ' tunicatus popellus ' and Naevius' early effort in this field, the ' Tunicularia '.) However, the word actually chosen was not descriptive of dress at all, but of the house of the characters ; ' tabernae ', says Diomedes, had once been a general term for private houses ' quod tabulis tegerentur ', and we remember that Horace uses it specifically for *poor* houses, ' pauperum tabernae '.   Modern writers usually regard tabernaria as a lower-class form of togata, and even suggest that it was Titinius who wrote tabernariae, plays about people who lived in ' booths ' (e.g. his play about the Fullers), whereas the more polite Atta and Afranius wrote *togatae*. It is surprising, in that case, that Diomedes refers to Atta and Afranius as writers of (togatae) tabernariae, while Titinius is nowhere spoken of except as a composer of togatae. True, Donatus twice mentions togata and tabernaria side by side, as though they differed in some way, and Evanthius, defining the terms, derives togata ' ab scaenicis atque argumentis Latinis ', tabernaria ' ab humilitate argumenti ac stili ' ; but this is a distinction without a difference ; the fragments show that all native comedy dealt (perhaps for reasons of prudence) with humble life. The grammarians are sometimes apt to be over-scientific ; having the two terms they tried half-heartedly to distinguish between them. Diomedes gives himself away when, contrary to his own theory, he refers to Atta as a togatarum scriptor, just as he weakens his argument about palliata by using palliati in the sense of *comic* actors. Finally, Donatus lets the cat out of the bag when he tells us that some people refer to togatae as tabernariae.

Our conclusion is that, in spite of some variation and confusion, the general usage of antiquity identified palliata and crepidata as denoting ' adaptations of Greek comedy ', togata and tabernaria as denoting ' native Latin comedy ', and that the modern attempts to explain crepidata as ' derivative *tragedy* ', and tabernaria as ' a *lower-class* form of togata ' are unsound.

APPENDIX E

THE ROMAN STAGE CURTAIN

(Hermathena, Vol. lviii. pp. 104–15).

THE drop-curtain was perhaps the most notable Roman contribution to stage technique. When was it introduced, and why? What was the relation of the aulaeum to the siparium, and how were they operated?

With the curtain as a form of decoration or scenery (παραπέτασμα) the Greeks of classical times may have been acquainted. Furthermore, the occasional use of a small portable curtain to conceal part of the stage, an unwanted door in the background, etc., is so obvious a device that it seems hazardous to deny it to the Greeks altogether.* For the use by the Greeks of a large drop-curtain, concealing the whole of the stage, there is no evidence ; indeed the development of Greek stage technique, especially in its later forms, as illustrated by our extant plays, seems to postulate a stage permanently open to view. The Latin adaptations by Plautus and Terence also read as if designed for a curtainless stage. The characters are brought on at the beginning and taken off at the end in a way which implies that opening or closing tableaux were impossible. An isolated passage such as *Capt.* 1,

> hos quos uidetis *stare* hic captiuos duos,

cannot outweigh the evidence of the plays as a whole. Still less was a curtain available within the course of a play ; hence objects no longer wanted have to be removed under the eyes of the spectators, whether without or with apology. Just as from Hamlet's remark :

> I'll lug the guts into the neighbour room,

we infer the absence of a drop-curtain in Elizabethan times, so when Lysimachus suggests that the dishes left by the cook in front of the door should be taken inside, adding the lame remark that they will supplement the family meal (*Merc.* 800-2), we clearly see the embarrassment to which the dramatist was put by the absence of a curtain on the Greek and Roman stages.

The aulaeum is said by Donatus (*de com.* 12. 3) to have been introduced in 133 B.C. (aulaea quoque in scaena intexta sternuntur, quod pictus ornatus ex Attalica regia Romam usque perlatus est ;

---

* Nevertheless I do not now think that doorways *were* concealed in this way : see Appendix F.

pro quibus siparia aetas posterior accepit) ; cf. Varro *de uit. pop. Rom.*, Serv. *ad Aen.* i. 697. These passages seem to mean that embroidered curtains were among the luxuries introduced from Attalus' palace, along with chlamides, pallae, plagae, uasa aurea ; the use of the aulaeum on the stage, at least in the form of a drop-curtain, was probably a Roman invention, which must have been subsequent to 133 B.C. It is first mentioned by Cicero, pro *Cael.* 65 (56 B.C.) ; he speaks of it as rising at the end of a mime. Our most detailed picture of the rising of the aulaeum is supplied by Ovid (Met. x. 111-4), who shows that the curtain rose smoothly and that only when it was fully raised did the figures embroidered on it become completely visible ; they then seemed to be standing on the edge of the stage. Similarly Virgil (*Georg.* iii. 25) refers to the 'embroidered Britons lifting the aulaea '. Clearly the curtain was raised to conceal the stage ; and Phaedrus,[1] who lived about this time, describes the lowering of the curtain (aulaeo misso) at the beginning of a pantomime. From Horace (*Ep.* ii. i. 189) we learn that the aulaeum was 'kept down' throughout an elaborate stage display, lasting for four hours or more, and that to wait for the aulaeum is to wait for the end of the play (*A.P.* 154).

We have seen that the drop-curtain had been introduced to the Roman stage by the year 56 B.C. at latest. Why it was introduced is further indicated by Cicero in the passage referred to. He is contrasting a regular, artistically constructed play with a mime, which comes to an abrupt halt at a given signal : mimi ergo iam axitus, non fabulae : in quo cum clausula non inuenitur, fugit eliquis e manibus, dein scabilla concrepant, aulaeum tollitur. In a regular play the spectators receive ample warning that the play is coming to an end, even before the final ' plaudite ' ; but it was precisely because of the formless nature of the mime that its con-clusion had to be marked by some external device—and the device used, according to Cicero, was the drop-curtain. The vogue of the mime and of similar performances may, therefore, explain the introduction of the drop-curtain itself.

Early in the first century B.C. we notice certain new features in Roman dramatic composition and theatrical production. Theatrical performances tend to become at once more splendid in display and more trivial in content ; the supply of new literary plays for the stage dries up, the writing of literary plays now becomes a private amusement for noble dilettanti, and the stage is given over to farce and display, with the occasional revival of an old play. We hear that Sulla was fond of the company of μῖμοι and γελωτοποιοί, that he wrote farces in Latin, and that Pomponius and Novius, writers of Atellane farces, were active about this time (Plut. *Sulla* 2 ; Athen. vi. 78). The introduction of painted scenery in 99 B.C. (Val. *Max.* ii 4) may also have helped to make the use of a front-curtain desirable.* Of course, once introduced, the drop-curtain would have been used not only for mimes but also for regular drama ; indeed, as we shall see, Cicero gives some evidence on this point.

In our modern theatres the curtain is drawn up towards the roof to leave the stage visible, and lowered so as to touch the stage at the end of the performance. Though the earliest drop-curtains in the post-Renaissance theatres appear to have worked in the opposite way, the convenience of the modern arrangement is obvious. The Roman method of working the aulaeum clearly raised two problems—how to prevent the curtain, when lowered, from encumbering the stage, and how to raise and lower it at all when, as is generally supposed, there was nothing overhead to which ropes could be attached. When we find in the remains of Roman theatres traces of a recess under the stage floor, near the front of the stage and running its full length, we seem to have the answer to the problem of where the curtain was housed during the performance. Indeed we have some evidence that this ' curtain-slot ' lent itself to other purposes, such as the emergence of ' ghosts ' from the under-world ; it was from here that Catienus appeared to address his famous ' mater, te appello ' to the deaf ears of his drunken fellow-actor Fufius in a revival of the *Iliona* of Pacuvius ; cf. Cic. *Sest.* 126 : emergebat subito, cum sub tabulas subrepserat, ut ' mater, te appello ' dicturus uideretur, and the scholiast : in eo est argumentum ita dispositum ut Polydori umbra secundum consuetudinem scaenicorum ab inferiore aulae(i) parte procedat. The operation of the curtain is thought to be connected with the row of holes sometimes found in the floor of the curtain-slot. Mazois suggested that a hollow post reached from the bottom of each hole to the level of the stage, while a narrower post could be made to slide down into the larger post or (by means of a rope attached to the bottom of the inner post and the top of the outer post) to project above stage level, raising the curtain with it. By this means it would be possible for some one in one of the wings to raise or lower the curtain by pulling a rope or releasing it, even though there was nothing overhead to which pulleys could be attached. For simplicity's sake I am giving Mazois' theory (so far as I understand it) in the form accepted by Fiechter (*Baugesch. Entwick. des ant. Theat.*), namely, that there were only two sections in each post. Fiechter reproduces Mazois' sketch (fig. 119). I do not feel competent to discuss the archaeological evidence, and am willing to accept the view that the holes were designed for narrower posts inside larger ones. Nor do I feel able to say whether the engineering problem involved in raising the huge curtain by this means could

---

* The words of Valerius Maximus and Pliny the Elder (35, 23) may mean only that the *scene-building* was painted decoratively for architectural effect ; see Appendix F.

be solved by the Romans. Since the posts must have risen above the stage when the curtain which they supported was raised, and since it is hard to suppose that when the curtain was lowered the posts were still left standing above the stage, thereby interfering with the spectators' view, we seem driven to accept the theory of telescoping sections. I still have two difficulties. First, is it not hard to believe that the Romans passed straight from the curtainless stage to this elaborate method of working the drop-curtain? Would it not be easier to imagine that the aulaeum was at first operated in some simpler and more obvious way? Second, if we find evidence that the working of the drop-curtain in the later empire cannot be explained on Mazois' theory, are we not bound to consider the whole matter afresh?

Leaving the aulaeum for the moment, I turn to the other form of stage-curtain, the siparium. The word is a varient of supparum, a topsail, or woman's upper garment.

The siparium is nowhere described as being raised or lowered; Apuleius twice refers to its being folded up. It must have already been in common use in Cicero's time, as is shown by his phrase post siparium, ' behind the scenes ', in contrast to in exostra, ' in full view ' (de prou. cons. 14). Donatus (l.c.), after observing that the aulaeum had been superseded on the stage by the siparium, defines this as a mimicum (v.l. minutum) uelum quod populo obsistit dum fabularum actus commutantur. Festus remarks : siparium, quo in scenis mimi utuntur, dictum ait Verrius a uelamento, quod uocetur alias aulaeum. Seneca (dial. ix. xi. 8) uses siparium = ' mime ' in contrast to cothurnus = ' tragedy '. Juvenal (viii. 185) speaks of a bankrupt noble hiring his voice out to the siparium as an actor in the Phasma of Catullus (a mime-writer), and the scholiast adds siparium uelum est sub quo latent paradoxi cum in scaenam prodeunt, aut ostium mimi. This last remark is perhaps the most illuminating. The siparium appears to have been a portable screen behind which jesters could hide when waiting their turn to appear (perhaps shown in Dieterich's Pulcinella, pl. 2). It served the mime-actors both as front-curtain and as back-scene. They could set it up where they chose ; they stood behind it until each actor's turn came to appear, when he made his way through a parting in the middle of the curtain[2] and so displayed himself to the audience. In the performance this parting would serve as the house-door, the need for which is seen in the Oxyrhynchus mime. When the mimes gained access to the theatre they would still bring their siparium with them. Diomedes gives as an alternative explanation of the term planipes the fact that the mimes had at one time stood not on the high stage but down in the orchestra, where they used to set up their instrumenta and give their performance. What can the instrumenta have been except the siparium? Festus says of the mimes : solebant (enim saltare) in orchestra dum (in scaena actus fa)bulae componerentur. In the Roman theatre, since the orchestra was occupied by the chairs of the senators, the mimi, like all other performers, must have appeared on the stage, as is shown by Cicero's statement that at the end of their performance the aulaeum was raised. Even on the Roman stage, however, the traditional siparium might still have been useful. We may picture the mime, when performed in the Roman theatre, as an interlude between other performances (embolium) or an after-piece (exodium) ; if the performers had appeared from the same house-doors and acted against the same background as the players in the drama which had just been staged, the dramatic illusion might have been disturbed.* We may perhaps conjecture that, when the aulaeum was raised at the end of the play, behind it the mimi set up their siparium and waited for the aulaeum to be lowered again. However we conceive the matter, it is clear from the evidence of Cicero and Juvenal that the aulaeum and siparium were both in use in their times.

For the use of the aulaeum and siparium together we have evidence in Apuleius, *Met.* x. 29. Lucius, the Ass, is waiting his turn to appear on the stage of the theatre at Corinth ; meanwhile he seizes the chance to crop the grass as he peers in at the open door. Presumably he is standing in the parodos, and thus commands a view of the stage and the orchestra. As a curtain-raiser boys and girls give a Pyrrhic dance ; then the trumpet sounds, and ' aulaeo subducto et complicitis sipariis scaena disponitur '. Butler translates : ' the great curtain fell away, the lesser curtains were drawn back, and the stage was arrayed before our eyes.' This translation gives a clear picture ; the preliminary dance must have taken place in the orchestra ; then the curtains are withdrawn, and the spectators see a most elaborate scene on the stage (' there was a mountain of wood,' etc.). Bulle (*Untersuchungen an griech. Theat.*, page 285, 1) takes a similar view, translating subducto as 'nach unten gezogen'. The trouble is that subducere nowhere means ' lower ' : it can, and frequently does, mean ' raise ' (for which meaning Georges quotes this very passage). Fiechter (*op. cit.*, page 120) understands Apuleius to mean that the aulaeum was raised to conceal the stage, the siparia being folded together for the same reason ; then, behind the curtains, the new scene is built up ; unfortunately Apuleius has forgotten to tell us that, when the new scene is ready, the aulaeum is lowered again to reveal it. This view at least does justice to subducto. But would the audience have sat patiently, gazing at the aulaeum, while so elaborate a scene was being prepared behind it ? In *Met.* i. 8, aulaeum tragicum dimoueto et siparium scaenicum complicato, the effect of folding the siparia is evidently to reveal something, not to conceal it ; therefore, in the present passage, complicititis sipariis must mean that the siparia

* This argument now seems to me to lack force ; see Appendix F.

were folded together so as to reveal the stage, and aulaeo subducto is part of the same process. A more plausible translation would be ' the aulaeum was removed ', this being a possible sense of subducere but if the process referred to is really the lowering of the curtain, subducere, which frequently means ' lift ', would be an unfortunate word to choose ; and if Apuleius' meaning is that the aulaeum is carried away altogether, we have to suppose that the method of operating it as a drop-curtain had been abandoned in the second century. Fiechter, indeed, though taking the aulaeum here to be a drop-curtain, worked in the classical method, believes for quite other reasons that the classical method of working it *was* altered in the second century. In three theatres of this period (at Dugga, Timgad and Athens) there are postholes, but there is no trace of a curtain-slot ; he therefore thinks that from this time on the curtain was attached on the morning of the performance to the movable posts and taken away again at the conclusion of the performance. If we try to apply such a suggestion on the present instance, we have to suppose *either* that the aulaeum rose and fell between the various items of the day's programme ; and when it fell, as there was no longer any curtain-slot, it must have remained heaped on the stage while the posts disappeared underground (a view which does not solve the difficulty presented by subducto, and adds the complication that the curtain is left lying on the stage during the main performance), *or* that the aulaeum is no longer used as a drop-curtain at all. But we have three references from the fourth century to the rising or falling of the aulaeum. Two come from Ammianus Marcellinus : (*a*) xvi. 6. 3, Dorus euanuit et Verissimus ilico tacuit uelut aulaeo deposito (where the lowering of the curtain marks the end of the performance) ; (*b*) xxviii. 6. 29 : ut ne quid cothurni terribilis fabulae relinquerent intentatum, hoc quoque post depositum accessit aulaeum (where, again, the lowering of the curtain marks the end of the tragedy, after which comes the exodium). The third passage refers to the *raising* of the curtain. Donatus (*Eun.* praef. 1. 5) tells us that Terence avoids pauses between the acts, ne ante aulaea sublata fastidiosus spectator exsurgeret, ' lest the spectator should grow weary and leave his seat before the curtain rose ' (for the new act, or at the end of the play ?).[3] Incidentally these passages suggest that the statement already quoted from Donatus to the effect that the aulaeum had been superseded by the siparium can scarcely have been universally true.

A drop-curtain was, then, known to Ammianus Marcellinus and to Donatus, and it worked just like our modern curtain, being raised at the opening of the performance and lowered at the end. The Thesaurus takes this view of the passages in Marcellinus. The passages quoted above from Apuleius can be explained, I think, only in this way. Nearly all our literary references to the drop-curtain subsequent to the age of Tiberius point, therefore, to its having

THE LARGE THEATRE, POMPEII

THE ROMAN THEATRE, VAISON-LA-ROMAINE
SHOWING CURTAIN-SLOT

worked in the reverse way to that which was known to Cicero, Virgil, Ovid and Phaedrus. It must now have been kept *up* during the performance in such a way as not to obstruct the view. But, according to Mazois' theory, the curtain could not have been raised higher than the top of the inmost poles, and to lift both curtain and poles out of sight would be impossible. So far as I know, the archaeologists are not aware of this new problem, and consequently have no solution to offer.

To keep a drop-curtain raised so that it does not obstruct the view of the stage necessitates the existence of some fixed object above the stage to which ropes can be attached. That ropes were used for drawing up other objects above the heads of the spectators is shown by Plutarch, *Sulla* xi, where we hear of a figure of Victory being made to soar aloft in the theatre at Pergamum. Juvenal (iv. 122) speaks of boys being hoisted to the awnings spread high above the spectators' heads :

> et pegma et pueros inde ad uelaria raptos.

The drop-curtain of the later period, at least, must have been drawn up *to* something. One might conjecture that permanent posts were erected, one at each end of the stage, perhaps concealed in the wings. Another possibility is that the curtain was drawn up towards the stage roof. But if we grant this for the later period, may we not grant it for the earlier period as well ? Fiechter thinks that the stage roof of the uncovered theatres is a vestige of the roof which covered the entire building in the theatrum tectum ; he also believes that the theatrum tectum in Pompeii dates from 80 B.C. The need to protect the stage with a permanent roof goes well with the other developments (such as the painting of the scene-building) which took place early in the first century. Once given a stage roof, whether high or low, the idea of a drop-curtain seems obvious. No doubt experiments were made, as in modern times ; the first plan, apparently, was to raise the curtain to conceal the stage and to lower it into a recess to reveal the stage. I suggest that the telescoping posts * were a development of this first plan ; they were designed not to supply the power which raised the curtain, but to ensure that it rose evenly, and perhaps to take some of the weight. There may have been some simple locking device which would hold the posts rigid when they were fully extended and which could be released when it was desired to lower the curtain again. In other words, the system of telescoping-posts was merely supplementary to the essential and common-sense principle that the curtain was raised and lowered by ropes attached to some fixed object, which was at least as high as the top of the fully raised curtain itself.

We have seen reason to believe that at some time between the

* If they ever existed.

life of Phaedrus and that of Apuleius the new system came in of operating the curtain as in the modern theatre. The top of the curtain must now have been permanently raised ; the bottom was drawn up to it to reveal the stage and let fall to conceal the stage. The telescoping posts and the curtain-slot were thus made useless ; and in fact Fiechter finds (page 123) that in the second century the curtain-slot disappears. We need not, however, suppose that the change of system occurred everywhere at the same time ; much must have depended on local circumstances, on the size of the theatre, the nature of the performances for which it was mainly designed, etc. At Verulamium the post-holes appear to have been filled up at an early period, while the curtain-slot remained in use. May we not suspect that each theatre had, at any given period, its own method of working its curtain ?

Apuleius twice speaks of the aulaeum and the siparium being used together for the purpose of concealing the stage ; when the aulaeum rises to reveal the stage, the siparia are folded together for the same purpose. The siparia in these references can scarcely have been the portable screens used by the mimes. Butler is perhaps right in translating complicitis sipariis as ‘ the lesser curtains were drawn back ’ ; the picture appears to be that whereas the aulaeum concealed the stage as a whole, the siparia were hung in the wings. When we roll up a window-blind and fold back the side-curtains we are performing a somewhat similar operation. Such siparia would be particularly useful if the aulaeum did not reach quite from end to end of the stage. It may be worth adding that at Dugga, where no trace of the curtain-slot has been discovered, an inscription records the presence of siparia : ‘ scaenam cum siparis et ornamentis omnibus et . . .’ The mention of σείφαροι in an inscription at Ephesus also suggests that the term siparia may sometimes have been used of a more permanent form of stage equipment than the portable screens of the mime-actors. We must not forget Festus’ remark that Verrius identified the siparium with the aulaeum. When Donatus tells us that the aulaeum has in his day been superseded by the siparium, he appears to be referring to the performance of Terence’s comedies. We have reason to believe that any such performances in the late empire were strongly influenced by the mime ; thus we are told by Donatus that actresses were now employed for female parts. So the influence of the mime may have helped to bring back the siparium into favour, and it is well to recall the frequent indication of small curtains in the illustrations to the manuscripts of Terence.

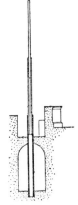

Mechanism of drop-curtain, according to Mazois

APPENDIX F

CHANGE OF SCENE AND CHANGE OF SCENERY : THE QUESTION OF 'SETS'

LIKE all Greek drama, the plays of Plautus and Terence were written for an open-air, curtainless theatre. So long as the stage lay permanently open to view, there was, in my opinion, no attempt to alter the visible background, though the imaginary scene might be changed at will. So in the medieval drama the stage might represent any desired place—a freedom satirized by Sidney but still retained by Shakespeare. Change of scene in Greek drama seems to be confined to the earlier period ; in the *Eumenides* the scene shifts from Delphi to Athens, in the *Peace* from Earth to Heaven, in the *Frogs* from Earth to Hades.

The innumerable theories as to Greek stage scenery which have been put forward may be arranged in two main groups. The common principle of the first group is that the actors' house, otherwise called the skené or permanent scene-building, was itself specially adapted to the needs of each play. The principle of the second group is that the permanent scene-building was concealed by 'sets'. In default of any real evidence in favour of either of these views, their supporters appeal to the text of the plays and to the evidence of vase-paintings and wall-paintings supposed to be in some measure inspired by theatrical performances. Unfortunately a major premiss is always lacking from such arguments ; we have no proof that verbal descriptions of the imaginary surroundings were pictorially represented in the physical setting, or that ancient illustrations, even when they contain details which are agreed to be theatrical in origin, are in other respects faithful copies, or copies at all, of theatrical performances.

Aristotle (*Poet.* iv) tells us that σκηνογραφία and the third actor were introduced by Sophocles. Vitruvius, however, asserts (vii. praef. §11) that it was Agatharchus who first made a scaena, and that he did so when Aeschylus was active as a dramatist (or perhaps 'under the instruction of Aeschylus'). In the view of Pickard-Cambridge (*Theat. of Dion.*, page 124) Agatharchus ' painted an architectural design in perspective on the flat background '. Apparently what he did was to paint the front of the scene-building so as to give it a decorative, architectural effect, sufficiently dignified to serve as the permanent background for dramatic performances of all kinds. The early plays of Aeschylus, *Suppliants, Persae, Seven Against Thebes, Prometheus Bound,* perhaps belong to a time when there was no scene - building. But from the *Oresteia* onwards the action of every extant play is specifically related to some sort of building or dwelling in the background, whether it be temple, palace, private house or houses, tent or cave. From the *Oresteia* onwards we also find the three-actor rule established. Apparently the purpose of the skené was to house the three actors, and the task of Agatharchus was to decorate the skené front. From now on all Greek drama was acted before a permanent background, the front of the scene-building, with its three doors. If this view is correct, it would be misleading to translate σκηνογραφία as ' scene-painting '.

Our modern convention of realistic scenery is bound up with a whole complex of circumstances utterly remote from the Greek theatre. Our theatre is an enclosed building, artificially lighted. By darkening the auditorium and lighting up the stage we concentrate the attention of the spectators on the stage, for that is all that they can see. The Greeks sat in theatres open to the sky ; if they turned their eyes away from the actors, they could look at real sunlit scenery of the most spectacular kind. Whatever Agatharchus and his successors tried to do, they can hardly have attempted to compete with Nature. If the spectators fixed their attention on the drama, it was because they were interested in the drama itself— the words of the actors and their actions.

There is no real evidence that the Greeks made any attempt to suit the background to the play. The assumption that they did so is based on nothing but our own convention of realistic scenery ; it always defeats itself by leading to most unrealistic results.

It is agreed that in the theatre of Dionysus several plays were performed in one day. In 431 B.C. Euripides presented the *Medea*, the *Philoctetes*, the *Dictys* and the satyric drama *Theristai*, after which presumably came a comedy. Thus the imaginary background changed from palace to sea-shore, then to country, and finally to two or three private houses. If we assume that the visible background was somehow changed between one play and another, we must allow that any such change was made in a very short time and in full view of the audience. If realism is what we desire, how do we suppose that a realistic-looking palace was changed (for example) into a realistic-looking cave ? If, on the other hand, we are content with slight and purely symbolical alterations ; if, with Professor Percy Gardner (' The Scenery of the Greek Stage ', *J.H.S.*, xix, 1899, pages 252-68) ' we may suppose that a few rocks strewn on the stage . . . would well suffice to satisfy the audience ' in the case of a satyric drama, then we have evidently abandoned our demand for realism, and may as well accept the convention in all its stark simplicity. A few rocks strewn on the stage would be of small aid to the imagination ; instead of helping the spectator to forget the inadequacy of the background, they would tend to underline it ; and they would presently (ex hypothesi) have to be cleared away before the next play could begin.

If we abandon the view that structural alterations, sufficiently convincing to be worth while, could be made in the brief interval between play and play, and if we still crave for a visible background corresponding to the imaginary setting, we may be tempted by the alternative hypothesis of ' sets '. This hypothesis has now received a notable adherent in Dr. Pickard-Cambridge. He holds (*Theatre of Dionysus*, pages 122-33) that changes of scene were indicated ' by the use of painted canvas or screens or panels, which could be easily moved into position ' ; in other words, that there were ' sets for each type of scene, easily transferable ', which the theatre servants could put in position ' openly in the presence of the spectators without offending their susceptibilities '. He does not claim that this is more than a theory ; in fact he discounts certain obscure remarks in ancient authors (page 122, note 2) which have sometimes been regarded as evidence for these screens.* (The καταβλήματα mentioned by Pollux, iv. 131, belong to the περίακτοι, on which see Appendix B. The reason for putting forward the hypothesis at all is presumably that it seems to offer an easy and practical way of suiting the background to the needs of each play in turn. Nevertheless it raises serious difficulties, some of which were pointed out by Professor Percy Gardner in the article already cited : cf. page 258 : ' There is no justification for the notion that the scene-painter of the fourth century would stretch across the upper part of the skené a great canvas screen representing the sky and across the lower part of that front another canvas screen representing some particular place, and pierced with doors corresponding to the doors from the skené on to the stage '.

I have already pointed out that the doors in Roman Comedy have to endure a good deal of knocking and kicking. This raises no difficulty if we are dealing with the sturdy wooden doors in the scene-building ; would it be possible if the doors were made of canvas or light wooden material ? I do not know how far in front of the skené these screens are supposed to have stood. Mercury, in the *Amphitruo*, standing on the house roof, empties pots on the head of Amphitruo below ; this is readily understandable if the house-front is also the front of the scene-building, not so convincing if the house-front is a canvas screen, separated by some space from the front of the scene-building. I do not see where these great screens were housed, nor how they were moved. As Navarre remarks (*Le Théâtre grec*, pages 80-1) ' Par quels moyens matériels

* He thinks, however, that the nickname proskenion applied to Nannion should be taken in the sense of ' screen ' (p. 157). I would give the term its ordinary sense, ' front of scene-building ', because this, like Nannion, owed its decorative appearance to paint.

ces divers decors étaient-ils obtenus ? Vraisemblablement â l'aide
de châssis peints, appliqués contre la façade de la skéné et glissant
sur une coulisse. Toutefois les dimensions considérables de ces
châssis (plus de 20 mètres de long au théâtre d'Athènes, par
exemple) les eussent rendus difficilement maniables.' He has
accordingly to suppose that the Greeks were already acquainted
with the scaena ductilis or some other Roman device ; in other
words he admits that the use of *sets* is a pure hypothesis, and one not
free from difficulties.

But the chief logical argument against the theory of ' sets '
is not that they would have been difficult to manipulate but rather
that they would (ex hypothesi) have afforded only too quick and
convenient a method of changing the scene. For if the Greeks really
felt the need of changing the visible background to suit the imaginary
setting, and if they solved the problem so successfully, we should
have expected that as Greek drama developed change of imaginary
setting would become more common. The opposite is the case.
The freedom from the unity of place which we notice in fifth-
century drama seems to have disappeared in the time of Menander.
If the fragments of his plays and the versions by Plautus and Terence
are any guide, the normal setting of New Comedy is a section of
street in front of one, two or three houses. I have already pointed
out that the wild scenery of the early part of the *Rudens* is completely
ignored for the greater part of the play, and was in all probability
left to the imagination, whereas Daemones' cottage remains
visible from first to last. Imaginary scenery can be forgotten when
no longer required, but physical objects would have to be physically
removed. The scene-building and its doors are the permanent
reality ; indeed the prologue to the *Menaechmi* (70-6) shows that
the same setting serves for play after play :

' This city is Epidamnus during the presentation of this play ;
when another play is presented it will become another town '
(Loeb. tr.).

> To change the play will change the town as well,
> And other folk within these doors will dwell ;
> For now a pimp you'll see, and now a lover,
> And now a cross old father you'll discover,
> Poor man or beggar, gipsy, toff or tout ;
> It all depends on what the play's about.

So far from any attempt being made to adapt the visible background to the imaginary setting, it was the setting which had to be
adapted to the permanent background. Where the background
helped, it was turned to good account ; where it did not help, it
had to be ignored. But the difficulty of ignoring it was felt more
keenly as the public grew more sophisticated ; and the result is
seen in New Comedy, with its stereotyped setting.

THE STAGING OF 'INTERIOR' SCENES: THYROMATA
OR PROTHYRA?

The action of every extant specimen of New Comedy is specifically related to one, two or three buildings, the doors of which are
used by the characters for their exits and entrances.   There can
therefore be no question of change of the imaginary setting.
Nevertheless it is supposed by some writers that special arrangements were made for the display of certain scenes which in real
life would probably take place indoors.   The two possible alternatives are :
   (1) that such scenes were staged in the doorway or a little
distance inside the doorway.   This implies that the doors in the
back-scene were wide—the so-called thyromata.   (For illustrations
of attempted reconstructions see Bieber, figs. 296, 297, 303, 306).
(The thyromata, according to Bieber (page 222), were ' wide open-
ings into which backdrops and other decorations were set, or which,
when left open, served to exhibit interior scenes '.)
   (2) that they were staged in front of the house-doors, but inside
the so-called prothyra.   These would be projecting open porches,
the roofs of which were supported by pillars.   (For illustrations see
Pickard-Cambridge, figs. 9-29).
   It will be seen at once that these two alternatives are opposed
to each other.   Nothing could well be more different from the
opening of a door wide in order to display an interior scene than
the partial concealment of that door behind a projecting porch.
Moreover the view just quoted concerning the use of the thyromata
contradicts itself ; if the doorways were filled with scenery, they
could not at the same time be used as doors ; and practicable
doors in the background are an absolute necessity, if New Comedy
is to be staged at all.
   The thyromata and prothyron theories have this in common :
they confine the actor in an enclosed space, where his movements
must necessarily be less free, his gestures less visible and his words
less audible than if he stood on the open stage.   To balance these
disadvantages, two claims are made :
   (1) that intimate scenes would be more convincing if framed
within a building ;
   (2) that instances where one character is not seen by another
are easier to understand if we suppose that the unseen character
was concealed within a doorway or a projecting porch.   Thus, for
example, Professor Nixon, in his Loeb edition of Plautus, assumes
that the banqueting-party in the *Asinaria* (line 830 ff.) takes place
inside Cleareta's house.   The weakness of this supposition has
already been pointed out (p. 179).
   A party takes place indoors in the *Bacchides*, but the spectators
do not see it ; Artamo opens the door an inch or two (832) and

Nicobulus and Chrysippus peer in and discuss what they see. Lines 720-3 show that the interior of the house is visible only to those standing at the open door. The spectators have to rely on the report given by the actor peering inside the door, just as they are accustomed to be told by the actor on the stage of an impending arrival from one of the wings.

There is no clear evidence that any character is thought of as visible to the spectators until he actually makes his entrance on the stage. The doors seem normally to be shut, except while a character is entering or coming out. If Theopropides is surprised to find his door shut in broad daylight (*Most.* 444), Antipho seems somewhat surprised too when he finds his daughter's door open (*Stich.* 87). The Loeb editor occasionally suggests that a character uses his own doorway as a place of concealment, while observing something taking place on the stage. This may seem plausible enough, but there is nothing in the text to support such a view. If Cleostrata is really standing in her doorway (*Cas.* 562) to spy on her husband, it is surprising that at line 573 he exclaims ' but there's my wife in front of the house ! I'm afraid she's not deaf and that she's heard all this.' In truth the conclusive argument against the theory that intimate scenes were staged inside the house-door is that the text usually speaks of the characters in such scenes as being in front of the house (*Pers.* 756 ; *Truc.* 490, 583, 631 ; *St.* 147, 683).

The alternative theory is that interior scenes were shown in a projecting prothyron or porch in front of the house-door. This is the view of Lundstrom (' Aussen oder Innen ', *Eranos*, i, page 95, 1896), Kelley Rees (' The Prothyron in Greek plays ', *C.P.* x, 1915, page 117 ff.) and Dalman (' *De aedibus scaenicis comoediae nouae* ', Leipzig, 1929) ; it has been searchingly criticized by Legrand (*Daos*, 1910, pages 434-444). While Pickard-Cambridge is in general opposed to the view that such porches were shown in the permanent back-scene (pages 75-100), he is willing to allow (page 174) that ' in the few plays in which scenes were certainly acted in a portico in front of the main house, such a portico could obviously be erected ad hoc in front of any of the doors of the skené ', referring in a foot-note to the *Mostellaria* and the *Stichus*.

The crucial passage on which the whole theory rests is admitted by both Kelley Rees and Dalman to be *Most.* 817. Two houses are mentioned in this play, the houses of Theopropides and Simo.* In line 817 Tranio, looking at Simo's house, says to Theopropides :

uiden uestibulum ante aedis hoc et ambulacrum quoiusmodi ?

' Do you see this porch in front of the house here, and what a fine promenade ? ' Theopropides replies ' Yes, very handsome, upon my word '. Rees comments : ' Thus the vestibulum formed a part of the stage building and was visible to actors and spectators '.

* See plan on p. 285.

Identifying it with the ambulacrum, he describes it as a ' promenade porch '. Having thus established the existence of a visible porch of some size, he proceeds to find a dramatic use for it. It would serve admirably, he thinks, for drinking-parties, toilet-scenes and the like, which the text expressly states to take place in front of the door ; it would also serve on occasion to explain why one character does not see another. In the *Mostellaria* he finds three such scenes. At line 157 we see Philematium, assisted by Scapha, preparing her toilet in front of Theopropides' house (cf. line 295), while Philolaches, who had arrived at line 84 from the forum and is therefore supposed to be standing in the street, looks on unobserved. Here, as Rees points out, ' if the women were busy with the toilet inside the house, Philolaches would have to stand upon the stage between the women and the audience in order to see them. In this case the women would have seen him '. Moreover, when at length he addresses them (ll. 295-6) he bids Scapha ' get inside and take this trumpery in with you '.

At line 308 slaves bring tables and couches, and the lovers, as they take their places at table, see their friends Callidamates and Delphium coming along the street (in uia, 326) to join them. Soon all four are carousing together. But at 348 Tranio arrives from the harbour with the bad news that Theopropides has returned ; he packs them all indoors (391) and locks the door behind them (425-6). These, then, are the two ' interior ' scenes which Rees supposes to have been acted inside an open porch in front of the door of Theopropides' house. Later in the play Callidamates' slaves, who have come to fetch their master, begin to knock at Theopropides' door (898) ; Theopropides comes out of Simo's door at 904, yet does not see them until 935. Rees infers that ' they were partially concealed ' from Theopropides owing to the fact that they were standing in the porch. Similar scenes occur, as we have seen, in other plays, though nowhere else do we have any indication as to the appearance of the porch.* For this Rees relies on vase-paintings supposed to be reminiscent of theatrical scenes and showing figures standing in or near a roofed and columned building like a small temple. If the argument from vase-paintings is valid at all, we seem compelled to suppose that such porches were a normal part of the visible background, not only in tragedy but also in comedy. There is great difficulty in supposing that such an imposing structure was run up merely to serve the purposes of a particular play, and removed afterwards. And as nothing in our comedies would suggest that one house front was more imposing than another, it is difficult to refuse all three doors their porches. Indeed Rees refers to a Pompeian wall-painting in the Casa dei Gladiatori which shows three doors, each with its portico. But if three porches formed part of the background, it is not easy to see

* But see *As.* 425 ; Plaut. *frag,* 146 (Lindsay).

how plays were staged in which only one or two houses are mentioned. It is one thing to ignore a plain door set unobtrusively in a flat wall : it is another matter to pretend that a visible pillared and roofed porch does not exist.

Everything turns on how we interpret *Most.* 817. According to Kelley Rees, ' ambulacrum is a descriptive term for the uestibulum.' At line 756 Tranio tells Simo that Theopropides is planning to improve his house in view of his son's approaching marriage. He wishes to add women's quarters, baths, an ambulacrum and a porticus ; he therefore proposes to visit Simo's house and take it as a model, having heard that it is well provided in these respects— especially with provision for shade in hot weather. (Simo retorts that, on the contrary, the sun stands at his door all day long, like a debt-collector.) Now the ambulacrum which Theopropides wishes to add to his house must be like the ambulacrum in Simo's house which he wishes to take as a model. If Simo's ambulacrum is a ' promenade porch ' in front of the door, then no such porch can be supposed to exist outside Theopropides' door ; for clearly, if the visible back-scene showed such porches in front of both doors, it would be absurd to say that Theopropides intends to build what is manifestly there already. But if Theopropides' door has no porch, then the ' interior scenes ' staged in front of his door cannot be supposed to take place inside a porch. Thus the prothyron- theory breaks down at the outset. In fact a ' porch ' would be irrelevant to Theopropides' building scheme ; the association of the ambulacrum with women's quarters, porticus and baths shows that what is meant is a covered walk in the interior of the house. It follows that his model, the ambulacrum in Simo's house, must also belong to the interior. Looking at line 817 again we notice that the phrase ante aedis goes with uestibulum and does not necessarily refer to ambulacrum. I imagine that at the words, ' Do you see this uestibulum in front of the house here ? ' Tranio opens the door slightly and then exclaims, ' And that promenade ? How fine ! ' pointing at the imaginary peristyle in the interior. The spectators cannot see it ; but there is much obvious make-believe in Tranio's description of what he sees. He asserts that he can see a picture of a crow making fun of two vultures, while Theopropides stubbornly denies that *he* can see anything of the kind. A little later Tranio scares the unhappy old gentleman by a sudden reference to the house-dog. Who can believe that there was a visible picture or a real house-dog ? The uestibulum is visible enough ; but all it need consist of is the door with its two doorposts and its joints (818-29), and the space just in front of it. As we have seen, Simo complains that the sun stands at his door all day long, like a debt- collector. Presumably the reference is to his *front* door, where the collector would naturally stand (so in this very play the money- lender Misargyrides makes his way to Theopropides' front door),

If so, then there was apparently no roofed porch to shade Simo's front door.

There is another indication that Simo's door leads straight from the house into the street, without any intervening porch. At line 1063 Theopropides, at last aware of the trick played upon him, sets a trap for Tranio. He tells Simo's slaves to stand inside the threshold of Simo's house, while he himself takes up his position 'in front of the house'. So far from wanting to conceal himself in a porch, his object is by a show of affability to lure Tranio to approach the door, inside which the invisible slaves are waiting. (In fact Tranio has already seen Theopropides coming out of Simo's door). A porch would have been very much in the way.

There remains the opening scene of the *Stichus*. In the background are the houses of Pamphila, Panegyris and their father Antipho.* The play opens with the appearance of the sisters. They seat themselves on a couch. Presently Antipho comes out of his own door on his way to Panegyris' house. He does not see his daughters, nor they him, for some thirty lines. At line 87 he approaches Panegyris' house, remarking 'I'll go in. But the door's open'. The two daughters then hear his voice, come up to greet him, and get him to sit down with them.

Is this opening scene supposed to occur inside Panegyris' doorway? or inside a porch in front of her door? The porch is ruled out by Antipho's words 'The door's open'. For if the daughters were sitting in the porch, they would be in front of the door, and he would see them before he noticed the door. If they are actually in the interior of the house, we have to infer that Antipho goes inside to sit down with them. It is clear from the text that they hear Antipho's voice before they see him. This would be inexplicable if at that moment he is entering the doorway inside which they are sitting. But it is readily to be understood if they are on the open stage, perhaps a little to one side, while Antipho stands behind them, looking with surprise at the door which Panegyris has left open. The open door makes him realize that she must have come out. When they hear his voice, they turn round and see him. The fact that for thirty lines they have failed to do so is nothing unusual in New Comedy; the actors took care not to look in the right direction. The only unusual feature is the presence of a couch, stool and cushions on the stage without any mention of their being brought out or taken in again. We may suppose that the two women bring these articles out with them at line 1, and perhaps that Panegyris carries them indoors at the end of the scene. However that may be, line 147 (nunc, soror, abeamus intro) shows that up till then the sisters have been on the open stage. Similarly the slaves' drinking-party with which the play concludes takes place on the open stage; as it ends Stichus remarks 'Let us go inside'; then, turning to the audience, he asks for their applause.

* See plan on p. 275.

THE OPENING SCENE OF THE *HEAUTON TIMORUMENOS*

The theory of ancient stagecraft which I have put forward will, I believe, be found applicable to every scene in New Comedy. Most of the difficulties which have been thought to exist are due either to baseless assumptions or to failure to read the text with care.

The opening scene of the *Heauton Timorumenos* is a case in point. Menedemus and Chremes are shown in conversation, Menedemus still carrying the heavy rake with which he has been working all day on his farm. The view that he is 'actually ' discovered ' at work on the farm (represented by the stage) is, I believe, quite foreign to ancient stagecraft ; it is, moreover, demonstrably out of keeping with the text. There was no curtain in the days of Terence, and therefore no opening ' tableau ' ; the stage represented merely the open space in front of the houses of the characters. As is normal in ancient drama, the play opens with an entry on the bare stage—in this case the entry of Chremes and Menedemus from the ' country ' side-entrance. (So the *Epidicus* opens with the entry of two characters from one of the wings.) The opening words of Chremes explicitly refer to Mene- demus' farm as being ' in the neighbourhood '. As the two are evidently walking from the country towards their own houses, the spectators will realize that they are going home. This obvious fact, taken in conjunction with Chremes' words (ll. 15-18 of this scene) ' I never go out so early or come home so late but I see you on your farm, digging or ploughing or else carrying something ' will make the situation clear. Chremes has evidently walked back with Menedemus from his farm, and therefore the time is evening. When Chremes urges Menedemus to put down his rake, his words ne labora mean not ' Don't go on working ' but ' don't distress yourself by holding so heavy an implement ' ; compare the meaning of labor in a few lines earlier (si quid laborist nollem) and of laborare in Cicero *Phil.* v. 6 §18 (' lest his friends should *suffer fatigue* if they had to carry the shields themselves ').

NOTE ON *SCAENA VERSILIS* AND *SCAENA DUCTILIS*

These terms occur in Servius' note on *Georg.* iii. 24-5. Virgil's meaning is (I think) clear : the play is ended, the periacti revolve (versis frontibus), the curtain rises and the stage disappears (scaena discedat). Servius seems by scaena versilis to mean the periactus, by scaena ductilis perhaps an alternative method of drawing the panels off the stands instead of revolving the periactus. When Servius says that this was done to show another picture behind the first, he can scarcely be referring to the back-scene, which, as Virgil expressly says, is concealed by the rising curtain. See pp. 258 ff. But Servius or his authority may have taken Virgil's discedat as ' parts asunder '.

APPENDIX G

THE DOORS SHOWN ON THE STAGE

THE view taken in this book is that, in addition to the entrances in the wings (open throughout the course of the performance) there were three practicable doors, perhaps all of the same size, in the permanent back-scene, set unobtrusively but visibly in the wall of the scene-building, and that these were the doors which the actors used for the purposes of the play ; it being understood that any door which was not required in a particular play was for the time being simply disregarded. This I imagine to have been the rule ever since the construction of the scene-building in the fifth century ; but it is particularly relevant to Roman Comedy. The theory that the projecting paraskenia, or wings, were themselves sometimes used to represent the houses of characters * seems to me to violate a general principle of staging in comedy—that the stage represented a section of street in front of the houses of the characters.†

The accompanying sketch will make clear the relation of the house-doors to the side-entrances, as I understand it.

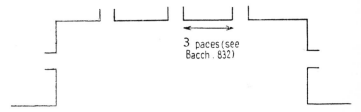

3 paces (see Bacch. 832)

That there were three doors at the back of the stage is stated by both Pollux and Vitruvius.‡ The statement of Pollux that the central door was reserved for the principal actor, the door to the right for the second actor and the door to the left for the least important character, absurd as it is, seems inspired by an attempt to connect the trinity of doors with the trinity of actors, and thus confirms the statement that there were three doors. It will be noticed that Vitruvius and Pollux speak of three doors in connexion with tragedy as well as with comedy, and offer explanations of the use to which each of the three doors is put in tragedy. These

* See e.g. Pickard-Cambridge, *Theatre of Dionysus*, p. 59.

† See Gomme, *Essays in Greek History and Literature*, p. 253, note 1.

‡ Cf. Haigh, *Attic Theatre*, p. 189, and p. 249 above.

explanations are difficult to reconcile with the needs of our extant tragedies, nearly all of which require only one entrance (sometimes, perhaps, a side-door is used as well). In comedy the usual setting requires two doors, but a few plays need three and a few only one. No comedy requires more than three doors. The problem is solved when we recognize that the number three was imposed not by the needs of the play but by the permanent background, and that Pollux and Vitruvius are merely endeavouring to suggest how this permanent background could be reconciled with the varying requirements of tragedy and comedy. When Haigh* tells us that ' it is necessary to distinguish carefully between the permanent doors in the wall surrounding the stage, and the temporary doors or entrances which were left when the scenery had been put up ', he is introducing a distinction which was entirely unknown to the Greeks.

To this extent I agree with the general view of Frickenhaus,† who by identifying the permanent structure of the scene-building with the visible background of all performances sweeps away the whole basis of the fanciful theories as to the stage setting of particular plays which have been advanced by Wilamowitz, Murray and many others. Unfortunately Frickenhaus puts forward an equally fanciful theory as to the number of permanent doors available in Athenian New Comedy. He admits (p. 8) that, in the fifth century, three doors were sometimes required—as in the *Acharnians*, the *Peace* and the *Lysistrata* ; he quotes a fragment of Eupolis (24 Kock) : ' they live here in three huts, each in his own home '. He thinks that the middle door was large and opened inwards (i.e. into the scene-building) in order to admit of the use of the ekkyklema, while the two side-doors were smaller, opened on to the stage, and had no ekkyklema. He supposes that the Athenian writers of New Comedy gave up the use of the ekkyklema and also of the central door, confining themselves to the two side-doors, each of which was used at least once in each act ; meanwhile plays written elsewhere than at Athens retained the use of the middle door. Therefore, when in Latin comedies translated from Attic originals we find that three doors are required, we are to take it that the third door has been introduced by the Latin writer, bent on ' contaminating ' Greek plays and influenced by such (supposedly) non-Attic originals as the *Curculio*, the action of which takes place at Epidaurus and requires three doors. A theory which depends on such uncertain assumptions as contamination, act-division, the ekkyklema and a fundamental difference between stage-convention in Athens and in other Greek towns, scarcely merits serious criticism, though Pickard-Cambridge ‡ thinks that Frickenhaus ' makes a strong case for supposing the third house in Plautus' *Stichus* and Terence's *Phormio* and *Hecyra* to

---

* *Attic Theatre*, p. 188.
† *Die altgriechische Bühne*, 1917.
‡ *Theatre of Dionysus*, p. 173, note 6. For ekkyklema see ib. 111–121.

be due to *contaminatio*.' It is always possible to argue that some detail in a Latin play is unsatisfactory, and one may, if one wishes, take the further step of supposing that the weakness is due to the Latin translator. I can only point to the obvious fact that Latin comedy requires sometimes one door, sometimes three, but usually two ; and as this is true of fifth-century Greek comedy also, the natural inference is that in this respect the Latin writers were following their originals. If Plautus and Terence sometimes added a third door for the fun of the thing, it seems surprising that they did not make more use of it. According to Frickenhaus himself, the added third door in the *Phormio* and the *Hecyra* is mentioned only once ; in other plays (e.g. the *Aulularia*) to remove it would necessitate a surgical operation. Perhaps it is enough to say that Frickenhaus has not convinced Dalman,* who quotes Jachmann's view that in the *Aulularia* the temple is essential to the plot, and cannot be supposed to have been added by Plautus.

I come now to a famous crux. Did the three house-doors open inwards or outwards ? Plutarch (*Life of Publicola*, ch. 20) tells us that ' whereas the doors of other houses at that time opened inwards, the street door of Publicola's house was made to open outwards, to show by such an honourable distinction that he was always ready to receive any proposals for the public service. All the doors in Greece, they tell us, were formerly made to open so, which they prove from those passages in the comedies where it is mentioned that those that went out knocked loud on the inside of the house first, to give warning to such as passed by or stood before them, lest the doors in opening should dash against them.' A similar statement with regard to early Greek practice is made by Helladius,[1] a grammarian of the fourth century A.D. (who is probably echoing Plutarch, or Plutarch's authority). The remarks of Plutarch and Helladius have been taken as reliable evidence with regard both to stage-practice and to real life, and are stated as fact by many editors. They were vigorously attacked more than a hundred years ago by Becker,† who rejected them as untrue both of Greek behaviour and of the construction of the house-door. The argument was taken up by W. W. Mooney,‡ who agreed with Becker that there was no such thing as ' knocking from within ', and that house-doors in real life usually opened inwards. Mooney was nevertheless led by other evidence, not considered by Becker, to conclude that the house-doors on the stage opened outwards. A different view of this evidence was taken by Dalman (op. cit.). But Plutarch's statement seems still to be accepted by most classical scholars, and we find Professor Murray § repeating it as recently as 1942.

* *De aedibus scaenicis comoediae nouae*, 1929.
† *Charicles*, Eng. ed., p. 54, note 32, and page 269.
‡ *The House-Door of the Ancient Stage*, 1914.
§ *Rape of the Locks*, p. 113.

I shall begin by examining Plutarch's words. As he says expressly that, according to his authorities, Greek doors ' formerly ' opened outwards, he clearly implies that this was no longer true in his own day. It is also apparent that the only evidence advanced by his authorities for their statement as to former practice was the (alleged) fact that in comedy persons going out of their houses gave a preliminary knock to warn passers-by, who might otherwise have been struck by the opening doors. This again implies that house-doors which opened outwards opened into the public street. They cannot, therefore, have been pictured as placed within a deep recess in the house-front, or alternatively as protected by a projecting porch ; for in either of these cases a door opening outwards would have opened into the recess or the porch, and would not have endangered any one in the public street. On this point we have evidence from Aristotle. He states* that ' Hippias of Athens offered for sale upper stories that projected over the public streets, together with flights of steps, railings and doors that opened outwards. The owners of the buildings bought them, and in this way a large sum of money was collected.' Evidently Hippias was exacting fines from persons whose houses encroached in one way or another on the street ; therefore doors that opened outwards opened on to the street.

Plutarch's authority is wrong in asserting that persons coming out of doors in comedy ' knock ' on their doors (κόπτουσι καὶ ψοφοῦσι τὰς αὑτῶν θύρας). The word κόπτω, like its Latin equivalent pulto or pulso, is never used in extant comedy of persons going out of doors. Moreover we have express statements in ancient authorities that κόπτω was used of knocking from outside, while the noise made by persons going out was denoted by the word ψοφῶ. It has been made clear by Becker and Mooney that ψοφῶ (Latin crepo) denotes not a deliberate knock but any kind of noise—in this case the noise made by the mere act of opening the door. The evidence of archaeology is accepted by Mooney as showing that in real life house-doors normally opened inwards ; from which it follows that persons coming out of doors had no need to warn passers-by. Nevertheless he concluded that stage-doors opened outwards because of the use of words for ' strike ' or ' push ' (πλήττω, pello) with reference to characters coming out of doors, especially when in a violent temper ; thus Menander, Sam. (Loeb ed.) 88–9, 154–5, 353, has the phrase τὴν θύραν πέπληχε, ' he has struck the door ', and Terence, Ad. 788, writes quisnam a me pepulit tam grauiter foris, ' who has banged so violently on my door ? ' (again of some one coming out). These phrases have apparently confirmed Murray in his view that persons coming out of doors gave a knock to warn passers-by ; though it is difficult on this view to understand the mental condition of Niceratus (Sam. 353),

* Econ. ii. 4.   I quote the Loeb translation.

who, in the act of bursting out of doors with threats of slaughter, pauses to give a polite warning to the general public. Mooney, on the other hand, understands the phrase to refer to the action of ' pushing ' the door open from within ; which of course implies that the door opens outwards. There is further the situation in the *Wasps* of Aristophanes. Here Philocleon is trying to force his way out of the house, while the other characters, standing outside the door, are trying to keep him in. If the door opened inwards, one would expect that Philocleon would try to pull it open, while his opponents would pull the other way, but Aristophanes speaks of pushing (line 152).

Dalman (op. cit.) disagrees with Mooney's interpretation of πέπληχεν, pepulit, and quotes A. von Gerkan's view that these verbs merely denote the shaking which necessarily accompanies the opening of a door. But I think it will be helpful if at this point I turn from the literary evidence to consider the structure and operation of an ordinary Greek or Roman house-door. Unfortunately this subject presents us with technical problems of the most delicate nature ; nevertheless certain fundamental points are clear, and seem to me decisive with regard to theatrical practice.

There are three distinct problems : (1) the construction of the house-door in real life ; (2) the construction of the stage house-door ; (3) the use of the stage house-door for dramatic purposes.

The main parts of a Greek or Roman doorway were the sill below, the lintel above and the doorposts or jambs at each side. In the space thus framed were hung the two wings (fores, ualuae) of the double door. Instead of being attached with hinges to the doorpost, each wing swung on metal-covered pivots set at top and bottom of the axis which turned in sockets excavated in the sill and lintel in an angle cut out of the inner side of the doorpost.

It is obvious that the position of the sockets in relation to the jambs decides the question whether the door opens inwards or outwards. The archaeological evidence shows that the sockets were on the inner side of the jambs. Moreover the sill was cut away on the inner side so that the door, when closed, should strike against it. It is evident that doors working on this principle would be clumsy and noisy in operation.

The house-doors were fastened by means of bars and bolts. The bar stretched from one post to the other, and fitted into sockets in each post. At the bottom of each wing, and near the central division, was a bolt which could be pushed down into a hole in the sill. These fastenings were on the inner side of the doors.

On general grounds we should expect the stage-doors to correspond to those of real life. The evidence of the plays suggests that they were similar in construction. The bars and bolts mentioned in the plays appear to be where one would expect to find them—on the inside of the doors. But the decisive point is the position of the

hinges, if we may use this term of the pivots and sockets. It has just
been said that the doors were noisy in operation. In real life,
persons who wished to enter the house without being heard had no
remedy but to open the door as gently as possible, lifting it at the
same time.* But persons wishing to leave the house quietly had
another resource : they could pour water in one of the sockets set
in the sill. So the wife in Aristophanes' *Thesmophoriazusae*, stealing
out of doors to meet her lover, pours water on the hinge (lines 487–8).

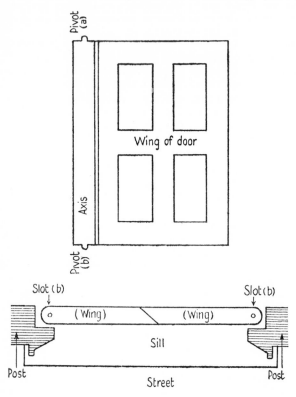

Here of course the speaker is referring to a real house-door. But
in the *Curculio* (lines 158–61) the old duenna ' pours a little water
underneath ' (suffundam aquolam) before opening the door from
within. Evidently the hinges of this stage-door were on the inside ;
therefore the door must have opened inwards, just like a real door.
(The object of pouring wine on the sill outside—line 80— was not to
silence the door but to tempt the old duenna to come out.)

I turn to the references to the stage-door in the *Wasps*. In the
opening scenes of this play, the inmate of the house is being kept

* Lucian, *Dial. Meret.* xii. 3.

indoors against his will. Therefore the house-door has the unusual function of keeping the occupant inside. To understand the passage where both sides are said to push against the door, we should note that, before old Philocleon had got to the door from the inside, Sosia had already, as a precautionary measure, been ordered to throw his weight against the door from outside (line 142). The effect of this, with a door which opened inwards, would be to force it against its bolts and thus make it difficult for any one inside to withdraw them. Now it is clear from the text that the bar and bolts are inside, and, also that Philocleon cannot undo them. Bdelycleon, addressing Sosia, who is pushing against the door from outside, expresses anxiety (line 155) lest his father will 'nibble off the door-pin' which fastened the bar in position.

Of course we must not fall into the error of supposing that everything mentioned as happening inside the house, and therefore out of sight of the spectators, does in fact happen. At line 177 Bdelycleon announces that he will go inside, disregarding the fact that the doors are supposed to be bolted. It is much easier for the spectator to forget what is unseen and imagined than what is visible. We have noticed that Euclio's instruction to his submissive housekeeper (*Aul.* 103-4) to 'shut the door with both bolts' cannot have been carried out; for in line 242 he enters his house without difficulty. In general I imagine that stage-doors were not really bolted, at least during the performance of a play. To bolt them could have had no effect on the spectators, who were unable to see the inside of the doors; it might, however, have had awkward consequences the next time some one on the stage was required by the plot to enter the door which had been bolted.

I turn to *Wasps* 199-201. Philocleon has again been driven indoors; then Bdelycleon, anxious to prevent him from escaping again, tells some one to

> "pile a heap of stones against the door,
> And shoot the door-pin home into the bar,
> And heave the beam athwart it, and roll up,
> Quick! the great mortar-block."

(Rogers' translation). These words would at first sight be taken to refer to visible action carried out on the stage—in other words, outside the closed door. If so, then the door could be barred on the outside, which seems to imply that it opened outwards? For otherwise what would be the use of piling stones against it? Those who take this view must, if they are consistent, suppose that all the elaborate measures referred to were actually carried out. If so, it is surprising that the chorus of Philocleon's fellow-judges, who presently appear, do not themselves offer to unbar the door and remove the stones, etc. But in fact they do not mention either the bar or the stones; and as their advice to Philocleon is to let himself down from the window,* it would seem that they cannot get at the fastenings of the door. I would therefore take the alternative course of assuming that Bdelycleon's words are addressed to some one within the house, who is asked to bolt and bar the door from within.† In fact it is plain that the door is not barred either on the outside or on the inside ; for at line 529 Bdelycleon bids some one ' bring out the memorandum-book ' ; and nothing is said about the need for removing the stones, mortar-block, etc. This inconsistency does not matter if the barring of the door at lines 199–201 is supposed to take place from within ; for as the spectators have never seen the stones, mortar-block or bar, they are ready to forget about them.

It seems to have been possible to lock a house-door, or sometimes one of the inner doors, from the outside by means of a key, in such a way that without the use of the key it could not be opened again, even by those inside.[2] The husband mentioned in Lysias' speech *De Caede Eratosthenis* complains that his wife had locked him into his bedroom, and had then taken the key away with her. In the *Mostellaria* Tranio, after sending the revellers indoors, has the key brought out to him. He bids the messenger fasten the door from inside, declaring that he himself will secure it from the outside. We must suppose that he does then lock the door, or at least go through the motions of locking it. The dramatic effect of his action is, I think, to assure the spectators that even if those inside the house forget or disregard Tranio's instructions, they will nevertheless not be able to open the door ; and in fact the door remains unused for the rest of the play.

In everyday usage the front door was normally closed, but not barred or bolted, except by night. Plutarch (*De Curios.* 3) remarks that it is not the ' done thing ' to enter another man's house without knocking ; and this implies that it would be physically possible to open the door. If people did not normally force their way into the houses of others, the reason was not that the door was barred : it was partly good manners, partly fear of the dog and the door-keeper ; indeed, given the abundance of domestic servants, the clumsy doors could scarcely have been opened without attracting the attention of some one. Evidently it was possible to close the door, so that it did not accidentally fly open, without having to use the bolts or bar. We hear of the use of door-handles and knockers, but we cannot be certain that there was anything corresponding to our modern door-handles, which operate a catch shutting the door securely yet leaving it possible for any one to open it from either side. Similarly in the theatre we may take it that the house-doors were

---

* ' So now to the window lash the cord ' (l. 379). But Philocleon seems to be on the roof, not at a window (350, 355). There is nothing to show that he comes out through a window.

† That some domestics have been left indoors is indicated in line 166, where Philocleon bids them give him a sword.

normally shut. Sometimes characters in plays express surprise to
find a house-door shut. I do not agree with Mooney that what
really surprises them is to find the house-door locked or bolted.
I do not see how any one could have known from outside whether
the door was locked, unless he tried to open it. But it has just been
pointed out that people did not normally try to open the doors of
others. Moreover we have a case of a character expressing surprise
at finding the door open (*St.* 87) ; and we can scarcely suppose that
by ' open ' Antipho meant ' unlocked ', as he has just declared his
intention of going in, which would have been impossible if the door
was locked. I take it that Panegyris' door is wide open, the reason
being that she has failed to pull it to when coming on the stage at
the beginning of the play. Taking the word ' shut ' in its plain

Woman unlocking front door   Woman looking out of door

sense, one has to admit that the closed but unbolted door of Roman
comedy displays surprising resistance to the violent thumping and
kicking to which it is so often subjected. Perhaps the stiffness of
the hinges kept the door in position. On one occasion it is deliberately left ajar (*Men.* 351, 362).

All our evidence supports the reasonable view that the doors
shown on the stage corresponded both in appearance and in construction with the doors of real life, except that, in the days when the
theatre was itself a temporary structure, the house-doors were
presumably slight affairs, made completely of wood. I imagine
that the scene-building was used as a store-room for theatrical
properties ; if so, it was presumably possible to lock the doors,
or at least one of them, from outside.

Everything on the inner side of the doors was invisible to the
spectators, and had to be left to their imagination. In *Bacch.* 834–5
the door is supposed to open into the dining-room, which is visible
to the characters on the stage when they open one wing of the door
an inch or two. In *Most.* 817 the (slightly opened) door gives a

view of the colonnade at the back of the house. All this and much
more the spectators were willing to take on trust. Of course they
knew that what really lay behind the doors was the interior of the
dressing-room, with actors waiting for their cues, perhaps changing
their masks or costumes under the watchful eye of the manager.*

The art of the theatre consists partly in making imaginative
use of material means and limitations. The very clumsiness of
ancient house-doors was turned to good account by the dramatists,
aided by the goodwill of the spectators, who were familiar with the
convention and readily joined in the game of make-believe without
which the theatre could never have come into existence. If we try
to see Roman drama with Roman eyes, we shall enjoy it more
keenly ; and the true end of all drama is enjoyment.

* For attractive Roman pictures of actors off duty see *D.F.*, Figs. 43, 44.

APPENDIX H

PASSAGES IN ANCIENT AUTHORS SUPPOSED TO REFER TO STAGE SCENERY

PHORMIS (Phormos), comic poet of Syracuse, fifth century B.C. Suidas (twelfth century A.D. ?) says of him : ἐχρήσατο δὲ πρῶτος ἐνδύματι ποδήρει καὶ σκηνῇ δερμάτων * φοινικοῦς. A. Körte (P.W., s.v.) calls this ' an unintelligible remark '. Emendations are :

(1) φοινίκων—' he introduced long cloaks and a stage of red skins ' (i.e. canvas scenery ?).
(2) ποικίλων : ' many-coloured '.
(3) Φοινικικῇ : ' Phoenician tent '.
(4) σκευῇ δερμάτων φοινίκων, ' outfit of red leather ' (i.e. phalloi ?).

Aristotle, *Eth. Nic.* IV. vi. : οἷον . . . κωμῳδοῖς χορηγῶν ἐν τῇ παρόδῳ πορφύραν εἰσφέρων, ὥσπερ οἱ Μεγαρεῖς.

Schol. on this passage : σύνηθες ἐν κωμῳδίᾳ παραπετάσματα δέρρεις ποιεῖν, οὐ πορφυρίδας.

Pickard-Cambridge, *T.D.* 122, note 4 : ' It is probably a mistake to ascribe the invention of movable decorated walls or screens to Phormos of Syracuse, the contemporary of Epicharmus. The passage relied on in Suidas is doubtful as regards both reading and sense. . . . There is no reason to suppose that, whatever Phormos did, it had any influence on Athenian performances, which, as Aristotle's language suggests, did not follow such " Megarian " practices ; nor to connect (as some do) his innovations at Syracuse with the καταβλήματα which Pollux iv. 141 describes as draped over περίακτοι to produce particular effects. In any case, nothing suggests that Phormos' invention was used to effect changes of scenery.'

Bieber, *H.T.* 141 : ' The decoration could be in real substantial architecture, or, more probably, painted screens could be used ; movable scenery (coulisse) is said to have been invented in Sicily as early as the fifth century. (Note : The inventor is said to have been Phormis or Phormos . . . Körte, however (in a letter to me), doubts whether Kaibel is right in assuming that Phormos was the inventor of the movable screens.) These must have been the katablemata mentioned by Pollux, that is the backdrops, curtains, pinakes or tablets, which were of wood or canvas and painted according to the requirements of each play. Vitruvius distinguishes between tragic, comic and satyric settings according to the three forms of dramatic poetry then existing. Movable painted settings of this sort may have belonged also to the scaena which, according to Vitruvius (VII, praef. 11), Agatharchus painted for Aeschylus and on which the research into perspective by Demokritos and Anaxagoras was based. (Footnote on katablemata : Bulle, *Unters.* 214 ff., is of the opinion that these decorations were movable scenery with pictures painted on canvas or wooden tablets and. attached to a permanent frame. This supposition would well explain the quick change of decoration in the relatively short intermissions between the four plays on each festival day.) '

Polybius xii. 28a : τηλικαύτην εἶναι φησι διαφορὰν τῆς ἱστορίας πρὸς τοὺς ἐπιδεικτικοὺς λόγους ἡλίκην ἔχει τὰ κατ' ἀλήθειαν ᾠκοδομημένα καὶ κατεσκευασμένα τῶν ἐν ταῖς σκηνογραφίαις φαινομένων τύπων καὶ διαθέσεων. 'He says that the difference between history and declamatory writing is as great as the difference between real buildings and furniture and the views and compositions we see in scene-paintings.'

Athen. xii. 536 : γενομένων δὲ τῶν Δημητρίων Ἀθήνησιν, ἐγράφετο ἐπὶ τοῦ προσκηνίου ἐπὶ τῆς οἰκουμένης ὀχούμενος (of Demetrius Poliorcetes). 'During the festival of Demeter at Athens a painting of him riding on the world appeared on the proscenium.'

Athen. xiv. §614 e. f. : (Demetrius Poliorcetes) τὴν Λυσιμάχου αὐλὴν κωμικῆς σκηνῆς οὐδὲν διαφέρειν ἔλεγεν : ἐξιέναι γὰρ ἀπ' αὐτῆς πάντας δισυλλάβους (τόν τε Βίθυν χλευάζων καὶ τὸν Πάριν . . .), παρὰ δ' αὐτοῦ Πευκέστας καὶ Μενελάους . . . ταῦτα δ' ἀκούων ὁ Λυσίμαχος ἐγὼ τοίνυν, ἔφη, πόρνην ἐκ τραγικῆς οὐχ ἑώρακα ἐξιοῦσαν : τὴν αὐλητρίδα Λαμίαν λέγων.

'He said that the court of Lysimachus was just like the scene-building in comedy ; for all who came out from it had names of two syllables (a taunting reference to Bithys and Paris), whereas from his own palace came such men as Peucestes and Menelaus. On hearing this Lysimachus remarked, ' Well, I have never seen a harlot coming out of the scene-building in tragedy,' the reference being to the flute-girl Lamia.'

(I take the phrases ' comic skené ', ' tragic skené ' as meaning the scene-building in comedy and tragedy, without any implication that its appearance was different.)

Vitruvius v. 6. 9 : genera autem sunt scaenarum tria : unum quod dicitur tragicum, alterum comicum, tertium satyricum. horum autem ornatus sunt inter se dissimili disparique ratione, quod tragicae deformantur columnis et fastigiis et signis reliquisque regalibus rebus ; comicae autem aedificiorum priuatorum et maenianorum habent speciem profectusque fenestris dispositos imitatione communium aedificiorum rationibus ; satyricae uero ornantur arboribus, speluncis, montibus reliquisque agrestibus rebus in topoedi speciem deformati. ' There are three types of scenery ; one which is called tragic ; a second, comic ; the third, satyric.

Now the subjects of these differ severally from one another. The tragic are designed with columns, pediments and statues and other royal surroundings ; the comic have the appearance of private buildings and balconies and projections with windows made to imitate reality, after the fashion of ordinary buildings ; the satyric settings are painted with trees, caves, mountains and other country features, designed to imitate landscape.' (Loeb trs.)

Vitruvius vii. 5. 5 : Trallibus cum Apaturius Alabandius eleganti manu finxisset scaenam in minusculo theatro . . . in eaque fecisset columnas, signa, centauros sustinentes epistylia, tholorum rotunda tecta, fastigiorum prominentes uersuras, coronasque capitibus leon- inis ornatas, quae omnia stillicidiorum e tectis habent rationem, praeterea supra ea nihilominus episcenium, in qua tholi, pronai, semifastigia omnisque tecti uarius picturis fuerat ornatus, itaque cum aspectus eius scaenae propter asperitatem eblandiretur omnium uisus. . . . Licymnius . . . ait ' qui uestrum domos supra tegularum tecta potest habere aut columnas seu fastigiorum expolitionis ? haec enim supra contignationis ponuntur, non supra tegularum tecta. . . .' itaque Apaturius contra respondere non est ausus, sed sustulit scaenam et ad rationem ueritatis commutatam postea correctam adprobauit. ' At Tralles Apaturius of Alabanda had invented scenery of fine technique for the tiny theatre which they call the Small Assembly. In this he showed columns, statues or centaurs supporting the architraves, the orbed roofs of domes, the projecting angles of pediments, and cornices having lions' heads, which all provided outlets for the rain from the roofs. Besides, the story above the scenery had domes, porticoes, half pediments and every kind of roof, with varied pictorial ornament. When, there- fore, the appearance of such a stage, by its high relief, charmed the eyes of all . . . Licymnius . . . said . . . " Who of you can have, above your roof tiles, buildings with columns and elaborate gables ? For the latter stand upon floors, not above the roof tiles." . . . Apaturius had not the courage to reply, and removed the scenery ; and when this was altered to resemble reality, he obtained sanction for his correction.' (Loeb trs.)

(By scenery here is meant the architectural decoration of the front of the scene-building. Apaturius was criticized for the fan- tastic character of his work. It is plain that such a background, whether fantastic or modest, could not be altered to suit the needs of the play. See Pickard-Cambridge, *T.D.* p. 226, note 1.)

Id. ib. vii. 2 (on wall-painting) : postea ingressi sunt ut etiam aedificiorum figuras, columnarum et fastigiorum eminentes proiecturas imitarentur, patentibus autem locis, uti exhedris, propter amplitudines parietum scaenarum frontes tragico more aut comico seu satyrico designarent, ambulationibus uero propter spatia longitudinis uarietatibus topiorum ornarent a certis locorum proprietatibus imagines exprimentes ; pinguntur enim portus, promunturia, litora, flumina, fontes, euripi, fana, luci, montes, pecora, pastores. 'Then they proceeded to imitate the contours of buildings, the outstanding projections of columns and gables ; in open spaces, like exedrae, they designed scenery on a large scale in tragic, comic or satyric style; in covered promenades, because of the length of the walls, they used for ornament the varieties of landscape gardening, finding subjects in the characteristics of particular places ; for they paint harbours, headlands, shores, rivers, springs, straits, temples, groves, hills, cattle, shepherds ' (Loeb ed.).

Valerius Maximus II. iv. 6 : Q. Catulus Campanam imitatus luxuriam primus spectantium consessum uelorum umbraculis texit. Cn. Pompeius ante omnes aquae per semitas decursu aestiuum minuit feruorem. C. Pulcher scaenam uarietate colorum adumbrauit, uacuis antea pictura tabu lis extentam, quam totam argento C. Antonius, auro Petreius, ebore Q. Catulus praetexuit. uersatilem fecerunt Luculli. argentatis choragiis P. Lentulus Spinther adornauit. translatum, antea poeniciis indutum tunicis, M. Scaurus exquisito genere uestis cultum induxit. ' Q. Catulus, imitating the luxury of the Campanians, was the first to cover the auditorium with shady awnings. Cn. Pompeius was the first to temper the summer heat by making cooling streams run down the gangways. C. Pulcher gave the front of the scene-building (which had previously consisted of unpainted boards) a many-coloured effect. C. Antonius faced it completely with silver, Petreius with gold, Q. Catulus with ivory. The Luculli made it capable of being turned. P. Lentulus Spinther adorned it with silver-plated equipment (?). The translatus [company ?], which had previously been dressed in scarlet tunics, were brought on in elegant attire by M. Scaurus.'

Pliny *N.H.* XXXV. ch. iv. 7. 23 : habuit et scaena ludis Claudi Pulchri magnam admirationem picturae, cum ad tegularum similitudinem corui decepti imaginem aduolarent. ' At the games of Claudius Pulcher the scene-building won great admiration ; crows flew to the painted tiles, thinking they were real.'

Vitruvius VII. praef. 11 : namque primum Agatharchus Athenis Aeschylo docente [tragoediam ad] scaenam fecit, et de ea re commentarium reliquit. ex eo moniti Democritus et Anaxagoras de eadem re scripserunt, quemadmodum oporteat, ad aciem oculorum radiorumque extentionem certo loco centro constituto, ad lineas ratione naturali respondere, uti de incerta re incertae imagines aedificiorum in scaenarum picturis redderent speciem et, quae in directis planisque frontibus sint figurata, alia abscedentia, alia prominentia esse uideantur. ' For to begin with, Agatharchus at Athens, when Aeschylus was presenting a tragedy, was in control of the stage, and wrote a commentary about it. Following his suggestions, Democritus and Anaxagoras wrote upon the same topic, in order to show how, if a fixed centre is taken for the

outward glance of the eyes and the projection of the radii, we must
follow these lines in accordance with a natural law, such that from
an uncertain object, uncertain images may give the appearance of
buildings in the scenery of the stage, and how what is painted upon
vertical and plane surfaces can seem to recede in one part and
project in another ' (tr. Frank Granger, Loeb ed. But see below.)

SCENE-PAINTING (σκηνογραφία)

Aristotle (*Poet.* ch. iv) says it was introduced by Sophocles : τρεῖς
δὲ καὶ σκηνογραφίαν Σοφοκλῆς. Vitruvius (vii. praef. 11) : primum
Agatharchus Aeschylo docente scaenam fecit et de ea re commentarium reliquit (see above).

Pickard-Cambridge, *T.D.* p. 124 : ' Vitruvius writes ' (above
words), ' adding that from the work of Agatharchus Democritus and
Anaxagoras learned the principles of perspective, about which they
also wrote, showing how the painted representations of houses on the
stage could be so made that ' quae in directis planisque frontibus
sint figurata, alia abscedentia, alia prominentia esse uideantur '.
In other words, he painted an architectural design in perspective
on the flat background. At a later date Apollodorus went further
and began the use of colour and shading to increase the illusion.
(He was known both as σκηνογράφος and as σκιαγράφος). Agatharchus
is also said to have painted the interior of the house of Alcibiades.'

Diogenes Laertius ii. 125 says that Kleisthenes and his son
Menedemus were skenographoi in fourth century.

Pliny *N.H.* 35. 65 : a picture by Zeuxis is called scaena.

Gregory of Nyssa, *ep.* ix (Migne 46. 1041) : τοιοῦτόν τι θαῦμα
ἐν τοῖς θεάτροις τοὺς θαυματοποιοῦντας τεχνάζεσθαι : μῦθον ἐξ ἱστορίας
ἤ τινα τῶν ἀρχαίων διηγημάτων ὑπόθεσιν τῆς θαυματοποιίας λαβόντες ἔργῳ
τοῖς θεαταῖς διηγοῦνται τὴν ἱστορίαν, ὑποδύντες σχήματά τε καὶ πρόσωπα,
καὶ πόλιν ἐκ παραπετασμάτων ἐπὶ τῆς ὀρχήστρας δι᾽ ὁμοιότητός τινος
σχηματίσαντες, καὶ τέως ψιλὸν τόπον τῇ ἐναργεῖ μιμήσει τῶν πραγμάτων
οἰκειώσαντες, θαῦμα τοῖς θεωμένοις γίγνονται, αὐτοί τε οἱ μιμηταὶ τῶν ἐν τῇ
ἱστορίᾳ πραγμάτων καί τὰ παραπετάσματα, ἡ πόλις δή.

' (It is related that) conjurors contrive such a marvel as this in
the theatres : taking a subject from history or one of the old tales
as the theme of their astonishing display, they set forth their narrative to the spectators by action. They put on costumes and masks,
and fashion a rough resemblance of a city on the stage by means of
curtains, and by adapting a bare space for the time being to their
mimetic display of their story, they win the admiration of the
spectators by means of their own miming of the story and by the
use of curtains, which give the effect of a city.'

Gregory lived in the fourth century A.D. I take ὀρχήστρα as meaning ' stage ' (Haigh, *A.T.* p. 107). The curtain here mentioned

seems to have been something more elaborate than the back-cloth used by the mimes. Apparently it was set up by the actors themselves.

Servius ad Virg. *Georg.* 3. 24 (uel scaena ut uersis discedat frontibus, utque purpurei intexti tollant aulaea Britanni) : scaena autem quae fiebat aut uersilis erat aut ductilis ; uersilis tunc erat cum subito tota machinis quibusdam eonuertebatur et aliam picturae faciem ostendebat ; ductilis tunc cum tractis tabulatis hac atque illac species picturae nudabatur interior ; unde perite utrumque tetigit dicens ' uersis . . . frontibus ', singula singulis complectens sermonibus.   quod Varro et Suetonius commemorant.

25 : nam Augustus postquam uictis Britannis plurimos de captiuis quos adduxerat donauit ad officia theatralia, dedit etiam aulaea, id est uelamina in quibus dipinxerat uictorias suas et quemadmodum Britanni, ab eo donati, eadem uela portarent.

I take the lines of Virgil to mean ' or how the stage disappears from view as the periacti revolve, and how the curtain is raised by the purple figures of Britons embroidered in it '.

Servius' meaning seems to be ' the stage (façade) of those times was capable either of being revolved or of being drawn along. It was capable of being revolved when it was turned round bodily by certain contrivances and displayed a new form of picture ; it was capable of being drawn along when by dragging board-work to left and right a painted scene was displayed behind. The poet has skilfully alluded to both these methods by his phrase ' when the fronts were turned ', each word referring to a separate contrivance. This is the explanation given by Varro and Suetonius. . . .

' For Augustus, after his conquest of Britain (!) gave many of his prisoners to the service of the theatre. He also presented curtains, that is screens on which he had displayed his victories and the way in which those very curtains were carried by the Britons whom he had given.'

Servius seems to be thinking of two different contrivances, revolving stands and sliding wooden sets. His words imply that Virgil has confused these two methods of changing the scenery.

NOTE ON THE PASSAGES QUOTED AS EVIDENCE FOR MOVABLE SCENERY

We must draw a distinction between theatrical practice *before* and *after* the introduction of the drop-curtain (first mentioned in 56 B.C.). Before that innovation was made changes (if any) in the scenery must have been made under the eyes of the spectators. The only passage quoted as evidence for movable screens in the early Greek theatre is Suidas' reference to Phormis. But the reading and meaning are so doubtful that no reliance can be placed on it. Pickard-Cambridge, though a believer in screens, rejects the Phormis reference as evidence. So does Körte. Bieber (as P.C. points out) has no warrant for identifying these hypothetical screens with the καταβλήματα mounted on the periacti.

P.C. himself relies on the reference to Nannion as a proskenion. But Nannion was not a ' screen ' to be put in front of something less attractive ; she herself was the unattractive object which needed to be disguised by paint and finery. When she was called proskenion (' front of scene-building '), she was being likened to the front wall of the skené, which, though naturally plain, was given a decorative appearance by σκηνογραφία. P.C. himself takes the view that this word refers to the painting of the front wall of the skené so as to give it an architectural effect. This view harmonizes with the other references from pre-Roman times. Polybius contrasts real buildings and scene-painting, i.e. the painting in perspective of a flat wall. The picture of Demetrius Poliorcetes on the proscenium could not have been specially appropriate to any one play, still less to all plays ; yet it must have been intended to be visible during the performance.

The references to the Roman theatre point to elaborate decoration of the front of the scene-building, which was far too large to be wholly concealed by the hypothetical sets, or even by the drop-curtain. The introduction of the drop-curtain enabled scenery to be built up on the stage, as described by Apuleius (see Appendix E). It may be noted that the scenery described by Apuleius is solid : ' there was a mountain of wood . . . planted with shrubs and living trees ', with a stream flowing from its peak. As we might expect, some time had been required to build up such a scene, while the spectators had been amused by a dance given in front of the curtain. At the end of this scene, the performers danced off the stage, the mountain spouted from its peak saffron mingled with wine, and ' while the whole theatre was sweet with the scent, a chasm opened in the ground and swallowed up the mountain of wood. Then, behold ! a soldier directed his steps across the middle of the theatre ' to fetch the woman who was to be thrown to the beasts, while a couch was spread for her and the ass. Here we have an intelligible account of how one item followed another in quick succession, but it contains no evidence of the use of sliding screens. For these the only authority is Servius. There is apparently some confusion in what he says ; Virgil cannot have meant that the back-scene was being revolved and was also being drawn aside so as to display other settings while the curtain was rising to conceal the back-scene. It is only too likely that Servius is trying to interpret the passage of Virgil in its own light.

Vitruvius' reference to the use in contemporary painting of three types of scenery corresponding to the three types of fifth-century drama is not easy to relate to actual stage-practice in his own day, when satyric drama must have been known only from literature. Painting and the stage were closely associated—the word 'scaena' was used for both. The reader of drama would naturally have in his mind a setting appropriate to the play—palace, private houses or open country ; and contemporary painting (i.e. wall-painting) gave these different effects.

The reference in Gregory is the strongest evidence I can find for the use of a back-curtain to give a scenic effect. He speaks of masked actors, but it is difficult to believe that these were other than mimes. Perhaps their back-curtain, the one indispensable piece of property of the mimes, was in this case painted or embroidered so as to give an architectural effect. It is striking to find that the Indian actors also used a curtain (which they called yavanika, yavana being the Sanskrit for ' Ionian ', ' Greek '). In Sanskrit plays ' the characters are surrounded by Nature. . . . The mango and other trees, creepers, lotuses and pale-red trumpet flowers, gazelles, flamingoes, bright-eyed parrots and Indian cuckoos, in the midst of which they move, are often addressed by them and form an essential part of their lives ' (Macdonell, *Sanskrit Literature*, p. 354). The scene may be transferred from one place to another ; the characters may even be spoken of as travelling through the air. Yet all this takes place in a room, and a mere curtain, divided in the middle, forms the background ; the flowers, the flamingoes, the aerial chariots are left to the imagination. ' It is somewhat curious that while there are many and minute stage directions about dress and decorations no less than about the action of the players, nothing is said in this way about change of scene ' (ib.). Not curious at all : the dresses and the actions are real, the sense of scenery must be conveyed by dialogue aloné.

External evidence for movable scenery in the Greek theatre does not exist. In the Roman theatre the drop-curtain made it possible to arrange special settings for certain occasions, and the back-cloth could no doubt give a decorative architectural effect, which *might* be dramatically appropriate in some cases ; but there was no attempt, it seems, to alter the appearance of the scene-building itself to suit particular scenes, and throughout the play it remained a decorative background, still visible above the curtain (when raised) to the spectators.

APPENDIX I

THE INTRODUCTION OF MASKS ON THE ROMAN STAGE

(*Classical Quarterly*, Vol. xxxiii. pp. 139–46, slightly modified.)

THE statement that masks were not introduced on the Roman stage until long after the time of Terence is still repeated by editors, and has the support of Pauly-Wissowa (Bieber, s.v. ' Maske ', 1930), Daremberg et Saglio (Navarre, s.v. *histrio*) and Pickard-Cambridge (*Dramatic Festivals*, p. 199). The contrary view was well put by A. S. F. Gow in 1912 (*J.R.S.* ii, 65–77), in support of whom we may refer to Navarre's (later) article on *persona* in Daremberg et Saglio, p. 415, note 20, where he completely abandons his denial of masks for the theatre of Terence. Duckworth (*N.R.C.*, p. 94) concludes that ' the evidence for the late introduction of masks in Roman comedy is weak '.

I will set forth the relevant passages in ancient literature, beginning with the most precise :

(*a*) Diomedes (p. 489, Keil) ; (fourth century A.D. ?) : antea itaque galearibus non personis utebantur, ut qualitas coloris indicium faceret aetatis, cum essent aut albi aut nigri aut rufi. personis uero uti primus coepit Roscius Gallus, praecipuus histrio, quod oculis peruersis erat nec satis decorus in personis nisi parasitus pronuntiabat. ' For previously they used wigs, not masks, in order that age might be indicated by its appropriate colour, as they were either white or black or red. The first to use a mask was the great actor Roscius Gallus, because he had a squint ; even when wearing a mask he was not handsome enough for his rôle, except when he played the part of a parasite.'

(*b*) Cicero, *de Orat.* iii. 221 : sed in ore sunt omnia, in eo autem ipso dominatus est omnis oculorum ; quo melius nostri illi senes qui personatum ne Roscium quidem magno opere laudabant. ' But the face is all-important, and in the face the dominating part is played by the eyes ; so our elders showed their superior sense in refusing to pay high praise even to Roscius when he had his mask on.'

In the preceding words the importance of gesture in setting forth the orator's meaning has been explained.

(*c*) Donatus, *de Comoedia*, 6.3 : personati primi egisse dicuntur comoediam Cincius [et] Faliscus, tragoediam Minucius [et] Prothymus. ' The first actors to wear masks are said to have been in comedy Cincius Faliscus, in tragedy Minucius Prothymus.'

(d) Donatus, praef. *Eun.* 1.6 : acta plane ludis Megalensibus L. Postumio L. Cornelio aedilibus curulibus, agentibus etiam tunc personatis L. Minucio Prothymo L. Ambiuio Turpione. ' The play was performed at the ludi Megalenses in the curule aedileship of L. Postumius and L. Cornelius ; the actors were L. Minucius Prothymus and L. Ambivius Turpio, who were wearing masks even at that early date.'

(e) Donatus, praef. *Ad.* 1.6 : haec sane acta est ludis scaenicis funebribus L. Aemilii Pauli, agentibus L. Ambiuio et L. (?) qui cum suis gregibus etiam tum personati agebant. ' This play was performed at the funeral games of L. Aemilius Paulus, the actors being L. Ambivius and L. (?), who, as well as their companies, were wearing masks even at that early date.'

(f) Festus, s.v. *personata* : personata fabula quaedam Naeui inscribitur, quam putant quidam primum (actam) a personatis histrionibus. sed cum post multos annos comoedi et tragoedi personis uti coeperint, uerisimilius est eam fabulam propter inopiam comoedorum actam nouam per Atellanos qui proprie uocantur personati quia ius est iis non cogi in scaena ponere personam quod ceteris histrionibus pati necesse est. ' There is a play of Naevius entitled *The Masked Play* (?), which some think was first acted by masked actors. But since it was not until much later that comic and tragic actors began to wear masks, it is more likely that because of the lack of comic actors this play was first performed by Atellane actors, who have a special claim to the title " masked actors " because they are not compelled to take off their masks on the stage, as all other actors are compelled to do.'

Of these passages only (a) can be regarded as a clear denial that masks were worn at an early period. That Roscius squinted we know from Cic. *N.D.* 1.28.79. While it has been usual to quote Cicero as supporting Diomedes, we must not disregard the possibility that Diomedes has founded his statement on a misunderstanding of the two passages in Cicero. It is not quite clear whether Cicero means that Roscius played sometimes without a mask ; personatum could conceivably be used as synonymous with ' on the stage ' (and therefore, like all actors, masked). There is no other evidence to connect Roscius with the introduction of masks. That his great tragic contemporary, Aesopus, wore a mask is stated by Fronto, *Eloq.* 5.1.37 : he tells us that Aesopus used to study his mask carefully before putting it on, in order that he might suit his voice and gestures to his appearance. Cicero, *de Div.* 1.37.80, speaks of his ardor uultuum atque motuum. This passage has been used to argue that he acted without a mask ; but we may compare Cicero's statement (*de Orat.* 2.46.193) that the eyes of an impassioned actor can seem to blaze out of the mask ; cf. p. 71).

Donatus, in (c), ascribes the innovation to Faliscus in comedy and Prothymus in tragedy. We have no information about these actors, other than the passages quoted here. To try, as Ribbeck did, to reconcile (c) with (a) by supposing that Roscius was the chief actor in a company, the manager of which was Faliscus (or Prothymus), is to indulge in perhaps unlikely hypothesis ; leading actors appear to have been themselves the managers of their companies.

In (d) and (e) Donatus tells us that the first performances of the *Eunuchus* and the *Adelphi* were given by actors who ' even then ' were wearing masks. (To suppose, with Leo, that Donatus was misled by miniatures of masked actors in the manuscripts he was using does not explain, as Gow pointed out, why ' only two of the plays should have been so decorated '.) In (f) Festus refers to a record of a masked performance as far back as the time of Naevius (third century B.C.). That Festus himself is puzzled by this record, and tries to explain it away, is strong evidence of its being genuine.

We have found no evidence in support of Diomedes' attribution of the introduction of masks to Roscius, and three independent records of masked performances at an early period. It seems that the matter was the subject of some controversy ; perhaps the only evidence available consisted of occasional records of masked performances, each of which was claimed by certain students as being the earliest. Indeed the statement that Prothymus had introduced masks (c) may well have been derived from (d).

That Greek drama (apart from mime) was a masked performance from the time of Aeschylus on is universally admitted. The Atellani of Campanian farce were invariably masked ; indeed it would not be easy to imagine how such a character as the manducus, with his huge clattering jaws, could be represented by an unmasked actor. Festus tells us in (f) that the Atellani never performed without masks, whereas all other actors might be compelled to lay aside their masks on the stage. Festus does not seem to realize that his explanation is inconsistent with itself : how could all other actors be compelled to lay aside their masks if in fact they never wore masks ? When we compare the Festus passage with Livy's statement (7.2) that even in Livy's own day the Atellani retained their rights as citizens, we may perhaps see an explanation of the problem : all actors wore masks, but a police regulation compelled the professionals to lay aside their masks on occasion in the theatre, in order to prevent persons who might be of low class from using the cloak of anonymity for attacks upon the government or upon leading citizens.

From the Pyrrhic War onwards there must have been a growing number of Romans who had witnessed the performances of Greek tragedies and comedies in the towns of Magna Graecia, and were thus familiarized with the use of masks, although, no doubt, they had also seen maskless performances by such mimes as Cleon

11

(pp. 150–1). From Campania came the Atellane plays, always performed in masks. From Etruria came the word persona itself (Etruscan φersu). Everywhere the Romans turned, they found the tradition of masked performances. Even in Rome ancient custom prescribed the wearing of the imagines of the dead at patrician funerals. From Tarentum came Andronicus, the founder of Roman drama. If Tarentum was like other Greek towns, a social gulf separated the masked actors of the respectable stage from the maskless mimes. What inducement could Andronicus have had to lay aside the mask, which was not merely an actor's badge of respectability, but an extremely convenient aid in dramatic production?

One of the most popular themes of Middle and New Comedy was the 'comedy of errors' produced by exact facial resemblance between two people. It may have been the existence of masks which suggested this theme to the dramatists. A feature of such plays appears to have been that the doubles should sooner or later confront one another; this is, at least, true of our only extant examples, the *Amphitruo* and *Menaechmi*. Nothing could be easier, if masks were worn; though it must be allowed that the *Comedy of Errors* is performed without masks on the modern stage.

The orthodox view is that Plautus wrote his plays for performance by maskless actors, and that lack of masks made all doubling of parts impossible. This view finds in both Plautus and Terence passages in which the play of expression on the actors' features is described—and must, therefore, have been visible. Among such passages are:

Miles Gloriosus : 201–2 :

illuc sis uide,
quem ad modum adstitit seuero fronte curans, cogitans.
Eun. 670 : illud uide, os ut sibi distorsit carnufex !
Phor. 210 ff.

AN. obsecro,
quid si adsimulo? satinest? GE. garris. AN. uoltum contemplamini : em
satine sic est? GE. non. AN. quid si sic? GE. propemodum.
AN. quid sic? GE. sat est.
Ad. 643 : erubuit : salua res est.

But we have similar references to facial expression in Greek drama : cf. Ar. *Lys.* 7 f. :

τί συντετάραξαι ; μὴ σκυθρώπαζ᾽, ὦ τέκνον.
οὐ γὰρ πρέπει σοι τοξοποιεῖν τὰς ὀφρῦς.

In reply to Hoffer's attempt to explain the reference to Aeschines' blush by supposing that the actor suddenly applies rouge to his face, Gow effectively quotes Seneca's remark (*Epist.* 11.7) that the one expression which artifices scaenici (? mimes) could *not* simulate was the blush. Reference to facial expression in Greek drama and in *Adelphi* 643 must have been directed to the imagination of the spectators, aided by the tones and gestures of the actors ; there is no need to assume a different explanation for the other passages which have been quoted.

We come finally to the question, 'Are there any situations in the plays of Plautus and Terence which demand the use of masks ? ' The orthodox view is that the Romans did not use masks, and that therefore doubling of rôles was impossible (because, presumably, no use of cosmetics could prevent the spectators from recognizing the features of an actor, and resenting his attempt to dupe them). Are we then to assume that there were two pairs of doubles in Plautus' company ? The *Amphitruo* turns on the exact resemblance of Mercury to Sosia and of Jupiter to Amphitruo. The doubles confront each other, as in the *Menaechmi* ; doubling of rôles would not, therefore, help us. The scene between Mercury and Sosia is the longest in Plautus (310 lines). Mercury has warned the spectators of the fact that his double is approaching, but has drawn their attention to the wings he is wearing under his hat ; these will help to distinguish him from Sosia. Then Sosia approaches, and for more than three hundred lines the spectators can compare the two. The resemblance is stressed : point by point Sosia compares Mercury to himself (lines 441 ff.) :

certe edepol, quom illum contemplo et formam cognosco meam,
quem ad modum ego sum (saepe in speculum inspexi), nimi' similest mei ;
itidem habet petasum ac uestitum ; tam consimilest atque ego ;
sura, pes, statura, tonsus, oculi, nasum uel labra,
malae, mentum, barba, collus : totus.

Could any employment of cosmetics make such a passage plausible ? When Jupiter and Amphitruo meet, Blepharo is unable to tell one from the other (1035). When the two Menaechmi meet, Messenio cannot tell which is his master (1074, 1085). We should further consider that, in a large open-air theatre, the resemblance would have to be not only close, but striking ; and the simplest way to achieve this would be by the use of masks.

Why are Bieber and others so confident that doubling of rôles was impossible ? Partly because of another statement of Diomedes : in Graeco dramate fere tres personae solae agunt . . . at Latini scriptores complures personas in fabulas introduxerunt, ut speciosiores frequentia faceret (Keil, 490–1) : ' In Greek drama as a rule there are only three characters on the stage at one time. . . . But the Latin dramatists brought on a large number of characters for the sake of the more effective appeal to the eye which number would give.' Whatever Diomedes had in mind, his words do not apply to the plays of Plautus, which could all be staged with a

company of not more than five actors, aided by an occasional
'super';* these numbers can hardly have differed much from
what was usual in New Comedy. Diomedes seems to be con-
fusing the number of characters with the number of actors ; in
any case his words have no bearing on the question of doubling
of parts. On doubling we have very little direct evidence in Latin
comedy (even in the case of Greek drama the earliest mention of
change of rôle quoted by Pickard-Cambridge is from Lucian,
Menipp. 16 (*D.F.*, p. 139, note 4)) ; but that the part of the prologue,
at least, could be doubled with that of one of the characters is
shown by *Poenulus* 123 (ego ibo, ornabor) and 126 (ibo, alius nunc
fieri uolo) ; † and why should the spectators have tolerated this
and not the doubling of two rôles in the play proper ? Another
point to consider is the frequency of minute personal descriptions
of characters who are present on the stage, or will soon appear.
In *As.* 400–1 ' Saurea ' is described :

> macilentis malis, rufulus aliquantum, uentriosus,
> truculentis oculis, commoda statura, tristi fronte.

Five lines later ' Saurea ' appears, so that the spectators can
compare him with the description. How disappointed they would
have been if it proved incorrect ! Indeed, even the holders of the
orthodox view are ready to concede that these passages are descriptions of masks—that is, of the masks worn in the Greek original,
which the Latin writer has copied word for word, although it is
supposed that the Roman actors were maskless.‡ This theory
not only attributes incredible lack of stage sense to Plautus, but is
quite inconsistent with the view (already quoted) that certain
passages in the Latin plays are descriptions of the play of expression
on the maskless features of the Roman actors.

Finally, we have direct references to masks in the Latin plays.
In *Amph.* 458–9, Sosia, gazing at his double, exclaims :

nam hicquidem omnem imaginem meam, quae antehac fuerat, possidet.
uiuo fit quod nunquam quisquam mortuo faciat mihi.

Here we have a reference to the wearing of imagines in funerals.
The very word *persona* occurs in *Pers.* 783 ; I accept Duckworth's
view (*N.R.C.* 94, note 44) that here it means ' personage ', ' person '.
Its diminutive, persolla, is found in *Curc.* 192, in an unflattering
reference to the heroine's face. By the time of Terence persona is

* How inconsistent the orthodox position is will appear from comparing
(a) the frequent assertions of thorough-going Plautine alterations in the *Stichus*
with (b) the stock view that doubling of rôles had no interest for Plautus, and (c) the
demonstrable fact that the *Stichus*, as we have it, with its eleven characters, could
be performed by a company of three.

† One of these two passages may conceivably be the work of a retractator ;
but they both seem written with an eye to performance, and are therefore evidence
for stage usage.

‡ See, for example, Pickard-Cambridge, *D.F.* page 199.

already established in the meaning ' character ' (*Eun.* 26, 32, 35) ;
it may well have had this meaning much earlier, but can only
have acquired it from the usage of the stage.

The Appearance of Roman Masks

Gellius (5.7), quoting Gavius Bassus (temp. Augustus) writes :
' " caput ", inquit, " et os coperimento personae tectum undique
unaque tantum uocis emittendae uia peruium, quoniam non
uaga neque diffusa est, in unum tantummodo exitum collectam
coactamque uocem ciet [et] magis claros canorosque sonitus facit,
quoniam igitur indumentum illud oris clarescere et resonare uocem
facit, ob eam causam ' persona ' dicta est, littera propter uocabuli
formam productiore " '. As Pickard-Cambridge says (*D.F.*,
p. 194), ' the suggested derivation, of course, does not bear looking
into, and some modern experiments with masks manufactured so
far as possible on ancient lines make it extremely doubtful whether
in fact masks ever did anything to increase sound '. Anyone who
has tried the acoustics of an ancient theatre will probably agree
that they are good. But Gellius' statement that they covered the
whole head (' like a visor ', L. C. Purser, Smith's *Dict. of A.*, s.v.
persona) appears to have been generally true ; the mask was
fastened with bands under the chin ; one of the terms used for
having the mask put on is περιτίθεσθαι. The material used was linen.

Pollux, writing in the second century A.D., has left us lists of
the masks used in drama. In comedy he gives nine for old men,
eleven for young men, seven for male slaves, three for old women
and fourteen for young women, in tragedy six for old or mature
men, eight for young men, three for male slaves, five for female
slaves, and seven for free women. See P.C., *D.F.* 177–212 for
details and illustrations. Pollux's list is no doubt far from complete,
as there were special masks for certain individuals. Pollux's
interest in masks, as in all other topics, is simply to give a list of
technical terms. Whether his list corresponds closely to the
practice of the Greek or Roman stage at an earlier period is uncertain. The illustrations which we possess may represent an
artistic rather than a stage convention. In general we are struck
by their grotesque quality, at least in the period after the fifth
century ; and Platonios (of unknown date) states that the characters
of Middle and New Comedy wore hideously exaggerated masks
to avoid all danger of accidental resemblance to some Macedonian
ruler. (This implies that fifth-century masks, even in Comedy,
were more naturalistic : cf. *Knights*, 230 ff.) If he is right, the
appearance of Menander's characters must have been very much
out of keeping, according to our notions, with their words. It
follows that we must either reject the evidence of Pollux, Platonios
and the illustrations, or disregard the evidence of the plays and our
own notions of fitness.

APPENDIX K

CONTAMINARE AND 'CONTAMINATION'

THE normal sense of contaminare is ' sully ', ' stain '. Donatus (ad *And.* 16) explains it as manibus luto plenis aliquid attingere, polluere, foedare, maculare. The opposite of contaminatus is integer (cf. Cic. *Top.* 69 : integra contaminatis, iucunda minus iucundis). It would thus be an appropriate word to use if the charge was that Terence had ' spoiled ' his Greek original (by altering it). The difficulty is that Terence appears to admit the truth of the charge (factum id esse non negat, *Heaut.* 18). As it is incredible that he would confess to having ' spoiled ' his original, he is supposed to be using the word in a special, technical sense, that of ' *combining* ' two originals. Yet this argument involves another absurdity. If contaminare meant ' combine two Greek originals ', and if such combination had been the normal and acknowledged practice of the Latin dramatists from the time of Naevius down to that of Ennius, who had died only three years before the production of the *Andria*, the accusation against Terence would amount to this—that he was following established practice. In order to give the necessary sting to the accusation, it is supposed that Terence's critics were using contaminare not merely as a technical word =' combine ', but also in its usual sense of ' spoil ' : that with them it meant not exactly ' spoil ', and not exactly ' combine ', but ' spoil by combining ', miscendo deprauare, as the Thesaurus explains it with special reference to the two passages in Terence's prologues. The first question, then, is whether contaminare contains the notion of ' combining '.

(1) Etymologically it comes from con, ' with ', and the root of tango. The prevailing view stresses the preposition : thus Walde translates ' in Berührung bringen, bes. mit Fremdartigen, daher besudeln . . .'. It is true that when explaining *And.* 16 (contaminari non decere fabulas) Donatus remarks id est ex multis unam facere. This, however, is not a definition of the word, but an attempt to interpret the line in the light of the context and of *Heaut.* 16–18 :

> nam quod rumores distulerunt maleuoli
> multas contaminasse Graecas, dum facit
> paucas Latinas : factum id esse non negat.

Donatus' comment would have made equally good sense if *And.*
16 had run :

> pollui non decere fabulas,

and if *Heaut.* 17 had been :

> multas polluisse Graecas, dum facit . . .

In certain contexts the root sense ' stain ' can mean ' stain by
mixture ' (with something base) ; thus Terence himself writes
(*Eun.* 552) :

> ne hoc gaudium contaminet uita aegritudine aliqua,

' lest life pollute this pleasure with some distress ' (Duckworth,
N.R.C. 203).   Similarly in Accius 208–9 (Ribb., *Tr. Rom.*) :

> matres inquinari regias,
> contaminari stirpem ac misceri genus.

But in all such cases one of Donatus' synonyms (polluere, etc.)
could take the place of contaminare.   On the other hand, there
are numerous cases where the idea of ' mixture ' is inappropriate :
e.g. Cic. *Catil.* 1.12.29 : sanguine . . . se . . . contaminarunt,
' they stained ' (not ' mixed ') ' themselves with blood ' ; id.
pro Rosc. Am. 40. 116 : fingi maleficium nullum posse, quo iste se
non contaminarit, ' stained ' (not ' mixed ') ' himself with crime ' ;
Suct. *Ner.* 56 : hanc mox ita spreuit ut urina contaminaret,
' sullied (the statue of the goddess) with urine '.   The prefix con-
does not necessarily imply ' mixing ' : cf. concacaui me (Señ.
Apoc. 4), comminxit lectum (Hor. *Sat.* 1.3.90) ; se conspuit (Petr.
Sat. 23) ; aquam conspurcat (Col. 8. 3) : illa maritum conuomit
(Juv. 6. 101).

(2) Terence nowhere says, ' I have contaminated my Greek
originals ' ; that is the charge against him, which he quotes in
Oratio Obliqua.   What he does say is, ' I have combined portions
of two very similar originals '.   The inference is not that ' contaminating ' meant ' combining ', but that it meant something
different.   The charge was that he had altered and so spoiled his
original ; his reply was that the only alterations made had been
the addition of some very similar material from the same Greek
author.   He claims precedent for what he has done ; he says that
he would rather imitate the ' carelessness ' of Naevius, Plautus and
Ennius than the ' dull carefulness ' of his critics.   But ' carelessness '
could never produce a deliberate fusion of two plays.   The only
common element which I can see in the accusation (of mistransla-
tion or altering his original), the defence (that he had merely
combined two Greek plays) and the appeal to the precedent set
by his ' careless ' predecessors, is that in all three some departure
from the ostensible original is implied.

(3) The frequent references in Latin literature to the translation of Greek plays into Latin always suggest that the Latin translator kept to one original at a time. Cicero goes so far as to say (see p. 74) that the Greek plays were translated ' word for word ', though elsewhere he states with more probability that the Latin dramatists rendered ' not the words but the sense '. He occasionally points out passages (see p. 82) in which the translator departs from his original, for example by changing the sense or expression in order to suit Roman taste ; but nowhere have we any reference to alteration of structure or to borrowing from another original. Apart from Terence's appeal to precedent there is no evidence at all that Plautus, Naevius or Ennius drew on more than one original at a time ; and even if we take Terence's appeal to precedent at its face value, it is no argument for a more elaborate form of combination than what we find in his own practice.

(4) The Latin plays have been eagerly scanned by scholars in quest of internal evidence of ' contamination ' in the modern sense of ' combination '. This would be a valid procedure if the a priori evidence for ' combination ' were beyond doubt. If, again, the hypothesis of ' combination ' had led to agreed and valuable results, that would be an argument in favour of taking Terence's words in the sense usually given to them. In fact the methods employed have been questionable and the results are conflicting. Every supposed imperfection has been taken as proof of Roman ' botching ', and every play in turn has been dissected by one enthusiast or another, anxious to lay bare the flawless structure of the Greek originals from which it has been ' botched together '. On the results of such studies I would refer the reader to Michaut's admirable chapter (*Plaute*, Vol. ii, p. 16) and Duckworth's more recent summary (*N.R.C.*, pp. 202 f.). It is always possible that some of these innumerable guesses may be near the truth ; the difficulty is to feel confidence in the procedure. To see ' contamination ' at work we need the power to compare a Latin play as a whole with its two originals as a whole. In fact all that we have to compare consists of passages, usually short. When we consider the Latin plays in themselves, the only convincing evidence of departure from the original is the presence of Roman material. But this is no argument for the use of a second Greek source.

It is true that we do not know much about how the Latin dramatists composed their plays. It is also true that other dramatists sometimes draw on more than one source : that, for example, Shakespeare used not only the *Menaechmi*, but the *Amphitruo* in composing his *Comedy of Errors*. Nevertheless the *Comedy of Errors* is not a mere combination of two Latin plays but an original play by Shakespeare. As Duckworth asks (*N.R.C.*, p. 388, note 11), ' If the originals . . . were lost and scholars attempted to restore the Plautine comedies utilized by Shakespeare, how closely, one wonders, would their reconstructions resemble the actual Roman models ? ' No mere use of scissors and paste can construct a play out of two plays ; and it is absurd to suppose that Plautus would work in so mechanical a way. Whatever he wrote was infused with his own spirit ; and if he did in fact combine two plots to form one, we may be sure that he added much of his own ; so much, indeed, that even with the originals before us we might have some difficulty in distinguishing what was borrowed from what was new. It is when the hypothesis of contamination is used as a means of *reconstituting* the Greek originals that its weakness is apparent. Contempt for the Latin versions which we possess, admiration for the Greek originals which have been lost, are dangerous motives for so hazardous a procedure. The uncertainties are enormous—the personality of the translator, of the Greek writer, of the scholar himself. We always come back to the Latin plays, such as they are : they seem to be unities ; they have held the stage, which is the test for which they were planned. To whom is their unity due ?

See also *Contaminatio* in *C.R.* 9 (1959) pp. 7-11.

11*

APPENDIX L

THE OXYRHYNCHUS MIME

(From a Papyrus of the Second Century A.D.)

(*See* Sudhaus, S., in *Hermes* xli, 1906, pp. 247–277)

Change of person denoted by ≡ (lines 116, 185).   At line 179
we have < in the margin.

Scene 1

107 . . .   ζώσωμαι. ἐρῶ νῦν παιδ(ός),
μάτην δὲ καλῶ αὐ]τόν, ἵνα με βεινήσῃ· τί οὖν
ὀκν(ῶ) ; φέρε τὰς μά]στιγας. δοῦλε. προσελθών
110 μοι σεμνύνῃ] ; μαστιγία. ἐγὼ ἡ κυρία.
τινὰ περὶ το]ύτου κελεύω καὶ οὐ γίνεται ; οὐ θέλεις,
ἄθλιε ; ἀλλὰ μ]αίνεσ(θαι) ποιήσ(εις). [κόμισο]ν τὰς μάστιγ(ας),
Μάλακε· οὐ θᾶ]ττ(ον) ποιήσ(εις) ; οὐδὲ σὺ θέλεις ; παῖδες, τοὺς
φύλακ(ας) καλῶ]· οὐδὲν γίνεται ; δὸς ὧδε τὰς μάστειγ(ας).
115 ἀλλὰ τί ἔτι] ἔστηκεν Αἴσωπ(ος) ὁ τὴν δούλ(ην) καταδεξό(μενος),
ἂν] τοὺς ὀδόντας ἀράσσουσα αὐτῷ ἐκτινάξω ; ἰδού,   ≡
κυρί'—εἰ δέ σε σκάπτειν ἐκέλευον, εἰ δ' ἀροτριᾶν.
εἰ δὲ λίθους βαστάζειν τῷ γυναικείῳ γένει συντεθραμμένον ;
118ᵃ πάντων οὖν τῶν ἐν τῷ ἀγρῷ ἔργων γενομένων
118ᵇ κενός σοι κύσθος σκληρότερος ἐφάνη ;
ἀλόγιστε, πονηρίαν τινὰ μένεις καὶ αὐχεῖς, καὶ τοῦτο σὺν τῇ πώλῳ
120 Ἀπολλωνίᾳ· ὥστε, παῖδες, συνλαβόντες τοῦτον ἕλκετε ἐπὶ τὴν
πεπρωμένην.—προάγετε νῦν κἀκείνην ὡς ἔστιν
πεφειμωμένη· ὑμῖν λέγω, ἀπαγαγόντες αὐτοὺς
κατὰ ἀμφότερα τὰ ἀκρωτήρια καὶ τὰ παρακείμενα
δένδρα προσδήσατε μακρὰν διασπάσαντες
125 ἄλλον ἀπ' ἄλλου, καὶ βλέπετε μή ποτε τῷ ἑτέρῳ
δείξητε, μὴ τῆς ἀλλήλων ὄψεως πλησθέντες
μεθ' ἡδονῆς ἀποθάνωσι· σφαγιάσαντες δὲ αὐτοὺς
πρός με ἔσω ἀντᾶτε. εἴρηκα· ἐγὼ δ' ἔνδον εἰσ-
ελεύσομαι.

Scene 2

τί λέγετε ὑμεῖς ; ὄντως οἱ θεοὶ ὑμῖν
130 ἐφαντάσθησαν, καὶ ὑμεῖς ἐφοβήθητε, καὶ ἐκεῖνοι ἀφανεῖς
γεγόνασι ; ἐγὼ ὑμῖν καταγγέλλω· ἐκεῖνοι

314

132 εἰ καὶ ὑμᾶς διέφυγον, τοὺς ὀρεοφύλακας οὐ μὴ λάθωσι.-
     νυνὶ δὲ τοῖς θεοῖς ἐπαρᾶσθαι βούλομαι. Σπινθήρ·
     ὄμοσον ἐπιπεσεῖν ὄντως ὑμῖν φαινόμενα. λέγετε
135 τὰ πρὸς τὰς θυσίας· ἐπειδὰν οἱ θεοὶ καὶ ἐπ' ἀγαθῷ
     ἡμῖν φαίνεσθαι μέλλωσιν, ὡς προσέχοντας ὑμνήσομεν
     τοὺς θεούς·—μαστιγία, οὐ θέλεις ποιεῖν τὰ ἐπιτασσόμενα ;
     τί γέγονεν ; ἢ μαίνῃ ; εἰσελθόντες ἴδετε τίς ἐστιν.
     τί φησιν ; ἐκεῖν' ἄρα. ἴδετε μὴ καὶ ὁ ὑπερήφανος
140 ἔσω ἐστί. ὑμῖν λέγω· ἀπαλλάξαντες ταύτην πα-
     ράδοτε τοῖς ὀρεοφύλαξι καὶ εἴπατε ἐν πολλῷ σιδηρῷ
     τηρεῖν ἐπιμελῶς. ἕλκετε, σύρετε, ἀπάγετε.
     καὶ ὑμεῖς δὲ ἐκεῖνον ἀναζητήσαντες ἀποσφά-
     ξατε, σπάσατε, προβάλετε, ἵνα ἐγὼ αὐτὸν νεκρὸν ἴδω.
145 εἴσιτε, Σπινθήρ, Μάλακε, μετ' ἐμοῦ.

SCENE 3

                    ἐξιοῦσα,
     παῖδες, ἀκριβῶς νῦν ἰδεῖν πειράσομαι, εἰ τέθνηκε
     ἐκεῖνος, ὅπως μή πάλιν πλανῇ μέ τις.—ὧδε μὲν
     οὖν, ἄθλιε κωμαστά, ὧδε. ἒ ἔ, ἰδοῦ οὗτος. αἱ ταλαί-
     πωρε· σὺ ἄρα ἤθελες οὕτω ριφθῆναι μᾶλλον ἢ ἐμὲ
150 φιλεῖν ; κείμενον δὲ κωφὸν πῶς ἀποδύρομαι ; νεκρῷ,
     εἴ τίς ποτε γέγονεν, ἦρται πᾶσα ἔρις. ἀνάπαυσόν
     με, ἵνα τὰς κεκλιμένας φρένας ἄρω.—
     Σπινθήρ, πόθεν σου ὁ ὀφθαλμὸς ἡμέρωται ; ὧδε ἄνω,
     συνείσελθέ μοι, μαστιγία, ὅπως οἶνον διυλίσω· εἴσελθε,
155 εἴσελθε, μαστιγία, ὧδε πάρελθε. ποταπὰ περιπατεῖς ;
     ὧδε στρέφου. ποῦ σου τὸ ἥμισυ τοῦ χιτωνίου, τὸ ἥμισυ ;
     ἐγώ σοι πάντα περὶ πάντων ἀποδώσω.

SCENE 4

                    οὕτω μοι
     δέδοκται, Μάλακε· πάντας ἀνελοῦσα καὶ πωλήσασα
     τὰ ὑπάρχοντά πού ποτε χωρίσεσθαι. νῦν τοῦ γέροντος
160 ἐνκρατὴς θέλω γενέσθαι, πρίν τι τούτων ἐπιγνοῖ. καὶ γὰρ εὐκαίρως
     ἔχω φάρμακον θανάσιμον, ὃ μετ' οἰνομέλιτος διηθήσασα
     δώσω αὐτῷ πιεῖν. ὥστε πορευθεὶς τῇ πλατείᾳ θύρᾳ κά-
     λεσον αὐτὸν ὡς ἐπὶ διαλλαγάς. ἀπελθόντες καὶ ἡμεῖς
     τῷ παρασίτῳ τὰ περὶ τοῦ γέροντος προσαναθώμεθα.
165 παιδίον, παῖ.

SCENE 5

165 τὸ τοιοῦτόν ἐστιν, παράσιτε—οὗτος τίς ἐστίν ;
     αὕτη δέ ; τί οὖν αὐτῇ ἐγένετο ; ἀποκάλυψον, ἵνα ἴδω
     αὐτήν.—χρείαν σου ἔχω, τὸ τοιοῦτόν ἐστιν, παράσιτε.

168 μετανοήσασα θέλω τῷ γέροντι διαλλαγῆναι. πορευθεὶς οὖν
    ἰδὲ αὐτὸν καὶ ἄγε πρὸς ἐμέ. ἐγὼ δὲ εἰσελθοῦσα τὰ πρὸς τὸ
170 ἄριστον ὑμῖν ἑτοιμάσω.—ἐπαινῶ, Μάλακε, τὸ τάχος.
    τὸ φάρμακον ἔχεις συνκεκραμένον καὶ τὸ ἄριστον
    ἑτοιμόν ἐστι ; τὸ ποῖον ; Μάλακε, λαβὲ ἰδοῦ οἰνόμελι.
    τάλας, δοκῶ πανόλημπτος γέγονεν ὁ παράσιτος : τάλας, γελᾷ·
    συνακολουθήσατε αὐτῷ, μὴ καί τι πάθῃ.—τοῦτο μὲν ὡς
175 ἐβουλόμην τετέλεσται· εἰσελθόντες περὶ τῶν λοιπῶν
    ἀσφαλέστερον βουλευσώμεθα· Μάλακε, πάντα ἡμῖν κατὰ
    γνώμην προκεχώρηκε, ἐὰν ἔτι τὸν γέροντα ἀνέλωμεν.

Scene 6

178 παράσιτε, τί γέγονεν ; αἲ πῶς ; μάλιστα· πάντων γὰρ αὐτῶν
    νῦν ἐνκρατὴς γέγονα.—ἄγωμεν, παράσιτε, τί οὖν θέλεις ;<
180 Σπινθήρ, ἐπίδος μοι φόνον ἱκανόν. παράσιτε, φοβοῦμαι
    μὴ γελάσω. καὶ καλῶς λέγεις· λέξω-τί με δεῖ λέγειν;
    πάτερ κύριε, τίνι με καταλείπεις ; ἀπολώλεκά μου τὴν
    παρρησίαν, τὴν δόξαν, τὸ ἐλευθέριον φῶς. σύ μου ἦς ὁ
183ᵃ κύριος τούτῳ μόνῳ, ἀληθῶς, οὐ λόγῳ.
    ἄφες, ἐγὼ αὐτὸν θρηνήσω· οὐαί σοι, ταλαίπωρε, ἄκληρε,
185 ἀλγεινέ, ἀναφρόδιτε, οὐαὶ σοί—ουαὶ μοί· οἶδα γάρ σε ὅστις
    ποτὲ εἶ, μεισούμενε. Σπινθήρ, ξύλα ἐπὶ τοῦτον. οὗτος πάλιν τίς
    ἐστιν ;
    μένουσι σῶοι, δέσποτα.

THE OXYRHYNCHUS MIME
(Free Translation and Notes)

THE FAITHLESS WIFE

Characters

The Mistress (performed by the archimima).
Aesopus, a slave, in love with Apollonia.
Apollonia, a female slave.
Spinther, a slave (apparently loyal to his master).
Malakos, a slave (siding with his mistress).
Parasite of the old man ; the Master, slaves.

Scene i

Mistress : I love a slave ; but in vain do I call him to love me.
Why do I hesitate ? Bring the whip. Slave, are you being
haughty with me ? You rascal, I am the mistress ; I give

orders and they are not obeyed? You refuse, you wretch? you will drive me mad. Bring the whip, Malakos. Quick ! . . . Why is Aesopus standing there, the slave who means to receive the love of his fellow-slave? I will knock the teeth out of his head. See that !

Aesopus : Mistress !

Mistress : If I was ordering you to dig, or plough, or carry stones, you woman's pet ! Does loving a woman seem harder than any toil in the fields? You fool, you're waiting for some knavery and giving yourself airs, with the help of the wench Apollonia. So seize him, slaves, and drag him off to his fate ; now bring her out also, gagged as she is. I bid you take them away to the two promontories, and bind them to the trees that border the place, after dragging them far apart, and take care that you keep each out of the other's sight, lest they die happy, feasting their eyes upon each other. And when you have slain them, come in to me. Enough ; I am going indoors.

Scene 2

Mistress : What are you slaves saying? The gods really appeared to you, and you were afraid? Although he has escaped you, they shall not escape the desert guards. Now I wish to propitiate the gods, Spinther. Swear . . . say the sacrificial prayers. Since the gods are about to appear to us auspiciously, sing the praise of the gods in expectation. Knave, won't you do as you're told? What has happened? . . . Go in and see who it is. What does he say? . . . Look if that haughty rascal is inside too. I tell you to remove this woman and hand her over to the desert guards, and tell them to load her with iron and keep her carefully. Take her, drag her off, away with her ! And do you search for him, and when you have killed him, fling out his body that I may see him dead. . . . Come, Spinther and Malakos, with me. . . .

Scene 3

Mistress : I will go out, slaves, and try to see for certain if he is dead, so that no one may fool me again. . . . So then, you unhappy reveller, so then ! . . . Ah, look at him ! Poor wretch ! So you chose to be flung out here rather than make love to me? Here he lies mute ; how shall I mourn for him? He is dead ; if I had a quarrel with him, it is all over now. Let me rest ; I must ease my troubled heart. . . .

Spinther, why is your eye so sad? Come up to me here, knave ! Come in, come in, knave ; come here ! Where are you walking from ? Turn in here. I will pay you in full for everything. . . .

SCENE 4

Mistress : This is my resolve, Malakos ; to kill them all and sell their property, and then to withdraw somewhere or other. Now I wish to get the old man into my power before he has any idea of this ; and I conveniently have a deadly drug which I will mix with mead and give him to drink. So go to the broad door and call him as though to a reconciliation ; let us go too, and communicate the affair of the old man to the parasite. Here, slave ! here !

SCENE 5

Mistress : The case is this, parasite.—Who is this ? Her very self ? Then what happened to her ? Unveil her, that I may see her.—I require your help. The case is this, parasite. I have repented and wish to be reconciled to the old man. Go then and see him, and bring him to me, and I will go in and prepare your dinner. . . . I commend your speed, Malakos. Have you got the drug mixed and is the dinner ready ? What ? Malakos ! here, take the mead. The wretch ! I think the parasite is panic-stricken. The wretch ! he laughs ! Go along with him, slaves, for fear anything should happen to him. . . . This has been done as I wished ; let us go in and deliberate more safely about the rest of the business. Malakos, everything has gone as I intended, if we can also make away with the old man.

SCENE 6

Mistress : Parasite, what has happened ? Ah, how ? Certainly, for I now have them in my power, all of them.

Spinther : Come, parasite ! What do you want, then ?

Parasite : Spinther, give me poison enough.

Spinther : Parasite, I'm afraid I shall laugh. You are right.

Parasite : I will say—what ought I to say ? My father and lord, to whom are you leaving me ? I have lost my freedom of speech, my glory, my light of liberty ! You were my lord. Do I not speak truly ?

Malakos : Let him alone, *I* will mourn him. Woe for thee, wretched, hapless, miserable one, unblest by Love ! Woe for thee !

Master : Woe for me ? I know what you are, you hateful rascal ! Spinther, bring the wood for this rascal ! . . . Who is this again ?

Spinther : They are still safe, master !

NOTES

SCENE 3. The opening word has the force of a stage-direction; the archimima comes out in front of the curtain. As between Scene 1 and 2, so between Scene 2 and 3, she has received a report from her slaves. The whole piece is performed in front of the house. As she enters, the body of Aesop is brought on from the side-entrance. . . . She has now transferred her passion to Malakos.

SCENE 4. After unfolding her plan to Malakos, she sends him into the house by the 'wide' or main door. The archimima summons another slave and they go off to fetch the parasite.

SCENE 5. The archimima and parasite enter to see a second body lying beside that of Aesopus; the concealed form is that of Apollonia. All the remarks are uttered by the archimima; it is surprising that she does not endeavour to discover how Apollonia met with her death, but the technical reason may be that only the archimima speaks in this scene. She is about to enter the house to prepare the fatal meal when Malakos meets her on the threshold, carrying the drink in his hand. At this point, perhaps, the parasite seizes the cup and puts it to his lips; hence the alarm of the mistress. The parasite is aware that the drink is not fatal, that the 'corpses' will come to life and that the mistress will pay the penalty.

SCENE 6. The part of the Archimima ends at 'all of them'; at the end of this line we find the sign <, indicating, doubtless, that her part is ended. Spinther and the parasite converse in amusement; Spinther, afraid that his mirth will overcome him, in response to a sign from the parasite, addresses a pretended lament to the 'corpse' of the old man. Malakos interrupts with *his* address to the corpse; suddenly the old man comes to life and orders the punishment of Malakos. The final words show that Aesopus and Apollonia are not really dead.

For the fact that the lovers are found to have been merely drugged, cf. Plutarch *de soll. an.* 19 for a story of a mime in which a dog pretended to be asleep. The drink handed to the old man cannot have had even this effect, as the parasite, after drinking, does not stop joking. The old man must simply have pretended to be dead.

The piece is intended for the stage, if we may judge by the indications of change of speaker. It is a 'hypothesis', intended to guide the company, but the chief performer would naturally expand her part at will. By means of question and answer she governs the action of the piece. She was also the producer and director, and probably the composer as well.

APPENDIX M

ACCENT, ICTUS AND RHYTHM : THE METRES OF LATIN DRAMA

MY object in this section is to set out the scheme of the metres used by Plautus and the other Republican dramatists, and to illustrate their rhythm for English-speaking students by adding approximate English equivalents. This procedure, though not new, invites the criticism that I am comparing two fundamentally different things. Latin (including Plautine) verse was quantitative : that is, it so arranged words that the long and short syllables formed a pattern. English verse is accentual : it so arranges words that the naturally stressed syllables form a pattern. For example, Byron's poem ' The Assyrian came down like the wolf on the fold ' may be regarded as containing four groups of three syllables to the line, the third syllable of each group bearing a natural stress (´)— that is, having a louder sound than the others :

The Assý/rian came dówn/ like the wólf/ on the fóld.

Once we have heard a line or two of this poem, we form a mental picture of its metre, and expect the other lines to conform to the pattern :

$$+ \ + \ \overset{+}{.} / \ + \ + \ \overset{+}{.} \ / \ + \ + \ \overset{+}{.} / \ + \ + \ \overset{+}{.}$$

each cross in this scheme representing an expected syllable, each dot under the line an expected stress. The actual words may not always quite conform to this scheme ; there may be a syllable too few or too many, and a natural stress may not come precisely where we expected it ; but this does not seriously disturb our enjoyment of the rhythm, provided that there is general agreement, both in the number of syllables and in the position of the stresses, between what we expect and what we hear. If, for example, the number of syllables were still twelve, but the natural stresses (marked (´)) no longer came at the places where we expected them (marked (.)), we should feel that the rhythm had been lost, or else changed. For example the line

Their soldiers were provided with bright uniforms

has the right number of syllables—twelve : but the stresses come in the wrong places. If we try to fit the words into our scheme, we get

Their sóldiers/ were províd/ed with bríght/ úniforms
. . . .

320

where the clash between the beat of the metre (.) and the actual stresses of the words is so great as to destroy the rhythm.

Evidently we must distinguish between stress-accent and metrical beat. The metrical beat belongs to the metrical scheme, not to the words ; it is the point at which anyone who was accompanying the speaking of the verse with hand or wand would make a heavy down-stroke. If we were setting the verses to music, we would try to choose a musical rhythm which corresponded with the metrical pattern, and the notes bearing the musical stress (the first after the bar-lines) should coincide with the metrical beats.

Rhythm (ῥυθμός, ' flow ') is explained by Aristoxenus (*Rhyth. Stoich.* ii, §§7, 8, Westphal's ed.) as ' a defined ordering of times '. For us it is rather that property in an ordered sequence of sensations which leaves upon the mind a satisfying and effective sense of proportion. Rhythm makes us want to *do* something—if it be only to go to sleep—and feel more able to do it. Metre is the formal pattern or scheme of verse. For the French these words are sharply distinguished ; metre is a measurement imposed from outside the verse, rhythm is an impulse from within, intimately connected with the emotion or meaning of each word spoken or sung. French verse is based on syllable-counting ; the slight stress on the last syllable of each ' rhythmical group ' is too variable in position to create that expectancy which we call ictus.

Greek, like French, was spoken with more or less level stress ; the Greek accent was one of pitch. Greek versification was based on the principle that syllables were either long (–) or short (⏑), a long being reckoned equal to two shorts. The smallest unit in the verse which displayed the metre was the foot. Feet were reckoned in values of short syllables (' times ' or morae). The main feet which concern us are :

> Feet of two times : the pyrrhic (⏑ ⏑).
> Feet of three times : the iambus (⏑ –), trochee (– ⏑), tribrach (⏑ ⏑ ⏑).
> Feet of four times : the spondee (– –), dactyl (– ⏑ ⏑), anapaest (⏑ ⏑ –), proceleusmatic (⏑ ⏑ ⏑ ⏑).
> Feet of five times : the cretic (– ⏑ –), and bacchiac (⏑ – –).

But in iambic, trochaic and anapaestic verse the real measure (metron) was the pair of feet, or dipody. If we think of ourselves as taking a pair of steps in time with the metre, we can see that a four-fold movement is involved, e.g. right foot *up*, right foot DOWN, left foot *up*, left foot DOWN. The down-movements correspond to the longs, the up-movements to the shorts. In origin the term ἄρσις seems to have meant the ' raising ' of the (dancer's) foot at the short or weak element of the metre, θέσις the ' setting down ' of the foot at the long or strong element. There is no evidence that the strong elements were marked by an artificial stress of the voice.

Later usage has inverted the meanings of ἄρσις and θέσις. So
used are we to the coincidence of stressed syllable with metrical
beat in our own verse that we stress the metrical beat in Greek
verse too, and equate *arsis* with our ' rise ', ' lift ' or ' crest ', *thesis*
with our ' fall ', ' dip ' or ' trough '. But the analogy of French
versification shows that a regularly recurring voice-ictus is not
essential to verse. Moreover, we do not stress syllables in English
verse merely because they come under the metrical beat : we give
them the natural stress which they would have in ordinary speech.

The two halves of the dipody in iambic and trochaic verse were
not quite alike. Greek usage allowed, and our ear approves, the
substitution of a long for a short in the ' outer fall '. Thus the first
foot of an iambic dipody, the second foot of a trochaic dipody,
might be a spondee. Adding the possibility of resolution (the
substitution of two short syllables for one long syllable) we get the
scheme :

Iambic dipody   Trochaic dipody

The dot under the line indicates the position of the metrical beat,
or ictus ; it falls on the compulsory long, or if that is resolved into
two shorts, on the first of these shorts. By compulsory long I mean
the element which cannot be replaced by a single short. I must
repeat that the dot is not intended to indicate any artificial stress
in the pronunciation of the syllable.

The ' inner fall ' (that which comes between the two compulsory
longs) was kept pure, the only exception being the occasional
occurrence of an anapaest in one of the even feet in iambic lines—
a licence confined to comedy, cf. *Wasps* 979 :

κατάβᾱ/ κατάβᾱ/ κατάβᾱ/ κατάβᾱ./—καταβή/σομαι.

Iambic, trochaic and anapaestic verses were named according
to the number of dipodies they contained ; thus the dimeter contains four feet, the trimeter six, the tetrameter eight. ' Catalectic '
means ' minus a half-foot at the end ' ; ' acatalectic ' means
' complete '.

Such were the metres taken over by the Latin poets into their
own language, which was certainly heavier in movement than
Greek, and may have differed in other ways as well. The only
native Italian verse known to us is the Saturnian, the structure of
which is a mystery. Whether based on quantity, stress-accent or
syllable-counting, it was a line of about thirteen syllables, falling
into two roughly equal parts, and (like Plautine verse) sometimes
alliterative. As for the position of the Latin accent, it seems to
be agreed that in primitive Latin the first syllable of every word

was prominent. For classical times we have the ' penultimate law ', as set forth by Cicero and Quintilian (that in all words of two syllables the first was accented, and in all words of more than two syllables the last but one, if long, took the accent ; if the last but one was short the accent went back to the last but two). The nature of this accent is always described by Roman writers as one of pitch, not stress ; and it is never spoken of as a factor in versification, which is described as purely quantitative. Not until medieval times do we find Latin verse which is clearly accentual, as, for example, the well-known

díes írae, díesílla,

and it is agreed even by French scholars that by the fourth century A.D. Latin was spoken with a stress-accent. In truth the most certain fact about classical Latin verse is that it accepted the quantitative principle (as, by way of contrast, English has refused to do).

Nevertheless the verse of Republican drama and certain other types of verse which we may call ' popular ' (soldiers' songs, riddles and lampoons, the beast-fables of Phaedrus, etc.—all of them iambic or trochaic) do differ markedly from the strictly quantitative verse which was written in these and other metres by the classical Latin poets. The differences are : (1) the occurrence of long ' inner falls ', contrary to the ' dipody law ' ; (2) the occurrence of other long syllables where quantitative rules demand short syllables ; (3) the extension of ' resolution ' to almost every position in the line. Only in the final foot of the line (and in the long lines the final foot of the half-line too) are these licences usually avoided.

Roman literary men like Horace were well aware that Latin dramatic verse did not quite conform with their own standards ; they seem to have regarded the differences as due to want of skill or care, or perhaps to a wish for special effects, but not to departure from the quantitative principle. This view cannot be rejected out of hand ; Lindsay says (*E.L.V.* p. 126) : ' although Plautus *allowed* a Spondee in the " even " feet of the Senarius, we may be sure that he *preferred* an Iambus.'

Nevertheless it is widely held that quantitative weakness was redeemed by the general agreement between stress accent and metrical ictus. In other words, it is believed (*a*) that the Latin accent was one of stress ; (*b*) that the Latin comic dramatists, aiming at reproducing the tones of conversation, contrived that, in a general way, the metrical beat fell on accented syllables. French scholars argue, however, that agreement of accent and ictus was largely the accidental result of the Latin insistence on the caesura (division between words inside a foot, especially important in the third or fourth foot of the iambic trimeter) and the diaeresis (division between words at the end of a foot, usual in the middle of the longer lines). If we compare, for example, the iambic senarii of Plautus with the strictly quantitative iambic trimeters of classical poets, we find that in both cases agreement is common in the interior of the lines, clash common in the first and fifth feet and universal in the sixth foot. In the poem of Catullus beginning :

phasélus ílle quem uidétis, hóspites,

there is general agreement, particularly in the interior of the lines ; yet no one argues that Catullus' iambics are accentual.

Many apparent violations of the quantitative principle are covered by the law of Brevis Brevians, or ' short making short '. A long syllable immediately preceded by a short syllable is often scanned as a short provided that the word-accent (or, as some would put it, the ictus) falls on the syllable (1) immediately preceding, or (2) immediately following the longer syllable : the two cases are (1) $\smile$ -, (2) $\smile$ - $\div$ (or (1) $\smile$ -, (2) $\smile$ - $\div$). Those who regard this metrical fact as due to the incidence of the stress-accent on the neighbouring syllable treat Brevis Brevians as one of the ways in which Plautine verse reflects speech ; thus Laidlaw (*Prosody of Terence*, p. 16) speaks of ' the simple reason that in everyday speech the Romans found difficulty in giving full value to a loud (unaccented) syllable succeeding a short (accented) syllable in the same word.* Thus male, bene became male, bene, as they are found in verse generally.' The alternative theory—that the metrical beat can affect the length of the syllable—is called by Lindsay (*E.L.V.* p., 49) ' surely the silliest theory that ever led respectable scholars astray '. Nevertheless the accentual theory is not free from difficulties ; Laidlaw's explanation does not cover case (2), where the accent *follows* the long syllable, e.g. uoluptatem in *Rud.* 459 :

uolupta/t(em) ines/se tan/t(am). ut hanc/traxi/lubens.

where the first foot must be an anapaest ($\smile$ $\smile$ -). In this, as indeed in most examples, accent and ictus coincide ; so that it is possible to uphold either theory. But in *Rud.* 895 :

sed uxor/ sceles/ta m(e) om/nibus/ seruat/ modis

the first foot must be taken as an anapaest ; yet not only is the first syllable of uxor naturally long, but it bears the accent.

Another way in which Plautine scansion is thought by some to mirror everyday speech is Synizesis, the fusing of two vowels into one syllable. Thus in *Poen.* 1142 :

lēn(o), ĕā/mus in/tus. ob/secro/ t(e) Agoras/tocles

the ea of eamus is thought to be fused into one syllable (yā).

---

* This view of Laidlaw, Lindsay, Skutsch and Victor Henry is rejected by Sonnenschein (*Cl. Phil.* vi., 1911, pp. 2, 3).

Embarrassing problems are raised by elision, the elimination from the metrical scheme of final vowels (or vowels followed by -m) before initial vowels (or h-). That this was something more than a metrical convention is suggested by forms like animaduerto (for animum aduerto), magnopere (for magno opere). Yet it is not easy to suppose that final syllables were entirely suppressed (thus making illum amo indistinguishable from illam amo or illa amo) ; and we have Vitruvius' warning (5. 3. 4) that the actor must make his case-endings audible even in the farthest seats. When we find elision in dramatic verse at change of speaker the logical problem becomes acute : are we to suppose that the first speaker did not utter his final syllable because he knew that the other speaker would begin with a vowel ? The opposite to elision is hiatus, including both the non-elision of a final vowel and the shortening of a final long vowel (prosodical hiatus). In drama we find sometimes elision, sometimes hiatus, at change of speaker. Lindsay suggests (*Capt.*, p. 52) that ' with elision the second speaker may be supposed to begin at the moment that the first has finished ' whereas hiatus would imply a pause ; thus in *Merc.* 762–3 :

CO. mihi/ quid(em) her/cle. LY. ita/m(e) ama/bit Iup/piter, uxor, /ut eg(o) il/lud nun/quam dix/(i) DO. etiam negas?

we can understand that the husband would pause a moment before protesting his innocence, while his wife would cut his protestations short. Yet Lindsay himself warns us (*Capt.*, p. 52) that ' there is a danger of being over-fanciful in these matters, and of attributing modern stage-conventions of enunciation to the ancient delivery of quantitative verse with or without musical accompaniment '.

The view that metre reflects actual pronunciation leads to one problem after another. Such a view could only have occurred to speakers of languages like German and English, in which verse is constructed so as to agree with the stress-accent of ordinary speech. This is manifestly not the case with Latin verse. If we believe in both stress-accent and voice-ictus, how do we suppose that words were pronounced where there was clash ? We find the same words placed differently with relation to the beat in different parts of the same line : cf. *Aul.* 415 : tene tene, and *Eun.* 8 :

ex Grae/cis bonis/ Lati/nas fe/cit non/ bonas

(in which bonis is an example of Brevis Brevians). Terence has hinc illae lacrimae at the beginning of a trimeter (*And.* 126) ; Horace (*Ep.* 1. 19. 41) quotes these words at the beginning of a hexameter : hinc illae lacrimae. How did Horace pronounce these words ? Did he sacrifice word-accent to beat, or beat to word-accent ? How did Terence pronounce ' bonas ' in the line just quoted ? Did he stress the first syllable, in accordance with the penultimate law, or the second, in accordance with the metrical beat ? Why are the favourite metres of Latin drama those in which clash is inevitable on the final syllable ?

There is no answer to these questions. An attempt to escape from the dilemma has been sought through phrase-accent. Quintilian tells us (1. 5. 27) that circum litora had only one accent ; the preposition and its noun were treated as a single word, circumlítora. It is supposed that there were many phrases (e.g. uoluptas mea) which were pronounced as single words (uoluptásmea), since in verse the ictus is u͝olup̆tas̄/mĕĕa. But we know little about phrase-accent ; there is no agreement as to what constitutes a phrase, and the only clue to the problem is precisely the metrical beat ; that is, we have to begin by assuming that the beat is an accurate guide to pronunciation in order to find out what the pronunciation was. This is clearly a petitio principii. Worse still, it involves a contradiction. For if the accentuation of words was altered according to their position with regard to other words, then we have to conclude that there was no such thing as a fixed word-accent.

It is not certain that there was even fixed quantity. The Greek division into shorts and longs was conventional and arbitrary ; and Lindsay admits (*Capt.*, p. 21) that many of the syllables of Latin ' as pronounced in ordinary discourse, were not definitely long or definitely short '. He also refers (ib. p. 37) to ' the tendency of every final syllable to be weakly articulated '. (There was also an opposite tendency to treat final syllables, at any rate before a pause, as in some way lengthened by the pause : hence syllaba anceps, a short doing duty as a long in pausa.)

While I do not pretend to have any explanation to offer for the peculiar deviations of dramatic verse from quantitative principles, it seems to me that a marked stress-accent is not consistent with quantitative versification. Lindsay admits (*L.L.* 152, 156) that the stress in Latin, as in modern Romance languages, was much less marked than it is in English and German. When the Greek accent became one of stress, as it seems to have done by about the third century A.D., the versification ceased to be quantitative and became one of syllable-counting, in which accent played an increasing part. French scholars hold that something similar happened in late Latin. The metre of a nation's verse is ultimately based, no doubt, on ordinary speech ; nevertheless all versification is something of a convention. Who would infer from the evidence of French verse alone that many of the ' mute e's ' which form an essential part of the metrical structure have in fact been mute for centuries in ordinary speech ? The metre of dramatic verse is always interesting, because it is a clue to the poet's mind, and perhaps an indication of how he uttered his own lines when ' proving ' them, but we are not entitled to regard it as a direction to the actors, or as a means of finding out how they actually spoke their words on the Roman stage.[1]

THE METRES

Iambic Trimeter : in Greek usage this was a line of three iambic dipodies :

$$\smile \bar{\;} / \breve{\;} \; \bar{\;} // \bar{\;} \; \bar{\;} / \breve{\;} \; \bar{\;} // \bar{\;} \; \bar{\;} / \breve{\;} \; \smile$$

By abandoning the dipodic structure (i.e. by allowing spondees in the second and fourth feet) the Latin dramatists converted this line into what modern scholars prefer to call the *iambic senarius*. (The Romans used the terms trimeter and senarius indifferently.) The further licence of resolving *any* long syllable (except the last) into two shorts gives the following alternatives in any of the first five feet : $\breve{\;} \bar{\;}$, $\bar{\;} \bar{\;}$, $\breve{\;} \breve{\;} \breve{\;}$, $\breve{\;} \breve{\;} \bar{\;}$, $\bar{\;} \breve{\;} \breve{\;}$, $\breve{\;} \breve{\;} \breve{\;} \breve{\;}$ $(= \breve{\;}_{\smile} \;_{\smile\smile})$.

The ictus is conventionally deemed to fall on the compulsory long, or, if that is resolved, on the first of the two shorts which take its place : $\breve{\;} \bar{\;}$, $\bar{\;} \bar{\;}$, $\breve{\;} \breve{\;} \breve{\;}$, $\breve{\;} \breve{\;} \bar{\;}$, $\bar{\;} \breve{\;} \breve{\;}$, $\breve{\;} \breve{\;} \breve{\;} \breve{\;}$. Thus Horace speaks of the 'six beats' (*seni ictus*) of the line (*A.P.* 252–3). When Roman metricians speak of the 'three beats' of the line, they are reckoning one (major) beat to each dipody.

There are 8,200 senarii in Plautus, 3,100 in Terence. The figures for the livelier trochaic septenarius are 8,800 in Plautus, 1,300 in Terence. Thus the senarius is the favourite metre of the reflective Terence, but comes only second with Plautus. It is used in general for matter-of-fact exposition or conversation, but considerable variety can be given to it, e.g. by the use of proceleusmatics to convey excitement :

fŭg(e), ŏp/sēcr(o) hēr/clĕ.   quŏ/ fŭgĭ(am) ?   ĕtĭ/am tŭ/ fŭgĕ.

(*Most.* 513). An important feature is the caesura (division between words *inside* a foot), regular in the third or fourth foot and common in the other feet, except the sixth. Caesura must not be confused with diaeresis, the division between words at the end of a foot. This is common in the middle of the *long* lines (septenarii, etc.), and almost has the effect of dividing each of them into two short lines (indeed, like the end of the line, diaeresis is often accompanied by metrical hiatus, or by syllaba anceps, a short allowed to do duty for a long) ; it is almost unknown in the middle of the senarius. (The caesura is *not* accompanied by metrical hiatus.)

The nearest English equivalent to the senarius is the 'Alexandrine' ; this, however, requires diaeresis to be tolerable :

Ŏf Āl/biŏn's glōr/iŏus īsle//thĕ wōn/dĕrs whīlst/ Ĭ wrītĕ/,

Thĕ sūn/drý vār/yĭng sōils,//thĕ plēas/ŭrĕs īn/fĭnĭte

(Drayton's *Polyolbion*). The English Alexandrine resembles the senarius in being iambic in movement ; the French Alexandrine is *not* iambic (or for that matter anapaestic), as the position of the stressed syllables varies from line to line : it affects the *rhythm*, it is not the principle of the *metre*.

Iambic Septenarius (*Iambic Tetrameter Catalectic*) : the Greek term denotes that this is a line of four iambic dipodies *lacking* the final half-foot. In Latin drama the fourth and seventh feet are usually pure iambi ; in the other feet spondees are allowed :

$$\breve{-}\ \bar{.}/\bar{-}\ \bar{.}/\bar{-}\ \bar{.}/\breve{}\ \bar{.}//\bar{-}\ \bar{.}/\bar{-}\ \bar{.}/\breve{}\ \bar{.}/\bar{-}$$

with the usual freedom of resolution of the longs.

There are about 1,300 examples in Plautus, 400 in Terence. It is essentially a metre of comedy—indeed of farce :

  fāc t(u) hōc/ mŏdŏ./ āt t(u) hōc/ mŏdŏ. / băbae ! / tătae ! /
  păpae ! / pāx !

(*Stichus* 771).

    The English equivalent is familiar, e.g. :

  In ent/erprise/ of mar/tial kind,/ when there/ was an/y fight/ing,
  He led/ his reg/iment from/ behind,/ he found/ it less/ excit/ing.

Iambic Octonarius (*Iambic Tetrameter Acatalectic*) : eight iambic feet or their substitutes (pure iambi in the eighth and usually in the fourth) :

$$\breve{-}\ \bar{.}/\breve{-}\ \bar{.}/\breve{-}\ \bar{.}/\breve{}\ \bar{.}//\bar{-}\ \bar{.}/\bar{-}\ \bar{.}/\breve{-}\ \bar{.}/\breve{}\ \bar{-}$$

There are about 420 examples in Plautus, 870 in Terence : cf. *Pers.* 9 :

  quae ĕrŏ/ plăcĕ/rĕ cĕn/sĕāt// praesēn/t(i) ātqu(e) ăb/sentī/ sŭŏ

(shortening the *quae* by ' prosodic hiatus ' seems preferable to eliding the diphthong before ĕ). Sometimes Plautus has a run of Iambic Octonarii without diaeresis :

  nūmquid/nam tĭbĭ/ mŏlēs/tŭmst, gnā/tĕ mī, ,s(i) haec nūnc/
  mēc(um) āc/cŭbăt ?

(*Asin.* 830).
    In English we may compare

      I quote in elegiacs all // the crimes of Heliogabalus ;
      In conics I can floor peculiarities parabolous.

The first of these lines has diaeresis, the second has not. The first line illustrates another point : shall we scan -ĭŏgáb- as an accentual anapaest (which is a procedure akin to the resolution of a long), or shall we pronounce yogáb-, fusing the vowels i and o (Synizesis) ? Similar problems often arise in scanning Plautus.

Iambic Dimeter (four iambi or their substitutes) : ⏑ ‾/⏑ ‾/⏑ ‾/⏑ ‾

> at un/(um) e prae/tura/ tua,
> Epidi/c(e), abest./ quidnum ?/ scies

(*Epid.* 27–8). Compare

> For duty, duty must be done ;
> The rule applies to everyone.

In *Trochaic* (‾ ⏑) metres a spondee (‾ ‾) is often substituted ; resolution gives the further possibilities ‾ ⏑ ⏑ , ⏑ ⏑ ‾ , ‾ ⏑ ⏑ , ⏑ ⏑ ⏑ ⏑.

The trochaic or ' running ' foot (also called the χορεῖος or ' dance ' foot) gives a rapid, bustling effect.

Trochaic Tetrameter Catalectic (*Trochaic Septenarius*) : seven trochees or their substitutes with an extra syllable : ‾ ⏑/‾ ⏑/‾ ⏑/‾ ⏑// ‾ ⏑/‾ ⏑/‾ ⏑/‾.

The seventh foot is usually a trochee (or tribrach). This old and popular march-measure is Plautus' favourite verse. Coincidence of accent and ictus is marked, cf. :

> ‾   ⏑ ‾ ‾   ‾   ⏑ ‾ ‾   ‾   ‾ ‾ ‾   ⏑ ⏑⏑ ⏑
> uos sce/lesti,/ uos ra/paces,/// uos prae/dones./ perii/mus,

(*Men.* 1015) where at each repetition of *uos* the speaker aims a blow at his antagonists. (Lindsay holds, mainly on the evidence of metre, that periimus was accented on the *first* syllable—cf. *L.L.* 158.)

The remarkable effects obtained by the use of resolved feet may be illustrated by *Curc.* 158 (see pp. 21, 218) :

> ⏑ ⏑ ´   ‾   ⏑ ⏑   ‾   ⏑ ⏑   ⏑ ‾   ⏑ ⏑   ‾
> placid(e) e/greder(e) et/ sonitum/ prohibe // fori(um) et /
>   ⏑ ⏑ ‾   ‾ ⏑ ‾
> strepitum/ cardi/num

Compare with the Roman soldiers' songs (in this metre) lines in English like

> Then the tuckets, then the trumpets, // then the cannon and he comes.

Trochaic Octonarius (*Trochaic Tetrameter Acatalectic*) : eight trochees or their substitutes :

‾ ⏑/‾ ⏑/‾ ⏑/‾ ⏑//‾ ⏑/‾ ⏑/‾ ⏑/‾ ⏑

> ‾ ⏑ ‾   ‾ ‾   ⏑ ⏑ ‾ ‾   ‾ ⏑   ‾ ⏑   ‾ ⏑
> atta/tae, ci/ues, popu/lares,// inco/l(ae), acco/l(ae), adue/n(ae)
>   ‾ ‾
>   omnes

(*Aul.* 406) illustrates the fact that this metre denotes intense excitement ; compare :

> This particularly rapid// unintelligible patter
>
> Isn't generally heard and// if it is it doesn't matter.

Trochaic Dimeter Acatalectic : four trochees or their substitutes :

$$\bar{\;}\,\breve{\;}/\bar{\;}\;\bar{\;}/\bar{\;}\;\bar{\;}/\bar{\;}\;\breve{\;}$$

quīd īam ?/ quĭ(a) ĕrus/ pĕrĕgrīst. / aīn tū ? (*Pers.* 29 a).

But, for all that we can see, it would be possible to regard two trochaic dimeters acatalectic as the equivalent of one tetrameter. There is no such doubt about the *Trochaic Dimeter Catalectic* :

$$\bar{\;}\;\bar{\;}/\bar{\;}\;\breve{\;}//\bar{\;}\;\breve{\;}/\bar{\;}$$

> respice/ uero,// Thespri/(o.)   Oh !
>
> Epidi/cumn(e) ego// conspi/cor ?   (*Epid.* 3, 4).

An English equivalent is

> Every day, as the days roll on,
> Bridesmaids' dress we gaily don.

Lyrical Metres (so-called).   The iambic and trochaic metres which have been described are almost the only metres used by Terence, who, as Lindsay says (*E.L.V.* 287), ' gets his effect by rapid transition from the one to the other metre (mutatis modis cantica) '.   It would therefore seem that, as Duckworth says (*N.R.C.*, p. 369), ' song is practically non-existent in Terence ', as he has ' almost no lyrical metres '.   Duckworth (p. 368) mentions as lyric measures the anapaest, the dactyl, the cretic and the bacchiac. (Lindsay says that bacchiacs are *not* lyrical : *E.L.V.* 293.)   Nevertheless Duckworth refuses (p. 369) to include a passage in anapaestic septenarii as song ' since there is no change of metre '.   The two criteria of ' song ' offered to us are inconsistent with each other.   If the anapaest is indeed a lyric measure, then passages in anapaests are songs whether there is change of metre or not ; but if frequent change of metre is necessary, then no metre can in itself be regarded as lyrical.

I will take first the Anapaestic metre, which is described by Lindsay (*Capt.* 80) as ' the favourite metre of Plautus in his Cantica ' (here by ' Cantica ' Lindsay evidently means song proper).   In Greek drama the anapaest is rather a march-measure, and, like the iambics and trochaics, it is reckoned in dipodies.   In Greek drama it is often regarded by scholars as transitional, something between speech and song ; cf. Haigh, *A.T.* 270.

Anapaestic Dimeter Acatalectic : ˘ ˘ ¯/˘ ˘ ¯//˘ ˘ ¯/˘ ˘ ¯. In Plautus, what with substitution of one long for two shorts, and resolution of a long into two shorts, it is often difficult to find a single pure anapaest in an anapaestic line ; cf. :

¯ ˘ ˘ ¯   ¯ ¯   ¯ ˘ ˘ ¯
hostibu'/ uictis// ciuibus/ saluis

¯ ˘ ˘ ¯   ¯ ¯ ˘ ˘ ¯   ¯
re placi/da pa//cibu' per/fectis

(*Pers.* 753–4.) Final s, as in hostibu', was scarcely pronounced before consonants : Lindsay, *L.L.* p. 103.
In English :

'Is it weakness of intellect, birdie ?' I cried,

'Or a rather tough worm in your little inside ?

Anapaestic Dimeter Catalectic : ˘ ˘ ¯/˘ ˘ ¯//˘ ˘ ¯/¯. In Plautus frequent substitution produces a spondaic effect :

¯ ¯   ¯ ¯   ¯ ¯   ¯
defes/ sus sum/pultan/do.

¯ ¯   ¯ ¯   ¯ ¯   ¯
hoc pos/tremumst./ uae uo/bis.

(*St.* 313–4.) In a less spondaic form the metre was used for sailors' songs :

˘ ˘   ¯   ˘ ˘ ¯   ¯ ¯   ¯
agit(e), O/ pelagi/ curso/res,

¯ ˘ ˘   ¯/   ˘ ˘¯   ¯ ¯ ˘
cupid(am) in/ patriam porta/te.

(tr. inc. 251–2; cf. Serv. *ad Aen.* iii. 192, ¯ ¯ ˘ ˘¯ ˘ ¯ ˘ ˘ ¯ Cretam proauosque petamus). In English we may compare the first two lines of the average Limerick :

There was/ a young la/dy of Ri/ga,

Who went / for a ride / on a ti/ger.

The catalectic dim. often concludes a run of acatalectics ; cf. Accius, *Philocteta* :

¯ ¯   ¯ ¯   ¯ ˘   ˘ ¯   ¯ ¯
fat(o) ex/pendis/se supre/mo.

Anapaestic Tetrameter Catalectic : ˘ ˘ ¯/˘ ˘ ¯/˘ ˘ ¯/˘ ˘ ¯//˘ ˘ ¯/ ˘ ˘ ¯/˘ ˘ ¯/¯ with freedom of substitution and resolution throughout.

¯ ¯   (¯)˘ ¯   ¯ ˘   ˘ ¯ ¯   ¯ ˘   ˘ ¯ ¯   ¯
qui sunt/ qui erunt / quique fu/erunt / quique fu/turi / sunt

¯ ¯   ¯
post/hac

(*Pers.* 777).

This is the well-known ' Aristophanic ' metre, used for nearly all the parabases. In English we may compare :

Then the blank/eting tick/les—you feel / like mixed pick/les—

so terr/ibly sharp / is the prick/ing.

And you're hot/ and you're cross/, and you tumb/le and toss/

till there's noth/ing 'twixt you/ and the tick/ing.

Plautus uses the Anapaestic Tetrameter Acatelectic as well, some-times in the same passage : ˘ ˘ ¯/˘ ˘ ¯/˘ ¯ ˘/˘ ˘ ¯//˘ ˘ ¯/˘ ˘ ¯/ ˘ ˘ ¯/˘ ˘ ¯, again with freedom of substitution and resolution throughout :

i̯ta mĕ/ Toxilus'/ perfabri/ cauit// itaque mĕ/am rem/ diuex/ auit

(*Pers.* 781 ; syllaba anceps before diaeresis).

In English the nearest equivalent in common use is a pair of four-foot anapaestic lines. But Schipper, *Hist. of English Versification*, p. 250) takes as an ' eight-foot iambic anapaestic ' verse

The small/ birds rejoice/ in the green/ leaves return/ing,

The mur/muring stream/let winds clear/ thro' the vale.

(*Bacchiacs* (˘ ¯ ¯) : there are about 400 bacchiac lines in Plautius.
Bacchiac Tetrameter : ˘ ¯ ¯/˘ ¯ ¯/˘ ¯ ¯/˘ ¯ ¯, with occasional substitution of a molossus (¯ ¯ ¯), and with occasional resolution. This metre (regarded by Lindsay, *E.L.V.* 293, as one of *sermo grauis* and therefore *not* a lyrical metre) is sometimes used in dignified passages, e.g. for the words of the priestess, *Rud.* 259 :

qui sunt qu(i) a/ patrona/ preces mea ex/ petessunt ?

but also for the tipsy entry of Pseudolus (*Pseud.* 1246) :

quid hoc ? si/cin(e) hoc fit,/ pedes ? sta/tin an non ?

In English we may perhaps compare :

Old Xeres/ we'll drink—Man/zonilla,/ Montero,

though it is different to reproduce in English a metre which has more than one long to the foot, and the English line just quoted is perhaps more properly scanned ˘ ¯ ¯/˘ ¯ ˘/˘ ¯ ¯/˘ ¯ ˘/.
Curtailed Bacchiac Tetrameter : ˘ ¯ ¯/˘ ¯ ¯ /˘ ¯ ˘ ¯ ¯. This is the most notable variant on the usual Bacchiac Tetrameter : cf. *Cas.* 662 :

insecta/tur omnes/ domi per aedes.

Cretic (¯ ˘ ¯) metres : there are about 400 Cretic lines in Plautus.

Cretic Tetrameter Acatalectic : ¯ ˘ ¯/¯ ˘ ¯/¯ ˘ ¯/¯ ˘ ¯. Occasionally we find a Molossus (¯ ¯ ¯) in the first or third foot (or even in the second if there is no diaeresis).

The Cretic is used to express panic in *Rud.* 664 ff. :

nunc id est/ qu(om) omnium/ copiar(um)/ atqu(e) opum.

In *Curc.* 147 it is used for the serenade :

pessul(i), heus/ pessuli,/ uos salu/to lubens.

Duckworth (*N.R.C.* 371) tries to reproduce the metre in English :

Bolts and bars, bolts and bars, gladly I greetings bring.

But again we notice the difficulty of reproducing two-beat feet in English verse.

Contracted Cretic Tetrameter : ¯ ˘ ¯/¯ ˘ ¯/¯ ˘ ¯ ˘

melius an/n(o) hoc mihi/ non fuit domi.

(*Most.* 690).

The fact that Bacchiacs are often found in conjunction with Cretics (Lindsay, *Capt.*, p. 87) and indeed that the distinction between these two metres sometimes depends on colometry (the division of the words into lines) makes it difficult to understand Lindsay's contrast of Bacchiacs as the ' vehicle of *sermo grauis* ' with Cretics as a ' metre of song '.

Glyconics (¯ ˘ ¯ ˘ ˘ ¯ ˘ ¯) may perhaps be found in *Bacch.* 979 f.

ut scias quae hic scripta sient

nil moror neque scire uolo.

Dochmiacs (˘ ¯ ¯ ˘ ¯) are recognized by Lindsay in *St.* 1–3 a, e.g. :

uiro suo caruit.

Choriambics (¯ ˘ ˘ ¯) : in *Men.* 110 we have a choriambic tetrameter :

ni mala, ni/ stulta sies,/ n(i) indomit(a) im/posqu(e) animi.

For a reproduction of the choriambic rhythm in English, we may take Swinburne's line (*Poems*, ii. 141) :

Love, what/ ailed thee to give/ life that was made/ lovely, we thought,/ with love ?

Dactyls (¯ ˘ ˘) : we find a dactylic tetrameter in Ennius (*Ribb.*, *Tr. R.* 50) :

iamque ma/ri mag/no clas/sis cita.

Dactylic Tetrameter Catalectic : Cas. 937 ff :

$$\text{maxim(o) e/g(o) ardeo/ flagiti/o,}$$

which is like the Christian Hymn to S. Agatha :

$$\text{fortior/ haec truci/busque ui/ris.}$$

Ionic a Maiore (‒ ‒ ˘ ˘) : *Amph.* 188 sqq., with occasional anaclasis
(‒ ˘ ‒ ˘) :

$$\text{noctesque di/esqu(e) assidu/o satis superqu(e) est.}$$

   Colon Reizianum : some of its many forms are ‒ ‒ ˘ ‒ ‒ , ‒ ‒ ˘ ˘ ‒ ‒ ,
˘ ˘ ‒ ˘ ‒ ‒. In *Aul.* 415 sqq. we find iambic dimeters followed by
Cola Reiziana :

$$\text{redi. quo/fugis/ nunc ? tene,/ tene// quid, stolide, clamas ?}$$

Cas. 752 sqq. show Cola Reiziana by themselves :

$$\text{scio : sic/ sin(e) habe/re ;}$$
$$\text{nugas/ agunt ; no/ui.}$$

   Colon Ithyphallicum (‒ ˘ ‒ ˘ ‒ ‒) : this occasionally follows a Cretic
passage, or a Cretic Dimeter may form the first part of the line,
e.g. *Rud.* 253 :

$$\text{sed quid hoc/ obsecr(o) est ? quid ? uiden, amabo ?}$$

APPENDIX N

THE SO-CALLED 'PHLYAX' VASE-PAINTINGS
OF SOUTH ITALY AS EVIDENCE FOR STAGING

A VERY large number of vases (about 159) have been discovered in South Italy, dating from the earliest to the latest years of the fourth century, which contain scenes strongly suggesting a connection with the stage. As Athenaeus tells us that the performers in Italy were known as phlyakes, and as Rhinthon is said to have written phlyax-plays about the beginning of the third century, it is natural to connect the paintings with the literary fragments and to speak of all comic and mock-serious drama and theatrical performance in southern Greece as phlyax, and of the actors, as well as the writers, as phlyakes. The word may be connected with the Greek word *phluarein*, ' to talk nonsense '; another suggestion is that it comes from *phleo* ' swell ', and so denotes the swollen figures of the performers in their padded costumes ; moreover *phleon* is an epithet of Dionysus as a vegetation god. The earliest of these paintings seem to have been made at Tarentum ; later we find them in Paestum and Sicily. They are rare in Campania.

The striking features of the paintings are the costumes and the occasional indications of a stage setting. The costume ' consists of close-fitting tights, intended to simulate nudity, with padding in front and behind, and a large phallos '; over this may be worn garments such as a tunic or cloak, where required . . . With this costume is worn a mask appropriate to the role being performed ; for women, who wear normal dress, the masks are often painted white '. The types of stage depicted have been divided into three classes :

(1) a low platform, sometimes with accessories like a column or a door, and posts supporting the platform, sometimes with draperies hung between them ;

(2) a platform supported by columns, sometimes with draperies between them ;

(3) a more elaborate stage, with taller supports, sometimes approached by a flight of steps. Whether or not a stage is shown, there are sometimes stage props such as doors, windows, porches.

The association with Dionysus is noticeable. The phlyax actor is shown with the god, perhaps also with a maenad. One picture shows Dionysus watching a female acrobat, while two phlyakes look on and two women watch from windows above.

The themes of the pictures are often comic versions of heroic legends ; even the gods are shown in very unfortunate circum-

335

stances. The heroes most frequently depicted are, as might be expected, Heracles and Odysseus. There are also scenes from daily life, feasting, quarrelling, stealing, flogging and so on.

The question is whether these paintings throw any light on the origins of the Roman stage, either in the types of themes chosen for performance, or in the construction of the stage, or in the costume of the actors. Briefly the answer seems to be that at present we know of no connection between these performances and developments at Rome. On the other hand it is certain that the paintings go back to about half a century after the time of Epicharmus and often depict the same themes ; that Rhinthon was already beginning to produce his phlyax-plays at Tarentum while the so-called phlyax-vases were still being produced there, or at least were very familiar objects to every Tarentine citizen ; and that while Rhinthon was active Livius Andronicus was born at Tarentum, from which town he made his way to Rome, there to give Rome her first performance of Greek plays in translation.

The missing link seems to be that between the drama of the great writers and the popular farces which amused the public all over the Greek world. The great theatre at Syracuse, still extant, was built by Damocopus and dedicated about 460 B.C. According to the Life of Aeschylus, Aeschylus retired to the court of Hiero I (478-467 B.C.) when Hiero was founding the city of Aetna, and produced his *Women of Aetna*. Thereafter Athenian tragedy was popular in Syracuse ; Euripides became the favourite, there as elsewhere, and Plutarch records (*Nic.* 29) that many of the Athenian prisoners in Sicily regained their liberty by reciting his verses to their masters—all this before our earliest phlyax vase had been made.

We still can see the remains of the theatres of Taormina and Segesta and we hear of a theatre at Tarentum.

Two points need comment ; which paintings seem to point back to Epicharmus or on to Rhinthon and Roman comedy, and how far the painting reflects or departs from stage usage.

The popularity of Heracles reminds us of his prominence in the plays of Epicharmus. A vase in Leningrad shows Heracles threatening Apollo, who has taken refuge on the roof of his temple, holding his bow and laurel branch. Heracles has mounted on to the sacred tripod, and is holding out in his left hand a basket containing fruit and cake, while less prominently he holds the club in his right hand. Apollo is evidently about to fall from the roof into the basin of holy water. Iolaus stands ready to catch the bow. A vase from Ruvo in Leningrad shows Heracles, accompanied by Iolaus, offering a sacrifice to Zeus, who is perched on a high throne. Heracles eats the food which he should have placed on the altar. We see Heracles in the Camarina vase-painting bringing the captured Kerkopes, little apes in cages, to his taskmaster Eurystheus. Heracles strides in boldly, helping himself along with his club. In the Berlin vase we see him banging with his club on a door ; in the background is his servant, seated on a mule. In the Lentini picture he drags a woman away from an altar in a shrine. In the Centuripe vase he has been led by Hermes to a woman ; but when she raises her veil he drops his club in fright. Most striking of all, in the Madrid vase-painting by Assteas we see the mad Heracles murdering one of his children ; but the style of this seems tragic rather than comic or satyric.

That other popular hero, Odysseus, is presented to Alcinous and Arete, king and queen of the Phaeacians, on a Campanian vase in the Louvre. On an Apulian krater he is seen threatening a woman (?Circe). On a bell-krater in Berlin, painted, it is thought, by Python, Odysseus is seen standing bound to the mast of the ship ; on the rocks near by are seated the Sirens, large birdlike creatures, one holding a lyre and the other a tambourine. The helmsman has wrapped himself in his cloak for safety's sake, while the crew, whose ears have been stopped with wax according to the story, row steadily on. There are dramatic possibilities in this scene, which is reminiscent of Epicharmus, but the picture as we have it does not suggest the stage. As we have seen from the Leningrad bell-krater, even Zeus is not spared. On the Paestan bell-krater in the Vatican he is seen putting a ladder up to a window from which a woman is looking out ; Hermes holds a lamp (see Plate IV). On an Apulian bell-krater an old man climbs up the steps to consult Zeus Ammon, who is seated on the platform, presumably the stage, if this scene is meant to be dramatic. A kalix-krater in London shows the fight between Ares and Hephaestus, while Hera sits in the middle, fettered to her magic chair, a gift sent her in revenge by her son Hephaestus (called Daedalus in the picture). In the end the quarrel will be solved by making Hephaestus drunk and bringing him triumphantly back to heaven. The picture on a Brussels hydria shows the Judgment of Paris ; in the centre sits Paris, dressed in Phrygian costume ; only one goddess appears in the picture. The subject recurs on a Berlin lekythos—and, one may add, in a relief in the Roman theatre of Sabratha, built in the second century A.D.* An Apulian vase in the British Museum shows the sick Cheiron climbing up the steps that lead to the stage ; his pupil Achilles stands modestly in the background. One slave pulls, while the other not only pushes Cheiron, but with him forms a group of centaur-like shape (see Plate I). On a vase in Bari the youthful Helen springs from the egg just as Hephaestus is about to cleave the egg with his axe ; an ugly Leda looks on from a half-opened door. On a Berlin vase we see Pyrrhus preparing to slay the aged Priam, who is seated on an altar and implores mercy. On a vase found in Lucania and painted by Assteas we see Ajax trying to carry off Cassandra from sanctuary and meeting with so fierce a resistance that he is forced to cling to the statue of Athena.

A number of scenes are from daily life. On a Syracusan vase a

---

* *Il teatro di Sabratha,* by Giacomo Caputo, 1959, figs. 79–83.

12

man and a woman play at seesaw. On a krater in Ruvo an old man and a young man struggle with drawn swords for a woman. On a vase painted by Assteas in Berlin we see two thugs trying to drag the prostrate form of an old man from the top of a chest. Two slaves, led by a pipe-player, carry an enormous roast and a pail of wine in a vase-painting in Leningrad. One krater from Capua in the British Museum shows an old man dragging his drunken son home from a party. The traditional theme of food-stealing recurs on a vase from Ruvo ; an old man and a woman are helping themselves to dainties from a large dish, while unknown to them a slave makes off with the best piece. A thief with a wine jar is seized by an old woman in a painting in Berlin from Ruvo. Boxers box in a Campanian hydria (B. 516) ; acrobats tumble, watched by Dionysus and two phlyakes ; above are two windows from which women look down. Slaves carry baskets to altars (B. 528) and tables with cakes (B. 527). A young man apparently hands a baby (or a bundle of clothes) to a woman, while a slave looks on (B. 507). We see a group of three soldiers discussing some matter ; one of them points at a dog (B. 497).

One of the most striking of these pictures (B. 512) shows three figures. One, an old woman, stands on a platform, which is presumably the stage, in front of a door ; a goose and some other property lie on the ground beside her. Below stands a man with his hands tied above his head ; near him stands an overseer with a stick. To drive home the point that this is a stage scene, a young man decently dressed and labelled *tragoidos* is shown in the background, and near him a comic mask. We may imagine that after the farce about the theft of the old woman's property and its detection there will be a tragedy. We see a slave running (B. 526), a slave being flogged (B. 513), an argument about an account (B. 514). On a bell krater by Python in the Vatican three elegant young men, perhaps actors, are playing a game of cottabos after a feast ; masks hang behind ; on one side is a girl pipe-player, on the other a young satyr is serving wine ; Papposilenus, still clutching the double pipes, lies in a drunken sleep.

When we ask ourselves what light these paintings throw on Greek or Roman staging, it is well to remember Trendall's warning (*P.P.* p. 111) : ' It is difficult to estimate the exact extent to which the stage had an influence upon the subjects of vases. As regards comedy there is little doubt, since some of the phlyax vases show the actual stage, but with regard to tragedy it is not easy to tell whether the artist is taking his subject directly from a play or whether he merely has the epic tradition in mind.'

It seems to me that these paintings are good evidence for per-formances on hastily-erected stages, and for the costumes worn by comic actors. But there are difficulties with regard to the dress of the women ; they do not look like men actors disguised. More-over, the artist is never a mere photographer ; he follows his imagination, his artistic sense and his whims.

What we see in these pictures seems often to be not a moment in a stage performance but an artist's impression of a central moment in a story—perhaps in the plot of a play. Thus we see Zeus getting ready to climb up to the window from which a woman looks out. If the woman is a courtesan, why the ladder? But if she is Alkmene, why has a vital part of the story—the god's trick of assuming exact resemblance to her husband—been abandoned? In fact the ladder is not easy to imagine in any play which really was a play ; and it raises problems of staging. The explanation seems to be that the picture is the free work of the artist, who is playing with the traditional story and has given it a decidedly satirical twist which he has *not* derived from the stage. Equally well the birth of Helen does not look like a moment in a performance, but as the artist's way of giving a satirical version of the story itself, even if he has a performance in his memory. The baby which the mad Heracles is about to throw on the fire is exactly the sort of touch which the artist can display and which the dramatist must convey by report.

The phlyax vases belong to a definite period, the fourth century. Aristoxenos, writing in Tarentum in the last quarter of that century (apud Athen. xiv. 632 : Trendall, *op. cit.* 105), deplores the fact that local theatrical production had become barbarised. We cannot explain what was in his mind ; but at any rate, as the phlyax-vases cease to be available, a new form of drama arises in Tarentum, the literary phlyax-play composed by such writers as Rhinthon of Tarentum (see p. 336).

APPENDIX O

THE MEANING OF XOPOϒ

(*Hermathena*, Vol. lxxxiv, 1954, 93–103)

THE DOUBTS expressed by me as to the validity of the Five-Act Law (*Hermathena* lxvii, 55; lxxii, 44 f.) have been briefly answered by Professor T. B. L. Webster (*Studies in Menander*, p. 181). He says : ' The *Epitrepontes* had, as we have seen, five acts, and at the three act ends where the text survives, the act break is marked by the word " (song) of the chorus ", an empty stage, and the need for a lapse of time '. But his detailed discussion of this play (ib. pp. 34–40) has made none of these points clear. The Five-Act Law is indeed assumed by him to hold good for Menander ; and any assumption which seems to be justified by results deserves respect ; but his second act begins with a lacuna (p. 37, ' the beginning of the second act is also lost ') ; the end of his second act is not mentioned in these pages ; at the end of his third act the text is defective, and there is a lacuna at the beginning of his fourth act ; finally ' the fragmentary concluding lines of the fourth act (640 f.) do not show what happens to the speakers ' (p. 39). The only tangible evidence for his theory is the three actual or alleged occurrences of XOPOϒ. To speak more precisely, the word XOPOϒ is once written in full ; in another place the letter . . P . . alone survives, and in the third place there is a *spatium uacuum*.

He goes on : ' an empty stage may mark a scene change rather than an act change . . . but the need for a lapse of time (e.g. to allow a character to get to the *agora* and back) is a sure guide at least to the limits within which an act must have ended in the Greek original. On these principles the act division can be restored in the *Perikeiromene* and *Samia* . . . the five-act structure can be restored without any difficulty and it seems likely that this was the normal form of Menander's plays . . . In the *Epitrepontes* the act ends are marked by a note for a choral song . . . The chorus presumably sings the choral interludes, but is not present during the action. In the last preserved play of Aristophanes, the *Plutus*, the chorus enter with a long dialogue with Karion (257–321), at the end of which the note XOPOϒ stands ; the note recurs at 626, 801, 958, 1097, and at 771 in the form KOMMATION XOPOϒ. The chorus also intervene three times in the dialogue and speak the closing lines of the play (328, 487, 631 f., 1208). Although the more elaborate forms of choral utterances known from the earlier plays of Aristophanes have gone, the play is still a string of shortish scenes separated by songs of the chorus and the chorus are present during the whole of the action after their entrance. The essential break between the late Aristophanic form and the Menander form comes where the chorus are no longer present during the action or, at least, take part in the dialogue '.

The question which I wish to discuss is the meaning to be attached to ΧΟΡΟΥ when it occurs in the manuscripts of Aristophanes' last surviving plays and in the fragments of later Greek drama. According to Pickard-Cambridge (*Dramatic Festivals*, p. 240) after the end of the fifth century ' in many plays the chorus simply sing interludes to break up the dialogue into scenes. This is so, for example, in Aristophanes' *Plutus*, and no words are provided by the poet for such interludes '. He holds (*Theatre of Dionysus*, pp. 160-7) that ' as regards the latest plays of Aristophanes himself, there is no reason why ΧΟΡΟΥ, which in the text takes the place of written choral odes, should not refer to such ἐμβόλιμα as Aristotle* mentions as occurring in tragedy, and the direction κομμάτιον χοροῦ, at *Plutus* 771, can hardly refer to a mere dance '. What Aristotle says is that the chorus should take part in the action like one of the actors, as in Sophocles, not as in Euripides ; in the other (tragic) dramatists the odes have no more to do with the plot than with that of some other tragedy ; ' accordingly they sing ἐμβόλιμα, a practice introduced by Agathon '. Fragments of a play, perhaps of the fourth century, dealing with the story of Oineus, include portions of two scenes separated by ΧΟΡΟΥ M . . ., which may perhaps be restored as χοροῦ μέλος, ' a song of the chorus '. In a number of fragments of Middle and New Comedy ' a speaker sees a κῶμος approaching which (in most of these fragments) he regards with some apprehension ' (ib. p. 164). These are Antiphanes, *Dodonis*, fr. 91K ; Alexis, *Kouris*, fr. 107 ; Menander, *Epitrepontes*, fr. incerti loci :

> ἴωμεν· ὡς καὶ μειρακυλλίων ὄχλος
> εἰς τὸν τόπον τις ἔρχεθ' ὑποβεβρεγμένων,
> οἷς μὴ 'νοχλεῖν εὔκαιρον εἶναί μοι δοκεῖ.

Under this passage Pickard-Cambridge puts χορου (strictly it should be . . P . .) and adds in a footnote that ' Körte doubts whether ' the passage ' belongs to this play '. His fourth example is Menander, *Perikeiromene*, ll. 141-6 in Allinson's edition :

> ΔΑΟΣ. παῖδες, μεθύοντα μειράκια προσέρχεται,
> πάμπολλ'. ἐπαινῶ διαφόρως κεκτημένην·
> εἴσω πρὸς ὑμᾶς εἰσάγει τὴν μείρακα·
> τοῦτ' ἔστι μήτηρ· ὁ τρόφιμος ζητητέος.
> ἥκειν γὰρ αὐτὸν τὴν ταχίστην ἐνθάδε
> εὔκαιρον εἶναι φαίνεθ', ὡς ἐμοὶ δοκεῖ.
> ΧΟΡΟΥ

' The fact that in the last two passages the revellers clearly form the chorus of the play makes it practically certain that they do so in

* *Poet.* xviii, 1456 a 25-30.

the two other (closely parallel) passages, and that we have in all a stock scene in which the actors make themselves scarce at the approach of a riotous band, and their alarm would scarcely seem so natural if they were already elevated above the revellers on a high stage. The argument is not indeed conclusive. If, as is probable, a regular division into Acts was already observed in Menander's time, and the only function of the chorus was to bring an Act to an end by its appearance, the actor might well sight the chorus at a distance from a high stage without arousing any strong sense of improbability '.

One problem is the meaning of ἐμβόλιμα. Pickard-Cambridge (*O.C.D.*, s.v. Agathon) says that his innovation was to make ' choral odes, for the first time, mere interludes . . . without reference to the plot '. This definition seems to be in harmony with what Aristotle has said about Sophocles and Euripides. But a new meaning was given by Flickinger's identification of ἐμβόλιμα with the use of the notation XOPOΥ (*C.P.* vii (1912), pp. 24–34), based on the statement in the *Vita Aristophanis** that when the supply of choruses had ceased Aristophanes wrote XOPOΥ in the *Plutus* in order to give the actors a rest and allow them to change their masks ' as we see the writers of New Comedy doing in imitation of Aristophanes '. ' As a result nearly everyone to-day accepts the view that the innovation which Agathon introduced was not merely stasima so loosely connected with the plot that they could have been moved from one play to another without difficulty— something that had already been done by Euripides and others— but that at least sometimes he wrote nothing at all for the chorus except XOPOΥ as an indication to the director to introduce a dance, a popular air of the day . . . or whatever else suited his fancy '.† Flickinger says ' It is significant that Aristophanes' use of embolima is still embryonic, has not yet been carried to the logical issue found in New Comedy. That is to say, the chorus of these two plays still figures in the action and converses with the actors. In the *Women in Council* it even has, in addition to embolima, several choral songs, the words of which are preserved '.

The MS. evidence for XOPOΥ is :

Ecclesiazusae : R (the Ravenna) shows it after 729 and 876 ; the other MSS., according to Rogers, do not.

Plutus : R has KOMMATION XOPOΥ after 770 ; a second hand (R²) has XOPOΥ after 801. V (the Venetian) has XOPOΥ in the margin at 321, 627 and 802, KOMMATION XOPOΥ between 769 and 770 ; the Byzantine scholia refer to XOPOΥ at 252–3, 626–7, 770–1 (KOMMATION XOPOΥ), 801–2, 958–9, and 1096–7‡. A, U and M do not mark XOPOΥ.

---

* πάλιν δὲ ἐκλελοιπότος καὶ τοῦ χορηγεῖν τὸν Πλοῦτον γράψας, εἰς τὸ διαναπαύεσθαι τὰ σκηνικὰ πρόσωπα καὶ μετεσκευάσθαι ἐπιγράφει Χοροῦ, φθεγγόμενος (v.l. φθεγγομένου) ἐν ἐκείνοις ἃ καὶ ὁρῶμεν τοὺς νέους οὕτως ἐπιγράφοντας ζήλῳ Ἀριστοφάνους.

† Weissinger, ' Act Divisions in Classical Drama ' (*Iowa Studies* ix), p. 49.

‡ E. W. Handley, ' XOPOΥ in the Plutus,' *C.Q.*, N.S. iii, pp. 56 61.

At line 729 of the *Ecclesiazusae* Chremes, alone on the stage, says that he will fetch his household goods ; at 730 he is bringing them out of his house (which is on the stage). At 876 the Citizen, alone on the stage, decides to leave for the public banquet ; in the next line a hag comes out of one of the houses on the stage. By analogy, as Rogers says, we should expect another XOPOΥ at 1111–2, separating the scene of the hags from the return of Praxagora's maid ; but it does not occur in the MSS.

At *Plutus* 252 the stage is empty, but the chorus of rustics has not yet arrived. At 253 Cario enters with the chorus. At 321, after an interchange of song between Cario and the chorus, he bids them quit jesting and turn to another ' shape '; he goes indoors, and Chremylus comes out to welcome the rustics. After 626 a night elapses, during which Plutus is cured of his blindness ; the stage is empty, except that (presumably) the chorus* do not withdraw. At 770 Cario goes off, leaving the stage empty, to meet the (approaching) god, who appears in the next line. At 801 Plutus and the other actors go indoors, leaving the stage empty ; at 802 Cario comes out to report the wonders that the god has wrought in the house. At 958 and 1096 the actors go indoors : in the next line new characters appear. At 1170 the stage is again left empty ; but here there is no evidence in the MSS. or the scholia for XOPOΥ though some editors insert it.

On the meaning of XOPOΥ there are two modern views :

(1) that Aristophanes composed a song which some later producer or editor suppressed, writing XOPOΥ to indicate that he had suppressed it. Thus Rogers ad *Eccl.* 729, 876 : ' the Chorus sing an ode which is now lost '; the two successive scenes were ' formerly separated . . . by a choral ode '. M. Platnauer (*New Chapters in Greek Literature,* Third Series, p. 167, note 3) : ' there was a time when choric lyrics were still written and sung, though they were omitted in reading editions, their place being marked by the word χοροῦ: cf. Schol. Ar. *Nub.* 889 '; and we have evidence (ib. p. 158) that in the second century A.D. a scribe in Egypt was hired to copy out the *Plutus.* We can understand that the *Ecclesiazusae* and the *Plutus,* because of their general themes, would interest a reading public ; and that a reading public might find choral songs difficult or boring.

(2) that Aristophanes did not compose a song, but instead wrote XOPOΥ in his manuscript to indicate that the chorus were here to give a performance which would not require words, or at any rate would not require words supplied by him. It is not easy to see why he should do this ; elsewhere in the play he has given the chorus words to utter.

But the *Vita Aristophanis* (quoted above) gives a third view : ' when the supply of choruses had ceased Aristophanes marked XOPOΥ on the MS. of the *Plutus* in order to give the actors a rest and to allow them to change their masks '. This means that there

---

* I assume that there was not yet a *raised* stage in the Athenian theatre.

was no chorus present, and that Aristophanes wrote ΧΟΡΟΥ as a modern playwright might write 'interval'. This view is doubly absurd ; there *is* a chorus in the *Plutus,* and even if there were not, Aristophanes is not likely to have written '(performance) of the chorus' when he knew that no chorus was present to give such a performance.

Yet we have other evidence that scholiasts sometimes thought of ΧΟΡΟΥ as unrelated to an actual chorus : schol. in *Plutum,* Paris, B.N., Coisl. 192, ad 253 : νοεῖται ἔξωθεν τόπος, ἵν᾽ ᾖ τόπος χοροῦ. ἐν γὰρ τῇ νέᾳ κωμῳδίᾳ οἱ χοροὶ ἤγουν αἱ παραβάσεις ἐπαύσαντο. ἔνθα οὖν βούλεται ὁ ποιητὴς διατρῖψαι μικρόν, τίθησι τὸ χοροῦ ἔννοιαν διδοὺς ἡμῖν ἀναμένειν βραχύ, ὡς καὶ ἐν Βατράχοις τὸ αὐλεῖ τις ἔνδον καὶ τὸ διαύλιον προσαυλεῖ, translated by Handley (l.c., p. 57) "τόπος is understood, to make τόπος χοροῦ. For in New Comedy the choruses, or rather the parabases, ceased. So where the poet wishes to pass away a short time, he puts ΧΟΡΟΥ, meaning that we should wait a little, just as, in the *Frogs,* he puts αὐλεῖ τις ἔνδον and διαύλιον προσαυλεῖ."

Similarly while the schol. ad *Plutum* 619 reads . . . ἐπὶ τῷ τέλει παράγραφος (i.e. ad 626) καὶ ἑξῆς τὸ χοροῦ κἀνταῦθα γὰρ χορὸν ὤφειλε θεῖναι καὶ διατρῖψαι μικρὸν ἄχρις ἄν τις ἐξ Ἀσκληπιοῦ ἀναστρέψειε τὴν τοῦ Πλούτου ἀπαγγέλλων ἀνάβλεψιν, at 627 we find the comment ἐπὶ τῷ τέλει παράγραφος. σημειώσαι ἐνταῦθα ὅτι δέον χορὸν διὰ μέσου θεῖναι μέχρις ἂν ἐκεῖνοι ἐξ Ἀσκληπιοῦ ἐλθόντες ἀναβλέψαιεν τὸν Πλοῦτον, ὁ δὲ παραχρῆμα τὸν Καρίωνα εἰσφέρει εὐαγγελίζοντα τοῖς γέρουσι περὶ τῆς τοῦ Πλούτου ἀναβλέψεως. ἐποίησε δὲ τοῦτο οὐκ ἀλόγως ἀλλὰ τῇ τε τῆς νέας κωμῳδίας συνηθείᾳ, ἐν ᾗ αἱ παραβάσεις ἐπαύσαντο, ὡς προείρηται, καὶ ἅμα δεῖξαι βουλόμενος ὡς ἄρα τάχιστα πάνυ ὁ Πλοῦτος ἀνέβλεψεν.

It is evident that the writers of the *Vita Aristophanis* and of these scholia were struck by the resemblance between the later plays of Aristophanes and New Comedy in the occurrence of ΧΟΡΟΥ and in the absence of the parabasis. From the absence of the parabasis they seem to have inferred the absence of the chorus ; it followed that ΧΟΡΟΥ had nothing to do with a chorus, but simply indicated that for some reason, whether aesthetic or practical, a 'pause' was to be assumed. Such a view was natural enough when the plays were no longer to be seen on the stage ; and though the author of the *Vita* refers to practical stage matters such as the need for the actors to rest and to change their masks, he has not thought of the problem in a realistic way ; the mere writing of ΧΟΡΟΥ in the manuscript could not provide for the changing of masks or for anything else.

It has been seen that our manuscripts differ widely as to the indication or otherwise of ΧΟΡΟΥ. Omission and interpolation are both conceivable explanations of such differences. As has been said, the Byzantine scholia include a ΧΟΡΟΥ at *Plut.* 252–3. Here, as Handley remarks (p. 59), 'there can be no question of a choral performance . . . the absurdity would be involved that the chorus must perform in order to give Carion time to meet it off stage, and then enter with him from the country '. Apparently XOPOϒ was here inserted by some reader who noticed that the stage was momentarily empty. V gives XOPOϒ at the end of the lyrical dialogue between Cario and the chorus. It is a rather forced interpretation of Cario's final remarks to see in them an exhortation to the chorus to sing an ode (316–21) :

> ἀλλ' εἶα νῦν τῶν σκωμμάτων ἀπαλλαγέντες ἤδη
> ὑμεῖς ἐπ' ἄλλ' εἶδος τρέπεσθ',
> ἐγὼ δ' ἰὼν ἤδη λάθρᾳ
> βουλήσομαι τοῦ δεσπότου
> λαβών τιν' ἄρτον καὶ κρέας
> μασώμενος τὸ λοιπὸν οὕτω τῷ κόπῳ ξυνεῖναι.

Some argue that ἄλλ' εἶδος means ' another kind (of song) '; others understand (ὀρχήσεως), a dance without words, and suppose that κόπος refers to ' the work involved in it '.* I agree with von Holzinger (quoted by Handley) that a song at 321 ' nicht nur überflüssig wäre, sondern geradezu störend wirken dürfte '. But his interpretation of κόπος as the ' work ' involved in dancing is against the text ; Cario, who promises to join in ' the work ', will not return to the stage until line 627. Here Rogers and the scholiast ad loc. give a much more plausible explanation : ' he has been speaking of them as metamorphosed, by means of his Circe-enchantments, into swine ; but now they are to take another shape, and become, I suppose, their natural selves ' (Rogers). τῷ κόπῳ : τῇ περὶ τὸν Πλοῦτον ἐπιμελείᾳ (sch.). Indeed the arguments of those who take XOPOϒ here as ' song ' and those who take it as ' dance '· may be left to destroy each other ; and the other favourite argument for XOPOϒ, the need for a pause, is inapplicable. Once more, as in 252–3, we have a moment when all the actors are absent, and some reader who noticed this may have inserted XOPOϒ.

The most strongly supported example of XOPOϒ in the *Plutus* is at line 770 ; but here, as the text shows, the absence of the actors need not be more than momentary ; Plutus' approach has been announced at line 749, and he may be supposed to enter immediately after Cario has run off to meet him. A whole night is supposed to elapse at 626–7 ; but here the scholiast ad loc. expressly says that Aristophanes avoids inserting a choral song ' in order to indicate the quickness of the cure '.

I do not feel certain that any of the examples of XOPOϒ in Aristophanes' plays can be traced to the poet himself ; but if they can, the supposition that he wrote a song which was subsequently suppressed out of indulgence for a reading public seems to be more likely than that he merely wrote a stage-direction, ' let the chorus perform '. Why should Aristophanes, of all men, be supposed unwilling or unable to write a brief passage of lyric when he had

* See Handley, pp. 59–60.

12*

himself provided the opportunity for it? (The stage-direction in the *Birds*, ad vers. 222, ' a note of the flute ', is quite another matter ; only by such a direction could the need for instrumental music be indicated ; moreover it is supported by the dialogue, cf. *Frogs* 313). When we are comparing (as readers did in the Byzantine period and even earlier) the use of XOPOY in Aristophanes and in New Comedy, a fundamental point to remember is that a chorus *was* present in Aristophanes' plays, and that he wrote words for it. Even in the *Plutus* he takes the trouble to compose a quite elaborate song for the chorus and Cario (290–321) ; for that this is a ' song ' (so far as this word can be used of anything in ancient drama) and not, as Webster says, ' a long dialogue ' (the dialogue ended at 289) is surely clear from the text : βούλομαι χορεῦσαι, line 288 ; θρεττανελὸ τὸν Κύκλωπα lines 290, 296 ; μέλη line 294 ; the refrains, the swing of the rhythm, and the changes of metre. All this, if found in Plautus, would undoubtedly be hailed as indicating a ' song '.

To the last, then, we find Aristophanes writing songs for his chorus. In view of this, remarks such as that the supply of choruses had ceased when he wrote the *Plutus,* or that, having secured a chorus which could sing as well as dance, he should leave others to decide what the chorus should sing or do, seem to need qualification. New Comedy is another matter*.

---

* See also *C.Q.* 5, pp. 49–52 ' XOPOY in the *Plutus*: a reply to Mr. Handley.'

APPENDIX P

PLAUTUS, TERENCE AND SENECA :
A COMPARISON OF AIMS AND METHODS

(From a paper read to the Seventh Congress of the Association,
Guillaume Budé, 1963).

WHAT criteria have we by which to measure the complete Latin
plays of the three dramatists which have come down to us? I
suggest that we ask three questions : first, what was the aim of
each of them? ; second, was this aim a good one? ; third, how far
was it achieved?

Everyone admits that Plautus was a man of the theatre. Everyone admits that Terence, though a practising dramatist, had something more in his mind than the mere entertainment of the multitude. Everyone admits that the Senecan tragedies are pieces of
rhetorical character intended to startle and dazzle the public. The
three dramatists differ markedly from one another in style.

Mr. Peter Arnott says : ' Plautus is no great literary figure . . .
he loses most through being read rather than seen '. Is it true that
Plautus is so dull to read? St. Jerome, after a night of weeping over
his sins, used to console himself by reading Plautus—but God
forbid that St. Jerome should be suspected of wanting to see the
plays performed.

The best performance of Plautus I have seen was that of the
Mostellaria in Italian by an Italian company—I think from the
University of Turin—at the Delphiad in Bristol. Careful rehearsal,
graceful, studied movement, almost developed into a dance, split-
second timing—all gave the performance a sophisticated quality.

I suppose one could claim that Plautus was 100 per cent. a
theatre man. Perhaps one would go on to claim that Terence,
who undoubtedly wrote for public performance but undoubtedly
had more in mind than mere stage success—that Terence was,
shall we say, only 50 per cent. a man of the theatre. And as for
Seneca, it is not certain, it is very much disputed, whether he
wrote for the theatre at all ; so that on the same line of reasoning
he might come out with a theatre sense approximating to zero.

I partly believe all this. But I do not think that it is the whole
of the truth. Contrary to Peter Arnott, I think that Plautus was a
considerable poet, who had a mastery of the Latin language and of
rhythm. I think that Terence longed for popular success, that he
had very definite theories as to how to achieve popular success,
and that to a large extent he *did* succeed on the public stage, not
only of his own day, but even of centuries later. As for Seneca, I
will maintain that whatever his aim in writing his plays, there are
scenes in them which are really dramatic, and that in certain ways
he comes nearer than the Greeks to our notion of the theatrical.

347

Plautus, the successful dramatist, I picture as a working dramatist wholly engaged in preparing Greek plays for the Roman stage. He knew men and he knew women. He knew the Roman streets, the forum, the shops ; he knew the rich quarters and the poor, the temples, the taverns, the Tiber and its bridge, the roads leading out of Rome. He probably did his own shopping ; he had a wide command of language when it came to consumer goods ; he had a great variety of meats in his mind—I think he was specially fond of bacon ; and it stands to reason that he was not a tee-totaller. He knew all the terms of fashion ; he had an astonishing vocabulary for women's dresses. He kept his eyes and ears open as he walked along the streets or listened to the orators in the Forum. He took stock of the Greek philosophers stalking along as gravely as a Scot on Sunday, not above slaking their thirst at a thermipolium, then going their way solemn-faced and half-seas over : ' tristes ebriolique incedunt '. He could deal with cheeky slaves, swaggering soldiers, street bullies, street-walkers. If you asked him his politics he might reply with a wink that he supported the ' boni viri '. A man with few illusions but with wide interests, he loved to note the racy dialogue of the streets, the ranting of the orators, the solemn rites of the public festivals ; and he could be thrilled to his finger-tips by rhythmic utterance and movement and by music.

In the theatre all his talents found their scope. Doubtless the physical equipment was meagre compared to ours ; but if we grant that in the Roman theatre players learn their parts, wear their costumes and move about, we have come a long way towards the fulness of dramatic production. If we add that the Roman theatre had a physical background, however slight, with three real double-doors, two side-entrances, and a practicable roof, then we have the essential—and all that we moderns have added to this is but frills.

In itself a Roman stage door is simply two panels of wood, turning rather noisily in their pivots. But the simplest physical things can assume importance when worked into the plot and the emotions of drama. Think of the opening scene of the *Curculio*, where the old hag who guards the heroine is tempted to the door by the fragrance of the wine poured by the lover on the threshhold—or a little later, when she softly ushers out the heroine :

placide egredere et sonitum cohibe forium et strepitum cardinum,
ne quod hic agimus erus percipiat fieri, mea Planesium.

Think of the knocking on the door in the *Rudens*. The girl, speaking in iambic rhythm, knocks somewhat uncertainly at the strange door :

heus ecquis in uillast? ecquis hoc recludit? ecquis prodit?

Whereupon the door bursts open, and framed in the doorway is the boorish Sceparnio snarling in trochaic rhythm :

quis est qui nostris tam proterue foribus facit iniuriam?

These are some of the effects obtainable in comedy. Need I remind you of the scene in tragedy where we hear knocking on a door?

In his stage with its limited equipment, its background and altar, and the occasional use of portable properties, chairs and tables, dishes, writing-materials, a fishing-net and the like— Plautus has his instrument, and he can play on it as a virtuoso on an old fiddle. As for his aims as a writer, and the way in which he treated his Greek texts, I think first of the prologue to the *Asinaria* :

> *inest lepos ludusque in hac comoedia;*
> *ridicula res est.*

No one doubts his power to make us laugh. But there is also the remark in the *Bacchides* about another play of his : ' even in the case of the *Epidicus*, a play which I am as fond of as I am of myself, there is no play which I see with less pleasure if Pellio is taking part '. Finally there are the prologue and epilogue to the *Captivi*, in which he praises the play for its good moral tone, and says that poets like himself find few plays of this type, showing good men becoming better.

The language, the jokes, the topical hits, the pungent dialogue, the abuse and the endearments, all poured effortlessly from his pen. The result is, I believe, something which is different from all the Greek originals which the sands of Egypt have ever disclosed, or will disclose to our successors.

* * * * *

We are told that Terence was a young man and a foreigner. A young man, perhaps of swarthy skin, befriended by the great, he has brooded long over this curious new industry which has grown up, the turning of Greek plays into Latin for the entertainment of the Roman public. There are no established rules governing Roman translators ; there is nothing corresponding to the French Academy ; but certain tendencies are becoming manifest. Terence, watching from the wings, has discerned the weakness in the productions of the Latin Muse. He has made up his mind to beat these *barbari* at their own game. He may pretend to admire the popular favourites, Naevius, Plautus and Ennius ; in fact he despises what he calls their *neglegentia*. But there is more behind. He intends to improve not only on the Roman adaptors but also on the Greek originals.

This is the central point, the vital secret in Terence's work. He says that his aim was to write plays which would please the people ; but he says elsewhere that he aims to give the people plays ' free from fault ', *sine uitiis*.

We have evidence that Terence did depart from the text of his Greek models. His wholesale dropping of the explanatory prologue —a Greek legacy, still found in Menander—is itself a criticism of this traditional expedient. The turning of the opening monologue of Menander's *Andria* into a dialogue of the father with a client (whom Terence has invented for the occasion, according to Donatus), the turning of the monologue of the excited young rascal Chaerea in the *Eunuchus* into a dialogue with a friend (whom, again according to Donatus, Terence has inserted for the occasion)— these are clear departures from the Greek. Why did he introduce them unless he thought that they were improvements? But the Roman audience would not have understood him, had he told them that he was improving on the Greek. They had come to hear a play of Menander or Diphilus or Philemon or some other Greek. The fact that a play by Plautus, or even by Caecilius, was verbally quite different from the Greek would not bother them— verbal changes were part of the job of translation. It was the changes in structure—e.g. the addition of a second lover—in the *Andria* which caught the jealous eye of the old rival playwright Luscius Lanuvinus and led to his denunciation of Terence for ' playing about ' with his originals.

If keeping close to an original was all that was asked of a Roman dramatist, success would not have been difficult to achieve. But mere fidelity was not what was really wanted, nor would it have guaranteed success. What the Romans enjoyed was a play in their own idiom.

It must not be thought that Terence was indifferent to stage success. The friendship of the great has its value. But it is a poor substitute for the dramatist's real reward, the applause of the multitude. The repeated failure of the *Hecyra* and the querulous tone of some of Terence's remarks about the public in his prologues—populus studio stupidus and the like—must not obscure the fact that Terence was a master of stage technique. But his mastery is of a different order from that of Plautus.

Now it is always possible that the difference was largely the result of choice of originals. Plautus liked one sort of Greek play, Terence another. We have learned a good deal from the discovery of the *Dyscolus*. Perhaps other plays will turn up all complete, and perhaps it will then be seen that what Terence did was simply to look for originals that had those dramatic qualities which he admired. What these qualities were is, I think, clear : intelligent intrigue and contrast of character.

Intelligent intrigue and contrast of character are scarcely to be found in Plautus. Plautus gives us farce—a succession of fireworks ; as one fades another lights up the sky. Terence gives us comedy. The difference between the *Menaechmi* and the *Adelphi* is the difference between farce and comedy.

To see Terence's mind at work, we may turn to his first play, the *Andria*. Right through the play runs a closely-knit plot. Pamphilus has formed a secret union with the poor girl Glycerium. His father Simo intends that he shall marry Philaenium, daughter of their wealthy neighbour Chremes. Davus, the slave of Pamphilus, intends to spoil this plan of Simo. But Davus has so over-reached himself that neither of the old gentlemen is likely to put any trust in anything he says. Glycerium has just given birth to a child— Pamphilus' child. This fact, if known to Chremes, would put an end to the preparations for his daughter's marriage to Pamphilus. But no statement by Davus would carry conviction. What does he do? Mysis, the woman-servant of Glycerium, is on the stage ; Davus brings out Glycerium's baby and tells Mysis to lay it on Simo's threshhold. Chremes is seen approaching ; Davus dashes off, leaving the bewildered Mysis alone to confront the astonished Chremes ; then Davus returns and accuses Mysis of trying to palm off some stranger's baby as that of Pamphilus. Mysis hotly denies this ; Chremes, listening, discerns in her voice the ring of truth. Horrified, he rushes into Simo's house to announce that he will not consent to give his daughter to a young man who has just had a child by another woman. Mysis, left alone with Davus, bitterly reproaches him for the way in which he has treated her. He replies : ' you silly woman, don't you see what I've been at? ' She asks : ' how should I know? ' He says ' that was the father-in-law to be ; it was the only way to let him into what we want him to know '. ' But ' she expostulates ' you should have told me beforehand '. He answers : ' do you think it makes so little difference whether one says a thing honestly and naturally or after preparation?'

Do not these words, and the whole scene, show a sense of acting as an art? I know no parallel in Plautus, or in Greek drama, to this scene. All the evidence points to one conclusion : Terence was an artist in comedy.

*   *   *   *   *

In turning to Seneca, I ring up the curtain on a different scene. We are in imperial Rome, the luxurious, treacherous atmosphere of Nero's court. On this gloomy stage Seneca appears—the great statesman, author and philosopher.

A cleavage of opinion separates the scholars of England and America from most European scholars with regard to the purpose for which Seneca's tragedies were written. We Anglo-Saxons believe that the plays were written for declamation, not for performance in the theatre. Moreover we think little of them as plays. Here is Mr. Barker, in the *Oxford Classical Dictionary* : ' In the tragedies we meet no product or promise of a balanced artist-mind, but the primitive thought-forms, rough-hewn idols, and nightmares risen out of a tortured egoist's unconscious mind. Everywhere are traceable the erratic ability and the limitations which are common stigmata of paranoiac abnormality '. This of the dramatist whom a European scholar has called the greatest writer of tragedy in the gulf of time between the death of Euripides and the birth of Shakespeare! Thus the Anglo-Saxons of today tend to depart not only from Europe but even from our ancestors and fellow-countrymen of the Elizabethan Age. For there can be no doubt that Shakespeare and his contemporaries read, admired and imitated Seneca. Moreover the plays of Seneca were acted at the University in sixteenth-century England.

On this vexed point, the purpose for which the plays were written, I have come to a fairly definite conclusion.

We know that Greek tragedy, written for performance, was forced to take into account the practical necessities of the stage. We know that in the Roman Empire plays were often written for declamation (witness Juvenal, Satire One, lines three to six). We have no certain information of any play being written under the Empire for performance. Now there are numerous scenes in Seneca's plays which would be difficult to present on the stage.

In Seneca's Hippolytus the hero's mangled corpse is brought on to the stage (or so it appears) and is pieced together under the spectators' eyes by his father Theseus :

> Be firm, my hands, for your sad purpose now ;
> Be dry, my eyes, and check the tears that flow
> While I the parts assemble, and employ
> My efforts to reconstitute my boy.
> What is this ugly, shapeless piece, I wonder,
> On every side with gashes torn asunder?
> What part of thee it is I cannot see ;
> I only know that part it is of thee.
> Here will I set it . . . not its proper home . . .
> Not . . . the right place . . . I know . . but . where there's room.

In the *Hercules Furens* the hero murders his wife and children before our eyes ; we see his club crashing through their skulls. In the *Medea* the heroine murders her children in full view of the spectators and throws the body of one down from the roof to his father below on the stage. Perhaps dummies could have been used in these scenes ; but this expedient, if used, would itself have been an innovation. What of the scene in the *Medea* where, after a speech has been attributed to Medea, another character asks her why she has been standing in gloomy silence?

At line 592 of the *Hercules Furens* Hercules and Theseus enter, dragging with them the monstrous three-headed dog Cerberus. Hercules warns all to avert their eyes from the dog. News of Lycus' plot summons Hercules off the stage ; but Theseus remains, and in the next two hundred lines gives a detailed account of how they brought the dog from Hades up to earth. I ask myself how this was staged. Dogs, indeed all animals, are difficult to manage on the stage ; three-headed dogs not easily obtainable. Why did Hercules ask all not to look at the dog, unless the dog is to be supposed present? And what is the tragic effect of Theseus' long speech, if all the time he is holding on to the dog? In fact it is plain that the dog neither comes nor goes ; he is simply forgotten.

For these and other reasons I cannot believe that these tragedies were meant for performance. They were meant to be declaimed. The object was to impress the listeners with the hammer-blows of rhetoric. In the constant straining for effect the subtle has no place, the simple and the natural gain no marks. Black and white character-drawing, ferocious villains, milkwhite victims, ghastly descriptions, Byronic defiance, flamboyant repartee, meet us on almost every page. Furthermore, we are bethumped and stunned by erudition. Juno, surveying the starry heavens, reads there the record of her husband's infidelities. ' Yonder the Bear, high up in the icy North, guards the Argive ships ; yonder he shines who bore the Tyrian Europa across the waves ; there the Atlantides put forth their band . . . here Orion terrifies the gods . . . and golden Perseus has his stars ; the bright constellation of the Tyndaridae shines yonder, and they at whose birth the unsteady land stood firm '. How many of us, unless we have written a Classical Dictionary, would recognize in these lines references to seven distinct amours of Jupiter? There is also the prominence of the gruesome and ghoulish. In the *Oedipus* Manto consults the omens : ' with no gentle motion do the entrails quake and shiver, but my whole hand do they cause to tremble. The heart, diseased through and through, is withered, and lies deep hidden, and the veins are of livid hue. A great part of the entrails is wanting, and from the rotting liver oozes forth BLACK GALL! '

And yet we have to admit that these plays were read, admired and imitated by the men who created our own drama. At a time when there was nothing with any dramatic form in the modern languages, these plays, with their efficient structure, their famous personages, their thrilling plots, their reflective choruses, had a fascination for all Europe. But further I find in Seneca a certain sense of the theatrical, of dramatic timing, which may have been nearer than was Greek tragedy to Elizabethan taste. In the *Troades* there is the scene where Andromache, trying to save her little son Astyanax from the Greek victors, conceals him in Hector's tomb, and then confronts Ulysses with the truthful statement that her son is gone to the tomb and lies among the dead. The gradual awakening of suspicion in Ulysses' mind, the cunning with which he plays on the mother's fears, till she calls the child to come out of its hiding-place, her plea for mercy and its failure, the child's one and only utterance, ' Pity me, Mother!', before he is led off to death, form a powerful scene.

Phaedra's disclosure of her passion to Hippolytus is quite different from the scene in Euripides, where it is the old servant who reveals the secret which Phaedra would have concealed till death. Is there not something to be said for Seneca's re-casting of the story? If Phaedra comes out of his treatment more tarnished, is she not also more real?

In scenes such as these—the search for the condemned victim, the disclosure of passion by woman to man—can we not see the Rome of Seneca's day and the woman-dominated, death-haunted palace of the Caesars?

A great moment in drama has something abrupt in its effect ; it must hit us like a blow. Such a moment we may find in Seneca's *Oedipus* when the king relentlessly forces the reluctant Phorbas to confess who the child was whom he rescued ; and when Oedipus knows that the child was himself he is still far from realising the full horror of his situation. He must still elicit the further point— born of what mother?—to which comes the dreadful reply ' born

of your wife '.   Here we have the sledge-hammer effect which
impressed the Elizabethans.

The dialogue is often powerful—especially in that Roman
feature, repartee.   When the Nurse points out to Medea the weakness of her position :

> Colchis is far away, your husband lost ;
> Of all your riches nothing now remains,

Medea flashes out the reply :

> Medea now remains! Land, sea, sword, fire,
> God and the thunderbolt are found in me!

There are also moving passages, especially in the choruses,
where we see that these are the works of a great mind.   There is
the address to Sleep over the prostrate body of Hercules : ' O
Sleep, conqueror of woes, rest of the soul, the better part of human
life, brother of Death ; O thou who art peace after wanderings,
haven of life, day's respite and night's comrade, who comest alike
to king and slave, sweetly and gently soothe his weary spirit '.
There is the terrible sense of blood-guiltiness : ' what Tanais,
what Nile, what Tigris can cleanse this hand?   Though cold
Maeotis should pour its northern sea upon me, though the whole
ocean should stream along my hands, yet will the deep stains
cling '.   May I remind you of the famous far-off echoes of these
passages in English literature :

> " Sleep that knits up the ravelled sleeve of care."
> " Will all great Neptune's Ocean wash this blood
> Clean from my hand?"
> " Sleepe after toyle, port after stormie seas,
> Ease after warre, death after life does greatly please." (F.Q. ix. 40)

The notion of universal doom lies heavy on Seneca.   There is
the choral passage on Death in the *Troades,* beginning ' is it true,
or does the tale cheat timid souls, that spirits live on when bodies
have been burned? ' and ending ' do you ask where you will be
when death has claimed you? You will be where they lie who were
never born '.

In his vision of the final destruction of the human race Seneca
is abreast of our own age.   In the *Thyestes* a certain consolation is
found in the prospect. ' Has the last day come in our time? Away
with lamentation! Greedy indeed for life is he who would not die
when the world is perishing in his company '.

But to end on a more cheerful note, and to show the range of
Seneca's imagination, and the secret of his appeal for the
Elizabethans, may I quote from the *Medea* the famous prophecy of
the voyage of Columbus :

> The billows have their masters now ;
> The Argo's bulk we need no more,
> For little ships undaunted plough
> The mighty deep from shore to shore.
> And in the distant years to be
> The Earth's last barrier shall unfold
> And Tethys spread her waters free,
> New worlds revealing to the old,
> Past Thule's bounds, for mariners bold,
> And ships that cross the Atlantic Sea.

NOTES AND SOURCES

CHAPTER II

1. *Hor. Sat.* 1. 5. 51-70.

2. Fronto, *epist.* 4. 6 : in torculari cenauimus . . . et rusticos cauillantes audiuimus libenter.

3. See Virg. *Georg.* 2. 385 ; Hor. *Ep.* 2. 1. 139 ; Festus, p. 85, M. Fescennini uersus, qui canebantur in nuptiis, ex urbe Fescennina dicuntur allati (so also Serv. *Aen.* 7. 695 ; Porph. ad Hor. *ep.* 2. 1. 145 ; Adn. ad Luc. 2. 368) siue ideo dicti quia fascinum putabantur arcere. Fesc. as wedding-songs : Catullus, poems 61, 62 ; Claudian, c. 11 ff. (Loeb ed. 1. 230). Sidon., *ep.* 1. 5. 10.

4. Varro, *L.L.* 6. 68 : sic triumphare appellatum quod cum imperatore milites redeuntes clamitant per urbem in Capitolium eunti : io triumphe. Tib. 2. 5. 117 ; Hor. *c.* 4. 2. 49 ; Ovid, *Tr.* 4. 2. 51. Livy 4. 20. 2 : longe maximum triumphi spectaculum fuit Cossus spolia opima regis interfecti gerens. in eum milites carmina incondita aequantes cum Romulo canere. id. 10. 30. 9 : milites triumphantes secuti sunt. celebrata inconditis carminibus militaribus non magis uictoria Q. Fabii quam mors praeclara P. Deci est. id. 45. 38. 12, 43. 8. Plut. *Marc.* 8 ; ὁ δὲ στρατὸς εἵπετο . . . ᾄδων ἅμα πεποιημένα μέλη καὶ παιᾶνας ἐπινικίους εἰς τὸν θεὸν καὶ τὸν στρατηγόν. Livy 7. 38. 3 ; id. 39. 7. 3. Appian *Lib.* 66 (i. 251 M.) : καὶ τῶν ἀρχόντων οὓς μὲν ἐπαινοῦσιν, οὓς δὲ σκώπτουσιν, οὓς δέ ψέγουσιν. Mart. 1. 4. 3 : consueuere iocos uestri quoque ferre triumphi, materiem dictis nec pudet esse ducem. Dionys. 7. 72. Livy 3. 29. 5 : epulantesque cum carmine triumphali et sollemnibus iocis comissantium modo currum secuti sunt. id. 5. 49. 7 ; 7. 10. 13, 17. 5. Plut. *Aem. Paul.* 34 : ᾄδων . . . ᾠδάς τινας πατρίους ἀναμεμιγμένας γέλωτι. Livy 4. 53. 11 : alternis inconditi uersus militari licentia iactati. Plin. 19. 144 : (the soldiers of Caesar at his triumph) alternis uersibus exprobauere lapsana se uixisse apud Durrachium praemiorum parsimoniam cauillantes. Dionys. 2. 34 : ἡ δ' ἄλλη δύναμις αὐτῷ παρηκολούθει . . . τὸν ἡγεμόνα κυδαίνουσα ποιήμασιν αὐτοσχεδίοις. Examples : Suet. *Diu. Iul.* 49, 51 (urbani, seruate uxores! moechum caluum adducimus). Others in Baehrens, *F.P.R.* 330 ; 383.

5. Suet *Vesp.* 19 : in funere Fauor archimimus personam eius ferens imitatusque, ut est mos, facta et dicta uiui.

6. Tert. *de Spect.* 12 ; Serv. ad Virg. *Aen.* 10. 519 ; Val. Max. 2. 4. 17 ; Liv. *Epit.* 16 ; Dio Cass. 43. 19.

7. See Plate I.

8. See Walde, *Lat. et. Wört.*, who accepts : φersu and rejects the older suggestions : (1) persŏnare, (2) πρόσωπον, (3) *per-sōnare from ζώνη.

9. See pp. 137 ff.

CHAPTER III

1. See Bieber, *Theater*, ch. x, and figs. 351-402. The φλύακες were a class of mime-actors known among the Greek towns of Italy. Athenaeus xiv. pp. 621 d, f., compares them with the deikelistai, phallophoroi, and autokabdaloi (' improvisers '). See Pickard-Cambridge, *Dithyramb*, etc., pp. 230, 232, 267 ff. Reich, *Mimus*, i. 17, 258, ii. 528. Heydemann, *Jahrb. Arch. Inst.* i. pp. 260 ff. Webster, South Italian Vases and Attic Drama, *C.Q.* xlii. (1948), pp. 15–27. Rhinthon is described by Suidas as Ταραντῖνος, κωμικός, ἀρχηγὸς τῆς καλουμένης ἱλαροτραγῳδίας, ὃ ἔστι φλυακογραφία. . . δράματα δέ αὐτοῦ κωμικὰ τραγικὰ λή. The poetess Nossis of Locri wrote an epitaph on him (*Anth. Pal.* 7. 414) ; she claims originality for his ' tragic phlyakes ', i.e. for ' raising the crude phlyax-drama by comic treatment of tragic themes ' (Waddell s.v. in *O.C.D.*). We possess six titles : *Amphitruon, Herakles, Iphigenia in Aulis, Iphigenia in Tauris, Orestes, Telephus.* One fragment (fr. 10) mentions ' the metre of Hipponax ', i.e. scazon ; a character in the play points out that a curse just uttered will not scan as a tragic iambic trimeter. Another writer of phlyakes was Sopater, *c.* 300 B.C., who lived in Alexandria. Fr. 6 (12 vv.) contains raillery at the Stoics.

The themes and fragments of the literary phlyakes seem considerably above the level of farce. The Italian vase-paintings are grotesque and obscene ; they present, in addition to burlesque, scenes from everyday life—the drunken son stealing home, the finding of the exposed infant, the lover at the window of the courtesan, the miser being dragged from his money chest by thieves, the nibbling of dainties, the stealing of wine, flogging, fighting, dancing. There is no proof that these pictures do represent the performance of the literary phlyakes ; they seem to point to some crude type of farce, in so far as they represent stage performances at all. Certainly the picture of the figure on a tunny fish (Bieber, fig. 372) cannot have been taken from the stage.

2. It is commonly said that all the actors of Old Comedy (including the plays of Aristophanes) wore the dress which we see on the South Italian vases—in particular that all the male characters wore a visible phallus, and that all the characters, female as well as male, were grotesquely padded. The evidence given for this view is (1) Aristotle's statement (*Poet.* ch. 4) that comedy took its rise from phallic performances. (But in these the phallus

was not something worn ; it was a pole carried in procession. We have some information about the dress of the performers, and it was not phallic ; see Athenaeus xiv. pp. 621 d, e ; 622, a–d.) (2) The scholiast's comment on Ar. *Clouds* 537 ff. ' for the comic actors came on wearing aidoia of leather to raise a laugh.' (This seems to be a mere inference from the words of Aristophanes ; similarly on 542 the scholiast tries to show (probably with no evidence but the text) that Aristophanes employs the practices which he has denounced—quoting the *Lysistrata* as à play where the phallus is introduced. This remark would be pointless if *all* characters were phallic.) (3) Aristophanes (*l.c.*) claims that his play is free from various vulgar tricks aimed at amusing children—the wearing of the ' dangling leather ' (σκύτινον καθειμένον), the kordax, jokes at baldness, the ' comic business ' with the old man's stick, torches, shouting. It is fair to infer that all these tricks were employed in Old Comedy ; but they cannot have been universal, still less compulsory, for in rejecting them he does not claim to be doing anything revolutionary. (4) There are numerous references to the male organ in Aristophanes' plays which are thought to prove that the actors were wearing a visible phallus. (But there are equally broad references to women : *Eccl.* 97 ; *Peace* 1350 ; *Ach.* 769 ff., and in particular *Wasps* 1374–7. If we do not demand visible effects of costume in these cases, we have to fall back on the use of language, aided perhaps by gesture ; and this will also explain other extravagantly indecent but non-phallic passages such as *Eccl.* 313 ff.) (5) We have references to padding as part of the actor's make-up (but these seem to apply only to tragedy : Lucian, *De Salt.* 27, *Iup. Trag.* 41 ; and the προστερνίδια and προγαστρίδια are meant to restore symmetry to the high-booted actor, ὡς μὴ τοῦ μήκους ἡ ἀρρυθμία ἐν λεπτῷ μᾶλλον ἐλέγχοιτο ; Photius, s.v. σωμάτια). (6) The passages quoted from the text to prove the use of the phallus can perhaps be explained as direct references to the peos itself, the male organ (not, of course, to be thought of as visible). *Clouds* 734 : Strepsiades, hidden under the bedclothes, is asked by Socrates ' caught anything yet? ' and replies ,' only my peos '. This is not a reference to anything visible—even the phallus, if worn, would be concealed by the blankets. Perhaps the most likely reference to something artificial is *Ach.* 158 ff. ; Dicaeopolis exclaims, ' who has docked the peos of the Odomantians? ' But at the most this would only suggest something unusual in the appearance of the Odomantians ; it cannot be used to prove that all actors (including Dicaeopolis here), presented a similar appearance. Similarly with padding ; Dionysus is called gastron, ' pot-belly ', in *Frogs* 200 : but to explain the epithet by a reference to padding would be pointless if all the other actors are supposed to have been similar in appearance. (7) The argument from vase-paintings, etc., cannot be shown to prove anything for Old Comedy ; but if we try to picture all the actors of Aristophanes dressed as in the South Italian

vase-paintings or the terra-cotta statuettes, then we cannot explain
how in the *Ecclesiazusae* the women can disguise themselves as men
by putting on their husbands' cloaks. (8) Much in Aristophanes'
plays is anything but farcical ; it is not easy to suppose that Aeschylus
in the *Frogs* is dressed in tights, padding and phallus, or that the
Just Argument in the *Clouds,* who praises the modesty of young men
in earlier days, is himself wearing a garb which flouts modesty
grossly. See further discussions in *C.Q.* 4. pp. 64–75 ; 5. pp. 94–95 ;
7. pp 184–185 ; and 9. pp. 126–127.

3. See *Pyrrhus* 16.

4. For the career of Andronicus, see Cic. *Brut.* 18. 72 ; *Tusc.*
i. 1. 3 ; *De Sen.* 14. 50. Cassiod., Chronic. for year 239 B.C. (p. 128
M.). Gellius 17. 21. 42–5. Hor. *ep.* 2. 1. 139 ff., 162. Jerome for
year 187 B.C. Suet. *gramm.* 1 : antiquissimi doctorum . . idem et
poetae et semigraeci erant—Liuium et Ennium dico. Glossae
Salomonis : tragoedias comoediasque primus egit idemque etiam
composuit Liuius Andronicus duplici toga inuolutus ('wearing
the toga praetexta '?). Livy 7. 2. 8. *C.Q.* 34 (1940), pp. 11–19.
H. de la Ville de Mirmont, *Études sur l'ancienne poésie latine,* Paris,
1903.

5. Hor. *ep.* 2. 1. 69.

6. Livy 27. 37. 7. Festus, p. 333 M. : cum Liuius Andronicus
bello Punico secundo scripsisset carmen quod a uirginibus est
cantatum, quia prosperius respublica populi Romani geri coepta
est, publice adtributa est ei in Auentino aedis Mineruae, in qua
liceret scribis histrionibusque consistere ac dona ponere, in honorem
Liui, quia is et scribebat fabulas et agebat.

7. 7. 2.

8. If that is what Livy means by ' descripto ad tibicinem cantu '.
But he may be referring to the words, not the notation.

9. Pl. *Curc.* 150.

10. *And.* 18.

11. See p. 117 f.

12. *Brut.* 18. 71 : et Odyssia Latina est sic tamquam opus
aliquod Daedali et Liuianae fabulae non satis dignae quae iterum
legantur.

13. *Golden Age,* p. 125.

14. See *Notes and Sources,* ii. 4.

15. See p. 168 and ch. xxvi.

CHAPTER IV

1. 1. 24. 2 : trium poetarum illustrium epigrammata, Cn. Naeui, Plauti, M. Pacuuii, quae ipsi fecerunt et incidenda sepulcro suo reliquerunt, nobilitatis eorum gratia et uenustatis scribenda in his commentariis esse duxi. epigramma Naeui plenum superbiae Campanae, quod testimonium esse iustum potuisset, nisi ab ipso dictum esset :

> immortales mortales flere si foret fas,
> flerent diuae Camenae Naeuiom poetam :
> itaque postquam est Orci traditus thensauro,
> obliti sunt Romai loquier lingua Latina.

2. 17. 21. 44–5 : anno deinde post Romam conditam quingentesimo undeuicensimo Sp. Caruilius Ruga primus Romae de amicorum sententia diuortium cum uxore fecit, quod sterilis esset, iurassetque apud censores uxorem se liberum quaerundorum causa habere, eodemque anno Cn. Naeuius poeta fabulas apud populum dedit, quem M. Varro in libro de poetis primo stipendia fecisse ait bello Poenico primo, idque ipsum Naeuium dicere in eo carmine quod de eodem bello scripsit.

3. See pp. 99 ff.

4. See Ribbeck, *Com. Lat.* 112 (p. 22), 9–20 (p. 6) ; id., *Trag. Rom.*, Naevius 63 (p. 14).

5. *Tusc.* 4. 31. 67 ; *ad Fam.* 5. 12 ; *ad Fam.* 15. 6 ; also Seneca *ep.* 17. 2.

6. *Curculio*, ll. 462–86.

7. *Orig.* 1. 25 : Ennius de quadam impudica.

8. *Sat.* 1. 5. 100.

9. uita insepulta laetus in patriam redux. See Ribbeck, *Trag. Rom.* p. 277.

10. On Ter. *Ad.* 537 : nam falsum est quod dicitur interuenisse lupam Naeuianae fabulae alimonio Remi et Romuli, cum in theatro ageretur.

11. *De Sen.* 14. 50 : quam gaudebat Bello suo Punico Naeuius ! quam Truculento Plautus ! quam Pseudolo !

12. Pseudo-Asconius ad Cic. *Verr.* 1. 29 (p. 215 St.) : dictum facete et contumeliose in Metellos antiquum Naeuii est : fato . . . consules ; cui tunc Metellus consul iratus uersu responderat senario hypercatalecto, qui et saturnius dicitur : dabunt . . .

13. 7. 8. 5.

14. 36. 2. M. : barbari dicebantur antiquitus omnes gentes exceptis Graecis, unde Plautus Naeuium poetam Latinum barbarum dixit.

3. 3. 15.

16. Naeuius comicus Vticae moritur pulsus Roma factione nobilium ac praecipue Metelli.

17. *Brut.* 15. 60.

18. See O. Skutsch, rev. of Marmorale's *Naevius poeta*, *C.R.* 1951, pp. 174–6.

19. See p. 93.

20. Cic. *de diuin* 1. 22. 43.

21. *Sest.* 58. 123 : nominatim sum appellatus in Bruto : ' Tullius qui libertatem ciuibus stabiliuerat '. miliens reuocatum est (' the line was encored again and again ').

22. *G.L.K.* 1. 490. 14.

CHAPTER V

1. See Gell. 3. 3. 14, 17. 21. 46 ; Cic. *Brut.* 15. 60, mortuus est Catone censore (184 B.C.). Jer. s.a. 200 B.C. : Plautus ex Umbria Sarsinas Romae moritur, qui propter annonae difficultatem ad molas manuarias pistori se locauerat, ibi, quotiens ab opere uacaret, scribere fabulas solitus ac uendere. F. Della Corte, *Da Sarsina a Roma* (Genoa, 1952).

2. 3. 3. 11–14.

3. Gell. 3. 3. 3.

4. *Ad.* 7 ; *Eun.* 25.

5. The Ambrosian (A) at the end of the *Casina*.

6. Westaway, *The Original Element in Plautus*, p. 76 ; Norwood, *Plautus and Terence*, p. 36. Havet and Freté, in their edition of the *Asinaria* (*Le prix des âmes*, 1925) ascribe it to ' Maccus '.

7. P. 239 M. Ploti appellantur qui sunt planis pedibus, unde et poeta Accius, quia Vmber Sarsinas erat, a pedum planitie initio Plotus, postea Plautus est dictus.

8. See p. 40 f.

9. 1. 202.

10. *De Sen.* 14. 50 ; see p. 30 and note. Cicero is speaking of the pleasure which *study* can give to a leisured old age (*otiosa senectus*).

11. Jer. s.a. 200 B.C. : Plautus ex Vmbria Sarsinas. Festus-Paulus p. 239 M. : Vmber Sarsinas erat. *Most.* 770.

12. Gell. 3. 3. 14 : Saturionem et Addictum et tertiam quandam, cuius nunc mihi nomen non suppetit, in pistrino eum scripsisse Varro ait et plerique alii memoriae tradiderunt, cum pecunia omni, quam in operis artificum scaenicorum pepererat, in mercatibus perdita inops Romam redisset et ob quaerendum uictum ad circumagendas molas, quae trusatiles appellantur, operam pistori locasset.

13. *Pers.* 75–6, *Trin.* 1057.

14. ' He whom the gods love dies young.' But proverbial expressions like this are common property ; and the Plautine context is farcical. The only other evidence that the *Bacchides* is

a version of the *Dis Exapaton* ('Twice a Deceiver') is in the two deceptions. But 'some critics find in the *Bacchides* three deceptions' (*N.R.C.*, p. 164 note), so that the argument from the Greek title is weakened.

CHAPTER VI

1. Ovid, *Trist.* ii. 369.

CHAPTER VIII

1. *Ep.* 2. 1. 175–6.
2. Pl. *Bacch.* 214–5.
3. *De Sen.* 14. 50.
4. See pp. 111 f.,
5. Vss. 54–7, 1029–1036.
6. *Ad.* 6–14.
7. 65–6.·
8. 462–86.
9. *Poen.* 930–49, cf. 982–1028. See Gray, *Am. Journal of Semit. Lang.*, 39 (1922), 73 ; Gottheil in Lodge's *Lexicon Plautinum* 1, 915.
10. Gell. i. 24. 3 : epigramma Plauti, quod dubitassemus an Plauti foret, nisi a M. Varrone positum esset in libro de poetis primo :

> postquam est mortem aptus Plautus, comoedia luget,
> scaena est deserta, dein Risus, Ludus Iocusque
> et numeri innumeri simul omnes conlacrimarunt.

11. Quint. x. 1. 99.
12. Hor. *ep.* 2. 1. 170, *A.P.* 270 ; Cic. *Off.* 1. 29. 104 ; Sid. Ap. c. 23, 149 (Graios, Plaute, sales lepore transis) ; St. Jerome, *ep.* 22 *ad Eustochium*.
13. *Cas.* 114 ; *Curc.* 178–80 ; *Pseud.* 683–6.
14. Ap. Don. *Vita Ter.* p. 9 W. (Perhaps comica goes not with uis but with uirtus.)
15. Kritik über die Gefangenen des Plautus (*Ges. Werk.* 4³ 192, ed. Lachm.).
16. *Capt.* 683–8.

CHAPTER IX

1. 52–3. See pp. 71, 116.
2. *Pseud.* 707.
3. Life of Ennius : Jer. ad ann. 1777 (=240 B.C.), p. 133 H. : Q. Ennius poeta Tarenti nascitur, qui a Catone quaestore Romam translatus habitauit in monte Auentino parco admodum sumptu contentus et unius ancillae ministerio. (*Tarenti* probably through confusion with Livius.) Cic. *De Orat.* 3. 42. 168 (quoting the line

of Ennius : nos sumus Romani, qui fuimus ante Rudini). Cic. *Pro Arch.* 10. 22 : Rudinum hominem. Sil. 12. 393 : Rudiae genuere uetustae. Strabo 6. 3. 5 p. 281 C : Ῥωδιῶν πόλεως.

Year of birth : Gell. 17. 21. 43 : consules secuntur Q. Valerius et C. Manilius, quibus natum esse Q. Ennium poetam M. Varro in primo de poetis libro scripsit. Arrival in Rome : Nepos, *Cato* 1. 4. Knowledge of languages : Gell. 17. 17. 1 : Q. Ennius tria corda se habere dicebat, quod loqui Graece et Osce et Latine sciret. Teacher and dramatist : Suet. *gram.* 1 : Liuium et Ennium dico, quos utraque lingua domi forisque docuisse adnotatum est.

Death : Cic. *Brut.* 20. 78 (169 B.C.) : mortem obiit Ennius. *De Sen.* 5. 14 : annos septuaginta natus (tot enim uixit Ennius). Jer. s.a. 1849=168 B.C. (p. 140 H.) : Ennius poeta septuagenario maior articulari morbo perit sepultusque in Scipionis monumento uia Appia intra primum ab urbe miliarium. quidam ossa eius Rudiam ex Ianiculo translata adfirmant.

4. *Glossae Salomonis* (Usener, *Kl. Schr.* 3. 38) : tragoedias Ennius fere omnes ex Graecis transtulit, plurimas Euripideis, nonnullas Aristarchiis.

5. Ribbeck *Tr.* p. 72 ; Cic. *De Amic.* 17. 64.

6. Eurip. *Iph. Aul.* 446 ; Enn. *Iph.* 7 (Ribbeck *Tr.* 42).

7. Cic. *De Fin.* 1. 2. 4.

8. See p. 99.

CHAPTER X

1. Life of Pacuvius : Cic. *Brut.* 64. 229. Jer. *ad. ann.* 1863=154 B.C. (p. 142 H.) : Pacuuius Brundisinus tragoediarum scriptor clarus habetur, Ennii poetae ex filia nepos, uixitque Romae, quoad picturam exercuit ac fabulas uenditauit. deinde Tarentum transgressus prope nonagenarius diem obiit. Pliny 35. 19 : celebrata est in foro Boario aede Herculis Pacuuii poetae pictura ; Enni sorore genitus hic fuit . . . Varro *sat. Menipp.* 356 B :

> Pacui discipulus dicor, porro is fuit Enni ;
> Ennius Musarum ; Pompilius clueor.

Cic. *De Amic.* 7. 24. Gell. 13. 2. 2. For the epitaph see Gell. 1. 24. 4.

2. Diomed. *G.L.K.* 1. 485 : olim carmen quod ex uariis poematibus constabat satira uocabatur, quale scripserunt Pacuuius et Ennius. Porphyrio ad Hor. *Sat.* 1. 10. 46.

3. Cic. *Opt. Gen. Orat.* 1. 2 ; Hor. *Ep.* 2. 1. 55 ; Quint. 10. 1. 97 ; cf. Vell. 2. 9. 3.

4. Cicero *Tusc.* 1. 44. 106 ; Hor. *Sat.* 2. 3. 60 and notes of Porphyrio (hoc uersu clamitabant qui est Pacuuii . . . hic Fufius actor tragoediarum fuit, qui cum uellet Ilionam dormientem exprimere, ut ad filii Polydori exsurgeret uocem, in scena obdormiuit ; and of Acro (hic Fufius actor tragoediarum fuit, qui cum Ilionam

tragoediam ageret ebrius et uellet eam simulare dormientem, grauitate uini ad uerum somnum ductus est . . .). Cic. *pro Sest.* 59. 126, with *Schol. Bobiens.* (est quippe argumentum ita dispositum ut Polydori umbra secundum consuetudinem scaenicorum ab inferiore aulae (i) parte procedat . . .).

5. Cic. de *Amic.* 7. 24.

6. Suet. *Caes.* 84 ; Appian *Bell. Ciu.* 2. 146. Ribb. *Tr. Rom.* (Pac.) 40.

7. Cic. *De Off.* 1. 31. 114.

8. Pacuvius, *Medus* 19 ; *Herm.* 20 ; *Dulor.* 13, in Ribbeck, *Tr.*

9. P. 74 and note †.

10. *Tusc.* 2. 21. 48–9.

11. 2. 26. 13.

12. Ribb. *Trag. Rom.* Pac. inc. fab. 45 ; *Herm.* 14 ; inc. 44.

13. *N.D.* 2. 36. 91, *de Diu.* 1. 57. 131.

14. Cic. *Brut.* 74. 258. Cf. Mart. 11. 90. 6. Tac. *Dial.* 20.

CHAPTER XI

1. See p. 18 and N. and S. iii. 6.

Jerome ad ann. 1838 179 B.C. : Statius Caecilius comoediarum scriptor clarus habetur natione Insuber Gallus et Ennii primum contubernalis. quidam Mediolanensem ferunt. mortuus est anno post mortem Ennii et iuxta Ianiculum sepultus. Gell. 4. 20. 13 : seruus fuit et propterea nomen habuit ' Statius '.

3. *Hec.* Prol. (2) 14 ff.

4. See pp. 91, 93.

5. *Sat. Menipp.* 399 B : in argumentis Caecilius poscit palmam, in ethesin Terentius, in sermonibus Plautus.

6. *Opt. Gen. Or.* 6. 19 ; *de Fin.* 1, 2, 41 ; Gell. 2. 23.

7. *Ep.* 2. 1. 59. Varro ap. Charisium *G.L.K.* i. 241. 28 : πάθη Trabea, Atilius, Caecilius facile mouerunt. Cic. *pro Cael.* xvi. 37 (Ribb. *Com. Lat.* p. 62) ; Vell. i. 17. 1.

CHAPTER XII

1. It is significant that we find the controversialists citing in support of their views no first-hand authority except Terence himself.

2. Cf. Auson. *epist.* 13, lines 15–16.

3. Quoted in the *Vita.*

4. Quoted in the *Vita.*

5. Was the idea of a fatal voyage suggested by *Ad.* 703 (periit, abiit, nauem ascendit) ?

6. See Schanz-Hosius, Röm. Lit.-Gesch. i. 109 : es ist kaum möglich . . . an eine Entlehnung aus der Perinthia zu denken.

7. St. Aug. *Ciu. Dei* ii. 7 (quoted by Rogers, ed. *Clouds*, line 1080).

8. Don. *ad Hec.* 840. Varro : see N. and S. xi. 5.

9. 11. 3. 178–82. See p. 227.

CHAPTER XIII

1. Varro ap Charis. *G.L.K.* i. 241. 28 : πάθη Trabea, Atilius, Caecilius facile mouerunt.

2. Cic. *Tusc.* 4. 11. 25 ; *ad Att.* 14. 20. 3 ; and preceding note.

3. Varro, *L.L.* 6. 89. Gell. 3. 3. 3. Ribbeck, *Comic. Lat.* pp. 27–8.

4. Gell. 13. 23. 16. Festus-Paulus p. 109 M. Livy 31. 12. 9.

5. Varro *L.L.* 7. 65 ; 6. 50 ; Gell. 18. 12. 2.

6. *Corp. Gloss. Lat.* 5. 8. 20 : Burrae Vatroniae, fatuae ac stupidae, a fabula quadam Vatroni auctoris quam Burra inscripsit.

7. Ribb. *Com. Lat.* p. 72.

8. Ter. *Eun.* 9 ; Donatus, 1. p. 272 W., gives the plots of the two plays. Ter., *And.* 7 ; *Phor.* 1, 13 ; *Heaut.* 22, 31.

9. Jer. ad. ann. 1914 (103 B.C.) : Turpilius comicus senex admodum Sinuessae moritur.

10. Servius ad *Aen.* 3. 279. See Ribb. *Com. Lat.* p. 84.

11. Cic. *ad Fam.* 9. 22 ; *Phil.* 2. 6. 15 ; *Rosc. Com.* 7. 20.

12 Gell. 1. 5. 24.

13. Ad *And.* 15 : Ennius namque ante Plautum fuit.

CHAPTER XIV

1. Life of Accius : Jer. *ad ann.* 1878=139 B.C. p. 144 H. : L. Accius tragoediarum scriptor clarus habetur, natus Mancino et Serrano coss. (=170 B.C.), parentibus libertinis, et seni iam Pacuuio Tarenti sua scripta recitauit. a quo et fundus Accianus iuxta Pisaurum dicitur, quia illuc inter colonos fuerat ex urbe deductus. (This last detail is false : the colony at Pisaurum was founded in 184 : Livy 39. 44.) Cic. *Brut.* 28. 107 (cf. 78. 271) ; *Phil.* 1. 15. 36. Quint. 5. 13. 43. Auct. *ad Herenn.* 1. 14. 24 ; 2. 13. 19. Val. Max. 3. 7. 11. Cic. *Pro Arch.* 11. 27. *Brut.* 64. 229. Gell. 13. 2. 2. Hor. *Sat.* 1. 10. 53. Pliny 34. 19 (in Camenarum aede maxima forma statuam sibi posuisse, cum breuis admodum fuisset).

2. Cic. *Pro. Sest.* 56. 120 ; *Pro Planc.* 24. 59. Hor. *ep.* 2. 1. 55. Quint. 10. 1. 97. Vell. 1. 17. 1 ; 2. 9. 3. Vitr. 9 praef. 16. Ovid *Am.* 1. 15. 19.

3. Ribb. *Tr. Rom.*, Att. 203–4, Enn. 379.

4. Cic. *Brut.* 48. 177. Marius Victor. *G.L.K.* 6. 8. 8. : primus de Tecmesa scripsit tragoediam et in scaena pronuntiari iussit.

Perhaps this merely means that Strabo ' ordered the play to be produced '. But see Lindsay, *E.L.V.* 147. Val. Max. 3. 7. 11. Asconius, p. 26, 28 St. : inter primos temporis sui oratores et tragicus poeta bonus admodum habitus est ; huius enim sunt tragoediae quae inscribuntur Iuli.

5. Cic. *Brut.* 45. 167.
6. Varro *L.L.* 7. 93. See N. and S. on life of Pacuvius, p. 332.
7. Nonius 2, p. 78 : Santra *Nuntiis Bacchis* (? *Nuptiis Bacchi*).
8. Auct. *ad Her.* 1. 14. 24, 2. 13. 19.
9. See Ribbeck, *Tr. Rom.* p. 229.
10. *Tr.* V. 7. 27 ; cf. II. 280, 497, 519, 553.

CHAPTER XV

1. Charis. *G.L.K.* 1. 241. 27 : ἦθη, ut ait Varro de Latino sermone libro v, nullis aliis seruare conuenit quam Titinio, Terentio, Attae.

2. Jer. ad ann. 1940 (77 B.C.). T. Quinctius Atta scriptor togatarum Romae moritur sepultusque uia Praenestina ad miliarium II. Hor. *Ep.* 2. 1. 79. Fronto p. 62 N. : animaduertas particulatim elegantis Nouium et Pomponium et id genus in uerbis rusticanis et iocularibus ac ridiculariis, Attam in muliebribus.

3. Vell. 2. 9. 3 : clara etiam per idem aeui spatium fuere ingenia in togatis Afranii, in tragoediis Pacuuii atque Accii ; id. 1. 17. 1 : dulces Latini leporis facetiae per Caecilium Terentiumque et Afranium suppari aetate nituerunt. Quint. 10. 1. 100 : togatis excellit Afranius ; utinam non inquinasset argumenta puerorum foedis amoribus mores suos fassus. Aus. *epigr.* 79, Loeb ed. : repperit obscenas ueneres uitiosa libido . . . quam toga facundi scaenis agitauit Afrani.

4. Macr. 6. 1. 4 : Afranius togatarum scriptor in ea togata quae Compitalia inscribitur, non inuerecunde respondens arguentibus quod plura sumpsisset a Menandro : fateor, inquit, sumpsi non ab illo modo, sed ut quisque habuit, conueniret quod mihi, quod me non posse melius facere credidi, etiam a Latino. Don., *Vita Ter.* p. 8 W. : hunc (Terentium) Afranius quidem omnibus comicis praefert, scribens in Compitalibus : Terenti num similem dicetis quempiam ? Cic. *Fin.* 1. 3. 7 : locos quosdam . . . transferam . . . ut ab Homero Ennius, Afranius a Menandro solet. Hor. *Ep.* 2. 1. 57 : dicitur Afrani toga conuenisse Menandro. Quintilian and Ausonius : see above. Cic. *Brut.* 45. 167 : quem (Titium) studebat imitari L. Afranius poeta. . . .

5. Ps. Ascon. ap. Cic. *Diu.* 48, p. 200, 14 St. : Latinae fabulae per pauciores agebantur personas, ut Atellanae, togatae et huiusmodi aliae.

6. Macr. 6. 5. 6 : Afranium sequitur, qui in prologo ex persona Priapi ait . . .

7. Donatus ad Ter. *Eun.* 57 : concessum est in palliata poetis comicis seruos dominis sapientiores fingere, quod idem in togata non fere licet.

8. Cic. *Sest.* 55. 118. *Incendium* : Suet. *Ner.* 11. 2.

9. Juvenal 1. 3.

10. Suet. *Gramm.* 21.

11. Suet. *Aug.* 45.4.

CHAPTER XVI

1. Hor. *Sat.* i. 5. 51–70.

2. *G.L.K.* i. 489. 32 : tertia species est fabellarum Latinarum, quae a ciuitate Oscorum Atella, in qua primum coeptae, appellatae sunt Atellanae argumentis dictisque iocularibus similes satyricis fabulis graecis.

3. *L.L.* 7. 29 : item significat in Atellanis aliquot Pappum senem, quod Osci casnar appellant. Strabo 5. 3. 6 : ἴδιόν τι τοῖς Ὄσκοις . . . συμβέβηκε : τῶν μὲν γὰρ Ὄσκων ἐκλελοιπότων ἡ διάλεκτος μένει παρὰ τοῖς Ῥωμαίοις, ὥστε καὶ ποιήματα σκηνοβατεῖσθαι κατά τινα ἀγῶνα πάτριον καὶ μιμολογεῖσθαι. Juvenal 3. 207. Cic. *ad Fam.* 7. 1. 3. Livy 7. 2.

4. Cic. *ad Fam.* 9. 16. 7 : secundum Oenomaum Accii non, ut olim solebat, Atellanam, sed ut nunc fit, mimum introduxisti.

5. *Ep.* 2. 1. 173.

6. Varro *L.L.* 7. 95.

7. 3. 175, and schol. ad loc. : exodiarius apud ueteres in fine ludorum intrabat, qui ridiculus foret, ut quidquid lacrimarum atque tristitiae, quae exissent ex tragicis affectibus, huius spectaculi risus detergeret. huius et Lucilius meminit : principio exitus dignus exodiumque sequetur. For the Atellana as exodium cf. Suet. *Tib.* 45 : in Atellanico exodio (id. *Dom.* 10. 4 : scaenico exodio sub persona Paridis et Oenones). Lydus mag. 1. 40 p. 41 W. Ἀτελλάνη ἐστὶν ἡ τῶν λεγομένων ἐξοδιαρίων.

8. Paul. ex Fest. p. 128 Müll.: manduci effigies in pompa antiquorum inter ceteras ridiculas formidolosasque ire solebat magnis malis ac late dehiscens et ingentem dentibus sonitum faciens. For the terror caused to children by masks, cf. Juv. 3. 175 and Mayor ad loc. Seneca *de ir.* 2. 11 : timetur a pluribus, sicut deformis persona ab infantibus ; id. *ep.* 24. 13 : (pueri) quos amant, quibus assueuerunt, cum quibus ludunt, si personatos uident, expauescunt. Mart. 14. 176. *Phaedo* 77 E (Timaeus lexicographus) : μορμολυκεῖα: τὰ φοβερὰ τοῖς παισὶ προσωπεῖα.

9. Festus p. 217 Müll. : personata fabula quaedam Naeui inscribitur, quam putant quidam primum (actam) a personatis histrionibus. sed cum post multos annos comoedi et tragoedi personis uti coeperint, uerisimilius est eam fabulam propter inopiam comoedorum actam nouam per Atellanos, qui proprie uocantur

personati, quia ius est eis non cogi in scaena ponere personam, quod ceteris histrionibus pati necesse est.

10. M. Aur. ap. Fronto, *ep. ad M. Caes.* 2. 3. Ps. Ascon ad Cic. *Diu. ad Caec.* 48, p. 200 St. (see N. and S. xv. 5).

11. Varro *sat. Men.* 198 B : putas eos non citius tricas Atellanas quam id extricaturos?

12. Quint. 6. 3. 47 : illa obscura [some emend to obscaena] quae Atellani e more captant.

13. See pp. 16f.

14. *Ann.* 4. 14. 4.

15. Plaut. *Bacc.* 1088 ; *Rud.* 535.

16. *de Orat.* 2. 69. 279 ; 2. 70. 285 ; *ad Fam.* 9. 16. 7.

17. 6. 71.

CHAPTER XVII

1. Jer. ad. ann. 1928=89 B.C. : L. Pomponius Bononiensis Atellanarum scriptor clarus habetur. Vell. 2. 9. 5 : sane non ignoremus eadem aetate (sc. as Rutilius, Claudius Quadrigarius, Valerius Antias) fuisse Pomponium, sensibus celebrem, uerbis rudem et nouitate inuenti a se operis commendabilem. Seneca *Controu.* 7. 3. 9 : auctorem huius uitii, quod ex captione unius uerbi plura significantis nascitur, aiebat (Cassius Seuerus) Pomponium Atellanarum scriptorem fuisse, a quo primum ad Laberium transisse hoc studium imitandi, deinde ad Ciceronem, qui illud ad uirtutem transtulisset.

2. Cic. *de Or.* 2. 69, 279 ; 70, 285.

3. Pl. *Merc.* 830. *Maccus Exul.* : Ribbeck *Com. Lat.* p. 221.

4. Cf. Aristoph. *Thesm.* 267–8 ; these are both farcical scenes. See p. 173.

5. Cic. *Phil.* 2. 27. 65 : exsultabat gaudio persona de mimo, modo egens, repente diues.

6. *Ep.* 89. 6.

7. Terentianus, *G.L.K.* 6. 396 :

frequens in usu est tale metrum comicis uetustis,
Atella uel quis fabulis actus dedit petulcos . . .
sonum ministrat congruentum motibus iocosis.

8. Athen. 6. 78, p. 261 C: ἐμφανίζουσι δ' αὐτοῦ τὸ περὶ ταῦτα ἱλαρὸν αἱ ὑπ' αὐτοῦ γραφεῖσαι σατυρικαὶ κωμῳδίαι τῇ πατρίῳ φωνῇ.

9. Macr. 1. 10. 3 : Mummius, qui post Nouium et Pomponium diu iacentem artem Atellanam suscitauit.

10. Suet. *Ner.* 89 : Datus Atellanarum histrio in cantico quodam ὑγίαινε πάτερ, ὑγίαινε μῆτερ ita demonstrauerat, ut bibentem natantemque faceret, exitum scilicet Claudi Agrippinaeque significans, et in nouissima clausula

Orcus uobis ducit pedes

senatum gestu notarat. histrionem . . . Nero nihil amplius quam urbe Italiaque summouit, uel contemptu omnis infamiae uel ne fatendo dolorem irritaret ingenia.

11. Quintilian 6. 3. 47.   See p. 141 and N. and S. xvi. 12.

12. Petr. *Sat.* 53. 13.

CHAPTER XVIII

1. Xenophon, *Symposium* 2. 11, 4. 54, 9. 2–6.

2. See Pickard-Cambridge, *Dithyramb*, etc., p. 229.   But the evidence seems to me to support the sense ' imitations ', ' representations ', rather than ' masks '.   Reich's argument (*Mimus*, pp. 257–8) rests on questionable assumptions, such as the supposed masklessness of Roman actors in early times.   The remark of Athenaeus (10, 452 f.) that Cleon the mimaulos was ' of the Italian mimes the best actor who displayed his own features ', Ἰταλικῶν μίμων ἄριστος αὐτοπρόσωπος ὑποκριτής, is, taken by itself, rather weak evidence for the view that there were other Italian mimes who wore masks.   The figures shown on the ' phlyax ' vase-paintings are often maskless, in Reich's view ;   and some of them—as, for example, the rider of the tunny-fish (Bieber *H.T.* fig. 372)—cannot be regarded as stage-actors at all.   My own feeling is that the wearing of a mask would tend to interfere with the essential feature of the mime's performance, which was mimicry ;   and if it is certain that the Roman mimes were maskless—as Reich holds—it seems reasonable to suppose that the Greek mimes also were maskless.   See Webster, *Greek Comic Costume*.

3. See Reich, p. 528 ;   Theophrastus, *Characters*, ch. 6 (the ' abandoned ' man, ὁ ἀπονενοημένος, is ready to ' dance the kordax though sober, and to take part in a comic chorus without a mask ', καὶ προσωπεῖον (μὴ) ἔχων ἐν κωμικῷ χορῷ : the negative is not in the MSS., but all editors since Casaubon have added it ;   Dem. *F.L.* 287 (433) : τοῦ καταράτου Κυρηβίωνος ὃς ἐν ταῖς πομπαῖς ἄνευ τοῦ προσώπου κωμάζει.

4. See Pliny 18. 286 ;   Reich, p. 559 ;   Smith, *Dict. Antiq.*, s.v.

5. Festus, p. 326 M., s.v. thymelici. libertinus mimus magnus natu qui ad tibicinem saltaret.   But see R. W. Reynolds, *Hermathena*, May, 1943, 56–62.

6. See p. 117.

7. ii. 23 ; see p. 87.

8. Reich, pp. 553–5.   Bieber, *H.T.*, pp. 204–5.

9. *Anthol. Lat.* 487 a (Schanz *Lit. Gesch.* i. 253) :

> fingebam uultus, habitus ac uerba loquentum,
> ut plures uno crederes ore loqui.
> ipse etiam quem nostra oculis geminabat imago
> horruit in uultus se * magis isse suos.
> O quotiens imitata meo se femina gestu
> uidit et erubuit totaque mota fuit !

10. *C.I.L.* I² 1861 ; Dessau 5221 ; Buecheler *Carm. Ep.* 361.
11. *C.I.L.* VI. 2. 10096 ; Reich, p. 561 ; Buecheler, *Carm. Ep.* 55 :

docta, erodita paene Musarum manu,
quae modo nobilium ludos decoraui choro
et graeca in scena prima populo apparui.

12. Reich 167–8, 558 ; *Anth. Pal.* ix. 587 :

ἡ καὶ ἔτ᾽ ἐκ βρέφεος κοιμωμένη Ἀντιοδημὶς
πορφυρέων Παφίης νοσσὶς ἐπὶ κροκύδων,
ἡ τακεραῖς λεύσσουσα κόραις μαλακώτερον ὕπνου
Λύσιδος ἀλκυονὶς, τερπνὸν ἄθυρμα Μέθης,
ὑδατίνους φορέουσα βραχίονας, ἡ μόνη ὀστοῦν
οὐ λάχεν (ἦν γὰρ ὅλη τοῦν ταλάροισι γάλα)
Ἰταλίην ἤμειψεν, ἵνα πτολέμοιο καὶ αἰχμῆς
ἀμπαύσῃ Ῥώμην μαλθακίνῃ χάριτι.

'Antiodemis, the nursling of Aphrodite, who from her babyhood slept on purple cloth, the glance of whose melting eyes is softer than sleep, the halcyon of Lysis, the delightful toy of Methe (Intoxication), whose arms flow like water, who alone among women has no bones at all (for she was all cream-cheese), has crossed to Italy, that by her softening charm she may make Rome cease from war and lay down the sword ' (tr. Paton). For Lysis see next note.

13. Plut. *Sulla* 36. Athen. 620 e, 621 c, d. Reich 235 note, 282–3. Aristocles (first century B.C.) identified magode and lysiode ; Aristoxenus (*circ.* 320 B.C.) said that Magodus is the name given to an actor who acts both male and female characters ; but that he who acts a woman's part in combination with a man's (?) is called a Lysiodist. Aristoxenus also said (Ath. 14. 621 c) that the art of the Hilarodus is solemn and akin to tragedy, but that the art of the Magodus is more like comedy : τὴν μὲν ἱλαρῳδίαν σεμνὴν οὖσαν παρὰ τὴν τραγῳδίαν εἶναι, τὴν δὲ μαγῳδίαν παρὰ τὴν κωμῳδίαν. The definition in the footnote is from Liddell and Scott. The name is derived from Lysis, who wrote songs for such parts ; see Strabo 648.

14. Dessau 2178 f. ; 5196 ; 5208 ; 5209. archimima : Dessau 5211 ; 5212. actores secundarum, tertiarum, quartarum : Suet. *Cal.* 57. 1 ; Dessau 5198–5201 ; Hor. *Ep.* 1. 18. 12. The mima is also called gesticularia and saltatricularia : Gell. 1. 5. 3. On the mimic dance see Reich 478.

15. *Orig.* 18. 49.

16. Festus, p. 274 M. : recinium omne uestimentum quadratum . . . unde reciniati mimi planipedes. Varro *L.L.* 5. 132 : antiquissimi amictui ricinium ; id, quod eo utebantur duplici, ab eo quod dimidiam partem retrorsum iaciebant, ab reiciendo ricinium

13

dictum. Nonius 14, p. 542, 1 M. ricinium, quod nunc mafurtium dicitur, palliolum femineum breue. Serv. *Aen.* 1. 282 : ricinus dicitur ab eo quod post tergum reicitur ; quod uulgo maforte dicunt. Also worn by men : Arnob. 6. 25 : riciniatus Iuppiter atque barbatus.

Apul. *apol.* 13 : mimi centunculus (as opposed to tragoedi syrma, histrionis crocota).

Painted face : Jer. *ep.* 22. 29. 4 : quae rubore frontis adtrito parasitos uicere mimorum. Apoll. Sid. *ep.* 2. 2. : absunt ridiculi uestitu et uultibus histriones pigmentis multicoloribus Philistionis supellectilem mentientes.

17. Schol. Juv. 6. 66 : penem, ut habent in mimo. Arnobius 7. 33 : delectantur (dei), ut res est, stupidorum capitibus rasis, salapittarum sonitu atque plausu, factis et dictis turpibus, fascinorum ingentium rubore. Cf. *N. and S.* iii. 1, 2.

Nonius I. p. 6 M. : a caluis mimicis. Juv. 5. 170 : pulsandum uertice raso praebebis quandoque caput. Reich 448–9, 578–9.

18. *Tr.* 2. 497–500. Cf. Mart. 5. 61 ; Reich. 59. Reynolds, The Adultery Mime, *C.Q.*, 1946, 77–84.

19. *Phil.* 2. 27. 65. Cf. Sen. *ep.* 114. 6.

20. Juvenal 6. 605–9.

21. Cic. *Cael.* 27, 65.

22. See Suet. *Aug.* 99.

23. Diomed., *G.L.K.* 1, 490. 3 : quarta species (fabulae Latinae) est planipedis, qui graece dicitur mimus. ideo autem Latine planipes dictus quod actores pedibus planis, id est nudis, proscaenium introirent, non ut tragici actores cum cothurnis neque ut comici cum soccis ; siue quod olim non in suggestu scaenae sed in plano orchestrae positis instrumentis mimicis actitabant. cuius planipedis Atta togatarum scriptor ita in Aedilicia fabula meminit :

daturin estis aurum? exultat planipes.

(For other references to the bare feet of the mime, cf. Sen. *ep.* 8. 8 : quam multa Publilii non excalceatis sed coturnatis dicenda sunt ! Juv. 8. 191 : planipedes audit (populus) Fabios. Macr. 2. 1. 9 : planipedis et sabulonis impudica et praetextata uerba iacientis. Donat *de com.* : planipedia autem dicta ob . . . uilitatem actorum, qui non coturno aut socco nituntur in scaena aut pulpito sed plano pede. Reich p. 600.)

24. P. 326 M. : solebant (enim saltare) in orchestra dum (in scaena actus fa)bulae componerentur. Cf. p. 271.

25. Jer. ad ann. 1974 (=43 B.C.) : p. 157 H. : Laberius mimorum scriptor decimo mense post C. Caesaris interitum Puteolis moritur. The ludi Caesaris at which he was forced to compete in his sixtieth year seem to have taken place in 46 B.C. (Cic. *ad Fam.* 12. 18. 2). Clodius : Macrob. 2. 6. 6.

26. Macrob. 2. 7. 2 : Laberium asperae libertatis equitem

Romanum Caesar quingentis milibus inuitauit ut prodiret in scaenam et ipse ageret mimos quos scriptitabat. id. 2. 7. 7 : cum mimos componeret (Syrus) . . . productus Romae per Caesaris ludos omnes qui tunc scripta et operas suas in scaenam locauerant prouocauit . . . superauit omnes, in quis et Laberium.

27. Plut. *de sollert. anim.* 19 (=973. 46).
28. *Sat.* 1. 10. 5.
29. Macrob. 2. 7. 6–7. Petron. 55. 5. Schanz, Röm. Lit. i, 260–1.
30. Seneca *Dial.* 9. 11. 8 ; *Ep.* 108. 8.

CHAPTER XIX

1. Antiphanes 191 Kock ; Menander 127 K.
2. Juv. vi. 67–70.
3. Val. Max. 2. 10. 8. Schol. ad Juv. 6. 250. Seneca *Epist.* 97. 8 ; Lactant. *Inst.* 1. 20.

CHAPTER XX

1. Cic. *Brut.* 18. 71.
2. *Eunuchus* bis die acta est meruitque pretium quantum nulla antea cuiusquam comoedia, id est octo milia nummorum. (*Vita Ter.*)
3. Macr. *Sat.* 2. 10 : mercedem diurnam de publico mille denarios sine gregalibus solus acceperit. Pliny *H.N.* 7. 39, 40.
4. *Phorm.* 18.
5. Lines 464 ff.
6. Macrob. *Sat.* 2. 10 : ceterum histriones non inter turpes habitos Cicero testimonio est, quem nullus ignorat Roscio et Aesopo tam familiariter usum ut res rationesque eorum sua sollertia tueretur . . . nam illam orationem quis est qui non legerit, in qua populum Romanum obiurgat quod Roscio gestum agente tumultuauerit ? . . . quae res ad hanc artis suae fiduciam Roscium abstraxit ut librum conscriberet quo eloquentiam cum histrionia compararet. . . . Aesopum uero ex pari arte ducenties sestertium reliquisse filio constat.
7. Pol. 30. 13.
8. Diomedes *G.L.K.* 1, p. 490 : at Latini scriptores complures personas in fabulas introduxerunt ut speciosiores frequentia facerent. Evanthius (Donatus, Teubner ed.) 2. 2 : qui quarti loci atque quinti actores essent.
9. Plaut. *Amph.* 69–74 ; *Poen.* 37–9.
10. Pliny *H.N.* 21. 4.
11. 7. 2. See Purser's article on Pantomimus (*Dict. of Ant.*).
12. *C.I.L.* 4. 1177, 1180, 1181, 1183, 1189, 1190, 1191. Inscr.

Orell. 6166.   Pliny *H.N.* 19. 23.   Mart. 14. 28.   Mau, *Pompeii*,
152, cf. 144.   These notices refer to gladiatorial shows.

    13. *Ars Am.* i. 139, 167.

    14. See article on Ludi by L. C. Purser, *Dict. of Ant.* ii, p. 88.

CHAPTER XXI

    1. 34. 54. 3 (194 B.C.) ;   40. 51 (179 B.C.) ;   41. 27 (174 B.C.) ;
Epit. 48 (155 B.C.).

    2. *Ann.* 14. 20.

CHAPTER XXII

    1. See p. 247.

    2. Suint. 6. 3. 63.

    3. See Purser, art. on Ludi, *Dict. of Ant.* ii, p. 88.

    4. Cic. *de Amic.* 7, 24 ; see p. 71.

CHAPTER XXIII

    1. Scaena :   *Capt.* 60, *Poen.* 20, *Pseud.* 568 ;   proscaenium :
Amph. 91, *Poen.* 17.

    2. See p. 249.

    3. Line 170 (if indeed it *is* used here ; see *Hermathena* 74 (1949),
p. 37.

    4. See Pickard-Cambridge, *Dramatic Festivals*, pp. 165–174.

CHAPTER XXIV

    1. Suet. *Aug.* 82 ;   Cass. Dio. 59. 7.

    2. Müller, *Frag. Hist.* i. 347. 45.   ' Among the Syracusans it
was the custom for women not to adorn themselves with gold or
to wear ἀνθινά unless they were courtesans.'   See Liddell and Scott
s.v. ἀνθινός , but for ' Athens ' read ' Syracuse.'

    3. There is a fundamental contradiction between the view that
costume indicated class and the view that it indicated mood.   The
plays would suggest that *neither* class *nor* mood was normally indicated by the costume ;   all that a character's appearance normally
indicates is age and sex.   There are few characters who do not
show some change of mood ;   yet we cannot suppose that this was
accompanied by a change of costume.

    4. 4. 18 :   τοῖς δὲ παρασίτοις πρόσεστι καὶ στλεγγὶς καὶ λήκυθος.

    5. xi. 3. 74 :   in comoediis . . . pater ille, cuius praecipuae partes
sunt, quia interim concitatus, interim lenis est, altero erecto altero
composito est supercilio, atque id ostendere maxime latus actoribus
moris est quod cum eis quas agunt partibus congruat.   I do

not see how this could be done ; but the general sense of this passage seems to be that the mask indicated not so much class as temperament.

6. See L. C. Purser, s.v., *Dict. Ant.* i. 557–8 ; J. T. Allen, *C.Q.* vol. i, pp. 226–8. There is no evidence in pre-Roman literature or art that the Greek tragic actor wore boots with thick soles, or that the word κόθορνος was associated with tragedy. The references to footwear in Greek tragedy suggest that the actors wore shoes suitable to the characters which they were representing, but not otherwise different from the footwear of everyday life ; thus Helen is said to wear golden sandals (Eur. *Or.* 1468) in which it would be possible to run or to dance (Eur. *I.A.* 1042) ; and when Agamemnon commands (*Agam.*, lines 944, 5) that his ἀρβύλαι, his ' servile footwear ' ; be ' unbound below ', he would seem to be referring to sandals. The conventional view would require us to suppose that the king sacrifices six inches of his stature ; and the effect could scarcely have been other than ludicrous. The ordinary meaning of κόθορνος is ' woman's boot ', easy to slip on (*Eccl.* 346) and therefore worn by the effeminate Dionysus (*Frogs* 47, 557), and contrasting ludicrously with the club and lion's skin which he wears in imitation of Heracles). The adaptability of the κόθορνος is apparent in both Greek (Xen. *Hell.* ii. 3. 31) and Roman (Cic. *Fin.* iii. 14. 46) references to it. It might thus come to be considered convenient for stage use, but we have no evidence for this before Roman times. It would also have Greek associations for the Romans ; and we could thus understand that they came to employ the cothurnus when performing Greek plays in translation. The earliest references to it in this sense show that it was already ' large ' and ' high ' (Hor. *Odes* II. i. 12, grandes cothurni, as opposed to the socci of comedy ; Ovid, *Am.* iii. 1. 63). It appears now to have denoted a leather upper with underneath it a rectangular block of painted wood, sometimes as much as six inches thick. Lucian, writing in the second century A.D., refers to the height and weight of the tragic actor's footwear (which he nowhere calls κόθορνος) and the difficulty of walking in it. Tragedy so acted must have been rather rigid and stylised ; and we can well believe that this was so in Imperial times. See now Pickard-Cambridge, *Dramatic Festivals*, p. 228.

7. See my article, *C.Q.* 33, 1939, pp. 139–146, and Duckworth, *N.R.C.*, pp. 92–4. Gellius (v. 7) quotes Gavius Bassus' derivation of persōna from persŏnare, ' sound through ', with the explanation that the mask made the voice more distinct and melodious. The etymology is disproved by the quantity of the vowel ; and the statement that the voice was made louder by the mask seems to be a mere invention. The effect of the mask would be, if anything, to muffle the voice, though this danger might be obviated by making the opening large. Another reason for having the mouth

large was to enable the same mask to fit different persons. (See *D.F.* 193–4 and Appendix I.)

8. Diomedes, p. 489 K. : antea galearibus, non personis utebantur, ut qualitas coloris indicium faceret aetatis, cum essent aut albi aut nigri aut rufi.
Donatus *de Com.* 26 W.
Cicero *De Orat.* iii. 59. 221.
Festus (*N. and S.* xvi. 9).

9. See Saunders, *Costume in Roman Comedy*, pp. 28 ff.

CHAPTER XXV

1. Mémoires présentées par divers savants, I. x. See Legrand, *Daos*, p. 465.

2. Mr. E. W. Handley asks (*Cambridge Review,* May 19, 1951) : " does our reading . . . suggest that the poets and their audience took such a rigid view of the function of the chorus and the nature of act-division as B.? Neither is committed, as he is, to an analysis or a definition.' But what I am discussing is the modern view that act-division was a reality in New Comedy ; and the first point to consider is what is meant by ' act-division '. In its ordinary modern sense the term carries with it implications which all would agree to be quite foreign to ancient drama. If it is not intended to be understood in its ordinary sense, then it is for those who use it in some other sense to explain what they mean by it.

CHAPTER XXVI

The quotations are from *Twelfth Night* II. iii. 53 ; *As You Like It,* II. v. 16 ; and *As You Like It,* V. iii. 36.

CHAPTER XXVII

1. Quintilian x. i. 98.

2. Didasc. in cod. Paris. 7530 s. VIII. et Casin. 1086 : Lucius Varius cognomento Rufus Thyesten tragoediam magna cura absolutam post Actiacam uictoriam Augusto ludis eius in scaena edidit ; pro qua fabula sestertium deciens accepit.

3. *Tr.* V. vii. 27 : nil equidem feci—tu scis hoc ipse—theatris. *Tr.* ii. 519 (et mea sunt populo saltata poemata saepe) probably refers to pantomime. Suet. *Nero* 25.

4. Suet. ap Hier. ed. Roth, p. 301, 25 ; Lucian *de Salt.* 35 ; and see Purser's article on pantomimus (*Dict. of Ant.*).

5. Lucani uita (att. to Vacca) : exstant eius . . . tragoedia Medea imperfecta, salticae fabulae xiv. Juv. vii. 82–92. Also Arbronius Silo : Sen. *Suas.* ii. 19.

6. Juv. vi. 60–6.

7. See Appendices F and H.

8. *Ep.* vii.

9. *Ep.* vi. 21.

10. xi. 3. 178–82 ; cf. x. 1. 99.

11. i. 3.

12. Suet. *Ner.* 11.

13. Aelius Lampridius, *Heliog.* 25.

14. Mart. *Lib. Spect.* 5 and 7, viii. 30. 15, x. 25 ; Friedlander ii. 444.

15. Suet. *Ner.* 39, *Dom.* 12 ; and see N. and S. on ch. xvi.

16. Petr. *Sat.* 53.

17. ii. 7. 3.

18. *Plin.* vi. 21.

19. *Ox. Pap.* 413 ; Herodas, ed. Crusius (1914) ; Appendix L.

20. Reich, *Mimus* i. 109–81.

21. ὄρνεα γῆς : Manetho, *Apotelesmata* iv. 282 (Reich, ii. 523).

APPENDIX A

1. Properly, as the termination shows, ' the means by which one sees '.

APPENDIX C

1. *Merc.* 219–22 : Charinus is warned not to take the direct route to the harbour but to go off-stage by the opposite wing (and make his way to the harbour by the back street). At line 330 he is seen returning from the harbour.

2. See now *C.R.*, N.S. iv. i. pp. 6–8.

APPENDIX E

1. V. vii. 23.

2. Cf. the ' Greek curtain ' used in the Indian theatre (App. H).

3. The other possible interpretation of this passage is that Donatus is using aulaea sublata in the familiar classical sense of ' end of the performance ', as Duckworth takes it (*N.R.C.*, p. 85), probably rightly. In other words, Donatus is not necessarily thinking of the theatre of his own day, still less is he to be taken as an authority for the stage usage of Terence's day.

APPENDIX G

1. Quoted, with most of the other authorities, by Becker, *Char.*, l.c. For ancient authorities on the door see *Excavations at Olynthus* (Robinson), part 12, pp. 399–452, and for door-fittings see ib., part 10, pp. 248–52 (with plates).

2. Cf. Xen. *Econ.* 9. 5 : ἔδειξα δὲ καὶ τὴν · γυναικωνῖτιν αὐτῇ, θύρᾳ βαλανωτῇ ὡρισμένην ἀπὸ τῆς ἀνδρωνίτιδος. . . . This door must have been fastened with something more than a bolt ; on which *side* would the bolt have been? the men's side, or the women's?

APPENDIX M

1. See also my articles in *Classical Philology*, 50 pp. 89–97 and *Heomathena* 87, pp. 3–20, and my book *Latin Verse and European Song*, 1957.

BIBLIOGRAPHY

The following list does not pretend to be complete. Fuller lists are given by Pickard-Cambridge and Duckworth (see below).

MANUSCRIPTS AND EDITIONS

Plautus. The only early MS. of Plautus is A, the Ambrosian Palimpsest, written in capitals in the fourth or fifth century A.D. It originally contained the twenty-one Varronian plays (see page 36). In the seventh or eighth century the original writing was erased and replaced by part of the Books of Kings and Chronicles. The MS. was discovered by Cardinal Angelo, who tried to decipher it (1815). In 1889 Wilhelm Studemund, after long and heroic labour, which cost him his eyesight, published his transcription (Apographum), on which all modern study is based. ' Aujourd'hui le palimpseste ambrosien, brûlé, troué, noirci par les réactifs, détérioré de toutes manières, n'est plus que l'ombre d'une ombre, et si nous pouvons l'utiliser avec certitude, c'est au dévoûment de Studemund que nous le devons ' (Ernout, *Plaute*, vol. 1, p. xxv).

The other extant MSS. (tenth century or later) are collectively known as the ' Palatine', descended from an original (now lost), probably of the eighth century.

The one early MS. of Terence is the Codex Bembinus (A), of the fourth or fifth century. The medieval MSS. belong to the ninth century or later. A few are illustrated by miniatures (most of them in colour) depicting each scene and showing the masks required for each play. The value of these illustrations as evidence for the staging of the classical (or indeed any) period is much debated.

The early MSS. contained didascaliae : these survive in the Ambrosian (in a mutilated form) for the *Stichus* and the *Pseudolus*., and in the MSS. of Terence. The MSS. contained scene-headings showing the names and social position of the characters taking part, and adding the letters C or DV (see page 210). These entries have largely disappeared, and the names of the characters, unless mentioned in the dialogue, are often unknown. The editio princeps of Plautus appeared in 1472. Among modern editors the great name is that of F. Ritschl, whose *Parerga* were published in 1845. His critical editions of nine plays appeared in 1849–54. His pupils, G. Goetz, G. Loewe and F. Schoell, edited all twenty plays (1879–1902). In 1895–6 appeared F. Leo's important but sometimes arbitrary text (adopted by P. Nixon for his Loeb edition, 1916–38). Not only does Leo bracket many passages on the purely subjective ground that he thinks them unworthy of Plautus, but he makes hazardous emendations. W. M. Lindsay's Oxford text reached its second edition in 1910 ; A. Ernout's Budé edition (introduction, text, translation and critical apparatus) appeared in 1932–40.

I have made much use of the following editions (with commentaries) of separate plays :

W. M. Lindsay, *The Captivi*, 1900.

E. A. Sonnenschein, *Rudens*, 1891. In 1901 appeared his editio minor of the *Rudens*, and in 1922 his *Mostellaria*.

F. Marx, *Rudens*, 1928.

P. J. Enk, *Plauti Mercator*, Leiden, 1932 ; *Truculentus*, 1953.

The editio princeps of Terence was published in 1470. Richard Bentley's text appeared in 1726, that of Dziatzko in 1884. The most useful edition (with commentary) for English readers is that of S. G. Ashmore, New York, 1908. In 1912 J. Sargeaunt published his Loeb edition. In 1926 appeared the Oxford text of R. Kauer and W. M. Lindsay ; the Budé text (with introduction, translation and critical notes) of J. Marouzeau was published in 1942–9. I have found A. Thierfelder's small edition of the *Andria* (Heidelberg, 1951) particularly useful. See now A. Pratesi's edition of *Phormio, Hecyra, Adelphoe*, Rome, 1952. Donatus is quoted from P. Wessner's Teubner edition (*Aeli Donati quod fertur Commentum Terenti*, 1902–8).

Those interested in textual study may consult :

L. Havet, *Manuel de critique verbale appliquee aux textes latins*, Paris, 1911 ; and W. M. Lindsay, *An Introduction to Latin Textual Emendation*, 1896.

For the illustrated MSS. consult :

L. W. Jones, and C. R. Morey, *The Miniatures of the Manuscripts of Terence Prior to the Thirteenth Century*, Princeton, 1930–1.

The fragments of Republican drama are cited from O. Ribbeck, *Tragicorum Romanorum Fragmenta*, 2nd ed., 1871, and *Comicorum Latinorum Reliquiae*, 1855.

E. H. Warmington's Loeb edition of the *Fragments of Old Latin*, 1935–6, is particularly useful to the English reader. See also A. Klotz, *Scaenicorum Romanorum Fragmenta*, vol. 1, 1953. In citing Seneca's plays I have used the Loeb edition by F. G. Miller, 1917.

G. E. Duckworth's *The Complete Roman Drama*, 1942, gives a translation of all extant Latin plays, including the post-classical *Querolus*, with notes.

ILLUSTRATED WORKS ON THE GREEK AND ROMAN THEATRE

J. T. Allen, *Stage Antiquities of the Greeks and Romans, and their Influence*, 1927.

Margarete Bieber, *Die Denkmäler zum Theaterwesen in Altertüm,* 1920, and *The History of the Greek and Roman Theater,* enlarged ed. ii, 1961.

H. Bulle, *Untersuchungen an griechischen Theatern,* 1928.

Giacomo Caputo, *Il Teatro di Sabratha e L'Architettura Teatrale Africana,* (reviewed by W. Beare in *C.R.* XI. 170).

W. Dörpfield and E. Reisch, *Das griechische Theater,* 1896.

E. Fiechter, *Die Baugeschichtliche Entwicklung des griechischen Theaters,* 1914.

R. C. Flickinger, *The Greek Theater and its Drama,* ed. iv, 1936.

A. Frickenhaus, *Die altgriechische Bühne,* 1917.

A. E. Haigh, *The Attic Theatre,* ed. iii, revised by A. W. Pickard-Cambridge, 1907.

J. A. Hanson, *Roman Theater-Temples,* 1959.

O. Navarre, *Le Théâtre grec,* 1925.

A. W. Pickard-Cambridge, *Dithyramb, Tragedy and Comedy,* 1927, and ed. ii, revised by T. B. L. Webster 1962 (references in the text are to the 1927 edition) ; *The Theatre of Dionysus in Athens,* 1946 (*T.D.*) ; *The Dramatic Festivals of Athens,* 1953 (*D.F.*) enlarged ed. ii, 1961.

A. D. Trendall, ' Phlyax Vases ', *London University, Institute of Classical Studies,* Bulletin Supplement 8, 1959.

For Aristophanes I have used Rogers' editions of the separate plays, and for Menander, E. Capps' *Four Plays of Menander,* 1910, the Loeb edition by F. G. Allinson, 1921, as these are generally available to English readers, and V. Martin, *Ménandre : Le Dyscolos,* Papyrus Bodmer iv, 1958. For the fragments I have used T. Kock, *Comicorum Atticorum Fragmenta,* 1880–8, and J. Demiańczuk, *Supplementum Comicum,* 1912.

For later Greek Comedy I have consulted :

J. U. Powell and E. A. Barber, *New Chapters in the History of Greek Literature,* 1921; Second Series, 1929; Third Series, 1933.

G. Norwood, *Greek Comedy,* 1931.

T. B. L. Webster, South Italian Vases and Attic Drama, *C.Q.* xlii, 1948, pp. 15–27 (discussed by Pickard-Cambridge, ib. xliii, 1959, p. 57, and by me, ib. xliii, pp. 30–1. ' The Masks of Greek Comedy ', *Bulletin of the John Rylands Library,* xxxii, 1949, pp. 97–135. *Studies in Menander,* 1950 (reviewed by P. W. Harsh, *Gnomon,* Band 25, 1953, pp. 40–4). *Studies in Later Greek Comedy,* 1950. ' Greek Comic Costume ': its History and Diffusion ', *Bulletin of the John Rylands Library,* xxxvi, 1954, pp. 563–88. *Greek Theatre Production,* 1956. ' Monuments illustrating Old and Middle Comedy ', 'Monuments illustrating New Comedy', and 'Monuments illustrating Tragedy and Satyrplay ', in *London University Institute of Classical Studies,* Bulletin Supplements 9, 11 and 14 (1960, 1961 and 1962) ; *Griechische Bühnenaltertümer,* 1963.

MIME

Herodas, O. Crusius (2nd ed. by R. Herzog, 1926) for text of the Oxyrhynchus Mime and the Oxyryhnchus Farce.

A. Olivieri, *Frammenti della Comedia Greca a del Mimo nella Sicilia e nella Magna Grecia*, 1930.

A. Dieterich, *Pulcinella*, 1897.

H. Reich, *Der Mimus*, 1903.

E. Wüst, excellent articles on *Mimus* and *Phlyakes* in P.W.

PUPPET-SHOWS

V. Prou, ' Les théâtres d'automates en Grèce ', published in 1884 in *Memoires presentées pars divers savants*, i. 10. Prou's views had already been discussed by H. Weil, *Journ. des savants*, 1882.

LATIN DRAMA

F. Arnaldi, *Da Plauto a Terenzio*, 1946–7.

E. Bignone, *Storia della letteratura latina*, vol. i, 2nd ed., 1946.

F. Della Corte, *Da Sarsina a Roma*, 1952.

G. E. Duckworth, *The Nature of Roman Comedy*, 1951 (with good bibliography). Referred to as *N.R.C.*

J. Wight Duff, *A Literary History of Rome from the Origins to the Close of the Golden Age*, new ed., 1953. *A Literary History of Rome in the Silver Age*, 1927.

P. S. Dunkin, *Post Aristophanic Comedy*, 1946.

P. J. Enk, ' Roman Tragedy ', *N. Ph.* 31 (1957), pp. 282–307.

P. Fabia, *Les Prologues de Terence*, 1888.

E. Fraenkel, *Plautinisches im Plautus*, 1922.

T. Frank, *Life and Literature in the Roman Republic*, 1930.

P. Grimal, *Le Siècle des Scipions*, 1953.

H. Haffter, ' Terenz und seine künsterische Eigenart ', *Mus. Helv.*, vol. 10, 1953.

G. Jachmann, *Plautinisches und Attisches*, Berlin, 1931.

P. W. Harsh, *Studies in Dramatic ' Preparation ' in Roman Comedy*, 1935. *Anthology of Roman Drama*, 1960 (reviewed by W. Beare in *C.R.*, XI, p. 296).

C. J. Herrington, ' Octavia Praetexta, a Survey ', *C.Q.* 11, pp. 18–30.

M. Herrmann, *Die Entstehung der berufsmässigen Schauspielkunst im Altertum und in der Neuzeit*, 1962.

W. E. J. Kuiper, *Grieksche Origineelen en Latijnische Navolgingen*, Amsterdam, 1936. ' Two Comedies by Apollodorus of Carystus : Terence's *Hecyra* and *Phormio* ', *Mnemosyne*, Supp. 1, 1938. (Reviewed by Tredennick, *C.P.* 53, 1939, p. 66).

P. E. Legrand, *Daos, Tableau de la comédie grecque pendant la période dite nouvelle*, 1910. Eng. Tr. by J. Loeb, ' *The New Greek Comedy* ', 1917.

P. Lejay, *Histoire de la littérature latine des origines à Plaute*, 1923 ; *Plaute*, 1925.

F. Leo, *Plautinische Forschungen*, 2nd ed., 1912 ; *Geschichte der römischen Literatur*, Vol. I, 1913.

G. Michaut, *Sur les tréteaux latins*, 1912 ; *Plaute*, 1920. I have found Michaut's work particularly valuable as giving a balanced and critical survey of the whole field.

A. Nicoll, *Masks, Mimes and Miracles*, 1931.

G. Norwood, *The Art of Terence*, 1923 ; *Plautus and Terence*, 1932.

E. Paratore, *Storia del Teatro Latino*, 1957.

R. Perna, *L'originalità di Plauto*, 1955.

M. Schanz, *Geschichte der römischen Literatur*, I, 4th ed. by C. Hosius, 1927. This gives the most complete summary of the literary evidence.

N. Terzaghi, *Prolegomeni a Terenzio*, 1931.

A. Thierfelder, *De rationibus interpolationum Plautinarum*, 1929.

K. M. Westaway, *The Original Element in Plautus*, 1917.

CHRONOLOGY OF PLAUTUS

C. H. Buck, *A Chronology of the Plays of Plautus*, 1940.

H. Mattingly and E. S. G. Robinson, ' The Prologue to the *Casina* of Plautus ', *C.R.* 47, 1933, pp. 52–4.

K. H. E. Schutter, *Quibus annis Comoediae Plautinae primum actae sint quaeritur*, Groningen, 1952.

W. B. Sedgwick, ' Plautine Chronology ', *A.J.P.* 70, 1949, pp. 376–83.

BOOKS AND ARTICLES ON SPECIAL LITERARY TOPICS

W. Beare, ' The meaning of XOPOY ', *Hermathena* 84, pp. 93–103 ; in the *Plutus* ', *C.Q.* 5, pp. 49–52 ; ' Contaminatio ', *C.R.* 9, pp. 7–11.

E. H. Clift, *Latin Pseudepigrapha*, Baltimore, 1945.

C. C. Conrad, *The Technique of Continuous Action in Roman Comedy*, Menasha, 1915.

G. E. Duckworth, ' The Structure of the Miles Gloriosus ', *C.P.* 30, 1935, pp. 228–46 ; ' Plautus : the other nineteen plays ', *C.W.*, Dec., 1947.

P. J. Enk, ' Quelques observations sur la manière dont Plaute s'est comporté envers ses originaux ', *R. Ph.* 64, 1938, pp. 289–94 ; ' Terence as an adaptor of Greek Comedies ', *Mnem.* 13, 1947, pp. 81–93.

T. Frank, ' Naevius and free speech ', *A.J.P.* 48, 1927, pp. 105–10 ; ' Status of actors at Rome ', *C.P.* 26, 1931, pp. 11–20 ; ' The actor Pellio ', *A.J.P.* 53, 1932, pp. 248–51.

R. C. Flickinger, ' XOPOY in Terence's Heauton, the Shifting of Choral Roles in Menander, and Agathon's Embolima ', *C.P.* 7, 1912, pp. 24–34.

A. Freté, ' Essai sur la structure dramatique des comédies de Plaute ', *R.E.L.* 7, 1929, pp. 282–94 ; 8, 1930, pp. 36–81.

J. N. Hough (see Bibliography in *N.R.C.*, pp. 449–50, 456, 457, 461).

Ruth Mildred Keller, '*Iste deiktikon* in the early Roman Dramatists', *T.A.P.A.* 77, 1946, pp. 261–316.

C. Knapp, 'The Sceptical Assault on the Roman Tradition concerning the Dramatic Satura', *A.J.P.* 33, 1912, pp. 125–48. See Bibliography in *N.R.C.*, passim.

A. M. G. Little, 'Plautus and Popular Drama', *Harv. Stud. in Class. Phil.* 49, 1935, pp. 205–28.

H. W. Prescott (see *N.R.C.*, p. 451).

E. G. Sihler, 'The Collegium Poetarum at Rome', *A.J.P.* 26, 1905, pp. 1–21.

R. Waltz, '*Contaminare* chez Térence', *R.E.L.* 16, 1938, pp. 269–74.

R. T. Weissinger, *A Study of Act Divisions in Classical Drama*, 1940 (Iowa Studies, no. ix).

STAGING

W. Beare, 'Angiportum', *C.R.* 4, pp. 6–8.

C. O. Dalman, *De aedibus scaenicis comoediae novae*, Leipzig, 1929.

P. Gardner, 'The Scenery of the Greek Stage', *J.H.S.* 19, 1899, pp. 252–68.

A. S. F. Gow, 'On the Use of Masks in Roman Comedy', *J.R.S.* 2, 1912, pp. 65–77.

P. W. Harsh, 'Angiportum, Platea and Vicus', *C.P.* 32, 1937, pp. 44–58.

M. Johnston, *Exits and Entrances in Roman Comedy*, New York, 1933.

C. M. Kurrelmeyer, *The Economy of Actors in Plautus*, Graz, 1932.

W. W. Mooney, *The House-Door on the Ancient Stage*, Baltimore, 1914.

H. W. Prescott, 'The Doubling of Rôles in Roman Comedy', *C.P.* 18, 1923, pp. 23–34.

L. C. Purser, Articles in Smith's *Dictionary of Greek and Roman Antiquities* on *cothurnus, ludi, mimus, pantomimus.*

Kelley Rees, *The So-called Rule of Three Actors in the Classical Greek Drama*, Chicago, 1908 ; 'The Function of the Πρόθυρον in the Production of Greek Plays', *C.P.* 10, 1915, pp. 117–138.

C. A. Saunders, *Costume in Roman Comedy*, New York, 1909 ; 'The Introduction of Masks on the Roman Stage', *A.J.P.* 32, 1911, pp. 58–73 ; 'Altars on the Roman Comic Stage', *T.A.P.A.* 42, 1911, pp. 91–103.

LANGUAGE

J. T. Allardice, *Syntax of Terence*, 1929 (St. Andrews University Publications, No. 27).

C. E. Bennett, *Syntax of Early Latin*, Boston, 1910–14.

L. H. Gray, 'The Punic Passages in the "Poenulus" of Plautus', *Am. Journ. of Semitic Languages* 39, 1922–23, pp. 73–88.

W. M. Lindsay, *Syntax of Plautus*, 1907.

G. Lodge, *Lexicon Plautinum*, 1924–33.

L. R. Palmer, *The Latin Language*, 1954.

MUSIC

D. B. Monro, *The Modes of Ancient Greek Music*, 1894.

J. F. Mountford, ' Greek Music in the Papyri and Inscriptions ', *New Chapters in Greek Literature*, ii, 1929, pp. 146–83 ; and R. P. Winnington-Ingram, article on ' Music ' in *Oxford Class. Dict.*, 1949 (with Bibliography).

METRE (GREEK AND LATIN)

W. Beare, *Latin Verse and European Song*, 1957 ; ' Pollicis ictus, the Saturnian and Beowulf, *Cl. Phil.* 50, pp. 89–97 ; ' The Origin of Rhythmic Latin Verse ', *Hermathena* 87, pp. 3–20.

A. M. Dale, *Lyric Metres of Greek Drama*, 1948.

J. D. Denniston, article on ' Metre, Greek ' in *O.C.D.*

W. R. Hardie, *Res Metrica*, 1920.

J. W. White, *The Verse of Greek Comedy*, 1912 (with bibliography).

C. E. Bennett, ' What was Ictus in Latin Prosody? ', *A.J.P.* 19, 1898, pp. 361–83.

F. Crusius, *Die Responsion in den plautinischen Cantica*, Leipzig, 1929.

H. Drexler, *Plautinische Akzentstudien*, Breslau, 1932–3.

P. W. Harsh, *Iambic Words and Regard for Accent in Plautus*, Stanford, 1949.

W. A. Laidlaw, *The Prosody of Terence*, 1938 (St. Andrews University Publications, No. 40).

F. Leo, *Die plautinische Cantica und die hellenistische Lyrik*, 1897 ; *Der saturnische Vers*, 1905.

W. M. Lindsay, *Early Latin Verse*, 1922 ; ' Plautus and the Beggar's Opera ', *C.R.* 37, 1923, p. 67 ; Edition of *Captivi*, pp. 12–102 ; ' The Saturnian Metre ', *A.J.P.* Vol. 14 (1893), pp. 139–70, 305–34.

J. F. Mountford, article on ' Metre, Latin ', in *O.C.D.*

L. Nougaret, ' La métrique de Plaute et de Térence ', *Mem. des Et. Lat. offert à J. Marouzeau*, 1943, pp. 123–148 ; *Traité de Métrique Latine Classique*, 1948.

W. B. Sedgwick, ' The Origin and Development of Roman Comic Metres ', *Classica et Mediaevalia* 10, 1949, pp. 171–81.

E. A. Sonnenschein, *What is Rhythm?*, 1925.

E. Vandvik, *Rhythmus und Metrum*, Oslo, 1937.

ENGLISH DRAMA, MUSIC, METRE, ETC.

E. K. Chambers, *Elizabethan Stage* (reprinted, with corrections), 1945.

M. Hunter, ' Act- and Scene-Division in the Plays of Shakespeare ', *Rev. Engl. Studies,* Vol. 2, 1926, pp. 295–310.

Dover Wilson, ' Act- and Scene-Division in the Plays of Shakespeare : a reply to Sir Mark Hunter ', *Rev. Engl. Studies,* Vol. 3, pp. 385–97.

R. Noble, *Shakespeare's Use of Song,* 1923.

Bruce Pattison, *Music and Poetry of the English Renaissance,* 1948.

WORKS OF REFERENCE

Daremberg et Saglio, *Dictionnaire des antiquités grecques et romaines,* 1877–1919.

Grammatici Latini, ed. H. Keil (8 vols.), 1855–1923. (*G.L.K.*)

Oxford Classical Dictionary, 1948. (*O.C.D.*)

Oxford Companion to the Theatre, 1951.

Pauly-Wissowa, *Real-Encyclopädie der classischen Altertumswissenschaft,* 1877–. (*P.W.*)

INDEX

accent, 223 f., 230, 320–7. (*See Hermathena* 81, 29–40, and Enk, *Mnem*. iv. vi. 93–109)
Accius, dramatist and critic, 26, 41, 42, 70–2, 74, 119–127, 233, 311, 364 f.
act, 196–218, 272, 340 ff.
acting, actor, 3, 16–23, 28, 81, 86, 132, 149, 166–8, 183, 213, 229, 237–40, 335–354, 371.
actress (in mime), 149, 151, 152, 239, 319
Aeschylus, 336
Aesopus (actor), 166, 371
Afranius, 106, 128–35, 365
Allen, J. T., 373
Allinson, F. G., 101, 205, 252
Ambivius Turpio, 89, 164–6
amphitheatre, 172, 243 f., 371 f.
Andronicus, Livius, 1, 26–32, 33, 71, 73, 86, 165, 336, 358
angiportus, –um, ('street', especially back street supposed to run behind houses fronting on stage), 181, 256–63. (*See C.R.* 68, 6–8, and *Enk. ad Truc.* 303)
Antiodemis (mime-actress), 152, 369
Antiphanes, 108, 341
Aprissius (dramatist), 147
Apuleius (on acts), 216 n.
(on curtain), 271 f., 274
(on scenery), 301
Aquilius (dramatist), 113
archimimus, –a, 153, 239, 319, 369
Aristophanes (dramatist), 50 f., 290 f., 340 ff., 356 f.,
(of Byzantium, on Menander), 54
Aristotle, *Eth. Nic.* 4. 6., 295 ; *Poetics* 4., 299, 357 ; 9. 8., 108, 341 ff.
Aristoxenus, 339
Atellana, 13, 17, 20, 21, 23, 25, 39, 47, 137–48, 192, 238 f., 366–8
Athenaeus 10.452 f., 368 ; 12.536, 296 ; 14.614, 296, 335, 339
Atilius (dramatist), 113
Atta, 128–35, 365
aulaeum. (*See* curtain)
awnings, *praef*. i, 170, 298, 371 f.

Balbus, L. Cornelius (amateur dramatist), 42, 44
Bassulus, M. Pomponius (amateur dramatist), 237

Bathyllus (pantomime dancer), 234
Becker, W. A., 287–88
Bieber, M., *praef*. i, 279, 295, 301
Bignone, E., 101
Brevis Brevians, 324
Bucco, 139 ff.
Bulle, H., 271
Butler, H. E., 271

Caecilius Statius, 71, 85–90, 91, 93, 117 f., 350, 363 f.
cantica, 29, 74, 75, 81, 169, 219–32, 234, 330
cantor, 229. (*See* actor)
Capps, E., 205
Catienus (actor), 81, 269
Catullus (mime-writer), 270
cauea ('pit'), 171
censor of plays, 169
centunculus (mime's jacket), 153, 155, 370
Chambers, Ed., 199
choragus (property manager), 166. (*See also* producer).
Choricius of Gaza (on the mime), 240
chorus, 29, 50–2, 75, 196–218, 340 ff. *See Hermathena*, 74, 26–38, and Appendix O
Cicero, on Andronicus, 27, 30 ; on Naevius, 41 f.; on Plautus, 47; on Ennius, 74–8 ; on Pacuvius, 82 ff. ; on Caecilius, 89 ; on Terence, 95 ; on Accius' *Brutus*, 42 f. ; on seated audience, 81, 175 (J. G. Griffiths, *C.R.* 66.72) ; on Roscius on Demiurgus, 116 ; on Roscius masked, 193, 303 f.; on Accius, 120 ; on Afranius, 131 ; on 'Oscan farce', 138 ; on Novius, 143 ; on mime, 153 f., 268 ; on Fufius, 269 ; on costume, 265 ; on delivery, 222 f.; on Roman methods of translation, 312
Cincius Faliscus (actor), 193, 303 ff.
Cleon (mime-writer), 150, 368
Clifford, H. R., 210
'cloakrooms', absence of. (*See* chaps. xix, xxii, xxv)
collegium poctarum, 28, 86, 126
commedia dell' arte, 148
conquistor (theatrical supervisor), 169
Conrad, C. C., 204

contaminare, 74, 82, 96–108, 310–2
Corte, E. della, 93
costume, 184–95, 264–6, 335, 356 f.,
    369, 372 f.
cothurnus ('buskin'), 188, 191, 265,
    370, 373
crepida, crepidata, 185 f., 264 f.
curtain, 81, 149, 154, 179 f., 267–74,
    284, 375
    (in Indian Theatre), 302

Dalman, C. O., 257, 287, 289
Dariocopus, 336
dance, 10–12, 16, 22, 222 f., 234, 341
Datus (Atellane actor), 367
Demetrius (actor), 237
didascaliae, 47 f., 91, 94 f., 116, 168,
    195
Dieterich, A., 148, 270
Diomedes (grammarian), 193, 209,
    220 f., 264, 270
dissignator (usher), 169, 173
diuerbium (deuerbium), unaccom-
    panied declamation, 219–32
dogs on the stage, 155, 319
Donatus, on act-division, 196–218
    on costumes, 185–7, 193
    on the curtain, 267–74
    on types of drama, 264–6
    on music, 220 ff.
    on Terence, 91–108, 349
door, 125, 176 f., 182, 257–63, 285–93,
    335, 375
Dörpfeld, W., praef. i, 244–6
Dossennus, 139 ff.
doubling, 167, 307 f.
dramatic time, 198 ff., 210 ff.
Duckworth, G. E., praef. i, ii, 53, 303,
    311–3, 373, 375
Duff, J. Wight, 31, 241

ekkyklema (alleged device for present-
    ing indoor scenes by 'wheeling
    out' interior of scene-building),
    286. (See T.D., 111–121.)
Enk, P. J., praef., 65
Ennius, 18, 27, 35, 37, 41, 70–8, 93,
    99, 349, 361 f., 364
Epicharmus, 336
Eucharis (mime-actress), 152, 369
Evanthius. (See Donatus)
exostra, 270

fabula, types of 264–6
farce, 1, 13, 16, 19, 20, 21, 25, 137 ff.,
    150, 156, 335 ff. (See article in
    Cassell's Encyclopaedia)
Fensterbusch, C., 249
Fescennine verses, 11–18, 355
Fiechter, E. R., 269, 272–4
Flaccus (musician), 168, 229
Flickinger, R., 204, 209, 212, 248, 342

flute, flute-player. (See tibia, tibicen)
Fraenkel, E., praef. i, 232
Freté, A., 201, 214
Frickenhaus, A., 286 f.
Fufius (actor), 81, 269

Gardner, Percy, 276 f.
Gerkan, A. von, 289
gesture, 140, 149, 183, 191
ghosts on stage, 81, 254, 269
gladiatorial shows, 21 f., 371 f.
Gomme, A. W., 285
Gregory of Nyassa, 299 f., 302
Grimal, P., 93, 105

Haigh, A. E., 203, 221, 244–6, 249,
    252, 285 f.
Handley, E. W., 374
Harsh, P. W., praef. i, 210, 256 f.
hilarotragoedia, 25
histrio, 16, 28, 142, 229. (See actor)
Holzinger, von, 345
Hunter, Mark, 199

ikria (benches supported on uprights);
    245 f.
illustrations in manuscripts, 111, 184,
    274
Indian theatre, 302
indoor scenes, 178 f.
interval and interlude, 196–218, 341

Jachmann, G., 209 f., 287
Johnston, Mary, 210, 248–54
Joseph, B. L., praef. i
Juventius (dramatist), 113
Juvenal, 352

katablemata (detachable pictures
    hung on periacti), 249, 254, 295 f.,
    301
Knocking. (See door)
Körte, A., 197, 204 f., 216, 295, 301
Kuiper, W. E. J., 200
Kurrelmeyer, Carrie, 163

Laberius, Decimus, 154–8, 370 f.
Laelius, 92 f.
Laidlaw, W. A., 324
'left' and 'right' on stage, 181, 248–54
Legrand, P., 204, 206, 374
Leo, F., 179, 201, 206 f., 217, 232
Licinius Imbrex (dramatist) 113
Lindsay, W. M., 219, 225, 231, 323 ff.
Livius. (See Andronicus)
Livy vii. 2–5, 10, 16–23, 141, 219
Lodge, Lexicon Plautinum, 257
Lucan (as writer of plays and libretti),
    234, 374

lucar (State grant for theatrical expenses, actors' pay, etc.), 142, 164–6, 351,
ludi, 162 f., 176
Lundström, V., 280
Luscius Lanuvinus, 94, 98, 102, 107, 114 f., 350, 364

Maccus, 47, 139 ff.
Maidment, K. G., 200, 204 f.
make-up, 370. (*See* 306)
Manducus, 139 ff., 366
manuscript, author's, 4–9, 164 f., 341
Marcipor (musician), 67, 168, 229
masks, 2, 5, 12, 14, 21–3, 81, 150, 183, 186–95, 303–9, 335 ff., 352–4, 368
Mazois' theory of curtain, 269 ff.
Melissus (dramatist), 136
Memmius (man of letters), 93
Menander, 51–5, 87–90, 94–109, 196–216, 340 ff., 349
metre, 31, 75, 124, 219–32, 320–34
Metrobius (mime-actor), 152
Michaut, G., 197, 217, 312
mime, 2, 5, 10, 14, 17, 19, 25, 47, 88, 127, 138, 140, 142, 149–58, 192, 239 f., 264, 268–74, 302, 306, 314–9, 348 f.
Minucius Prothymus (actor), 193, 302–5
Mirmont, H. de la Ville de, 358
Mommsen, T., 112, 138
Monro, D. B., 223 f.
Mooney, W. W., 287–93
Mountford, J. F., *praef.* i
Mummius (dramatist), 147, 367
Murray, Gilbert, *praef.* i, 286–8
music, 3, 11–25, 29, 67, 167–9, 218–32

Naevius, 33–43, 47 f., 67, 71, 73, 85, 87, 99, 104, 128, 193 f., 304, 311, 349, 259 f.
Nauplios puppet-show, 196, 206–8
Navarre, O., 186, 277 f.
Neoptolemus of Parium, 208. *Cf.* 217
Nepos (on Terence), 93
Nero, emperor (as singer), 233 (in the *Octavia*), 235 f.
New Comedy, 50–5, 248–55, and *passim*
Nixon, P., 179, 227, 279
Noble, R., 231
Norwood, G., 47
Novius, 142–8, 268, 367

occentare, 40, 228
orchestra, 4, 22, 154, 176, 270 f.
Oscan farce, 137 f. (*See* Atellana)
Ovid, 127, 224, 233

Oxyrhynchus farce, 156 ; mime, 156, 239, 270, 314–9
Pacuvius, 79–84, 119 f., 359, 362 f.
palliata, 184, 264–6
pantomime, 2, 234, 238, 371, 374
Pappus, 139–42, 145, *Papposilenus*, 338
Pattison, Bruce, 231
pay, actor's, dramatist. (*See* lucar, and *cf.* 149, 163)
Pellio (actor), 67, 164
performance, notice of, 170
    preliminary, 104, 169 f.
periacti (revolving scenery-stands set in wings), 248–55, 277, 284 (295 f.), 300 f.
persona, 22, 193. (*See* mask)
phallus, 13, 25, 153, 335, 350, 356 f. (*See C.Q.*, N.S. iv. 1–2, pp. 64–75)
Phersu, 22, 193, 356
phlyakes, viii, 6, 23–5, 150, 335 ff., 356 f., 368
Phormis (–os), 295, 300 f.
Pickard-Cambridge, A. W., *praef.* i, ii, 180, 203, 250, 275, 277, 279, 285, 295, 303, 308 f., 341, 373
planipes, 47, 151, 154, 163 (264), 369 f.
Platnauer, M., 343
' Plautius,' 46
Plautus, *passim*, especially 45–69, 346, 347
Pliny, elder, on Curio's revolving theatres, 172 ; on painting of scene-building, 298 f.
Pollux, on costume, 186 ; on masks, 195, 309 ; on periacti, 249 ff.; on doors, 285 f.
Polybius, on the musician's battle, 167 ; on scenic decoration, 296
Pompilius, dramatist, 126
Pomponius, dramatist, 142–8, 268, 367
Pomponius, mime-actor, 151, 338
Porcius Licinus, 26, 92 f.
praeco (crier), 169 ; cf. *Amph.* 3
praetexta (ta), 39, 41–4, 192, 235 f., 264 f., 359
producer, actor-manager, 7–9, 17, 28, 164–6, 177. (*See* acting, actor)
programmes, 170, 198
prologue, 4, 7, 8, 38, 50 ff., 91–108, 132, 155, 159–61, 201 ff., 241–7
property-manager. (*See* choragus)
proscenium, 171, 176, 301
protasis, epitasis, catastrophe, 217
protatic character, 97
prothyron (porch), 279–83
Protogenes (mime-actor), 152, 369
Prou, V., 196, 206–8
Publilius Syrus, 155–8, 371
puppet-show. (*See* Nauplios puppet-show)
Purser, L. C., 234, 343 f.
Pylades (pantomime dancer), 234

Quintilian (on Terence), 93, 112, 237;
    (on theatrical decorum), 174 ;
    (on variable mask), 191 ;
    (on Roman tragedy), 233

recitationes, 1, 23, 233–7 ; *cf.* 218
Rees, Kelley, 249, 280–2
Reich, H., 149, 368 ff.
revivals, 4, 7, 8, 85, 135, 164 f., 237
Rhinthon, Rhinthonica, 25, 155, 264,
    335, 336, 356
rhythm, 109, 219–32, 320 f., 322–7
ricinium (recinium), mime's hood,
    153, 369 f.
Ritsch, F., 3, 171, 247
roof (of scene-building), 56, 177, 180
    (of stage), 177, 273
Roscius, 166, 193, 303–5, 371
Rupilius (actor), 81

sannio (buffoon), 148
Santra (dramatist), 126
    (grammarian), 92
satura, satire, (medley), 16–23, 28 f.,
    80, 130, 134, 147, 339, 362
Saunders, C. (on costume), 195, 374
scabillarii (time-keepers), 154, 169 ;
    cf. 268
scaena (stage-scene), ludi scaenici
    (scenic shows or games) 16, 17,
    23, 25, 171 f., 176, 275, 302, 335 ff.
scaena ductilis, scaena uersilis, 278,
    284, 300 f.
scene, scenery, scene-painting, 180,
    269, 275–84, 295–302, 335 ff., 341.
    (*See Phoenix*, 7.2. 77–9)
Scipio Africanus—
    the elder, 40
    the younger, 91–3, 95
seats, 3, 22, 170–2, 240–7
Seneca (dramatist and critic), 1 f., 81,
    125, 158, 217 f., 233–6, 270,
    347 ff., 351
Servius *ad Georg.*, 3. 24–5, 284, 300 f.
Shakespeare, 1, 6, 198–200, 230 f., 275,
    312, 351, 354
side-entrances, 177, 180 f., 248–55
siparium (small curtain?), 154, 267–74
Skutsch—
    F., 209, 324
    O., 360
soccus, 185, 188, 266
song, 11–19, 29, 150, 168, 209, 219–
    32, 233 f., 323, 330–3, 355, 340 ff.,
    346
spectacula (seats. grand-stands), 3,
    22, 242–7, 375
spectators, 3, 4, 7, 8, 11, 20–22, 70 f.,
    81, 95 ff., 149, 160 f., 167, 169 f.,
    171–5, 178, 198, 201, 212, 216,
    238. 241–7

stage, 25, 176 f., 335 ff., 340 ff.
stage conventions, 178–83, 335 ff.
stage-directions, 177, 314, 319
Statius, Caecilius. (*See* Caecilius)
Statius, Papinius (as writer of libretti),
    234
Stephanio (actor), 136
Strabo (dramatist), 125 f., 364 f.
Strabo (geographer), on ' Oscan
    farce ', 138, 366
Stratocles (actor), 237, 375
Sulla (dictator), as patron of theatre
    and writer of farces, 141, 147, 152,
    268, 369
Syracuse, 335 ff.
Syrus. (*See* Publilius Syrus)

tabernaria, 129, 264–6
Tarentum, 335 ff.
Terence, 34 f., 46, 85–90, 91–112,
    159–61, 196–218, 237, 310–2,
    330, 347, 363 f., 365, 371
Theatre Royal, Bristol, 172
Theodora (empress) as mime-actress,
    240
Theirfelder, A., 101
thyromata (wide doors in back-scene),
    279 f.
tibia (pipe), 168, 219
tibicen (piper), 28 f.. 168 f., 206, 212,
    213, 219–32, 338
tickets, 170
Titinius, 128 ff., 365
Titius (dramatist), 126, 365
togata, 39, 128–36, 192, 237, 264–6
Trabea (dramatist), 113, 364
trabeata (middle-class comedy), 136,
    366
tragoidos, 338
Turpilius, 115–7, 364
Tyrrell, R. Y., 120 f.

uersura (projecting wing of scene-
    building, perhaps = ' parascen-
    ium '), 177, 249
unities, 39, 200, 210 ff.

vacant stage, 211–3
Valerius (dramatist), 114, 364
Varius (author of *Thyestes*), 127, 233,
    374
Varro (scholar and student of theatre
    history), 4, 8, 18, 34, 46 f., 67,
    87, 214 f., 268
Vatronius (dramatist), 113 f., 364
Vergilius Romenus (amateur drama-
    tist), 237, 375
Virgil (Georgics iii. lines 24 f.), 268,
    284, 300 ff.
Vitalis (mime-actor), 152, 368

Vitruvius—
    (on audibility), 177, 183
    (on periacti), 249 ff.
    (on stage-doors), 285 f.
    (on scenery), 296–9
Volcacius Sedigitus, 73, 117 f.

Warmington, E. H., 83, 129
Webster, T. B. L., *praef.* i, ii, 101, 216,
    340 ff., 356, 368

Weil, H., 207 f.
Weissinger, R.T., 197 f., 205, 208, 210 f.
Westaway, K. W., 47
wigs (galearia), 193, 373 f.
Wilamowitz, U. von, 232, 286
Wilson, Dover, 199
window—
    (=skylight?) in scene building, 292
    (in vase-paintings), 335

INDEX TO LINES OF LATIN PLAYS
QUOTED OR DISCUSSED

References to Ribbeck, Trag. (2nd ed., 1871 ; cf. Klotz, 1953) and Com·
(2nd ed., 1873). W. = Warmington. Plautus, Terence : Lindsay's text.

ACCIUS
Trag.

4 ff. (W. 452 ff.) (*Myrmidones*) : 123
24 (W. 6) (*Aegisthus*) : 125
29 (W. 244) (*Clutemestra*) : 124
123 (W. 82) (*Antenoridae*) : 125
156 (W. 123) (*Armorum Iudicium*) : 122
187 f. (W. 151 f.) (*Astyanax*) : 122
207 f. (W. 171 f.) (*Atreus*) : 311
220-2 (W. 187-9) (*Atreus*) : 121
239 (W. 209) (*Bacchae*) : 124
272 (W. 263) (*Diomedes*) : 123
281 (W. 266)(*Diomedes*) : 125
292 (W. 280) (*Epigoni*) : 125
318 (W. 305) (*Epinausimache*) : 125
391-402 (W. 381-96) (*Medea*) : 125
493-6 (W. 509-12) (*Oenomaus*) : 125
499 (W. 495) (*Oenomaus*) : 125
554, -7 (W. 557 f.) (*Philocteta*) : 125f.
581-4 (W. 585-8) (*Phoenissae*) : 121
596 (W. 599) (*Phoenissae*) : 124
597 f. (W. 600 f.) (*Phoenissae*) : 123
619 f. (W. 625 f.) (*Telephus*) : 122
636-9 (W. 639-42) (*Tereus*) : 121
640 f. (W. 648 f.) (*Tereus*) : 121
653 ff. (W. 1 ff.) (inc. fab.) : 124
693 (W. 41) (inc. fab.) : 125

Praetext.

1-16 (W. 1-16) (*Aeneadae* siue *Decius*) :
    41 f.
17-38 (W. 17-38) (*Brutus*) : 42 f.
39 f. (W. 40 f.) (*Brutus*) : 43

AFRANIUS

25-30 (*Compitalia*) : 108, 131
48 (*Diuortium*) : 132
52-4 (*Diuortuim*) : 133
104-6 (*Epistula*) : 132, 192
104-32 (*Epistula*) : 133 f.
133 f. (*Exceptus*) : 192 n.

136-52 (*Exceptus*) : 133
156-62 (*Fratriae*) : 133
189-91 (*Incendium*) : 134
272 (*Prodigus*) : 135
282 f. (*Prosa*) : 135
301-14 (*Simulans*) : 131
301 (*Simulans*) : 133
346-403 (*Vopiscus*) : 131
405 f. (fab. inc.) : 132

ANDRONICUS, LIVIUS

Trag.

18 (W. 18) (*Andromeda*) : 31
20-2 (W. 20-2) (*Equos Troianus*) : 31

Com.

1 (W. 1) (*Gladiolus*) : 30
2 (W. 6) (*Ludius*) : 30

ATTA

1 (*Aedilicia*) : 350
8 f. (*Lucubratio*) : 132

CAECILIUS

142 ff. (W. 136 ff.) (*Plocium*) : 88 f.
232 ff. (W. 226 ff.) (inc. fab.) : 89

ENNIUS
Trag.

2 f. (W. 16 f.) (*Achilles*) : 77
13-5 (W. 1-3) (*Achilles Arstarchi*) : 78
41 (W. 59) (*Alexander*) : 77
57-9 (W. 76-9) (*Alexander*) : 76
81 f. (W. 101 f.) (*Andromache Aech-
    malotis*) : 76 (cf. Cic. De Orat.
    3, 102)
163 (W. 203) (*Hecuba*) : 76
177 ff. (W. 222 ff.) (*Iphigenia*) : 75 ff.
183-90 (W. 241-8) (*Iphigenia*) : 74.
191-6 (W. 229-34) (*Iphigenia*) : 65,
    76 f.

ENNIUS—*continued*

Trag.

197 f. (W. 235 f.) (*Iphigenia*) : 78
199–201 (W. 249–51) (*Iphigenia*) : 76
219 (W. 266) (*Medea Exul*) : 78
222 f. (W. 268 f.) (*Medea Exul*) : 75 f.
235 f. (W. 289 f.) (*Medea Exul*) : 75
237–9 (W. 291–3) (*Medea Exul*) : 75
298 (W. 355) (*Thyestes*) : 229
302 (W. 351) (*Thyestes*) : 77
388 (inc. fab.) (W. 216 *Hecuba*) : 77

Praetext.

1–4 (W. 374–8) (*Ambracia*) : 42
5 f. (W. 379 f.) (*Sabinae*) : 41

LABERIUS

4 f. (*Aquāē Caldae*) : 156
10 (*Aulularia*) : 156
11 f. (*Belonistria*) : 156
13 f. (*Cacomnemon*) : 156
15 f. (*Gaetuli*) 9 156
42–5 (*Ephebus*) : 156 f., 192
47 f. (*Fullo*) : 156
59 (*Late Loquentes*) : 156
61 (*Natal*) : 192
63 f. (*Necyomantia*) : 156
72–9 (*Restio*) : 157
80 (*Salinator*) : 157
86 (*Sorores*) : 156
98–126 (inc. fab.) : 155
134 f. (inc. fab.) : 157
141–3 (inc. fab.) : 156

LUSCIUS LANUVINUS

Phasma : 114
Thesaurus : 114 f.

NAEVIUS

Trag.

17 (W. 17) (*Hector Proficiscens*) : 35 f.
24–6 (W. 27–9) (*Lycergus*) : 36
63 (W. 34) (inc. fab.) : 36

Praetext.

2 (W. 1) (*Clastidium*) : 39
5 f. (W. 2 f.) (*Romulus siue Lupus*) : 39

Com.

1–4 (W. 1–4) (*Acontizomenos*) : 38
5–8 (W. 5–8) (*Agitatoria*) : 38
9 f. (W. 9 f.) (*Agitatoria*) : 38
11 f. (W. 13 f.) (*Agitatoria*) : 38
17 (W. 15) (*Argrypnuntes*) : 38
18 f. (W. 20 f.) (*Apella, Appella*) : 38

21–4 (W. 22–6) (*Ariolus*) : 36
75–9 (W. 74–9) (*Tarentilla*) : 37
99–102 (W. 97–100) (*Tunicularia* : 36 f.
108–10 (W. 1–3) (inc. fab.) : 40
113 (W. 27) (inc. fab.) : 35

NOVIUS

2 (*Agricola*) : 192
17 (*Dou Dossenni*) : 146
45 f. (*Maccus*) : 146
49 f. (*Maccus Exul*) : 144
75 f. (*Pappus Praeteritus*) : 145
113 f. (inc. fab.) : 145

PACUVIUS

Trag.

2–8 (W. 4–10) (*Antiopa*) : 83
40 (W. 45) (*Armorum Iudicium*) : 81
64 (W. 59) (*Atalanta*) : 79
83–92 (W. 104–114) (*Chryses*) : 83 f.
101 (W. 100) (cf. 365 f.) (*Chryses*) : 81, 175
133 (W. 154) (*Dulorestes*) : 81
177 (W. 187) (*Hermiona*) : 83
185 (W. 189) (*Hermiona*) : 81
197–201 (W. 205–10) (*Iliona*) : 80 f., 342 f. (Cicero's 'septenarios' may be a mere mistake for 'octonarios')
200 f. (W. 209 f.) (*Iliona*) : 223
215 (W. 224) (*Iliona*) : 79
238 (W. 251) (*Medus*) : 81
244–6 (W. 266–8) (*Niptra*) : 82 f.
268 f. (W. 294 f.) (*Niptra*) : 72
327 ff. (W. 345 ff.) (*Teucer*) : 81, 82, 304
365 f. (inc. fab.) (W. 163 f.) : 81
413 f. (inc. fab.) (W. 357 f.) : 83

Praetext.

1–5 (W. 1) (*Paulus*) : 42

PLAUTUS

Amphitruo

Summarized, 56 f.
15 (appeal for silence), 161
52 f. (tragedy unpopular ?), 70
65 (usher), 69
68 (toga worn by spectators), 187
83–5 (organized applause), 168
116 f. (slave-costume), 190
142–6 (clue for distinguishing doubles), 307
153 (metre of soliloquy), 225
153–462 (Plautine expansion of street-scene ?), 66, 307

PLAUTUS—*continued*

Amphitruo

248 ('lyric' verses described as 'spoken'), 230
333 ('left' and 'right'), 181
343 (slave or free?), 191
441–5 (exact resemblance), 307
458 f. (wearing of imago at funeral), 14, 308
999 (garland), 189
1008 (roof used), 180, 277
fr. iv, v (roof used), 180, 277
1035 (exact resemblance), 307
1062, 1130, 1143 (stage 'thunder'?), 254

Asinaria

Date and metrical structure, 67
Stage setting, 259 f.
3 (organization of troupe), 166
4 (praeco), 169
8 (promise to be brief), 161
11 (author called Maccus), 47
13 f. (promise that play will be funny), 161
400 f. (mask?), 308
740–3 (angiportum), 259
745, 809 f., 941 (banqueting-party), 179, 279
751 ff. (reading aloud of document), 225
830 (banquet), 179, 279

Aulularia

Summarized, 57 f.
Stage setting, 285
103 f., 242 (bolting of door), 289
120 ff. (bacchiac metre used for discussion), 229
415 (pronunciation of tęne tęne?), 325
791 (seated spectators wearing togas), 241 f.

Bacchides

Study in debauchery, 61
106 (vestige of Greek chorus?), 209
214 f. (reference to Pellio in *Epidicus*), 48, 63, 164
720–3, 832 (party held indoors), 279 f.
816–7 ('he whom the gods love dies young'), 49, 340
833 (door opened slightly), 179, 285, 293
997 ff. (document read aloud), 225

Captiui.

Summarized, 58 f.
1 (opening tableau?), 267

11–14 ('if you can't hear, come closer'), 174
12 (seated audience), 241
37 (exchange of clothes), 189 f.
54 (appeal for attention), 161
61 f. (special outfit needed for tragedy?), 191
461, 497 (movements of Ergasilus), 248
647 f. (red hair in freeman), 190
659 ff. (abrupt change in metre), 225 f.
795 (platea), 257
1033 f. (high moral tone of play), 257

Casina

Indecency and popularity of play: 62, 64 f.
Rhythmical variety, 68
Prologue, 85, 159, 165, 241
114 (forceful abuse), 68
213 (whisper?), 230
562, 574 (convention of 'invisibility'), 280
613 f. (stage setting), 260
767–70 (man dressed as bride), 188 f.
799 (platea), 257; (instrumental music), 227 f.
814–936 ('lyric' metres distributed among all the actors), 230
855 f. (uia), 256 f.

Cistellaria

Comédie larmoyante, 62
Date and source, 49
149–202, ('deferred' prologue), 161
197–202 (reference to Hannibalic War), 47, 67 f., 179
747 (significant change of metre), 225
782–end (rewards and punishments for actors), 167

Curculio

1, 9 (opening before daybreak), 62, 178
36 f. (permitted and forbidden loves), 134
147–54 (serenade), 227 f.
156, –8 (metrical effects), 226, 228
178–80 (love-song), 68, 228
192 (masks?), 194, 308
288 (Graeci palliati), 187
392–5, etc. (patch worn over one eye), 189
341 (scene laid in Epidaurus), 243
429 ff. (document read aloud), 225
462–86 (monologue of property-manager), 65 f., 166
464–6 (hiring of actor's costume), 187
644–7 (seats in theatre), 241–7

PLAUTUS—*continued*

Epidicus

Complex plot, 62
1 (opens with entry from wing), 284
660 f. (garden), 260
725 (slippers), 187
733 (seated spectators), *see* pp. 241 ff.

Menaechmi

Summarized, 59
3 (' Plautus '), 159
5 f. (promise to be brief), 161
72–6 (no movable scenery ?), 180, 278
190 f. (woman's palla), 188
351, 362 (door left ajar), 293
555 (' left ' and ' right '), 181
753 ff. (metrical effect), 226
1074, 1085 (exact resemblance), 307
881–2 (' dramatic time '), *see* pp. 300 ff.

Mercator

Date, character, etc., 47, 49, 65, 67
10 (Maccus Titus), 47
225 ff. (recounting of dream), 225
408 (occentare), 228 n.
762 f. (hiatus and elision), 325
800–2 (pretext for removal of properties no longer required), 180, 267
1009 (garden), 260 f.

Miles Gloriosus

Summarized, 59 f.
Stage setting, 258
81–3 (seated spectators), *see* pp. 241 ff.
156 ff. (roof), 180
210 ff. (imprisonment of Naevius), 40, 47
690 (cock's ' song '), 230
791 f., 872 (courtesan posing as matrona), 188 n.
1171–81 (disguise), 188 f.

Mostellaria

Summarized, 60 f.
Stage setting, 258
Opening scene, 190
157 (intimate scenes, how staged), 281
348, 431 (metrical contrast), 226
384 (sandals taken off at table), 188
405, 426 (locking of doors from outside), 292
444 (door shut in daytime), 280
770 (Sarsina), 48
817 (uestibulum), 280 ff., 293

928–30 (side-entrances and back-door), 258
1063 ff. (a ' porch ' would be inconvenient), 283

Persa

155 f. (disguise), 189
157–60 (hiring of costume), 187
444–6 (angiportum), 261
464 (crepida in comedy), 265
676–9 (angiportum), 261
758 (intimate scene staged in front of house), 280
829–31 (disguise almost penetrated), *see* pp. 188 f.

Poenulus

1 ff. (parody of Ennius), 78
3 f. (appeal for silence), 161
5–10 (seated audience), 241
6–43 (description of audience), 174
123, 126 (actor's costume, prologue takes another part), 194, 308
504–816 (aduocati), 209
930 ff. (Punic passages), 62, 66
1224 (seated audience), 241 f.
1298, 1303 (trailing tunic), 188
1342 (synizesis), 324

Pseudolus

Date, didascalia, 49, 163
1 f. (spectators warned to ' stretch their legs '), 159, 163, 180, 212
343 (ornamenta), 109
366 (cantor), 230
573 a (instrumental interlude), 212 f., 228
610 (slave or free ?), 190
683–6 (moralizing), 68
507 (parody of tragic style), 71
735 (disguise), 189
738 (sleeved tunic), 188
960–2, 971 (angiportum), 262
1184–6 (hire of costume), 187
1235 (angiportum), 258, 262

Rudens

Summarized, 61
Title, 64
Setting, 181, 250
85 ff. (roof), 180
156 (' left ' and ' right '), 181
220–43 (scenery), 180
259 (metre), 226
413 (metre), 226

PLAUTUS—continued

Rudens

428 f. (wearing of phallus ?), cf. pp. 337 f., and *see D.F.* 234, n. 3
450 ff. (metre), 225
535 f. (manducus), 140, –2
593, 1338 (metre), 225

Stichus

Date and didascalia, 49, 163, 168
Title, 64
Structure, 66, 308 n.
Stage setting, 261 n.
Opening scene, 283
87 (door left open), 283, 293
147 (staging), 280
431–52 (back-door), 261 f.
729 ff. (' drinking-song '?), 228
758 ff. (metre and music), 222, 228

Trinummus

Moralizing tone, 61
prologue, 95
4 f. (promise to be brief), 161
287 (canto), 230
720 (slave's socci), 187
767, 851 (disguise), 189
840, 1006 (platea), 257
857 (cost of costume), 187
1008 (metre), 222

Truculentus

(Structure, etc. *See* Enk's edition)
Study in debauchery, 61
date, 48
248 f., 303 f. (garden), 262
478f., 631 (sandals removed when reclining), 188
490, 583, 631 (staging), 280
968 (seated audience), 241

Vidularia.

Theme, 62
Prologue, 95 n.

Fragmenta

146 (uestibulum), cf. p. 280

POMPONIUS

10 f. (*Aruspex uel Pexor Rusticus*) : 145
18 (*Auctoratus*) : 145
19 f. (*Bucco Auctoratus*) : 145
27 f. (*Campani*) : 146
57–60 (*Kalendae Martiae*) : 144 f.

67 f. (*Macci Gemini*) : 144
75 f. (*Maccus Virgo*) : 146
94 f. (muffling of head) (*Pannuceati*) : 145
99 f. (*Pappus Agricola*) : 145
109 f. (*Philosophia*) : 146
11 f. (*Pictores*) : 142
119 (*Piscatores*) : 192
131 (*Praeco Posterior*) : 145
135, –7 (*Praeco Posterior*) : 192
147 (muffling of head) (*Praefectus Morum*) : 145

SENECA

Agamemnon

108–26 (silent thoughts reported), 235

Hercules Furens

990 ff., 1296 ff. (unstageable ?), 235

Hippolytus

1256 ff. (fragments of corpse pieced together), 235

Octauia

See pp. 1, 217, 235 f.

Phoenissae

See p. 217

Thyestes

760 ff. (banquet prepared for Thyestes), 122

Troades

See p. 236

TERENCE

Adelphi

Summarized, 105 f.
1–14 (charge of ' stealing '), 96, 102
7 ff. (*Commorientes*), 46, 65
15 ff. (help from noble friends), 93
578 (angiportum non perium), 256
643 (blushing), 193, 306 f.
788 (' striking ' door from within), 288
855 (Demea's change of behaviour), 98, 108
908 f. (garden wall), 263

Andria

Summarized, 96 f.
Alterations introduced by Terence, 97– 101
5 (' prologues '), 95
16 ff. (contaminare), 96 ff.
43 f. (good manners), 110
61 f. (nequid minus), 110
119 f. (Glycerium), 110
126 (hinc illae lacrimae), 110
129 ff. (midwife), 101

TERENCE—*continued*

Andria

250, 428–30 (Roman touches ?), 97 f.
368 f. (slave), 101
732 ff. (sudden change of plan), 108

Eunuchus

Summarized, 103 f.
Alterations made by Terence, 104 f.
8 (metre), 325
20 (purchase of play), 164
21 (preliminary performance), 104, 169 f.
23 ff. (' theft '), 96, 104, 106
25 (collaboration between Plautus and Naevius ?), 46
26, 32, 35 (persona = ' character '), 193, 308 f.
343 f., 1064 (platea), 257
552 (contaminare), 311
670 (facial expression ?), 306

Heauton Timorumenos

Summarized, 102 f.
prologue, 164, 170, 301 f.
4 (ex integra Graeca), 102 ; cf. p. 310
17 ff. (multas contaminasse Graecas), 95, 96–102, 310 ff.
22 ff. (helped by friends), 93, 96
30 (artistic standards), 107
40 (need to declaim loudly), 230
opening scene, 102, 284
170 f. (choral interlude in Greek play ?), 209. *See Hermathena*, 84, 36–48
409 f. (lapse of a night), 212

Hecyra

Two prologues, 95, 165
4 (populus studio stupidus), 107
9 (ornatu prologi), 194 f., 354
14 ff. (Ambivius Turpio), 164

35 (clamor mulierum), 174
39 (primo actu), 214
57 (pretio emptas meo), 164
361 ff. (Pamphilus' discovery), 108

Phormio

Stage setting, p. 262 f.
4 (charge of weakness of style), 96
13 ff. (taunt about nature of prologues), 95 f.
18 (failure means starvation), 166
210 ff. (facial expression ?), 306 f.
215 (platea), 257
891 ff. (angiportum), 262
941 ff. (use of surprise), 108

TITINIUS

4 f. (*Barbatus*), 134
15 f., 26, 32 f. (*Fullonia*), 131
25 (*Fullonia*), 192
26 f. (*Fullonia*), 134
43 f. (*Gemina*), 134
44 (*Gemina*), 192
58 (*Gemina*), 135
60 f. (*Hortensius*), 132
85 (*Psaltria siue Ferentinatis*), 135
104 (*Quintus*), 135
107 f. (*Setina*), 133
111 (*Setina*), 135
116 (*Setina*), 132
138 f. (*Veliterna*), 192
167 f. (inc. fab.), 192
171 (inc. fab.) (affecting woman's voice ; *see* p. 145)

TURPILIUS

Demiurgus (Roscius performs in), p. 116
50–3 (*Epiclerus*), 116
100–125 (*Leucadia*), 115 f.

Key to the meaning of the metrical terms used in this book

acatalectic, 322
accent, Greek, 321
accent, Latin, 321 f.
accentual verse, 320
Alexandrine, 327 f.
anapaest, 321, 330–2
arsis, 321 f.

bacchiac, 321, 332 f.
Brevis Brevians, 324

caesura, 323
catalectic, 322
choriambic, 333
colon, a coherent group of feet, forming part of a verse ; Hardie, *R.M.* 264
colon ithyphallicum (e.g. ' Riding down from Bangor '), 334
colon Reizianum (e.g. ' and a fig for the Vicar ! '), 334
compulsory long, 322
cretic, 321, 333

dactyl, 321, 333 f.
diaeresis, 323 f.
dimeter, 322
dipody, 321
dochmiac (e.g. ' rebel, serfs, rebel ! '), 333

elision, 325

foot, 321

glyconic (e.g. ' lads and lasses, come out to play '), 333

hiatus, 325

iambus, 321, 327–9
ictus, properly the ' beat ' of hand, wand, etc., when counting the ' measures ' (or the feet or even the half-feet) of verse. Modern usage reckons one ' beat ' to each compulsory long ; and the false analogy of our own verse leads us to accompany this 'beat' with an artificial, i.e. false voice-stress on the syllable
in pausa, at a metrical break, i.e. the end of the line (or half-line)
ionic a maiore (e.g. ' Sing " Hey to you—Good day to you " '), 334 (Contrast ionic a minore (e.g. ' at the midnight, in the silence of the sleeptime ")

measure (metron), the unit of measurement. In the conversational or 'marching' or 'running' metres (iambic, anapaestic, trochaic), the 'measure' is a dipody ; in other metres it is a foot
metre, 321
mora (in modern metrical phraseology = 'time'), 321

octonarius, 328 ff.

phrase-accent, 326
prosodical hiatus, 325

quantitative verse, 320

resolution, 322, 329
rhythm, 321

senarius, 327
septenarius, 328, 329
syllaba anceps, 326
synizesis, 324, 329

tetrameter, 323
thesis, 321 f.
trimeter, 322
trochee, 321, 329 f.